TOWER BIBLIOGRAPHICAL SERIES

NUMBER SIXTEEN

Elizabeth Bowen

A BIBLIOGRAPHY

by

J'NAN M. SELLERY

and

WILLIAM O. HARRIS

Humanities Research Center

THE UNIVERSITY OF TEXAS AT AUSTIN

Frontispiece: a snapshot of Elizabeth Bowen taken in 1946
by Alfred Knopf. Used by permission.

CONTENTS

INTRODUCTION

This study combines a bibliography (descriptive and enumerative) of the writings of Elizabeth Bowen with a checklist of writings about her. Sections A-G embody the former aim, and sections H-J embody the latter. There are, however, two modifying exceptions to this dichotomy: reviews of Bowen's published works are for convenience subsumed under each of the relevant entries in section A; and the manuscripts and typescripts of unpublished letters written to her are included in section E, following those of her own letters.

The bibliography is designed to be useful primarily to literary as well as to textual scholars, and only secondarily to collectors of books as artifacts. For example, we have sought to help the critical scholar apprehend the sequence of a Bowen work from manuscript to its first appearance in a periodical, to a revised version in one or more published volumes, and even to adaptations for radio or television readings or performances, and appearances in anthologies and translations that give some sense of the history of Bowen's influence and reputation.

To accomplish that end, we have modified the standard bibliographical form by subsuming into the Collation section the descriptions conventionally cited under the section on Contents, freeing this latter section for a full enumeration of Bowen's pieces which appear in the particular volume and affording a context for notes on prior appearances and reprintings. Also included in the Contents are cross-references to the pertinent manuscripts, radio and television scripts, broadcast records, translations, and anthologies. For other, more unified works (novels, autobiographies, etc.), we have relegated such annotations to the very end of Notes. To simplify and to clarify the network of cross-references throughout the bibliography, we have made the first appearance in one of her published works (Section A) the nexus for these citations, including only there the full range of pertinent references. Subordinate entries in all latter sections refer only to this parent citation in section A. If the study or critical essay was never collected in her published works but appears in a published work to which Bowen contributed, then its citation in the appropriate entry in section B becomes the locus for the parent reference. And so through section C and following, the first citation becomes the key reference, except in a few instances in the manuscript and broadcast sections (E and F).

We have not described paper or typography and have made only general references to binding materials, although we have adopted the color system proposed by G. T. Tanselle[1] for citing Centroid terminology and numbers for binding, lettering, and dustjacket colors (as well as for colors other than black in the printing within the volumes). Finally, citation of dust jackets is not intended to be considered complete, representing as it does only those seen. Whenever notations on the jackets themselves indicate that a particular impression had been enclosed or a book club copy involved, that information is provided in brackets at the beginning of the description.

Within these limits, we have sought to arrange chronologically, in Section A, descriptions of all books and pamphlets written wholly by Bowen. One salient feature of her publication history has significantly shaped this arrangement—that is, the nearly balanced Anglo-American nature of her publishing. From the outset, her works appeared under imprints in both countries; and as her affinities with this country grew and especially as her close association with the Knopfs and their company developed, the English and American publications became, with a few exceptions, essentially collateral.[2] Thus, with the single exception of the first edition of *Seven Winters* by the Cuala Press in Dublin (A14a), we have described, when appropriate, the first edition/first impression copies in each of the two major publishing nations. When a first American publication is, in actual fact, an issue derived from the first impression of the English edition (or vice versa), it is described, providing a collateral parent entry for that country, but is entitled *First Edition* (*American* [or *English*] *issue*). Under the Notes to each of these entries are included (1) information, when known, on all subsequent impressions and (2) records of all new editions based simply upon that parent.[3] Only in those few instances when Bowen's revisions

---

[1] 'A System of Color Identifications for Bibliographical Description,' *Studies in Bibliography*, 20 (1967):203–34.

[2] It should be noted that, although the title pages of Dial Press volumes (*e.g.* A3b) indicate also publication in Canada by Longmans, and Knopf copyright pages (*e.g., A4c) sometimes indicate that volumes are 'published simultaneously' by McClelland & Stewart or Random House in Canada, these are purely copyright necessities to accommodate territorial sales by these companies; no such Canadian editions or issues are actually known to exist, although occasional reviewers in Canada refer to McClelland & Stewart copies. To be understood similarly are references in the *Cumulative Book Index* to Jonathan Cape editions with Canadian counterparts by Irwin Clarke, etc

[3] It might be noted that all Penguin editions of Bowen's works have been cited only under the English parent edition, since they were published only in the United Kingdom and not also by Penguin, U.S.A.

or additions after publication led to reset editions (*e.g.*, A1c and A13c) have descriptions been provided for later publishing.[4]

Arranged chronologically in section B are abbreviated descriptions of the first English and American editions of those books and pamphlets to which Bowen contributed; and cited under Contents within each entry in this section are the specific contributions made by Bowen, the pages on which they appear, and the appropriate cross-reference as indicated earlier. In facing the major difficulty of differentiating between items appropriate to this section and those anthologized reprintings appropriate only to section G, we chose a severe principle of including here only those books containing some Bowen material appearing in print for the first time. Thus, volumes containing pieces printed earlier in periodicals were excluded and cited in G.

Arranged chronologically in section C are all of the Bowen contributions to periodicals we have been able to verify. While we believe the listing approaches inclusiveness, there remains at least a handful of items which we have reason to believe did appear in journals but which we have not actually been able to locate. In order to avoid as much redundancy of citation as possible, we have included under the entry of first periodical appearance all approximately simultaneous appearances in other periodicals (*e.g.*, C6) and all periodical reprintings (*e.g.*, C7). Each of the remaining sections devoted to primary materials (D–G) contains its own introductory statement of principle and protocol.

Elizabeth Bowen's death while at work on yet another novel as well as on a major retrospective piece provides an unfortunate *terminus*, more apparent than real, for a bibliography. For even the posthumous publication of these fragments and other pieces in *Pictures and Conversations* (A31) affords no clear demarcation since not only do reprintings, translations, etc. continue to appear but significant new editions have recently been undertaken (such as the Avon project to provide new paperback editions of all her novels, and the Poolbeg Press collection of her Irish short stories [A33]), and Victoria Glendinning's authorized biography has appeared and more recently been reprinted in paperback. In view of such developments after Bowen's death, the compilers are especially aware of how likely they are to have overlooked relevant material of very recent date and welcome any additions, corrections, and criticisms.

---

[4] One partial exception to this principle has been the collation description for those volumes in the Jonathan Cape Collected Edition which were set as new editions (*e.g.*, *The Hotel* [A3a]) rather than being late impressions of the original Cape edition, cut and bound in the new Collected Edition format.

Obviously, this bibliography does not clearly reflect Elizabeth Bowen's contribution to drama. Partly, this is a consequence merely of formal arrangement: her nativity play in *Pictures and Conversations* (A31) and her radio play on Trollope (A16) are included among her published works; an earlier 'New Judgement' of Jane Austen (F1) was broadcast though unpublished, as was a play on Fanny Burney's London (F2) and another on the year of 1918 (F23). Typescripts exist for all of these broadcasts (E115, 116, 121) as do others for 'The Confidante' (E117) and notes for a *son et lumière* production at Kinsale in County Cork (E112). Add to all this the fact that she prepared many of the BBC dramatizations of her works, and one perceives how much theatrical work is actually included. Not included, however, is the fact that *Castle Anna*, her play in collaboration with John Perry, was produced at the Lyric Theatre in Hammersmith between 24 February and 20 March 1948. In addition, there are suggestions that she contributed in some way to Kate O'Brien and John Perry's *The Last of Summer*, produced at the Phoenix in London on 7 June 1947. She may even have written for at least one film, treating an aspect of the Norwegian resistance to the Nazis, since a contract to that effect exists in the collection of Bowen materials at the Humanities Research Center.

J'nan M. Sellery
Harvey Mudd College
William O. Harris
University of California, Riverside

ACKNOWLEDGMENTS

The compilers greatly appreciate all who have helped with the bibliography during the past decade. Numerous libraries and their staffs have been among our prime resources not only for volumes shared but for searches undertaken and guidance offered. Our debts to them are deep, most particularly to the Humanities Research Center at The University of Texas at Austin. The printed books, manuscripts, and letters, by and about Elizabeth Bowen, found in the Humanities Research Center are incomparable for their variety and completeness. F. W. Roberts, William R. Keast, and David Farmer have provided continuing support, even to supplementing HRC's extensive Bowen collection with manuscripts, typescripts, letters, and translations which became available after her death. Many on the staff bore our enquiries with continual assistance, and particular appreciation goes to librarians Mary M. Hirth and Sally Leach, to the managing editor James E. Bagg, Jr., and his assistant Dave Oliphant.

Especially for English imprints and for information regarding their accession dates, the British Library has been indispensable. The Reading Room and Colindale staffs have been unfailingly helpful to each of us on visits there and in correspondence answering a multitude of queries. In its specialized way, the BBC Written Archives Centre at Reading has also provided assistance, especially through Dorothy L. Phillips, P. Longuehaye, E. Munro, Dennis Perry, and V. Schuck. We are similarly grateful to W. A. Munford of the National Library for the Blind, and E. R. S. Fifoot of the Edinburgh University Library.

John D. Gordan and Lola L. Szladits, successive Curators of the Berg Collection at the New York Public Library, made available the significant collection of Bowen manuscripts there; from the general collection at the library we have used a number of crucial volumes and and scarce periodicals; and it was in their *Bulletin* that the preliminary work toward the present study was first published. The Library of Congress as well as the libraries at UCLA, UC Berkeley, The University of Texas at Austin, and Stanford University have also been of major help. But, of course, it is to our home libraries at the Claremont Colleges and at UC Riverside that we owe a special kind of debt. From the very beginning and reliably over the years, Hazel Schupbach has contributed immeasurably to the bibliography. Robert Lang, Assistant Librarian at UCR, and Betty Lang, Librarian to the UCR English Department, have actively sought to procure important Bowen pieces; and Clif Wurfel, Elizabeth Weeks, and Geff Selth have helped on numerous occasions. In addition, we offer thanks to the many libraries in the United States and Canada which responded to our inter-library requests and sought answers to our queries.

Publishers and booksellers as well have been of fundamental importance to our work. We relied upon The Covent Garden Bookstore, Crane Bookshop, and Bertram Rota through the assistance of Anthony Rota and George Lawson. Much more widely diverse has been our reliance upon publishers for information which sometimes only they can supply. William A. Koshland, the Director of Alfred A. Knopf, not only ferreted out detailed publishing data but supplied them with a generosity and good will reflecting the fondness he recalls for Elizabeth Bowen. We also wish to thank Pyke Johnson, Jr., the Managing Editor at Doubleday & Co.; Graham C. Greene, Managing Director, and Suzanne Battle at Jonathan Cape; Benjamin K. Glazebrook at Constable & Co.; Stewart Reid-Foster at William Collins Sons & Co.; John Bush, Director, and Angela Morrell at Victor Gollancz; P. E. Atkinson and Sheila Redfern at Longman Group, Inc.; Georgina Horley, Eleo Gordon, and Peter Carson at Penguin Books; William Armstrong at Sidgwick & Jackson. Additional aid was given by those at Edward Arnold, Publisher; Arno Press; Avon Books; Barrie & Jenkins; B. T. Batsford; Blond & Briggs; Books for Libraries Press; Buccaneer Books; The Dramatic Publishing Company; Ecco Press; Harcourt Brace Jovanovich; Harper & Row, Publishers; George C. Harrap & Co.; William Heinemann, Ltd.; Hodder and Stoughton; Houghton Mifflin Co.; Hutchinson Publishing Group; Irish University Press; Allen Lane; Little, Brown & Co.; Liveright Publishing Corp.; New American Library; New English Library; Oxford University Press; Poolbeg Press; S. A. Purnell & Sons; Scholarly Press; Charles Scribner's Sons; Martin Secker & Warburg; Simon Schuster; Sphere Books; Stein and Day; and George Weidenfeld & Nicolson. Finally, F. J. Furneaux, former Managing Director of the Alden Press, provided meticulous information on the early printing of *The Heat of the Day*.

Various scholars have given each of us help on particular problems; from among them we would acknowledge especially Vinton A. Dearing, David Farmer, Edward R. Hagemann, Ralph Hanna III, Austin R. Sellery, John B. Vickery, and George W. Williams. The office staffs in our respective departments have been of repeated assistance, and we would like to thank Margaret Thompson for typing a difficult manuscript, Lisa Farrell and June Clee for preparing the groundwork for the indexing, and Joan Reclam for typing the index. Finally, we wish to acknowledge our indebtedness for the financial support provided by the Committee on Research of the Academic Senate at UC Riverside, by a Shell Assist Award, and by the Research Committee at Harvey Mudd College.

ABBREVIATIONS

AmerRev	*American Review* [replaced *Bookman* after March 1933]
Among Our Books	*Among Our Books* [in *Pittsburgh Monthly Bulletin,* a publication of the Pittsburgh Carnegie Library]
ArchR	*Architectural Review*
Atlantic	*Atlantic Monthly* [1857–1959]; *The Atlantic* [1959 +]
ArQ	*Arizona Quarterly*
BA	*Books Abroad*
B&B	*Books and Bookmen*
BD	*British Digest*
BETrans	*Boston Evening Transcript*
BOMCNews	*Book-of-the-Month Club News*
BuffEN	*Buffalo Evening News*
CanF	*Canadian Forum*
CathW	*Catholic World*
ChCent	*Christian Century*
ChiDTrib	*Chicago Daily Tribune*
ChiST	*Chicago Sun-Times*
ChiSTrib	*Chicago Sunday Tribune*
ChScM	*Christian Science Monitor*
ChScMM	*Christian Science Monitor Magazine*
ColD	*Columbus Dispatch*
COS	[Cleveland] *Open Shelf*
CSunBW	[*Chicago Sun*] *Book Week*
CTribMB	[*Chicago Tribune*] *Magazine of Books*
CTribBW	[*Chicago Tribune*] *Book World*
EB Reviews	[book review column written by Elizabeth Bowen in *Tatler and Bystander* under the titles, 'Elizabeth Bowen's Bookshelf', 'Elizabeth Bowen's Book Reviews', and 'Elizabeth Bowen Reviewing Books']
EJ	*English Journal*
F&C	*Forum and Century*
Guardian	*Manchester Guardian*

HopR	*Hopkins Review*
ItalQ	*Italian Quarterly*
JO'LW	*John O'London's Weekly*
Kirkus	*Kirkus Bookshop Service* [1940s–1967]; *Kirkus Service* [1967–1969]; *Kirkus Reviews* [1969+]
LJ	*Library Journal*
ManGW	*Manchester Guardian Weekly*
ManG&EN	*Manchester Guardian and Evening News*
N&A	*Nation & Athenaeum*
NLB	National Library for the Blind [London]
NAmerR	*North American Review*
NCDN	*North Carolina Daily News*
NCF	*Nineteenth-Century Fiction*
N&D	*Night & Day*
New Statesman	*New Statesman* [1913–1931]; *New Statesman and Nation* [1931+]
NewSt (rev)	*New Statesman* [book reviews by Elizabeth Bowen]
NY	*New Yorker*
NYEPost	*New York Evening Post*
NYEPostLR	[*New York Evening Post*] *Literary Review*
NYHTB	[*New York Herald Tribune*] *Books* [1924–1943]; *Weekly Book Review* [1943–1949]; *Book Review* [1949–1960]; *Book Week* [1960–1967]
NYRB	*New York Review of Books*
NYTBR	*New York Times Book Review*
NYTimes	*New York Times*
NYWorld	*New York World* [1860–1931]
ObsWeekRev	*Observer Weekend Review*
O&I	*Outlook and Independent* [London *Outlook* merged with *Independent* on 24 Oct. 1928]
Outlook	*The Outlook: A Weekly Review* [New York, 1880–1928]
Outlook (London)	*Outlook, A Weekly Review of Politics, Art, Literature and Finance* [London]
PIBR	[*Philadelphia Inquirer*] *Book Review*

PIQB	[Pratt Institute Library] *Quarterly Booklist*
SatN	*Saturday Night*
SatRev	*Saturday Review of Literature* [New York, 1924–1951]; *Saturday Review* [1951+]
SatRevPLSA	*Saturday Review of Politics, Literature, Science and Art* [London, 1855–1930]; *Saturday Review* [1930–1938]
SFChron	*San Francisco Chronicle*
SFChronTWM	[*San Francisco Chronicle*] *This World Magazine*
SpRep	*Springfield Republican* [Springfield, Mass.]
SR	*Sewanee Review*
Tatler	*Tatler* [1901–1940]; *Tatler and Bystander* [1940+]
T (rev)	*Tatler* [book reviews by Elizabeth Bowen in *Tatler and Bystander* which do not appear in the 'EB Reviews' columns]
T&T	*Time and Tide*
TLS	*Times Literary Supplement*
VQR	*Virginia Quarterly Review*
WD	*World Digest of Current Fact and Comment*
WiscLB	*Wisconsin Library Bulletin*
WWGaz	*Weekly Westminster Gazette*
YR	*Yale Review*

BOOKS AND PAMPHLETS BY
ELIZABETH BOWEN

a. *First edition*:

Encounters: Stories | by Elizabeth Bowen | London: Sidgwick
& Jackson, Ltd. | 3 Adam Street, Adelphi, W.C. 1923

Collation: 7⅛ x 5¼"; [A]⁴ B–O⁸; pp. [8], 1–203 [204–208].
[1]: half title. [2]: publisher's advertisement. [3]: the title page. [4]: blank.
[5]: 'To M.J.' [6]: blank. [7]: contents. [8]: blank. 1–[204]: text. [204],
at bottom: 'The Westminster Press | 411a Harrow Road | London W.9'.
[205]: publisher's device. [206–208]: publisher's advertisements.

Binding: Bound in vivid dark greenish blue (175) cloth lettered across
the spine in gold: '[triple rule] | ENCOUNTERS | ELIZABETH |
BOWEN | SIDGWICK | & JACKSON | [triple rule]'. On the front cover
in gold: '[within an ornamental design of frames] Encounters | Elizabeth
Bowen'.
Dust jacket: Entire wrapper in light olive gray (112) paper. Front:
'[triple-ruled frame in black (267)] ENCOUNTERS: | Stories by |
ELIZABETH BOWEN | CONTENTS | Breakfast | Daffodils | The Re-
turn | The Confidante | Requiescat | All Saints | The New House |
Lunch | The Lover | Mrs. Windermere | The Shadowy Third | The Evil
that Men do — | Sunday Evening | Coming Home | LONDON: SIDG-
WICK & JACKSON, Ltd.' Spine: '[triple rule] | Encounters: | Stories by |
Elizabeth | Bowen | 5/– | net | Sidgwick | & Jackson | [triple rule]'.
Back: '[within a single-rule frame] UNIFORM WITH THIS VOLUME |
[rule across] | [reference and reviews on the following four books] *Third
Impression | The Celestial Omnibus: and other Stories* by E. M. Forster,
The Temple on the Hill. A Tale of Transylvania by Elsa de Szász, *The
Third Miss Symons* by F. M. Mayor, and *Vain Oblations: and other
Stories* by Katharine F. Gerould | [rule across] | LONDON: SIDGWICK
& JACKSON, LTD.' Front and back flaps are blank.

Contents:
'Breakfast'. Reprinted in A20 and A28.
'Daffodils'. Reprinted in A20.
'The Return'. Reprinted in A20.
'The Confidante'. Reprinted in A20.
'Requiescat'. Reprinted in A20.
'All Saints'. Reprinted in A20. Published in anthology, G1.
'The New House'. Reprinted in A20.
'Lunch'. Reprinted in A20.
'The Lover'. Reprinted in A20.
'Mrs. Windermere'. Reprinted in A20.
'The Shadowy Third'. Reprinted in A20. Published in anthology, G2.

19

'The Evil that Men do —'. Reprinted in A20.
'Sunday Evening'. Reprinted in A20.
'Coming Home'. Reprinted in A20 and A23. Published in anthology, G1.1.

Notes: Published 1 May 1923, in an edition of 2,000 copies at 5/0.
Transcribed in Braille 1949, in NLB.

Reviews:
unsigned, *TLS* 22 (10 May 1923): 320
Raymond Mortimer, *New Statesman* 21 (26 May 1923):201
V. Sackville-West, *Nation* (London) 33 #10 (9 June 1923): 336–37
Gerald Bullett, *Challenge* 2 #12 (15 June 1923): 234
unsigned, *Spectator* 131 (21 July 1923): 91–92

b. *First edition (American issue)*:
Encounters: Stories | by Elizabeth Bowen | [publisher's device] |
Boni and Liveright | Publishers | New York

Collation: $7\frac{1}{2}$ x 5"; [A]⁴ B–N⁸ O⁸ (–O₇, ₈); pp. [8], 1–203 [204].
Contents remain as in the first edition through [204], except in the fol-
lowing respects: [2]: blank. [4]: '*Printed for Boni and Liveright | in
Great Britain*'.

Binding: As in the first edition, except for the omission of the triple rules
on the spine.

Dust jacket: Not seen.

Contents: As in the first edition.

Notes: Published in September 1924, at $2. From sheets printed in Eng-
land and bound in the U.S., Boni and Liveright was to have issued 500
copies. Since publisher's records no longer exist, one cannot determine
whether these plans were carried out.

Reviews:
unsigned, *NYTBR* 29 (21 Sept. 1924): 14
E. McD. J., *NYWorld* 65 (21 Sept. 1924): 7E
John Ferris, *NYEPostLR* (27 Sept. 1924):14
unsigned, *NYHTB* 1 (5 Oct. 1924): 13
H. B., *NCDN* (12 Oct. 1924): 8
unsigned, *SatRev* 1 (25 Oct. 1924): 234
unsigned, *Outlook* 138 (17 Dec. 1924): 648

c. *Second edition* (re-set):
ENCOUNTERS | [swelled rule] | *Early Stories by* | ELIZA-
BETH BOWEN | SIDGWICK & JACKSON · LONDON | 1949

Collation: $7\frac{3}{8}$ x 5"; [A]⁸ B–L⁸ M¹⁰; pp. [i–iv] v–xiii [xiv–xvi], 1–178
[179–180].

[i]: half title. [ii]: blank. [iii]: title page. [iv]: 'To M. J. | PRINTED IN GREAT BRITAIN BY RICHARD CLAY AND COMPANY, LTD., | BUNGAY, SUFFOLK.' v–xiii: preface, dated '*April,* 1949.' [xiv]: blank. [xv]: contents. [xvi]: blank. 1–178: text. [179–180]: blank.

Binding: Bound in strong blue (178) cloth lettered across the spine in gold: 'EN– | COUNTERS | [triple rule] | ELIZABETH | BOWEN | SIDGWICK | AND | JACKSON'.

Dust jacket: Front and spine contain a moderate blue (182) outside border with black (267) printing on yellowish white (92) background. Back white. Front: '[one heavy and three light lines forming black-ruled frame on yellowish white (92)] ENCOUNTERS | [list of fourteen stories] | *early stories by* ELIZABETH | BOWEN'. Spine: 'EN– | COUNTERS | [three black rules] | ELIZABETH | BOWEN | SIDGWICK & | JACKSON'. Back recommends *The Collected Short Stories* of E. M. Forster. Front flap carries a photograph of Elizabeth Bowen followed by a blurb on the contents; back flap is blank.

Contents: As in the first edition, to which is added a preface, later revised and reprinted in A20 [combined with a previously unpublished preface to *Ann Lee's* (A2)]. Further revised, the preface was again reprinted in A25 and A26. MS, E1.

Notes: Published 28 October 1949, in an impression of 2,930 copies at 7/6.
A third English edition (in paperback) was published 28 April 1961, by Four Square Books in an impression of 20,000 copies, at 2/6. Not seen by the compilers.

Reviews:
Angus Wilson, *New Statesman* 38 (3 Dec. 1949): 656
Sylva Norman, *Spectator* 184 (24 March 1950): 400, 402
E. K., *Dublin Magazine* n.s. 25 #2 (Apr.–June 1950): 74

A2　　　　　　**ANN LEE'S AND OTHER STORIES**　　　　**1926**

a. *First edition*:
Ann Lee's: & other stories | by Elizabeth Bowen | London: Sidgwick & Jackson, Ltd. | 44 Museum Street, W.C.1 1926

Collation: 7¼ x 4¾"; π⁴ A–S⁸ [T]⁴; pp. [8], [1–2] 3–288 [289–296]. [1]: half title. [2]: 'BY THE SAME AUTHOR | Encounters | (published 1923)'. [3]: title page. [4]: blank. [5]: 'To | A.C.C.' [6]: blank. [7]: contents. [8]: 'NOTE | [six lines]'. [1]–288: text; 2, 24, 52, 78, 80, 106, 108, 140, 164, 166, 190, 212, 214, 234, 236, 264, and 266 blank. 288, at bottom: 'Printed in Great Britain by T. and A. CONSTABLE LTD. | at the University Press, Edinburgh.' [289]: publisher's device. [290]: blank. [291–296]: publisher's advertisements.

Binding: Two different bindings have been noted. All copies seen are bound in moderate brown (58) cloth, but some are lettered across the spine in gold and others in dark grayish brown (62): 'Ann Lee's | and other | stories | Elizabeth | Bowen | SIDGWICK | & JACKSON'. Blind-stamped on front cover: 'Ann Lee's | & other stories | Elizabeth Bowen'.

Dust jacket: Not seen.

Contents:
'Ann Lee's'. First printed in abridged form in *The Spectator* (C4). Reprinted in A20. MS, E2.
'The Parrot'. First printed in *Everybody's Magazine* (C6). Reprinted in *The London Mercury* (C6) and in A20. MS, E2.
'The Visitor'. Reprinted in A20. MS, E2.
'The Contessina'. First printed in a different version in *The Queen* (C5). Reprinted in A20.
'Human Habitation'. Reprinted in A20. MS, E2.
'The Secession'. Reprinted in A20. MS, E2.
'Making Arrangements'. First printed in *Everybody's Magazine* (C3). Reprinted in *Eve* (C3) and in A20. MS, E2.
'The Storm'. Reprinted in A20 and A23. MS, E2.
'Charity'. Reprinted in A20. MS, E2.
'The Back Drawing-Room'. Reprinted in A20. MS, E2.
'Recent Photograph'. Reprinted in A20. Translated, D59.

Notes: Published 14 April 1926, in an edition of 2,000 copies at 7/6.

Reviews:
unsigned, *Morning Post* (3 Apr. 1926):17
unsigned, *TLS* 25 (22 Apr. 1926):300
A. E. Coppard, *Guardian* (30 Apr. 1926):9
H. C. Harwood, *Outlook* (London) 57 (22 May 1926):360
unsigned, *N&A* 39 (29 May 1926):211–12
L. P. Hartley, *SatRevPLSA* 141 (5 June 1926):686–88
Gerald Gould, *Observer* 8 (6 June 1926):8
unsigned, *Daily Telegraph* (18 June 1926):15
unsigned, *Bookman* (London) 70 (July 1926):229
P. C. Kennedy, *New Statesman* 27 (17 July 1926):388
V. Sackville-West, *Vogue* (British edition) (late July 1926):47

b.   *First edition (American issue)*:
Ann Lee's: & other stories | by Elizabeth Bowen | [publisher's device] | Boni and Liveright | Publishers New York

Collation: 7½ x 5″; π^4 A–S^8; pp. [8], [1–2] 3–288.
Contents as in the first edition through p. 288, except in the following respect: [4]: *'Printed for Boni and Liveright in Great Britain'*.

Binding: Bound in dark blue (183) cloth, lettered across the spine in gold: 'ANN LEE'S | ELIZABETH | BOWEN | BONI & | LIVERIGHT'. On the front cover in gold: '[within an ornamental design of frames] Ann Lee's | Elizabeth Bowen'.

Dust jacket: Not seen.

Contents: As in the first edition.

Notes: Published 15 September 1926, at $2. Liveright no longer has records to indicate the number of copies issued; and T. & A. Constable (printer of the first edition) reports that, after printing the 2,000 copies ordered, it provided the molds presumably for shipment to the United States and printing there. However, as indicated above, the note on p. [4] indicates that the printing was in Great Britain. On 15 December 1969, Books for Libraries, Inc. reprinted 700 copies of this edition by photolithography, at $9.

Reviews:
unsigned, *NYTBR* 31 (3 Oct. 1926):9
H. W. Boynton, *Outlook* 144 (13 Oct. 1926):214
Mary Kolars, *NYHTB* 3 (31 Oct. 1926):21
unsigned, *BETrans* (17 Nov. 1926):7
Frances Newman, *NYEPostLR* (11 Dec. 1926):3
unsigned, *SpRep* (12 Dec. 1926):7f
Gladys Graham, *SatRev* 3 (15 Jan. 1927):514

A3   **THE HOTEL**   **1927**

a. *First edition*:
THE HOTEL | by | ELIZABETH BOWEN | LONDON | CON-STABLE & CO LTD | 1927

Collation: 7⅜ x 4⅞"; [A]² B–U⁸ X⁶; pp. [4], 1–314 [315–316].
[1]: half title. [2]: list of Bowen's works and review excerpts. [3]: title page. [4]: 'Printed in Great Britain by Butler & Tanner Ltd., Frome and London. 1–314: text. 314, at bottom: imprint as on [4]. [315–316]: publisher's advertisements.

Binding: Bound in grayish purplish blue (204) cloth lettered across the spine in moderate purplish pink (250): '[all within a frame] [rule] | THE | HOTEL | *by* | ELIZABETH | BOWEN | [rule] | [rule] | CONSTABLE'. On the front cover in pink: '[all within a frame] THE HOTEL | *by* | ELIZABETH BOWEN'.

Dust jacket: Entire jacket is pale yellow (89). Front: '[at center is a line sketch in black (267) and strong red (12) of a man and three women, with the shadow of a waiter holding a tray with three glasses in the background;] | [all block script letters with black edges and red centers] *The Hotel* [signed by artist D. Nachshen] | *Elizabeth Bowen'*. Spine: '[black and strong red] *The* | *Hotel* | *Elizabeth* | *Bowen* | [red and black line sketch of two tennis rackets tied with a bow, and a bird with a playing card in his beak] | *Constable'*. Back carries names and authors of fourteen novels printed by Constable. Front flap has a blurb on *Encounters* and *Ann Lee's*; back flap is blank.

Notes: Published 18 August 1927, in an unknown number of copies, at 7/6. The publisher's records were destroyed during World War II, but the dust jacket on a copy retained by the publisher indicates a second impression in October 1927.

A second English edition (in paperback) was published March 1944 by Penguin Books, at 0/9. Although on p. [4] of this edition appears 'Published in Penguin Books 1943', *The Bookseller* records publication during the week of 20 April 1944, and the deposit receipt stamped in the British Library copy dates from 15 March 1944.

The Collected Edition was published by Jonathan Cape 15 May 1950, at 7/6, and collated as follows: 7⅛" x 4⅝"; [A]⁸ B–R⁸; pp. [1–8] 9 [10] 11–270 [271–272]. It was reprinted August 1960 and October 1969.

Translated, D1. MS, E3. Transcribed in Braille 1950, in NLB.

Reviews:
unsigned, *Spectator* 139 #5173 (20 Aug. 1927):291
unsigned, *TLS* 26 (25 Aug. 1927):574
Cyril Connolly, *New Statesman* 29 (3 Sept. 1927):651–52
L. P. Hartley, *SatRevPLSA* 144 (3 Sept. 1927):311
Gerald Gould, *Observer* #7110 (4 Sept. 1927):5
unsigned, *N&A* 41 (17 Sept. 1927):784

b. *First American edition*:
[within an ornamental double frame] THE HOTEL | *By* | ELIZABETH BOWEN | [publisher's device] | NEW YORK | LINCOLN MAC VEAGH · THE DIAL PRESS | LONGMANS, GREEN & COMPANY | TORONTO | 1928

Collation: 7⅞ x 5⅛"; [1–18⁸ 19⁴]; pp. [1–6] 7–294 [295–296].
[1]: half title. [2]: blank. [3]: title page. [4]: [copyright notice] | *'First issue in America | April, 1928* | MANUFACTURED IN THE UNITED STATES OF AMERICA | BY THE VAIL-BALLOU PRESS, INC., BINGHAMTON, N.Y.' [5]–294: text, 6 blank. [295–296]: blank.

Binding: Bound in black cloth, lettered in black across a moderate orange (53) label on the spine: '[ornamental border] | THE | HOTEL | *By* | ELIZABETH | BOWEN | [publisher's device] | LINCOLN MAC VEAGH

| THE DIAL PRESS | [ornamental border]'. Blind-stamped on the front cover: the publisher's device.

Dust jacket: Cover in strong orange (50) and lettered in dark pale blue (201). Front: 'The | Hotel | By | Elizabeth | Bowen'. Spine: '[across in dark pale blue] THE | HOTEL | [ornamental leaf] | ELIZABETH | BOWEN | [publisher's device] | LINCOLN MAC VEAGH | THE DIAL PRESS'. Front flap and back of jacket include review comments on the novel. Back flap is blank.

Notes: Neither publisher nor printer has any information on this edition other than that it was published in April of 1928 as cited on p. [4] of the volume. However, the Book-of-the-Month Club distributed 55,600 copies at $2.50 as its April selection that year. The novel was not considered by the Club as a successful offering (Charles Lee, *The Hidden Public: The Story of the Book-of-the-Month Club* [Garden City, N. Y.: Doubleday & Company, Inc., 1958], p. 162). According to *Publisher's Weekly*, A. L. Burt Company published a paperback reprint of this edition for $.75 during the week of 2 February 1929; however, no copy of this reprint has been located by the compilers. On 10 October 1972, Greenwood Press, Inc. reprinted 150 copies by photolithography, at $12.50.

A second American edition (in paperback) was published on 19 April 1966, by Popular Library, Inc., (115,350 copies), at $.60.

A third American edition (in paperback) was published on 21 February 1980, by Avon Books (45,000 copies), at $2.25.

Reviews:
Christopher Morley, *SatRev* 4 (7 Apr. 1928):740
Margery Latimer, *NYHTB* 4 (8 Apr. 1928):4
John Chamberlain, *NYTBR* 33 (8 Apr. 1928):8
Tess Slesinger, *NYEPost* (21 Apr. 1928):13
unsigned, *SpRep* (13 May 1928):7f
unsigned, *BETrans* (19 May 1928):4
unsigned, *Independent* 120 (26 May 1928):509
John Macy, *Bookman* 67 (June 1928):431
unsigned, *Among Our Books* 33 (June 1928):320
Clifton Fadiman, *Nation* 126 (6 June 1928):652
Francis Lamont Robbins, *Outlook* 149 (6 June 1928):236
John R. Chamberlain, *NYTBR* 33 (24 June 1928):2
unsigned, *Booklist* 24 (July 1928):402
Deirdré O'Shea, *VQR* 4 (July 1928):447–48
D. B. W., *New Republic* 56 (12 Sept. 1928):107

A4　　　　　　**THE LAST SEPTEMBER**　　　　**1929**

a. *First edition*:
THE | LAST SEPTEMBER | by | ELIZABETH BOWEN | CONSTABLE & CO LTD | LONDON

Collation: $7\frac{3}{8}$ x $4\frac{7}{8}''$; [A]⁴ B–U⁸ X⁴; pp. [8], 1–312.

[*1*]: half title. [2]: excerpts from reviews of *The Hotel*. [3]: title page. [4]: [publisher's imprint] | *First published* 1929 | Printed in Great Britain by Butler & Tanner Ltd., Frome and London'. [5]: 'TO | JOAN GRACE REED'. [6]: ' "Ils ont les chagrins qu'ont les | vierges et les paresseux. . . ." | *Le Temps Retrouvé*.' [7]: contents. [8]: blank. 1–312: text. 312, at bottom: 'Printed in Great Britain by Butler & Tanner Ltd., Frome and London'.

Binding: Two different bindings have been noted: moderate yellowish brown (77) cloth with very deep yellowish green (138) lettering, and grayish purplish blue (204) cloth with black (267) lettering. Across the spine in each case: '[all within a frame] [rule] | THE LAST | SEPTEM-BER | *by* | ELIZABETH | BOWEN | *Author of* | *"The Hotel"* | [rule] | [rule] | CONSTABLE'. On the front, in each case: '[all within a frame] THE | LAST | SEPTEMBER | *by* | ELIZABETH | BOWEN | *Author of "The Hotel"* '.

Dust jacket: Cover in yellowish white (92) with large stripes of grayish olive green (127) on spine and bordering the painting on the front center. Front: '[grayish olive green bands, painting by 'P.V.P.' of house in trees, in moderate yellowish green (136) light gray (264) and dark reddish gray (23)] | [dark reddish gray] THE LAST SEPTEMBER | BY | ELIZABETH BOWEN | Author of "The Hotel" etc.'. Spine: '[green background and lettering in yellowish white boxed frame across] THE LAST | SEPTEMBER | BY | ELIZABETH | BOWEN | CONSTABLE'. Front flap contains excerpts of press opinions of *The Hotel* from *Morning Post, TLS, SatRevPLSA,* and *Spectator*. Price 7/6 net. Back flap blank. Back lists thirteen volumes of fiction published by Constable.

Notes: Published 31 January 1929, in an unknown number of copies, at 7/6; and reprinted 19 February 1931 (number of copies unknown), at 3/6.

A second English edition (in paperback) was published by Penguin Books, at 0/9, in December 1942. The British Library has record of a 5 December 1942 deposit.

The Collected Edition was published by Jonathan Cape, 26 July 1948, at 7/6, and collated as follows: $7\frac{1}{2}$ x $4\frac{5}{8}''$; [A]⁸ B–S⁸; pp. [1–8] 9–283 [284–288]. It was reprinted October 1949, August 1960, and October 1969.

Translated, D2–3. MS, E4. An excerpt appears in an anthology, G6.

Reviews:
Robert Lynd, *Daily News* and *WWGaz* (1 Feb. 1929):4
unsigned, *TLS* 28 (7 Feb. 1929):96
L. P. Hartley, *SatRevPLSA* 147 (9 Feb. 1929):184
unsigned, *Spectator* 142 #5250 (9 Feb. 1929):210
unsigned, *N&A* Supp. (9 Mar. 1929):812
Nora Meade, *Nation* 128 (15 May 1929):589–90

b. *First American edition*:
[within an ornamental double frame] THE LAST | SEPTEM-
BER | *By* | ELIZABETH BOWEN | *Author of "The Hotel"* |
[publisher's device] | NEW YORK | LINCOLN MAC VEAGH ·
THE DIAL PRESS | LONGMANS, GREEN & COMPANY |
TORONTO | 1929

Collation: 7⅜ x 5⅛"; [1–20⁸ 21⁴]; pp. [*10*], [1–2] 3–315 [316–318].
[*1–2*]: blank. [*3*]: half title. [*4*]: blank. [*5*]: title page. [*6*]: [copyright
notice] | 'MANUFACTURED IN THE UNITED STATES OF AMERI-
CA | BY THE VAIL-BALLOU PRESS, INC., BINGHAMTON, N. Y.'
[*7*]: ' "*Ils ont les chagrins qu'ont les vierges et les paresseux.*" | LE
TEMPS RETROUVÉ. [*8*]: blank. [*9*]: contents. [*10*]: blank. [1]–315:
text, 2, 104, and 212 blank. [316–318]: blank.

Binding: Bound in grayish purplish blue (204) cloth lettered in gold
across the spine: 'THE | LAST | SEPTEMBER | [publisher's device] |
BOWEN | LINCOLN MACVEAGH | THE DIAL PRESS'. The publish-
er's device is also blind-stamped on the front cover.

Dust jacket: Not seen.

Notes: Neither publisher nor printer has any information on this edition;
however, second impression copies include the following beneath the
copyright notice on page [*6*]: '*First printing January, 1929* | *Second
printing January, 1929*', and the title entry in the *Catalog of Copyright
Entries* is dated 25 January. On the other hand, *Publisher's Weekly*
records publication as of the week of 9 February 1929, at $2.50; and
the earliest review dates from this time.

Reviews:
unsigned, *NYTBR* (3 Feb. 1929):9
unsigned, *NYWorld* (10 Feb. 1929):11m
T. S. Matthews, *Bookman* 69 (March 1929):89
Mary Ross, *NYHTB* 5 (10 March 1929):22
W. T., *New Republic* 58 (13 March 1929):105
unsigned, *BETrans* (30 March 1929):4
unsigned, *SpRep* (31 March 1929):17e
unsigned, *Booklist* 25 (May 1929):321
unsigned, *COS* (May 1929):77

c. *Second American edition*:
[title and author's name within a double frame, with the publisher's device superimposed upon the center of lower frame]
THE LAST | SEPTEMBER | *by Elizabeth Bowen* | New York |
ALFRED · A · KNOPF | 1952

Collation: 7½ x 5⅛"; [1–10]¹⁶; pp [2], [i–iv] v–xi [xii-xiv], [1–2] 3–303 [304].

[1]: blank. [2]: list of Bowen's works. [i]: half title. [ii]: *'Ils ont les chagrins qu'ont les vierges et les paresseux.* | LE TEMPS RETROUVÉ'. [iii]: title page. [iv]: LC number, publisher's imprint, and copyright notice, concluding, *'Manufactured in the* | *United States of America. Published simultaneously in Canada by Mc-* | *Clelland & Stewart Limited.'* |'FIRST BORZOI EDITION'. v–xi: preface. [xii]: blank. [xiii]: contents. [xiv]: blank. [1]–303: text, 2, 98, 100, 204, and 206 blank. [304]: colophon, concluding, *'The book was set up in type, printed, and bound by* KINGSPORT | PRESS, INC., *Kingsport, Tenn.'*

Binding: Bound in dark reddish orange (38) cloth lettered in gold across the spine, all enclosed within a gold frame except the publisher's name: '[square and ornamental frames enclosing 4 stars] | [within a frame] THE | LAST | SEP- | TEM- | BER | ELIZABETH | BOWEN | [square and ornamental frames enclosing 4 stars] | ALFRED A | KNOPF'. Blind-stamped on the front cover: '[within a frame] EB'. On the back cover, publisher's device blind-stamped at the lower right.

Dust jacket: Front, spine, and back of pale purplish blue paper (203) with black (267) background for lettering. Front: '[centered rectangular design of black bordered by yellowish white (92) rule with concave corners to accommodate flower design] [yellowish white] THE | LAST | SEPTEM- | BER | *A Novel of Ireland in the* | *Nineteen-Twenties* | [outside frame] *Elizabeth Bowen* | [black] *WITH A NEW PREFACE BY THE AUTHOR'*. Spine: '[frame design similar to the design enclosing the front lettering] THE | LAST | SEP- | TEM- | BER | · | *Elizabeth* | *Bowen* | [publisher's device] | *Knopf'*. Back carries a photograph of Elizabeth Bowen by Angus McBean. Front flap carries a blurb on the contents, back flap a blurb on Elizabeth Bowen.

Contents: As in the previous editions, to which is added the 'Preface' [pp. v–xi]. Reprinted in A25 and A26. MS, E5.

Notes: Published 22 September 1952, in an impression of 3,500 copies, at $3.50 ($4.25 in Canada); a second impression of 1,500 copies in October 1952, varies in the deletion on p. [iv] of 'FIRST BORZOI EDITION' and the substitution of 'PUBLISHED SEPTEMBER 22, 1952 | SECOND PRINTING, OCTOBER 1952'; a third impression of 1,500 copies in January 1964, varies in the following respects:
[2]: list of Bowen's works is expanded and reset. [iii]: date on the title page is changed to '1964'. [iv]: copyright notice is modified to conclude, *'Manufactured in the* | *United States of America and distributed by Random House, Inc. Published* | *in Canada by Random House of Canada, Limited'*; a third line is added to the publishing register: 'THIRD PRINTING, JANUARY 1964'. [304]: Colophon is modified to conclude, *'The book was set up in type by* KINGSPORT PRESS, INC., *Kingsport,* | *Tenn. Printed and bound by* THE HADDON CRAFTSMEN, INC., | *Scranton, Pa.'*

A third American edition (in paperback) was published by Avon Books 21 December 1979 (50,000 copies), at $2.25.

Reviews:
Mark Schorer, *New Republic* 127 (3 Nov. 1952):18–19
Mary Lowrey Ross, *SatN* 68 (15 Nov. 1952):38 (review of 'McClelland & Stewart' issue)
H. Strickhausen, *SR* 73 (Winter 1965):158

A5   JOINING CHARLES AND OTHER STORIES   1929

a. *First edition*:
JOINING CHARLES | and other stories | by | ELIZABETH BOWEN | CONSTABLE & CO LTD | LONDON

Collation: 7¼ x 4⅝″; [A]⁴ B–O⁸ P⁴; pp. [2], [i–iv] v [vi], 1–216.
[1–2]: blank. [i]: half title. [ii]: list of Bowen's works and excerpted reviews. [iii]: title page. [iv]: '*First Published 1929* | Printed in Great Britain by Butler & Tanner Ltd., Frome and London'. v: contents. [vi]: blank. 1–216: text. 216, at bottom: imprint as on [iv].

Binding: Bound in red (11) cloth lettered across the spine in strong blue (178): 'JOINING | CHARLES | [double rule] | ELIZABETH | BOWEN | author of "The | Last September" | CONSTABLE'. On the front cover in strong blue: 'JOINING | CHARLES | and Other | Stories by | ELIZABETH | BOWEN | author of | "The Last | September" | "The Hotel" '.

Dust jacket: Cover of deep red (13) paper with vertical gold stripes ¼″ apart. Pasted rectangles of 1¼ x 1¾″ printed with identical information about the book are placed on the front cover top right hand and on the top of the spine. Front and spine collage: '[vivid reddish orange (34) with black printing across inside black ruled frame] JOINING CHARLES | & OTHER STORIES | ELIZABETH | BOWEN | Author of "THE | LAST SEPTEMBER" '.

Contents:
'Joining Charles'. First printed in a different version as 'The White House' in *The Royal Magazine*, (C7). Reprinted in A17. MS, E6. Published in anthology, G7.
'The Jungle'. MS, E6.
'Shoes: An International Episode'. Translated, D59. MS entitled 'The Shoes', E6.
'The Dancing-Mistress'. Reprinted in A17 and A28. MS, E6.
'Aunt Tatty'. First printed in *The Queen* (C9). Translated, D58.
'Dead Mabelle'. MS, E6.
'The Working Party'. Reprinted in A17. MS, E6.
'Foothold'. MS, E6. Published in anthology, G8.

'The Cassowary'. MS, E6.

'Telling'. First printed in B1 and reprinted in A17. Translated, D59. MS, E6. Radio script, E28. Broadcast, F19. Published in anthology, G4.

'Mrs. Moysey'. MS, E6.

Notes: Published 11 July 1929, in an unknown number of copies, at 6/o. The edition was reprinted in 1972 by The Scholarly Press, St. Clair Shores, Michigan, at $19.50.

The Collected Edition was published by Jonathan Cape 1 July 1952, at 8/6, and collated as follows: $7\frac{1}{8}$ x $4\frac{5}{8}''$; [A]^8 B–N^8; pp. [1–6] 7–205 [206–208].

Translated, D4. Transcribed in Braille 1929, in NLB.

Reviews:

B. E. Todd, *Spectator* 143 #5273 (20 July 1929):104

E. S., *New Statesman* 33 (27 July 1929):500

L. P. Hartley, *SatRevPLSA* 148 (27 July 1929):108

Gerald Gould, *Observer* (28 July 1929):6

Hon. Mrs. Robert Hamilton, *Sunday Times* (London) (28 July 1929):9

unsigned, *TLS* 28 (1 Aug. 1929):606

E. B. C. Jones, *T&T* 10 (2 Aug. 1929):939

I. H., *Irish Statesman* 12 (3 Aug. 1929):438

Sylvia Lynd, *Daily News* (20 Aug. 1929):4

N. M. H., *Guardian* (23 Aug. 1929):5

G. F., *Bookman* (London) 76 (Sept. 1929):310

b. *First American edition*:

[within a leaf and floral frame] JOINING CHARLES | *And Other Stories* | BY | ELIZABETH BOWEN | *Author of "The Hotel," Etc.* | [publisher's device] | LINCOLN MAC VEAGH | THE DIAL PRESS | NEW YORK · MCMXXIX | LONG-MANS, GREEN & COMPANY, TORONTO

Collation: $7\frac{1}{2}$ x $5\frac{1}{8}''$; [1–19^8 20^4]; pp [*10*], 1–302.

[*1–2*]: blank. [*3*]: half title. [*4*]: blank. [*5*]: title page. [6]: 'COPY-RIGHT, 1929, BY DIAL PRESS, INC. | MANUFACTURED IN THE UNITED STATES OF AMERICA | BY THE VAIL-BALLOU PRESS, INC., BINGHAMTON, N. Y.' [7]: contents. [8]: blank. [9]: half title. [*10*]: blank. 1–302: text.

Binding: Bound in boards covered with grayish olive green (127) plaid paper. The spine is covered with grayish olive green cloth lettered across in gold: 'JOINING | CHARLES | [waved rule] | BOWEN | [publisher's device] | LINCOLN MACVEAGH | THE DIAL PRESS'.

Dust jacket: Not seen.

Contents: As in the first edition.

Notes: Neither publisher nor printer has any information on the edition; however, *Publisher's Weekly* registers its publication during the week of 9 November 1929, at $2.50. In 1972 The Scholarly Press reprinted 81 copies of the edition under its own imprint.

Reviews:
Florence Haxton Britten, *NYHTB* 6 (24 Nov. 1929):4
unsigned, *NYTBR* 34 (24 Nov. 1929):7
Gertrude Daimant, *NYWorld* (5 Jan. 1930):11m
Gladys Graham, *SatRev* 6 (25 Jan. 1930):669

A6   FRIENDS AND RELATIONS   1931

a.   *First edition*:
FRIENDS AND | RELATIONS | A Novel | by | ELIZABETH BOWEN | LONDON | CONSTABLE & CO LTD | 1931

Collation: 7½ x 4¾"; [A]⁴ B–S⁸ [T]⁴; pp. [8], [1–2] 3–280.
[1]: half title. [2]: list of Bowen's works and excerpted reviews. [3]: title page. [4]: [publisher's imprint] | 'Printed in Great Britain by Butler & Tanner Ltd., Frome and London'. [5]: '*To* | B.' [6]: blank. [7]: contents. [8]: blank. [1]–280: text, 2, 84, and 192 blank. 280, at bottom: 'Printed in Great Britain by Butler & Tanner Ltd., Frome and London'.

Binding: Bound in moderate reddish brown (43) cloth lettered in dark blue (183) across the spine: 'FRIENDS & | RELATIONS | [heavy broken rule] | ELIZABETH | BOWEN | constable'. On the front cover in dark blue: 'FRIENDS & | RELATIONS | [heavy broken rule] | ELIZABETH | BOWEN'.

Dust jacket: Cover in strong greenish blue (169) paper lettered in dark blue (183). Front: 'FRIENDS & | RELATIONS | [heavy broken rule] | ELIZABETH | BOWEN | [twenty-seven line blurb on contents]'. Spine: 'FRIENDS & | RELATIONS | [heavy broken rule] | ELIZABETH | BOWEN | author of | THE HOTEL | etc. | Constable'. Back includes brief blurbs on *The Hotel, The Last September,* and *Joining Charles.* Front flap notes price at 7/6 net; back flap is blank.

Notes: Published 21 May 1931, in an unknown number of copies, at 7/6. Second impression copies vary from the first in the omission of the date on the title page and in the addition of the following, between the publisher's and the printer's imprints on p. [4]: '*First Published May 1931* | *Reprinted · June 1931*'.
    A second English edition (in paperback) was published by Penguin Books, at 0/9, in October 1943. The British Library has record of a 13 October 1943 deposit. It was reprinted October 1946.
    The Collected Edition was published by Jonathan Cape 9 July 1951, at

8/6, and collated as follows: $7\frac{1}{8}$ x $4\frac{5}{8}''$; [A]⁸ B–O⁸; pp. [1–8] 9–224. It was reprinted June 1966.

MS, E7. Radio script, E8. Broadcast, F36.

Reviews:
unsigned, *TLS* 30 (21 May 1931):406
H. C. Harwood, *SatRevPLSA* 151 (30 May 1931):797
L. A. G. Strong, *Spectator* 146 (30 May 1931):872

b.   *First American edition*:

[within an ornamental border] FRIENDS | AND | RELATIONS | *By* | ELIZABETH BOWEN | Author of *"The Hotel,"* etc. | [publisher's device] | LINCOLN MAC VEAGH | THE DIAL PRESS | NEW YORK · MCMXXXI | LONGMANS, GREEN AND CO., TORONTO

Collation: $7\frac{1}{2}$ x 5"; [1–19]⁸ [20]⁶; pp. [8], [1–2] 3–307 [308]. [*1*]: half title. [*2*]: blank. [*3*]: title page. [*4*]: [copyright notice] | 'MANUFACTURED IN THE UNITED STATES OF AMERICA | BY THE VAIL-BALLOU PRESS, INC., BINGHAMTON, N. Y.' [*5*]: 'TO | B.' [*6*]: blank. [*7*]: contents. [*8*]: blank. [*1*]–307: text, 2, 92, and 210 blank. [*308*]: blank.

Binding: Bound in grayish purplish blue (204) cloth, lettered in brilliant yellow (83) across the spine: 'FRIENDS | AND | RELATIONS | [wavy rule] | BOWEN | LINCOLN MACVEAGH | THE DIAL PRESS'. The publisher's device is blind-stamped on the front.

Dust jacket: Not seen.

Notes: Neither publisher nor printer has information on this edition; however, the title entry in the *Catalog of Copyright Entries* is dated 21 September 1931, whereas *Publisher's Weekly* records publication during the week of 10 October, at $2. Second impression copies tend to confirm the earlier date in that, following the copyright notice on p [*4*], a printing register is added: '*First printing September 1931* | *Second printing September 1931*'. Third impression copies contain an additional line: '*Third printing January 1932*'; and the title page dateline is changed to 'MCMXXXII'.

A second American edition (in paperback) was published on 21 April 1980, by Avon Books (40,000 copies), at $2.25.

Reviews:
Iris Barry, *NYHTB* 8 (27 Sept. 1931):6
unsigned, *NYTBR* 36 (1 Nov. 1931):6
V. P. Ross, *O&I* 159 (18 Nov. 1931):379
Dorothea Brande, *Bookman* 74 (Dec. 1931):465–66
unsigned, *F&C* 86 (Dec. 1931):xii
Hazel Hawthorne, *New Republic* 69 (2 Dec. 1931):76

unsigned, *Booklist* 28 (Jan. 1932):200
unsigned, *SatRev* 8 part 2 (16 Jan. 1932):463

a. *First edition*:
TO THE NORTH | by | ELIZABETH BOWEN | LONDON |
VICTOR GOLLANCZ LTD | 14 Henrietta Street Covent Gar-
den | 1932

Collation: 7¼ x 4⅞″; [A]⁸ B–U⁸; pp. [1–5] 6–318 [319–320].
[1]: half title. [2]: list of Bowen's works. [3]: title page. [4]: 'To | D.C. |
Printed in Great Britain by | The Camelot Press Ltd., London and South-
ampton | *on paper supplied by* Spalding & Hodge Ltd. | *and bound by*
The Leighton-Straker Bookbinding Co. Ltd.' [5–318]: text. [319–320]:
blank.

Binding: Bound in purplish black (235) cloth lettered across the spine in
moderate greenish yellow (102): 'TO | THE | NORTH | BY | ELIZA-
BETH | BOWEN | GOLLANCZ'.

Dust jacket: [2nd impression] Cover is brilliant greenish yellow (98) and
lettered in black (267) and vivid purplish red (254). Front: '[lettered in
black] *First Cheap Edition* | [scrolled boxed letters] A NOVEL BY |
Elizabeth Bowen | [vivid purplish red] TO THE | NORTH | [heavy rule] |
[two-line blurb signed by Sylvia Lynd] | [heavy rule] | 3/6 | Net'. [At top
right in heavy black ink are publisher's initials]. Spine: '[across in black]
TO THE | NORTH | By | ELIZABETH | BOWEN | 3/6 | NET | [pub-
lisher's device] | GOLLANCZ'. Front and back flap and back list 74 titles
from Gollancz's Cheap Editions.

Notes: Published 10 October 1932, in an impression of 3,000 copies, at
7/6; and reprinted 25 March 1935 (3,000 copies), at 3/6. This second
impression is bound in vivid red (11) cloth lettered in black (267). In
1946 the Continental Book Company in Stockholm, Sweden, photolitho-
graphed the edition (in paperback) in its series of Zephyr Books, as Vol.
72 of "A Library of British and American authors"; the gatherings of this
impression are signed [1]⁸ 2–20⁸ and the page size reduced to 7¼ x 4¼.
    A second English edition (in paperback) was published by Penguin
Books, at 1/0. Although on p. [4] of this edition appears 'Published in
Penguin Books 1945', *The Bookseller* records publication during the week
of 31 October 1946, and the deposit receipt stamp in the British Library
copy dates from 27 October 1946.
    The Collected Edition was published by Jonathan Cape 15 May 1950,
at 7/6 in the United Kingdom and $1.60 in Canada, and collated as

follows: $7\frac{1}{8}$ x $4\frac{5}{8}''$; [A]^8 B–T^8 [U]^4 X^8; pp. [3–8] 9–329 [330]. It was re-printed March 1961 and July 1970.

Translated, D5–8. MS, E9.

Reviews:

L. A. G. Strong, *Spectator* 149 (15 Oct. 1932):491
unsigned, *TLS* 31 (20 Oct. 1932):756
R. E. Roberts, *New Statesman* 4 (22 Oct. 1932):488
Gwendolyn Raverat, *T&T* 13 (22 Oct. 1932): 1144; (29 Oct. 1932):1181–82; (5 Nov. 1932):1214; (12 Nov. 1932):1250
Helen Morgan, *London Mercury* 27 (Dec. 1932):171

b.   *First American edition*:

[all within the narrowest but tallest of three strong yellowish green (131) frames] ELIZABETH BOWEN | TO THE NORTH | [publisher's device, in green] | [design of vertical lines] | NEW YORK | ALFRED · A · KNOPF | 1933

Collation: $7\frac{3}{4}$ x $5\frac{3}{8}''$; [1–20]^8; pp. [10] 1–306 [307–310].
[1]: blank. [2]: list of Bowen's works. [3]: half title. [4]: blank. [5]: title page. [6]: [copyright notice] | '*Manufactured in the United States of America* | FIRST AMERICAN EDITION'. [7]: 'TO | *D. C.*' [8]: blank. [9]: half title. [10]: blank. 1–[307]: text. [308]: colophon, concluding, '*This book was composed, printed, and bound by Vail-Ballou* | *Press, Inc., Binghamton, N.Y. The paper was manufactured by* | *S. D. Warren Co., Boston*'. [309–310]: blank.

Binding: Two different bindings have been noted:
Some copies are bound in light gray (264) cloth, lettered across the spine in very light yellowish green (134): '[between two pair of vertical lines, extending the length of the spine, the inner lines of each pair stepped inward in two stages toward the top] TO | THE | NORTH | ELIZABETH | BOWEN | ALFRED A. KNOPF'. Most of the front is covered by three blocks of colors, superimposed in the following order: the widest but shortest is very light yellowish green; narrower but taller is moderate yellowish green (136); narrowest but extending from bottom to top is black (267). Through the blocks of colors the title is lettered by the light gray cloth: 'ELIZABETH BOWEN | TO THE NORTH'. On the back, at the lower right, in moderate yellowish green, is the publisher's device.
Other copies are bound in light yellowish green cloth, lettered across the spine in black: '[all within a decorative vertical frame] TO | THE | NORTH | ELIZABETH | BOWEN | ALFRED · A · KNOPF'. Down the middle of the front runs a wide band of black from top to bottom, through which is lettered by the light yellowish green cloth, 'ELIZABETH BOWEN | TO THE NORTH'. On the back, at the lower right in black, is the publisher's device.

Dust jacket: Not seen.

Notes: Published 15 February 1933, in an impression of 2,060 copies, at $2.50, and reprinted February 1933 (1,000 copies), and January 1950 (2,500 copies). This third impression, announced for publication on 20 February 1950 in *Publisher's Weekly*, varies from the first two impressions in the following respects:

Title page transcription: [title and author's name within a double frame, with the publisher's device superimposed upon the lower sides] TO | THE NORTH | by *Elizabeth Bowen* | New York | ALFRED · A · KNOPF | 1950
Collation: 7½ x 5⅛"; pagination as in the first impression.
[2]: reset with a new list of works. [6]: as in the first impression, with 'FIRST AMERICAN EDITION' omitted. [308]: as in the first impression, with the final sentence on composition, printing, and binding omitted.
Binding: Bound in black cloth lettered in gold across the spine, all enclosed within a gold frame except the publisher's name: '[square and ornamental frames enclosing 4 stars] | [title within a frame] TO | THE | NORTH | ELIZABETH | BOWEN | [square and ornamental frames enclosing 4 stars] | ALFRED A. | KNOPF'. Blind-stamped on the front cover: '[within a frame] EB'. On the back cover, publisher's device blind-stamped at the lower right.
A second American edition (in paperback) was published by Avon Books 21 October 1979 (50,000 copies), at $1.95.

Reviews:
Isabel Paterson, *NYHTB* 9 (19 Feb. 1933):2
Louis Kronenberger, *NYTBR* 38 (19 Feb. 1933):7
T. S. Matthews, *New Republic* 74 (22 Feb. 1933):53
Dorothea Brande, *Bookman* 76 (Mar. 1933):292
unsigned, *New Outlook* 161 (Mar. 1933):57–58
E. C. P., *BETrans* (4 Mar. 1933):1
unsigned, *SatRev* 9 #2 (4 Mar. 1933):469
unsigned, *Nation* 136 (26 Apr. 1933):481–82
unsigned, *Booklist* 29 (May 1933):268
unsigned, *ChiDTrib* (10 June 1933):18

A8   **THE CAT JUMPS AND OTHER STORIES**   **1934**

THE CAT JUMPS | *AND OTHER STORIES* | by | ELIZA-BETH BOWEN | LONDON | VICTOR GOLLANCZ LTD | 14 Henrietta Street Covent Garden | 1934

Collation: 7¼ x 4⅞"; [A]⁸ B–S⁸; pp. [1–8] 9–285 [286–288].
[1]: half title. [2]: list of Bowen's works. [3]: title page. [4]: *'Printed in*

Great Britain by | The Camelot Press Ltd., London and Southampton | *on paper supplied by* Spalding & Hodge, Ltd. | *and bound by* The Leighton-Straker Bookbinding Co. Ltd.' [5]: contents. [6]: blank. [7]–285: text, 8, 22, 24, 40, 42, 60, 62, 72, 140, 162, 178, 180, 202, 216, 218, 244, 246, and 264 blank. [286–288]: blank.

Binding: Bound in purplish black (235) cloth, lettered in vivid yellow (115) across the spine: 'THE | CAT | JUMPS | AND OTHER | STORIES | ELIZABETH | BOWEN | GOLLANCZ'.

Dust jacket: Cover is brilliant greenish yellow (98) and lettered in black (267). Front: '[an insignia in the upper left-hand front in vivid purplish red (254)] | [black] THE | CAT JUMPS | *short stories by* | ELIZABETH | BOWEN | [a four-line blurb on new novel of Miss Bowen by L. P. Hartley [(*Week-End Review*)]'. Spine: '[across] THE | CAT | JUMPS | by | ELIZABETH | BOWEN | 7/6 | net | [publisher's device] | GOLLANCZ'. Front and back flaps and back blank.

Contents:
'The Tommy Crans'. First printed in *The Broadsheet Press* (C12), again in *The Listener* (C12), and reprinted in A11b, A23, and A33. Radio script, E30. Broadcast, F12. Published in anthology, G10.
'The Good Girl'. First printed in *Time and Tide* (C14). Translated, D59.
'The Cat Jumps'. First printed in B3 and reprinted in A11b, A17, and A28. Translated, D59, D60, D61, D72. Radio script, E29. Broadcast, F6. Published in anthology, G9.
'Last Night in the Old Home'. Reprinted in A11b.
'The Disinherited'. Reprinted in B10, A11b, A23, and A28. Translated, D72. MS, E35.
'Maria'. First printed in B2. Translated, D59. Broadcast, F57. Published in anthology, G5.
'Her Table Spread'. First printed as 'A Conversation Picture' in *The Broadsheet Press* (C13), again as 'Her Table Spread' in *The Listener* (C13), and reprinted in A11b, A23, A28, and A33. MS, E31. Published in anthology, G11.
'The Little Girl's Room'. First printed in *The London Mercury* (C15). MS, E34.
'Firelight in the Flat'. MS, E36. Radio script, E37. Broadcast, F58.1.
'The Man of the Family'.
'The Needlecase'. Reprinted in *Harper's Bazaar* (C89) and in A11b and A17. Translated, D59, D62, D63.
'The Apple-Tree'. First printed in B4 and reprinted in A11b. Radio script, E32. Broadcast, F45. Published in anthology, G12.

Notes: Published 6 July 1934, in an impression of 1,500 copies, at 7/6 in the United Kingdom and $2. in Canada. A second impression (500 copies) was printed in September 1934.
  The Collected Edition was published by Jonathan Cape 11 July 1949, at 7/6 in the United Kingdom and $2. in Canada, and collated as follows:

$7\frac{1}{8}$ x $4\frac{5}{8}''$; [A]^8 B–M^8; pp. [1–6] 7–191 [192]. It was reprinted March 1955, June 1967, and again in 1971.

Reviews:
unsigned, *Times* (London) (17 July 1934):8e
unsigned, *TLS* 33 (19 July 1934):508
William Plomer, *Spectator* 153 (20 July 1934):98
Peter Quennell, *New Statesman* 8 (21 July 1934):93
L. P. Hartley, *The Sketch* 167 (25 July 1934):174

A9   **THE HOUSE IN PARIS**   **1935**

a. *First edition*:

THE HOUSE IN PARIS | by | ELIZABETH BOWEN | LON-DON | VICTOR GOLLANCZ LTD | 1935

Collation: $7\frac{1}{4}$ x $4\frac{7}{8}''$; [A]^8 B–U^8; pp. [1–9] 10–318 [319–320].
[1]: half title. [2]: list of Bowen's works. [3]: title page. [4]: '*Printed in Great Britain by* | The Camelot Press Ltd., London and Southampton'. [5]: contents. [6]: blank. [7]–318: text, [8], 80, 250, and 252 blank. [319–320]: blank.

Binding: Bound in black (267) cloth, lettered across the spine in gold: 'THE | HOUSE | IN | PARIS | BY | ELIZABETH | BOWEN | GOLLANCZ'.

Dust jacket: Cover is brilliant greenish yellow (98) and lettered in black (267) and vivid purplish red (254). Front: '[five black lines consisting of two blurbs by Sylvia Lynd in the *Book Society News* and L. P. Hartley in the *Week-End Review* on *The Cat Jumps* and *To the North*] | [vivid purplish red] THE HOUSE | IN PARIS | *a novel by* | ELIZABETH | BOWEN | [seven black lines consisting of two blurbs on *To the North* and *The Cat Jumps* by Clemence Dane in *Good Housekeeping* and Gerard Hopkins in *The Landmark*]'. Spine: '[across] THE HOUSE | IN | PARIS | by | ELIZABETH | BOWEN | 7/6 | net | [publisher's device] | GOLLANCZ'. Front flap includes excerpts from reviews on *To the North* by Sylvia Lynd (*News Chronicle*), Frank Kendon (*JO'LW*), L. P. Hartley (*Week-End Review*), Kate O'Brien (*Sunday Referee*). Back flap and back include excerpts of reviews on *The Cat Jumps* by Richard Church (*JO'LW*), unsigned (*Times*), and Sylvia Lynd (*Book Society News*).

Notes: Published 26 August 1935, in an impression of 5,000 copies, at 7/6, and reprinted September 1935 (2,000 copies). A third impression on 16 October 1936 (2,000 copies), at 3/6, varies from the first two in the omission of the date from the title page and in the addition of the following at the top of p. [4]: '*First published August 1935 | Second impression September 1935 | Third impression (first cheap edition) October 1936*'.

A second edition (based on the Gollancz text) was published in English in Hamburg, Germany, as no. 299 in *The Albatross Modern Continental Library* in 1936. The compilers have been unable to see a copy of this edition; however, a contract in the collection at the Hmuanities Research Center indicates that publication was to have been between 1 May and 8 October 1936.

A third English edition (in paperback) was published by Penguin Books, 23 August 1946, at 1/0. This was reissued in 1976 as one of the "Penguin Modern Classics," with an Introduction by A. S. Byatt. See H17.1.

The Collected Edition was published by Jonathan Cape 11 July 1949, at 7/6, and collated as follows: 7⅛ x 4⅝"; [A]⁸ B–Q⁸; pp. [1–6] 7–256. It was reprinted August 1952, September 1959, and June 1966.

A fifth English edition (in paperback) was published by Sphere Books Ltd., 6 June 1967 (20,000 copies), at 4/0.

A large-print edition, for the near blind, was published by Cedric Chivers Ltd. in 1978.

Excerpt reprinted in B20. Translated, D9–17. MS, E10. Radio script, E11. Broadcast, F25, F27, F32, F38.

Reviews:
Edwin Muir, *Listener* 14 (21 Aug. 1935):335
Peter Quennell, *New Statesman* 10 (24 Aug. 1935):253
L. P. Hartley, *The Sketch* 171 (28 Aug. 1935):422
unsigned, *TLS* 34 (29 Aug.. 1935): 536
William Plomer, *Spectator* 155 (30 Aug. 1935):334
unsigned, *T&T* 16 (31 Aug. 1935):1256
unsigned, *Daily Express* (19 Nov. 1951)
unsigned, *Daily Telegraph* (19 Nov. 1951)

b.   *First American edition*:
[all within 4 thin frames, within a thick frame, within a thin frame] *The House in* | PARIS | *by* | ELIZABETH BOWEN | [ornament] | [publisher's device] | NEW YORK · ALFRED · A · KNOPF | 1936

Collation: 7½ x 5⅛"; [1–18]⁸; pp. [14], [1–2] 3–268 [269–274].
[1–5]: blank. [6]: list of '*RECENT BORZOI FICTION*'. [7]: half title. [8]: blank. [9]: title page. [10]: [copyright notice] | '*Manufactured in the United States of America* | FIRST AMERICAN EDITION'. [11]: notice of fictional intent. [12]: blank. [13]: contents. [14]: blank. [1]–[269]: text, 2, 64, 210, and 212 blank. [270]: colophon, concluding, '*This book was composed, printed and bound by H. Wolff, New York. | The paper was manufactured by S. D. Warren Co., Boston.*' [271–274]: blank.

Binding: Bound in dark purplish red (259) cloth, lettered in grayish purplish pink (253) across the spine: 'THE HOUSE | IN PARIS | [in script] *Elizabeth* | *Bowen* | [ornamental panel] | [in script] *Knopf*'. On the front cover, the author's initials within a circle. On the back cover, at the lower right, the publisher's device.

Dust jacket: [Book-of-the-Month Club jacket] Grayish yellow (90) paper. Front: '[drawing of room with photograph of the Eiffel Tower seen through a window in three colors: moderate yellowish brown (77), dark yellowish pink (30), and light bluish green (163) and signed by 'Martinot'] [moderate yellowish brown] THE HOUSE | [tapered rule] | IN PARIS | [light bluish green] ELIZABETH BOWEN'. Spine: '[centered drawing of Eiffel Tower in the three colors] | [moderate yellowish brown] THE | HOUSE | IN | PARIS | [tapered rule] ELIZABETH | BOWEN | [light bluish green square background] [publisher's device] ALFRED · A · | Knopf'. Back has blurb on Elizabeth Bowen. Front flap has blurb about the novel. Back flap: 'What the English Critics say of | THE HOUSE IN PARIS | by A. G. Macdonnell, Gerald Bulltee, L. A. G. Strong, James Hilton, and Sylvia Lynd'.

Notes: Bowen's contract with Knopf dates from 8 November 1932; however, over three years passed before the book was actually published on 24 February 1936, in an impression of 2,500 copies, at $2.50. This is the date of publication cited by William Koshland of Knopf in correspondence with the compilers, although it should be noted that copies drawn from later impressions contain statements that publication was on 2 March 1936.

The novel was offered as a March selection by the Book-of-the-Month Club, which paid royalties on 83,000 copies printed from plates obtained from Knopf and modified in the following respects:

[6]: excerpt from a review of *To the North*. [9]: title page is partially printed in strong reddish orange (35), as are various ornaments throughout the volume. [10]: 'PUBLISHED MARCH 2, 1936' is substituted for 'FIRST AMERICAN EDITION'. [270]: in the final line, '*P. F. Glatfelter Co., Spring Grove, Pa.*' is substituted for '*S. D. Warren Co., Boston*'.

Binding: As in the original binding, except for deep reddish orange (36) cloth lettered in gold. The ornamental panel on the spine, the initials on the front, and the publisher's device on the back are blind-stamped.

Knopf records an alleged 'second impression' during February 1936 (7,500 copies), which William Koshland says was actually drawn from the BOMC printing. Also, in March 1936, Knopf records an alleged 'third impression' of 2,500 copies. It seems probable that these copies were also drawn from a BOMC printing, since an exhaustive search has brought to light no copies bearing the usual Knopf printing register of a second or third impression. In January 1949, however, an impression of 1,500 copies was printed; it varies from the first impression in the following respects:

Title page transcription: As in the first impression, with the date changed to '1949'.

Collation: size as in the first impression; [1]⁸ [2–9]¹⁶ [10]⁸; pp. [*12*], [*1–2*] 3–268 [269–276].

[*1–3*]: blank. [*4*]: list of Bowen's works. [*5*]: half title. [*6*]: blank. [*7*]: title page. [*8*]: [publisher's imprint] | [copyright notice] | '*Manufactured in the United States of America*'. [*9*]: notice of fictional intent. [*10*]: blank. [*11*]: contents. [*12*]: blank. [1]–[269]: text, as in the first impression. [270]: blank. [271]: colophon, with the final two lines omitted. [272–276]: blank.

Binding: Bound in moderate yellowish green (136) cloth, lettered in very deep purplish red (260) across the spine: 'THE | HOUSE | IN PARIS | [in script] *Elizabeth* | *Bowen* | [ornamental panel] | [in script] *Knopf*'. On the front cover, the author's initials within a circle. On the back cover, at the lower right, the publisher's device.

A fifth impression of 1,000 copies, printed in June 1961, varies from the first in the following respects:

Title page transcription: As in the first impression, with the date changed to '1961'.

Collation: [1–9]¹⁶; pp. [*14*], [*1–2*] 3–268 [269–274].

[*1–5*]: blank. [6]: list of Bowen's works (expanded upon the list in the fourth impression). [7]: half title. [8]: blank. [9]: title page. [10]: [completely reset] [publisher's device] | [copyright notice] | 'PUBLISHED MARCH 2, 1936 | REPRINTED THREE TIMES | FIFTH PRINTING, JUNE 1961'. [*11*]: notice of fictional intent. [*12*]: blank. [*13*]: contents. [*14*]: blank. [1]–[269]: text, as in the first impression. [270]: blank. [271]: biographical note. [272]: blank. [273]: colophon, as in the fourth impression. [274]: blank.

A sixth impression of 1,000 copies, printed in October 1966, varies from the fifth in that, on the title page, the dateline is changed to '1966' and, on page [*10*], for the final two lines is substituted 'REPRINTED FOUR TIMES | SIXTH PRINTING, OCTOBER 1966'.

A second American edition (in paperback) was published by Vintage Books 16 September 1957, in an unknown number of copies, at $.95 in the United States and $1. in Canada. It was reprinted October 1962 (3,884 copies) and December 1966 (1,002 copies).

A third American edition (in paperback) was published by Avon Books 21 August 1979 (46,000 copies), at $2.50.

Reviews:
unsigned, *COS* (Mar. 1936):8
unsigned, *F&C* 95 (Mar. 1936):iv
Isabel Paterson, *NYHTB* 12 (1 Mar. 1936):5
Edith Walton, *NYTBR* 41 (1 Mar. 1936):6
unsigned, *SpRep* (1 Mar. 1936):7e
unsigned, *Time* 27 (2 Mar. 1936):79
M. E. P., *BETrans* (7 Mar. 1936):5
Fanny Butcher, *ChiDTrib* (7 Mar. 1936):12
unsigned, *Newsweek* 7 (7 Mar. 1936) 44; (9 May 1936):3
George Stevens, *SatRev* 13 (7 Mar. 1936):6
M. W., *ChScMM* (11 Mar. 1936):11

Mason Wade, *AmerRev* 7 (Apr. 1936):126
Edward Weeks, *Atlantic* 157 (Apr. 1936):n.p.
unsigned, *Booklist* 32 (Apr. 1936):232
unsigned, *Review of Reviews* 93 (Apr. 1936):21
Dorothy Van Doren, *Nation* 142 (1 Apr. 1936):425–26
T. S. Matthews, *New Republic* 86 (1 Apr. 1936):229
Herschel Brickell, *QB* ser. 5 (Summer 1936):35

A10   **THE DEATH OF THE HEART**   **1938**

a.   *First edition*:

THE DEATH OF | THE HEART | by | ELIZABETH BOWEN | LONDON | VICTOR GOLLANCZ LTD | 1938

Collation: 7¾ x 3⅞″; [A]⁸ B–EE⁸; pp. [1–9] 10–445 [446–448].
[1]: half title. [2]: list of Bowen's works. [3]: title page. [4]: [notice of fictional intent] | 'PRINTED IN GREAT BRITAIN BY PURNELL AND SONS, LTD. (T.U.) | PAULTON (SOMERSET) AND LONDON'. [5]: contents. [6]: blank. [7]–445: text, [8], 168, 170, 318, and 320 blank. [446–448]: blank.

Binding: Bound in black (267) cloth, lettered across the spine in gold or moderate greenish yellow (102): 'THE | DEATH | OF THE | HEART | BY | ELIZABETH | BOWEN | GOLLANCZ'.

Dust jacket: Cover is brilliant greenish yellow (98) paper with lettering in black (267) and deep purplish red (256). Front: '[black] ELIZA-BETH | BOWEN'S | *new novel* | [deep purplish red] THE DEATH | OF THE | HEART | [black thick rule]'. Spine: '[across in black] THE DEATH | OF | THE HEART | *by* | ELIZABETH BOWEN | 8/- | net | [black thick rule] | [vertically up] [deep purplish red] ELIZABEH BOWEN | [black thick rule] | [across] GOLLANCZ'. Back blank, as are front and back flaps.

Notes: Published 3 October 1938, at 8/0, in an impression of 15,000 copies according to the publisher's records. However, the printer's records indicate that this number represents two separate impressions prior to publication: 3 August (5,000 copies) and 20 September (10,000 copies). The publisher states that no further copies were printed at that time, but the printer states that 2,000 additional copies were printed 21 October 1938. The title was offered as an October choice by The Book Society, which apparently drew its copies from the impressions cited above, since the printer has no record of special printings for the Society. Thus, Book Society copies are distinguishable only by their bookplates inside the front covers. A third impression was printed 16 October 1939 (2,000 copies), at 3/6.
    The second edition (based on the Gollancz text) was published in

English in Leipzig, Germany, as No. 501 in *The Albatross Modern Continental Library* in 1939. While the compilers have been unable to see a copy of this edition, a contract in the collection at TxU indicates that publication was to have been between 28 January and May of 1939.

The Collected Edition was published by Jonathan Cape 26 July 1948, at 7/6, with collation as follows: 7⅛ x 4⅝"; [A]⁸ B–AA⁸; pp. [1–6] 7–384. A second impression in November 1949 consisted of two issues, one bearing the imprint of the Readers Union "for sale to its members only", and the other, dated 1950, with the Cape imprint. The publisher records a third impression in July 1952 while the register in later impressions cites a fourth impression in 1957 as well. Reprintings subsequent to these were in October 1959, June 1963, and June 1967.

A fourth English edition (in paperback) was published by Penguin Books 22 February 1962 (35,000 copies) at 4/0.

Translated, D18–28. MS, E12. Radio script, E13. Broadcast, F29, F35, F37. Excerpt published in anthology, G17.1.

Transcribed in Braille 1938, in NLB.

Reviews:
unsigned, *TLS* 37 (1 Oct. 1938):625
Wilfrid Gibson, *Guardian* (7 Oct. 1938):7
Graham Greene, *Spectator* 161 (7 Oct. 1938):578
Raymond Mortimer, *New Statesman* 16 (8 Oct. 1938):534
Edwin Muir, *Listener* 20 (13 Oct. 1938):795
Wilfrid Gibson, *ManGW* (14 Oct. 1938):314
Tullis Clare, *T&T* (15 Oct. 1938):1435–36
L. P. Hartley, *The Sketch*, 184 (19 Oct. 1938):140, 142
Humbert Wolfe, *Living Age* 355 (Nov. 1938):282–83
Marie Scott-James, *London Mercury* 39 (Nov. 1938):89–90
Sir Hugh Walpole, *JO'LW* Christmas No. (2 Dec. 1938):349

b. *First American edition:*
[title in script] The Death | of the | Heart | ELIZABETH | BOWEN | [all within a double frame] [publisher's device] | NEW YORK · ALFRED · A · KNOPF | 1939

Collation: 8 x 5½"; [1–12¹⁶ 13¹⁰ 14¹⁶]; pp. [12], [1–2] 3–418 [419–424]. [1–3]: blank. [4]: list of Bowen's works (2 titles). [5]: half title. [6]: blank. [7]: title page. [8]: copyright notice, concluding, '*First American Edition*.' [9]: notice of fictional intent. [10]: blank. [11]: contents. [12]: blank. [1]–418: text, 2, 156, 298, and 300 blank. [419]: blank. [420]: colophon, concluding, '*This book was composed, printed, and bound by* | H. WOLFF, *New York*. | *The paper was made by* S. D. WARREN CO., *Boston*. | *Designed by* GEORGE SALTER'. [421–424]: blank.

Binding: Bound in deep red (13) cloth. Over a spinal design of alternating very light blue (180) and dark grayish blue (187) curved lines: '[title and author's name lettered across in deep red upon a dark grayish

blue background] THE | DEATH | OF THE | HEART | · | ELIZA-
BETH | BOWEN | [in black] [ornamental design] | KNOPF'. On the
front cover: '[title lettered in deep red script upon a dark grayish blue
background] The Death of the Heart | [ornamental border of alternating
very light blue and dark grayish blue lines]'. Publisher's device in dark
grayish blue on the back cover.

Dust jacket: [3rd impression] Top portion of front and spine in deep
blue (179) and bottom portion in dark reddish orange (38). A line
sketch of a room interior, signed by 'Salter', divides the colors and is
centered between the front and spine. Front: '[yellowish white (92)]
The Death | of the | Heart | [printed at a slant] A NOVEL BY | ELIZA-
BETH BOWEN | *Author of* | *The House in Paris* | *Salter*'. Spine:
'[yellowish white] *The Death | of the | Heart* | BY | ELIZABETH |
BOWEN | [publisher's device] | Alfred · A · Knopf'. Back carries a
blurb on Elizabeth Bowen. Front flap carries a blurb on the contents and
comments by Isabel Paterson of *NYHTB* and by *SatRev*, in addition to
the publisher's device. Back flap carries commentaries on *The House in
Paris* by Fannie Hurst, Harry Hansen, Herschel Brickell, Lewis Gannett,
Isabel Paterson, and Robert van Gelder.

[8th impression] Front and spine same as the third impression. Back
carries photograph of Elizabeth Bowen by Alfred A. Knopf. Front flap
carries a blurb on the contents and a brief commentary by Isabel Paterson; back flap carries a blurb on Elizabeth Bowen.

Notes: Published 23 January 1939, in an impression of 6,000 copies at
$2.50. Copies from later impressions are characterized as follows:

IMPRESSION (Quantity)	PAGE [4]	PAGE [7]	PAGE [8]	PAGE [420]
2nd (3,300 copies)			copyright notice reset; 'First American Edition.' deleted and 'Published | January 23, 1939. Second Printing, January 1939.' added.	
3rd (3,150 copies)			'Third Printing, | February 1939.' added.	
4th (1,500 copies)			'Fourth Printing, March 1939.' added.	
5th (1,500 copies)	6 titles	'1939' deleted; '1948' added.	'Fifth Printing, August | 1948.' added.	'The paper was made by S. D. WARREN CO., Boston.' deleted
6th (1,550 copies)	11 titles (reset)	'1948' deleted; '1952' added.	'Sixth Printing, May 1952.' | publisher's imprint added.	
7th (1,000 copies)	13 titles	'1952' deleted; '1961' added.	'Seventh Printing, May 1961.' added to register; publisher's device added beneath imprint.	

Collation and pagination of the eighth and later impressions are modified to: $[1-11^{16}\ 12^8\ 13-14^{16}]$; [10], [1–2] 3–418 [419–422]. [1]: blank. [2]: list of Bowen's works. [3]: half title. [4]: blank. [5]: title page. [6]: copyright notice and printing register | publisher's imprint | publisher's device. [7]: notice of fictional intent. [8]: blank. [9]: contents. [10]: blank. [1]–[419]: as in the first impression. [420]: colophon. [421]: biographical note. [422]: blank.

IMPRESSION (Quantity)	PAGE [2]	PAGE [5]	PAGE [6]	PAGE [421]
8th (1,200 copies)	14 titles	'1961' deleted; '1963' added.	|'Eighth Printing, January 1963.' added.	
9th (1,200 copies)	15 titles	'1963' deleted; '1965' added.	'Ninth Printing, March 1965.' added.	biographical details added.
10th (2,039 copies)	16 titles	'1965' deleted; '1966' added.	'Tenth | Printing, December 1966.' added.	
11th (2,058 copies)	17 titles	'1966' deleted; '1969' added.	[re-set, with 'Eleventh Printing, August 1969.' added.]	biographical details added.
12th (1,000 copies)	[as in the 10th impression]	'1969' deleted; '1975' added	[as in the 10th impression, with 'Eleventh Printing, January 1975.' added.]	[as in the 10th impression]

A second American edition (in paperback) was published by Vintage Books 12 September 1955, at $.95, and reprinted January 1958 and October 1959. In correspondence, William Koshland at Knopf indicates that Vintage Books records lack information on early printing quantities and that, although the records are unclear, he believes a fourth impression was printed between 1959 and 1961. Further printings were in May 1961 (5,147 copies), November 1961 (4,950 copies), and February 1963 (7,741 copies). Of this 1963 printing (designated the seventh impression), 962 copies were hardbound for libraries. Further reprintings were in August 1965 (6,066 copies), September 1966 (6,833 copies), April 1967 (3,986 copies, of which 963 were hardbound for libraries), July 1969 (4,613 copies), October 1971 (4,782 copies), November 1972 (4,987 copies), and March 1974 (3,835 copies).

A third American edition (in paperback) was published by Avon Books 21 June 1979 (55,000 copies in the United States and 8,000 copies in Canada), at $2.25.

Reviews:
unsigned, *COS* (Jan. 1939):4
George Dangerfield, *SatRev* 19 (21 Jan. 1939):6
Isabel Paterson, *NYHTB* 15 (22 Jan. 1939):4
A. H. Eckstein, *NYTBR* 44 (22 Jan. 1939):7
Olga Owens, *BETrans* (28 Jan. 1939):1
Louise Bogan, *Nation* 148 (28 Jan. 1939):123–24
Clifton Fadiman, *NY* 14 (28 Jan. 1939):52
unsigned, *Time* 33 (30 Jan. 1939):65–66
M. M. Colum, *F&C* 101 (Feb. 1939):77–78
unsigned, *Booklist* 35 (1 Feb. 1939):190
T. S. Matthews, *New Republic* 97 (1 Feb. 1939):376
unsigned, *SpRep* (5 Feb. 139):7e
Herschel Brickell, *Commonweal* 29 (24 Feb. 1939):499–500
Margaret Williamson, *ChScMM* (25 Feb. 1939):10
Ralph Thompson, *YR* n.s. 28 (Spring 1939):xii
C. W. M. Hart, *CanF* 19 (Apr. 1939):28
unsigned, *QB* ser. 5 (Summer 1939):29
Lucy Cores, *NAmerR* 247 (Sept. 1939):186–87
Karl Arns, *Englische Studien* 74 (July 1940–41):249

A11 **LOOK AT ALL THOSE ROSES** **1941**

a. *First edition*:

LOOK AT ALL THOSE ROSES | *SHORT STORIES* | by | ELIZABETH BOWEN | LONDON | VICTOR GOLLANCZ LTD | 1941

Collation: 7¼ x 4⅞"; [A]⁶ B–Q⁸ R⁶; pp. [1–7] 8–263 [264].
[1]: half title. [2]: list of Bowen's works. [3]: title page. [4]: [notice of fictional intent] | 'To | SUSAN BUCHAN | PRINTED IN GREAT

BRITAIN BY PURNELL AND SONS, LTD. (T. U.) | PAULTON (SOMERSET) AND LONDON'. [5]: contents. [6]: blank. [7]–263: text. [264]: blank.

Binding: Bound in moderate blue (182) cloth, lettered in dark blue (183) across the spine: 'LOOK | AT ALL | THOSE | ROSES | BY | ELIZABETH | BOWEN | GOLLANCZ'.

Dust jacket: Cover in brilliant greenish yellow (98) with lettering in black (267) and deep purplish red (256). Front: '[deep purplish red] *Just Out* | [black double rule] | ELIZABETH | BOWEN'S | new volume of short stories | [deep purplish red printing and black rule] LOOK AT | [rule] | ALL THOSE | ROSES | by | ELIZABETH | BOWEN | 7/6 | net | [publisher's device] | GOLLANCZ'. Back and front flaps and back blank.

Contents:

'Reduced'. First printed in *The Listener* (C16) and reprinted in A17, A23, and A28. Translated, D64, D65, D72. MS, E38. Radio script, E39. Broadcast, F8, F43. Published in anthology, G13.

'Tears, Idle Tears'. First printed, in a different version, in *The Listener* (C31). Reprinted in A17 and in *The Blarney Magazine* (C31). Translated, D59, D72. Radio script, E43. Broadcast, F16. Published in anthology, G15.

'A Walk in the Woods'. First printed in *The London Mercury* (C64) and reprinted in A17. Translated, D72.

'A Love Story'. First printed in *Horizon* (C98) and reprinted in A23, A28, and A33. Published in anthology, G21.

'Look at All Those Roses'. First printed in *The Listener* (C59) and reprinted in A17, A23, and A28. Translated, D59, D72. MS, E44. Radio script, E45. Broadcast, F18. Published in anthology, G16.

'Attractive Modern Homes'. First printed in *The Listener* (C25) and reprinted in A17. MS, E40. Radio script, E41. Broadcast, F47.

'The Easter Egg Party'. First printed in *The London Mercury* (C73) and reprinted in A23. MS, E46. Broadcast, F49. Published in anthology, G17.

'Love'. First printed in *The Listener* (C94). Broadcast, F15.

'No. 16'. First printed in *The Listener* (C83), again in *Living Age* (C83), and reprinted in A23 and A28. Published in anthology, G18.

'A Queer Heart'. First printed in a different version as 'The Same Way Home' in *The London Mercury* (C81), revised and printed as 'A Queer Heart' in *Living Age* (C81). Published in anthology, G19.

'The Girl with the Stoop'. First printed in *JO'LW* (C82).

'Unwelcome Idea'. First printed in *New Statesman* (C100), and reprinted in A33. Published in anthology, G22.

'Oh, Madam . . .'. First printed in *The Listener* (C103), again in *Living Age* (C103).

'Summer Night'. Reprinted in A23, A28, and A33. Translated, D66, D67. Published in anthology, G23.

Notes: Published 20 January 1941, in an impression of 2,000 copies, at 7/6, and reprinted February 1941 (500 copies). The second impression copies are collated [A]⁸ B–R⁸; pp. [*4*], [*1–7*], 8–263 [264–268]. The additional eight pages are blank, with the first and last leaves (pp. [*1–2*] and [267–268]) glued as end papers.

The Collected Edition was published by Jonathan Cape 9 July 1951, at 8/6, and collated as follows: 7¼ x 4⅝"; [A]⁸ B–O⁸; pp. [1–8] 9–222 [223–224]. It was reprinted November 1967.

Transcribed in Braille 1941, in NLB.

Reviews:

L. P. Hartley, *The Sketch*, 193 (22 Jan. 1941):118
Charles Marriott, *Guardian* (24 Jan. 1941):7
Kate O'Brien, *Spectator* 166 (24 Jan. 1941):94, 96
unsigned, *TLS* 40 (25 Jan. 1941):41
Tullis Clare, *T&T* 22 (25 Jan. 1941):71
Desmond Hawkins, *New Statesman* 21 (8 Feb. 1941):144–45

b. *First American edition:*

[all within an ornamental double frame] *LOOK* | *AT ALL THOSE* | *ROSES* | SHORT STORIES BY | *Elizabeth Bowen* | 19 [publisher's device] 41 | *NEW YORK* · ALFRED · A · KNOPF

Collation: 7¾ x 5¼"; [1–20⁸ 21⁴ 22⁸]; pp. [*12*], [*1–2*] 3–329 [330–332]. [*1–3*]: blank. [*4*]: list of Bowen's works. [*5*]: half title. [*6*]: blank. [*7*]: title page. [*8*]: [copyright notice] | '*Manufactured in the United States of America* | FIRST AMERICAN EDITION'. [*9–10*]: contents. [*11*]: notice of fictional intent. [*12*]: blank. [1]–329; text, 2 blank. [330]: colophon, concluding, 'COMPOSED, PRINTED, AND BOUND BY H. WOLFF, NEW | YORK. PAPER MADE BY S. D. WARREN CO., BOSTON.' [331–332]: blank.

Binding: Two different bindings have been noted: light gray (264) cloth stamped with grayish blue (186) and strong purplish red (255), and yellowish gray (93) cloth stamped with moderate blue (182) and moderate red (15). In each case, a design of alternating blue and red curves runs down the spine, which is lettered across as follows: '[title and author's name in gray upon a panel of blue] LOOK | AT ALL | THOSE | ROSES | · | ELIZABETH | BOWEN | [in blue] [ornament] | KNOPF'. On the front cover: '[in gray script upon a panel of blue] Look at All Those Roses | [a horizontal band of the alternating curves]'. On the back cover, the publisher's device in blue.

Dust jacket: Not seen.

Contents:
'The Tommy Crans'. See A8.

'The Cat Jumps'. See A8.
'Her Table Spread'. See A8.
'The Needlecase'. See A8.
'The Apple-Tree'. See A8.
'The Disinherited'. See A8.
'The Last Night in the Old Home'. See A8.
'Reduced'. As in the first edition.
'Tears, Idle Tears'. As in the first edition.
'A Walk in the Woods'. As in the first edition.
'Look at All Those Roses'. As in the first edition.
'The Easter Egg Party'. As in the first edition.
'A Queer Heart'. As in the first edition.
'No. 16'. As in the first edition.
'The Girl with the Stoop'. As in the first edition.
'A Love Story'. As in the first edition
'Love'. As in the first edition.
'Oh, Madam . . .'. As in the first edition.
'Summer Night'. As in the first edition.

Notes: Published 4 August 1941, in an impression of 4,000 copies, at $2.50. A second impression of 950 copies was printed in January 1949, with variants as follows:

> The title page is identical to that of the first impression, except that the dateline reads '19 [publisher's device] 49'.

Collation: [1–11]¹⁶; pp. [*14*], [*1–2*] 3–329 [330–338].
Contents as in the first impression, except in the following respects: [*4*]: expanded list of Bowen's works. [8]: [publisher's imprint and copyright notice] | '*Manufactured in the United States of America* | *Published August 1941* | *Second Printing, January 1949*'. [9]: notice of prior publications. [*10*]: blank. [*11–12*]: contents. [*13*]: notice of fictional intent. [*14*]: blank. [330]: blank. [331]: colophon, as in the first impression. [332–338]: blank.

Reviews:
M. E. Clark, *LJ* 66 (Aug. 1941):669
Basil Davenport, *SatRev* 24 (2 Aug. 1941):13
Rose Feld, *NYHTB* 17 (3 Aug. 1941):3
Margaret Wallace, *NYTBR* 46 (3 Aug. 1941):7
unsigned, *SpRep* (3 Aug. 1941):7e
Vincent McHugh, *NY* 17 (9 Aug. 1941):53–54
unsigned, *Time* 28 (18 Aug. 1941):76
Robert Littell, *YR* n.s. 31 (Autumn 1941):xvi
unsigned, *Booklist* 38 (Sept. 1941):12
Kappo Phelan, *Decision* 2 #4 (Oct. 1941):84–86
Louise Bogan, *Nation* 153 (25 Oct. 1941):405–06
James Stern, *New Republic* 105 (27 Oct. 1941):550
P. T. Hartung, *Commonweal* 35 (14 Nov. 1941):96
unsigned, *QB* ser. 6 (Dec. 1941):12
Frederick Wilcox Dupee, *Kenyon Review* 4 (Winter 1942):116–17

a. *First edition*:

ENGLISH NOVELISTS | [swelled rule] | ELIZABETH BOW-
EN | [swelled rule] | *WITH* | *8 PLATES IN COLOUR* | *AND* |
19 ILLUSTRATIONS IN | *BLACK & WHITE* | [publisher's
device: colonade] | WILLIAM COLLINS OF LONDON |
MCMXXXXII

Collation: 8¾ x 6¼"; [A]⁴ B⁴ C⁸ D–E⁴; pp. [1–6] 7–47 [48]; eight plates
(in pairs between pp. 8 and 9, 16 and 17, 32 and 33, 40 and 41).
[1]: 'BRITAIN IN PICTURES | THE BRITISH PEOPLE IN PICTURES
| [swelled rule] | ENGLISH NOVELISTS'. [2]: 'GENERAL EDITOR |
W. J. TURNER' | [star] | [seven-line acknowledgment note]. [3]: title
page. [4]: 'PRODUCED BY | ADPRINT LIMITED LONDON | [star] |
PRINTED | IN GREAT BRITAIN BY | WM. COLLINS SONS AND
CO. LTD. GLASGOW'. [5–6]: illustrations. 7–[48]: text.

Binding: Bound in boards covered in dark grayish red (20) paper lettered in pale yellow (89) up the spine: '[triple rule] ELIZABETH
BOWEN · ENGLISH NOVELISTS [triple rule]'. On the front cover in
pale yellow: [all within a triple frame] ENGLISH NOVELISTS | [quill
and inkstand] | ELIZABETH BOWEN'. On the back cover, a triple frame
in pale yellow.

Dust jacket: Front cover and spine in dark grayish red (20) with pale
yellow (89) lettering and design; back cover reverses printing and back-
ground colors. Front: '[pale yellow, three-line ruled border] ENGLISH |
NOVELISTS | [line drawing of quill pen and inkstand] | ELIZABETH
BOWEN'. Spine: '[vertically up] ELIZABETH BOWEN · ENGLISH
NOVELISTS'. Back cover carries twenty-six titles in the series: BRITAIN
IN PICTURES. Front flap has blurb on contents; back flap carries six
titles of 'The British Commonwealth in Pictures' already published and
future books 'In Preparation'.

Notes: Published prior to *The Sketch* review (6 May 1942) and probably
after 13 April, the date of the deposit receipt stamp in the British Library copy. This first impression (20,485 copies) was offered at 4/6 in
the United Kingdom and $1.35 in Canada. A second impression of 1945
(14,905 copies) varies from the first in the following respects: the title-
page dateline is changed to 'MCMXXXXV'; and at the bottom of p. [4]
is added 'SECOND EDITION'. In 1973, the first-impression text was reprinted under the imprint of Richard West, Haverton, Pennsylvania, at
$10. And it is available in xerographic reproduction through University
Microfilms at $6.

According to *Cumulative Book Index, 1943–1948*, Hastings House of
New York published the title at $2.00. *The National Union Catalogue*,

Pre-1956 Imprints cites a copy without date: however, this copy has not been located by the compilers, nor have inquiries to Hastings House and Collins been fruitful. We have, however, located an undated copy bearing the following imprint on the title page in substitution for the Collins imprint and date: 'BRITAIN IN PICTURES PUBLISHERS | Bahamas'. It has not been determined if this copy is drawn from an issue of the first impression or represents a separate impression.

Translated, D29–30. MS, E14. Appeared in anthology as a chapter in G27. Transcribed in Braille 1942, in NLB.

Reviews:
L. P. Hartley, *The Sketch*, 196 (6 May 1942):262
unsigned, *TLS* 41 (16 May 1942):250
Michael Riga, *T&T* 23 (13 June 1942):488
Yvonne Ffrench, *Life and Letters* 34 (July 1942):64

b. *Second edition* (reset):
ENGLISH NOVELISTS | [swelled rule] | ELIZABETH BOW-EN | [swelled rule] | *WITH* | *8 PLATES IN COLOUR* | *AND 16 ILLUSTRATIONS IN* | *BLACK & WHITE* | [publisher's device: colonade] | COLLINS · 14 ST. JAMES'S PLACE · LONDON | MCMXLVI

Collation: 8¾ x 6¼"; [1–2]⁴ [3]⁸ [4–5]⁴; pp. [1–6] 7–47 [48]; eight plates (in pairs between pp. 8 and 9, 16 and 17, 32 and 33, 40 and 41).
[1]: 'BRITAIN IN PICTURES | THE BRITISH PEOPLE IN PIC-TURES | [swelled rule] | ENGLISH NOVELISTS'. [2]: 'GENERAL EDITOR | W. J. Turner' | [seven-line acknowledgment note]. [3]: title page. [4]: 'PRODUCED BY | ADPRINT LIMITED LONDON | THIRD IMPRESSION | PRINTED IN GREAT BRITAIN BY | CLARKE & SHERWELL LTD NORTHAMPTON | ON MELLOTEX BOOK PAPER MADE BY | TULLIS RUSSELL & CO LTD MARK-INCH SCOTLAND'. [5–6]: illustrations. 7–[48]: text.

Binding: As in the first edition .

Dust jacket: Not seen.

Notes: Although described internally as the 'THIRD IMPRESSION', this printing is completely reset. Bowen's text shows no signs of authorial revision, but the black-and-white illustrations are rearranged (having been reduced from the original 19 to 16). Publication in 1946 was in an impression of 6,006 copies, at 5/o. In July 1947 a second impression (4,154 copies) varies in the following respects: the title-page dateline is changed to 'MCMXLVII' and on p. [4] the words 'THIRD IMPRES-SION' are replaced by 'FIRST PUBLISHED 1942 | FOURTH IM-PRESSION 1947'.

a. *First edition*:

BOWEN'S COURT | BY | ELIZABETH BOWEN | Author of *The Death of the Heart* | and *The Last September* | *WITH ILLUSTRATIONS* | LONGMANS, GREEN AND CO. | LONDON : NEW YORK : TORONTO

Collation: 8½ x 5⅜″; [A]⁴ B–Y⁸ Z⁴; pp. [i–v] vi–viii, 1–340 [341–344]; four plates (frontispiece and facing pp. 86, 140, 236); one folding genealogical table facing p. 1.
[i]: half title. [ii]: blank. [iii]: title page. [iv]: [publisher's imprint] | 'First Published 1942 | [code number] | Printed in Great Britain by the KEMP HALL PRESS LTD. | in the City of Oxford'. [v]: 'TO MY FATHER | HENRY CHARLES COLE BOWEN' | [acknowledgments]. vi: contents. vii: illustrations. viii: map. 1–332: text. 333–340: 'AFTERWORD', dated 'December, 1941'. [341]: bibliography. [342–344]: blank.

Binding: Bound in moderate yellowish green (136) cloth lettered in vivid reddish orange (34) across the spine: 'BOWEN'S | COURT | [swelled rule] | ELIZABETH | BOWEN | LONGMANS'.

Dust jacket: Front and spine of moderate bluish green (164) with lettering and design in yellowish white (92). Front: '[rectangular ruled border enclosed by scalloped design] *Bowen's | Court* | [diamond design] ELIZABETH | BOWEN | [two-line blurb on contents]'. Spine: '*Bowen's | Court* | [diamond design] | ELIZABETH | BOWEN | Longmans'. Back carries blurbs on three books by other authors. Front flap carries blurb on contents; back flap carries a blurb on the radio news program 'London Calling'.

Contents:
'Bowen's Court'.
'Afterword'.

Notes: Bowen's contract with Longmans dates from 17 May 1939; however, over three years passed before the book was published on 15 June 1942, at 16/0 in the United Kingdom and $5. in Canada. A second impression in September of that year is gathered [A]⁸ B–Y⁸ (with Y₈ serving as end paper) and varies on p. [iv] in the following respects: for 'First Published 1942' is substituted 'First Published 1942 | Reprinted by Novographic Process September 1942' and for the original printer's imprint is substituted 'PRINTED IN GREAT BRITAIN BY | LOWE AND BRYDONE PRINTERS LIMITED, LONDON, N.W. 10'. The publisher declines to reveal the number of copies issued in either impression. MS, E13.

Reviews:

Alice R. Eaton, *LJ* 67 Part 1 (15 June 1942):581
unsigned, *TLS* 41 (27 June 1942):322
unsigned, *Observer* (28 June 1942):3
Kate O'Brien, *Spectator* 169 (3 July 1942):15
unsigned, *Guardian* (22 July 1942):3
Edward Sackville-West, *New Statesman* 24 (25 July 1942):62–63
L. P. Hartley, *The Sketch* 197 (29 July 1942):78
unsigned, *Bell* 4:5 (Aug. 1942):368–71
Winifred Bryher, *Life and Letters* 34 (Aug. 1942):141–42
Renée Haynes, *T&T* 23 (12 Sept. 1942):726
Constantia Maxwell, *Dublin Magazine* n.s. 17:4 (Oct.-Dec. 1942):46–48
David Mathew, *Dublin Review* 212 (Jan.-Mar. 1943):92–94

b. *First American edition:*

[within an ornamental frame] BOWEN'S | COURT | BY | *Elizabeth Bowen* | [publisher's device] | ALFRED · A · KNOPF | NEW YORK: 1942

Collation: 8⅜ x 5⅝″; [1–28⁸ 29⁶ 30⁸]; pp. [*12*], [*1–2*] 3–458 [459–464]; eight plates (opp. pp. 20, 24, 114, 118, 146, 204, 318, and 362). [*1–3*]: blank. [*4*]: list of Bowen's works. [*5*]: half title. [*6*]: blank. [*7*]: title page. [*8*]: [copyright notice] | 'FIRST AMERICAN EDITION'. [*9*]: contents. [*10*]: blank. [*11*]: illustrations. [*12*]: blank. [1]: half title. [2]: map. 3–447: text. 448–458: 'AFTERWORD', dated 'December 1941'. [459]: Bowen genealogy. [460]: blank. [461]: colophon, concluding, 'COMPOSED, PRINTED, AND BOUND BY | THE PLIMPTON PRESS, NORWOOD, MASS.' [462–464]: blank.

Binding: Bound in vivid green (139) cloth. On the spine: '[ornamental border, in brilliant violet (206)] | [lettered across in strong blue (178)] BOWEN'S | COURT | *Elizabeth* | *Bowen* | [ornamental border, in brilliant violet] | [in strong blue script] Knopf'. On the front cover, an ornamental device in brilliant violet. On the back cover, the publisher's device in brilliant violet.

Dust jacket: Not seen.

Contents: As in the first edition.

Notes: Bowen's contract for the book with Knopf dates from 12 October 1937; however, nearly five years passed before it was published on 3 August 1942, in an impression of 4,000 copies, at $3.50. The edition is available in xerographic reproduction through University Microfilms at $23.50.

Reviews:
Isabel Paterson, *NYHTB* 19 (2 Aug. 1942):5
Herbert Gorman, *NYTBR* 47 (2 Aug. 1942):4
unsigned, *Time* 40 (3 Aug. 1942):79–80
unsigned, *NY* 18 (8 Aug. 1942):47
Harry Lorin Binsse, *Commonweal* 36 (21 Aug. 1942):424–25
Louise Bogan, *Nation* 155 (22 Aug. 1942):156
unsigned, *Booklist* 39 (Sept. 1942):10
Mary Colum, *SatRev* 25 (5 Sept. 1942):3–4, 17–18
Kay Boyle, *New Republic* 107 (21 Sept. 1942):355–56
M. M. Colum, *QB* ser. 6 (Dec. 1942):13
unsigned, *WiscLB* 38 (Dec. 1942):184

c. *Second American edition*:
[all within an ornamental double frame] BOWEN'S | COURT |
BY | *Elizabeth Bowen* | SECOND EDITION | [rule] | [publish-
er's device within ornamental borders] | [rule] | NEW YORK |
Alfred A. Knopf | 1964

Collation: 8¾ x 5⅝″; [1–13¹⁶ 14¹⁴ 15¹⁶]; pp. [2], [i–vii] viii, [1–2] 3–459
[460–466]; twenty plates (six on two sheets between pp. 22 and 23, four
on two sheets between pp. 118 and 119, three on one sheet between pp.
198 and 199, two on one sheet between 326 and 327, five on two sheets
between pp. 390 and 391).
[1]: blank. [2]: list of Bowen's works. [i]: half title. [ii]: blank. [iii]:
title page. [iv]: copyright notice, concluding, 'Manu- | factured in the
United States of America, and distrib- | uted by Random House, Inc. |
Published August 3, 1942 | *Second Edition, August 24, 1964*'. [v]: con-
tents. [vi]: blank. [vii]–viii: illustrations. [1]: half title. [2]: map. 3–447:
text. 448–459: 'AFTERWORD', dated *'Old Headington, Oxford, 1963'*.
[460]: blank. [461]: genealogical table. [462]: colophon, concluding,
'PRINTED AND BOUND BY | THE HADDON CRAFTSMEN, INC.,
SCRANTON, PA.' [463–466]: blank.

Binding: Bound in strong purplish blue (196) cloth, lettered in gold
across the spine: '[ornamental border] | BOWEN'S | COURT | *Elizabeth*
| *Bowen* | [ornamental border] | [in script] *Knopf*'. Blind-stamped orna-
mental design on front cover. Blind-stamped publisher's device at lower
right of back cover.

Dust jacket: Not seen.

Contents:
'Bowen's Court'. As in the previous editions.
'Afterword'. Revised.

Notes: Published 24 August 1964, in an issue of 2,044 copies, from an
impression of 4,068, at $6.95. By offset, the Ecco Press reprinted this

edition under its own imprint 15 September 1979 (4,000 copies), at $6.95.

Reviews:
George Walsh, *Cosmopolitan* 157 (Nov. 1964):28

d. *Second edition* (*English issue*):
The title page is identical to that of the second American edition, except that the following is substituted for the final five lines: '[publisher's device within ornamental borders] | [rule] | Longmans'.

Collation: 8¼ x 5½"; foliation and pagination as in the second American edition, except for the following:
[iv]: [publisher's imprint and copyright notice] | *'Printed in the United States of America'*.

Binding: Bound in deep red (16) cloth, lettered across the spine in red: '[rule] | [ornamental border] | [rule] | BOWEN'S | COURT | [rule] | *Elizabeth Bowen* | [rule] | [ornamental border] | [rule] | Longmans'.

Dust jacket: Moderate yellowish green (120) background, black (267) sketches and white (263) and black lettering. Front: '[white oval rule and circular scalloped design enclosing printing at top] [white] *Bowen's* | *Court* | *Elizabeth Bowen* | [black sketch of Bowen's Court]'. Spine: '*Bowen's* | *Court* | [white oval rule and scallop design enclosing black sketch of Bowen's Court] [black] *by* | [white] *Elizabeth* | *Bowen* | [black] Longmans'. Back carries same design and sketch as on spine. Front flap carries sketch and blurb on contents; back flap carries blurb on Elizabeth Bowen and commentaries on two of her books, *A Time in Rome* and *Afterthought*.

Contents: As in the second American edition.

Notes: Published 22 February 1965, in an issue of 2,024 copies from the American impression (A13c), at 42/0 in the United Kingdom and $9.25 in Canada.

Reviews:
John Davenport, *Spectator* 214 (19 Mar. 1965):367–68
D. A. N. Jones, *New Statesman* 69 (26 Mar. 1965):503
G. Harrison, *B&B* 10 (July 1965):34

A14   **SEVEN WINTERS**   **1942**

a. *First edition*:
SEVEN WINTERS | BY | ELIZABETH BOWEN | [a circular

Celtic device in deep reddish orange (36)] | THE CUALA
PRESS | DUBLIN IRELAND | MCMXLII

Collation: 8½ x 5⅝"; [a]⁴ b–i⁴; pp. [8], [1] 2–57 [58–64].
[*1–4*]: blank. [*5*]: title page. [*6–8*]: blank. [*1*]–57: text. [*58*]: blank.
[*59*]: [in red] 'Here ends "Seven Winters" by | Elizabeth Bowen. Four
hun- | dred and fifty copies of this | book, of which four hundred |
and forty are for sale, have been | set in Caslon type, and printed |
by Esther Ryan and Maire Gill, | on paper made in Ireland, and |
published by the Cuala Press, | 46 Palmerston Road, Dublin, | Ireland.
Finished in the last | week of August, nineteen hun- | dred and forty
two. | This is Number   '. [*60–64*]: blank.

Binding: Quarter-bound in grayish yellow (90) cloth, with boards covered in grayish yellow paper. The spine is lettered in black (267) on a
paper label: [vertically up] 'SEVEN WINTERS BY ELIZABETH
BOWEN'. On the front: 'SEVEN WINTERS | BY | ELIZABETH
BOWEN'.

Dust jacket: Unprinted glassine wrapper.

Notes: Published, at 13/6, in late 1942, the colophon indicating comple-
tion of the volume in late August, and the deposit receipt stamp in the
British Library copy being dated 15 October 1942. Although the colophon
states that the edition was limited to 450 copies, there are copies extant
(as in the Sellery collection) which are unnumbered and inscribed 'out of
series.' On 29 March 1971, the Irish University Press reprinted 257
copies by photolithography under its imprint, at $10.50.
   An excerpt was reprinted in *The Bell* (C129), another in *WD* (C211.1).

Reviews:
unsigned, *TLS* #2126 (31 Oct. 1942):539
Naomi Royde Smith, *T&T* 24 (2 Jan. 1943):15
Desmond Shawe-Taylor, *New Statesman* 25 (19 June 1943):403–4

b.   *First English edition*:
SEVEN WINTERS | MEMORIES OF A DUBLIN CHILD-
HOOD | By | ELIZABETH BOWEN | Author of | *Bowen's
Court, The Death of the Heart,* | *The Last September, etc.* |
LONGMANS, GREEN AND CO. | LONDON   NEW YORK
TORONTO

Collation: 6¾ x 5¼"; [A]⁴ B–F⁴; pp. [1–4] 5–48.
[*1*]: half title. [*2*]: blank. [*3*]: title page. [*4*]: [publisher's imprint] |
'*This Edition first published 1943* | CODE NUMBER: 12410 | PRINTED
IN GREAT BRITAIN | BY WESTERN PRINTING SERVICES LTD.,
BRISTOL'. 5: contents. 6: blank. 7–48: text.

Binding: Bound in very deep red (14) cloth, the spine lettered in gold: [vertically up] '*Seven Winters*'. On the front cover in gold: '*Seven Winters | by | Elizabeth Bowen | Longmans*'.

Dust jacket: Pale yellow (89) cover lettered in deep reddish orange (36). Front: 'SEVEN | WINTERS | by | ELIZABETH BOWEN | [small design] *Memories of* | A DUBLIN CHILDHOOD'. Spine: [vertically up] '*Elizabeth Bowen*—SEVEN WINTERS'. Back has blurbs on 'BOWEN'S COURT' by *Liverpool Daily Post, Sunday Times, Listener*, and *New Statesman*. Front flap has a blurb on the contents; back flap has a 29-line blurb on BBC program 'BRITAIN CALLS THE WORLD'.

Notes: Published 12 May 1943, at 3/6 in the United Kingdom and $1.25 in Canada. The publisher declines to reveal the number of copies printed.
   Transcribed in Braille 1943, in NLB.
   For the First American edition, see A25.

Reviews:
Desmond Shawe-Taylor, *New Statesman* 25 (19 June 1943):403–4
M. J. MacM., *Irish Press* 13 (11 Aug. 1943):2
unsigned, *Spectator* 171 (3 Sept. 1943):226
Robert Speaight, *Dublin Review* 213 (Oct.-Dec. 1943):196

A15   THE DEMON LOVER AND OTHER STORIES   1945

a. *First edition*:
THE | DEMON LOVER | *and Other Stories* | *by* | ELIZABETH BOWEN | [publisher's device] | JONATHAN CAPE | THIRTY BEDFORD SQUARE | LONDON

Collation: $7\frac{3}{8}$ x $4\frac{7}{8}''$; [A]8 B–M8; pp. [1–4] 5–189 [190–192]. [1]: half title. [2]: blank. [3]: title page. [4]: 'FIRST PUBLISHED 1945 | [publisher's imprint] | [wartime economy notice] | PRINTED IN GREAT BRITAIN IN THE CITY OF OXFORD | AT THE ALDEN PRESS | BOUND BY A. W. BAIN & CO. LTD., LONDON'. 5: contents. 6: notice of previous appearances. 7–189: text. [190–192]: blank.

Binding: Bound in light greenish gray (154) cloth, spine lettered across in red (11): 'THE | DEMON | LOVER | [ornamental rule] | ELIZABETH | BOWEN | [publisher's device]'. On the front cover, in red: 'THE DEMON LOVER'.

Dust jacket: Background color of front and spine is grayish yellow green (122) with a stripe an inch deep across the top front of moderate reddish brown (43). Front: '[upon the moderate reddish brown is lettered in grayish yellow green] ELIZABETH BOWEN | [yellowish white on grayish yellow green background] *The | Demon | Lover | and other Stories'*. Spine: '[lettered vertically up in moderate reddish brown against a grayish greenish yellow (105) background] *The Demon Lover and other Stories by* [grayish yellow green] *Elizabeth Bowen'*. Back is blank, in yellowish white. Front flap is yellowish white with blurb on the novel lettered in black, and priced at 7s. 6d. net; back flap is yellowish white and blank.

Contents:
'In the Square'. First printed in *Horizon* (C117). Translated, D59, D68. MS, E47. Published in anthology, G25.
'Sunday Afternoon'. First printed in *Life and Letters Today* (C113) and in *The Bell* (C113), and reprinted in A23 and A33. Published in anthology, G24.
'The Inherited Clock'. First printed in *Cornhill* (C135) and reprinted in A23. MS, E53. Broadcast, F42.
'The Cheery Soul'. First printed in *The Listener* (C130) and reprinted in A28. Published in anthology, G28.
'Songs My Father Sang Me'. First printed in B14 and reprinted in A23. MS, E55. Radio script, E56. Broadcast, F20. Published in anthology, G32.
'The Demon Lover'. First printed in *The Listener* (C122) and reprinted in A23 and A28. Translated, D59, D67.1, D72. Radio script, E49. Broadcast, F10, F41. Published in anthology, G26.
'Careless Talk'. First printed as 'Everything's Frightfully Interesting' in *The New Yorker* (C120).
'The Happy Autumn Fields'. First printed in *Cornhill* (C139) and reprinted in A23, A28, and A33. Translated, D72. Published in anthology, G31.
'Ivy Gripped the Steps'. First printed in *Horizon* (C147) and reprinted in A23 and A28. Translated, D59, D72. Published in anthology, G34.
'Pink May'. First printed in B13 and reprinted in *Argosy* (C204.1). Radio script, E51. Broadcast, F28.
'Green Holly'. First printed in a substantially different version in *The Listener* (C141).
'Mysterious Kôr'. First printed in *Penguin New Writing* (C136) and reprinted in A23 and A28. Translated, D59, D69, D70, D71, D72. MS, E54. Published in anthology, G30.

Notes: Published 22 October 1945, at 7/6. While production figures are not available, it is known that within a month an increase of 5,000 sheets was being considered. Then a second impression was printed the following March.
Translated, D31–34. Transcribed in Braille 1946, in NLB.

Reviews:
Harold Brighouse, *Guardian* (2 Nov. 1945):3
Henry Reed, *New Statesman* 30 (3 Nov. 1945):302–3
unsigned, *TLS* 44 (3 Nov. 1945):521
V. C. Clinton-Baddeley, *Spectator* 175 (9 Nov. 1945):444

Diana Witherby, *Horizon* 12 (Dec. 1945):431–32
Hugh Bradenham, *Life and Letters* 47 (Dec. 1945):216, 218
Marie Scott-James, *T&T* 26 (8 Dec. 1945):1036–38
unsigned, *Bell* 12.1 (Apr. 1946):76–79

b. *First American edition:* IVY GRIPPED THE STEPS AND OTHER STORIES
[all within an ornamental double frame] *Ivy* | *Gripped the Steps* | AND OTHER STORIES | BY | Elizabeth Bowen | 19 [publisher's device] 46 | NEW YORK · ALFRED · A · KNOPF

Collation: 7½ x 4⅞"; [1–8]¹⁶; pp. [i–vi] vii–xiv [xv–xvi], [1–2] 3–233 [234–240].
[i]: blank. [ii]: list of Bowen's works. [iii]: half title. [iv]: blank. [v]: title page. [vi]: [note, citing previous appearance of a story] | [copyright notice] | 'FIRST AMERICAN EDITION'. vii–xiv: 'Preface', signed and dated 'Elizabeth Bowen, October 1945'. [xv]: contents. [xvi]: blank. [1]–233: text, 2 blank. [234]: blank. [235]: colophon, concluding, 'COMPOSED, PRINTED, AND BOUND BY H. WOLFF, NEW YORK'. [236–240]: blank.

Binding: Bound in moderate blue (182) cloth lettered in gold across the spine: '[ornamental border] | *Ivy* | *Gripped* | *the* | *Steps* | [rule] | Elizabeth | Bowen | [ornamental border] | [double rule] | *Knopf*'. On the front cover, blind-stamped: '[within a round ornamental frame] *EB*'. Publisher's device blind-stamped at lower right of back cover.

Dust jacket: The front and spine are in moderate purplish red (258), black (267) and yellowish white (92). Front: '[background moderate purplish red] [yellowish white] IVY | GRIPPED | THE STEPS | & | OTHER STORIES | [double black rule frames author's name] [background yellowish white] [moderate purplish red] by ELIZABETH BOWEN | [background black] [yellowish white] [three lines describing twelve new stories]'. Spine lettered across: 'IVY | GRIPPED | THE | STEPS | & | OTHER | STORIES | *Elizabeth* | *Bowen* | [publisher's device] | *Knopf*'. Back: yellowish white bordered by thin black rule, design outside top and bottom enclosing photograph and blurb on Elizabeth Bowen. Front flap carries blurb on book; back flap carries the titles of five other books by Elizabeth Bowen.

Contents: As in the first edition, with the addition of the 'Preface', dated 'October 1945' (p. xiv). Prior to publication Knopf printed an unknown number of copies of the following promotional brochure: [dark blue (183)] [all within an ornamental double frame] This is a reprint of *Miss Bowen's* Preface | to her new volume of short stories | *IVY* | *Gripped the Steps* | By Elizabeth Bowen | It is a brilliant and

59

moving statement of a | distinguished writer's artistic credo | for these times. | *To be published on April 11th at $2.50 net.* | ALFRED A. KNOPF [publisher's device] NEW YORK 22, N.Y.

Collation: 8⅛ x 5⅜"; one unsigned gathering of six leaves.
[1]: title page. [2]: copyright notice. [3–10]: text. [11]: list of Bowen's works. [12]: blank.

Binding: Single-stapled. The outer sheet of the gathering is of heavier yellowish white (92) paper, serving as a cover.
The preface-text of the brochure (pp. [3–10]) collates with that of the published book (pp. vii–xiv), but is gathered differently and lacks pagination.
The preface was reprinted in *Cornhill* (C194) and in A19. Slightly revised, it appears as "Postscript' in the second English edition of *The Demon Lover* (A15c). MS of preface, E16.

Notes: Published 11 April 1946, in an impression of 5,000 copies, at $2.50. The second impression (2,500 copies) varies in that, on p. [vi], 'FIRST AMERICAN EDITION' is replaced by '*Published April 11, 1946* | *Second Printing, May 1946*', as a printing register. The third impression (950 copies) varies in that, on the title-page dateline, '46' is replaced by '48'; and, on p. [vi], '*Third Printing, May 1948*' is added to the printing register. The third impression is bound in grayish purplish pink (253) cloth, lettered in strong purplish red (255). The edition is available in xerographic reproduction of the first impression, through University Microfilms, at $12.60.

Reviews:
unsigned, *Kirkus* 14 (1 Mar. 1946):108
unsigned, *LJ* 71 (1 Apr. 1946):484
Virgilia Peterson, *NYHTB* 31 (7 Apr. 1946):5
John Farrelly, *NYTBR* 51 (7 Apr. 1946):1, 37
Sara Henderson Hay, *SatRev* 29 (13 Apr. 1946):70
Jack Conroy, *CSunBW* (14 Apr. 1946):3
unsigned, *Time* 47 (15 Apr. 1946):104, 108
D. S., *ChScM* (20 Apr. 1946):16
Diana Trilling, *Nation* 162 (20 Apr. 1946):484
unsigned, *NY* 22 (20 Apr. 1946):98
James Stern, *New Republic* 114 (29 Apr. 1946):628–30
Orville Prescott, *YR* n.s. 35 (Summer 1946):766
unsigned, *Booklist* 42 (1 June 1946):317
Kappo Phelan, *Commonweal* 44 (12 July 1946):311

c. *Second English edition*:
The title page is identical to that of the first edition.

Collation: 7¾ x 4⅞"; [A]⁸ B–M⁸ N⁴; pp. [1–4] 5–197 [198–200].

The contents are as in the first edition, second impression, with the following exceptions: [4]: 'FIRST PUBLISHED OCTOBER 1945 | SECOND IMPRESSION MARCH 1946 | THIRD IMPRESSION APRIL 1947 | PRINTED IN GREAT BRITAIN IN THE CITY OF OXFORD | AT THE ALDEN PRESS | BOUND BY A. W. BAIN & CO. LTD., LONDON'. [5]: (added to the table of contents is the line, 'POSTSCRIPT BY THE AUTHOR 190'.) 7–197: text. [198–200]: blank.

Binding: As in the first edition.

Contents: As in the first edition, to which has been added the postscript (see A15b). The postscript is dated (on page 197) as 'October 1944'; as the preface to the American edition of *Ivy Gripped the Steps*, it had been dated 'October, 1945'. The 1945 dating is correct since the piece refers to various short stories in the collection which were not published serially until that year.

Notes: Although identified by the publisher as the third impression of its original edition, this printing contains, in the added postscript, substantial new authorial material, making the printing in effect a new edition, dating from April 1947.

The Collected Edition was published by Jonathan Cape 1 July 1952, at 8/6, and collated as follows: $7\frac{1}{4}$ x $4\frac{5}{8}''$; A–O^8; pp. [1–6] 7–224. It was reprinted May 1970.

A fourth edition (in paperback) was published by Penguin Books 21 February 1966 (20,000 copies), at 4/6.

Reviews:
unsigned, *ObsWeekRev* (27 Feb. 1966):22 (review of Penguin edition)

A16 ANTHONY TROLLOPE: A NEW JUDGEMENT   1946

a. *First edition*:
ANTHONY | TROLLOPE | A NEW JUDGEMENT | [triple rule] | ELIZABETH BOWEN | GEOFFREY CUMBERLEGE | OXFORD UNIVERSITY PRESS | LONDON NEW YORK TORONTO | 1946

Collation: $7\frac{1}{4}$ x $4\frac{3}{4}''$; [1]^{16}; pp. [6], 1–22 [23–26]; four plates (in pairs between pp. 6 and 7, 14 and 15).
[1–2]: blank. [3]: half title. [4]: '*This "New Judgement" of Anthony Trollope | was first broadcast by the BBC on | 4 May 1945*'. [5]: title page. [6]: illustrations. 1–20: text. 21–22: bibliography. [23]: blank. [24]: 'PRINTED IN GREAT BRITAIN | AT THE CURWEN PRESS PLAISTOW'. [25–26]: blank.

Binding: Bound in yellowish gray (93) paper. On the front cover in black (267), within a deep orange (36) quadruple frame: 'ANTHONY | TROLLOPE | [triple rule] | ELIZABETH BOWEN | OXFORD UNIVERSITY PRESS'. At the bottom of the back cover in deep orange: 'PRICE: TWO SHILLINGS AND SIXPENCE NET.'

Dust jacket: Not seen.

Notes: First presented as a BBC radio broadcast on 4 May 1945 (see F7). Published 16 May 1946, in an impression of 5,000 copies, at 2/6. Reprinted in A19. MS, E17. Broadcast, F7.

Reviews:
Humphrey House, *New Statesman* (29 Sept. 1945): 215 (review of broadcast)
Malcolm Edwin, *Observer* (2 Apr. 1946)
unsigned, *TLS* 45 (1 June 1946):263
unsigned, *News & Book Trade Review* (8 June 1946)
V. S. Pritchett, *New Statesman* 31 (8 June 1946): 415
unsigned, *The Wind and the Rain* 3 #3 (Autumn 1946):162–63
William Brown, *CanF* 27 (Apr. 1947):23

b. *First American edition:*
[in deep brown (56), shaded block letters] ANTHONY | TROL-LOPE | [in black (267)] *A New Judgement* | [deep brown swelled rule] | [in black] BY ELIZABETH BOWEN | [deep brown swelled rule] | [in black] 1946 | Oxford University Press | *New York & London*

Collation: 6 x 4¼"; [1]²⁴; pp. [8], [1–2] 3–35 [36–40].
[1–2]: blank. [3]: half title. [4]: frontispiece. [5]: title page. [6]: [copyright notice] | 'FIRST AMERICAN EDITION | PRINTED IN THE UNITED STATES OF AMERICA'. [7]: illustrations. [8]: blank. [1]–32: text, 2 blank. 33–35: bibliography. [36]: blank. [37]: colophon. [38–40]: blank.

Binding: Trade copies are bound in boards, covered in marbled paper of a deep brown (56) background, with pale green (149), moderate yellow (87), and yellowish white (92) print. On the front cover, upon a printed black (267) label with a wavy edge partially defined by swelled moderate yellow lines: '[in pale green block letters, shaded with deep brown] ANTHONY | TROLLOPE | [in yellowish white] *A New Judgement* | [in moderate yellow block letters] ELIZABETH BOWEN | [signed at the lower right in yellowish white] Eckardt'. 'Christmas Keepsake' copies are stapled in heavy paper of the same design.

Dust jacket: None for either binding. Binding cover of Keepsake copies is wrapper, folded with flaps.

Notes: Published 12 December 1946, at $1. While the number of copies printed in the impression is unknown, it is known that 25,000 copies were distributed *gratis* by Oxford University Press as its 'Christmas Keepsake' that year. See E195, E207–8.

Reviews:
Eric Forbes-Boyd, *ChScM* (24 Aug. 1946):12
Kappo Phelan, *Commonweal* 46 (15 Aug. 1947):433–34

A17   **SELECTED STORIES**   **1946**

SELECTED STORIES | *by* | ELIZABETH BOWEN | [publisher's device: hourglass] | MAURICE FRIDBERG | DUBLIN : LONDON

Collation: $7\frac{1}{8}$ x $4\frac{1}{2}''$; [A]⁸ B–H⁸ (gatherings B, D, F, & H inserted and sewn in the center of gatherings A, C, E, & G respectively; B signed irregularly on B5); pp. [1–6] 7–127 [128].
[1]: half title. [2]: series note. [3]: title page. [4]: 'FIRST PUBLISHED NINETEEN-FORTY-SIX | MAURICE FRIDBERG | DUBLIN : LONDON | PRINTED BY HELY'S LIMITED DUBLIN | SET IN TEN POINT PLANTIN'. [5]: contents. [6]: blank. 7–126: text. 127: acknowledgments. [128]: blank.

Binding: Bound in yellowish white (92) paper patterned with dark blue (183) pen-and-scrolls and hourglasses. Spine: '[vertically up] [dark blue hourglass of the paper design] [title only in two lines] [black (267)] SE-LECTED | STORIES : ELIZABETH BOWEN [dark blue hourglass of the paper design]'. On the front cover in black: '[within a dark blue ornamental frame opening onto the top edge] HOUR-GLASS LIBRARY | [within a dark blue ornamental frame] SELECTED STORIES | ELIZA-BETH BOWEN | [within a dark blue ornamental frame opening onto the bottom edge] MAURICE FRIDBERG | DUBLIN : LONDON'. On the back cover in black within a dark blue ornamental frame is a list of titles in series.

Dust jacket: None.

Contents:
'The Dancing-Mistress'. See A5a.
'Look at All Those Roses'. See A11a.
'Reduced'. See A11a.
'Attractive Modern Homes'. See A11a.
'The Cat Jumps'. See A8.
'A Walk in the Woods'. See A11a.
'The Needle-Case'. See A8.
'Joining Charles'. See A5a.

'Telling'. See A5a.
'Tears, Idle Tears'. See A11a.
'The Working Party'. See A5a.

Notes: Published, at 2/6, in late 1946: *Whitaker's Cumulative Book List* indicates publication in October, and the deposit receipt stamp in the British Library copy is dated 16 September. Although nowhere acknowledged in the volume itself, Reginald Moore compiled the selection of stories.

Reviews:
L. P. Hartley, *T&T* 27 (7 Dec. 1946):1193
unsigned, *Bell* 13:4 (Jan. 1947):80–81

A18   **THE HEAT OF THE DAY**   **1949**

a. *First edition*:
[title and author's name within a double frame, with the publisher's device superimposed upon the center of the frame] THE HEAT | OF THE DAY | by Elizabeth Bowen | New York | ALFRED · A · KNOPF | 1949

Collation: 7½ x 5⅛″; [1–12]¹⁶; pp. [8], [1–2] 3–372 [373–376].
[1]: blank. [2]: list of Bowen's works. [3]: half title. [4]: blank. [5]: title page. [6]: [publisher's imprint and copyright notice] | 'FIRST EDITION'. [7]: '*To* CHARLES RITCHIE'. [8]: blank. [1]–372: text, 2 blank. [373]: blank. [374]: colophon, concluding, '*The book was set up in type, printed, and bound by* KINGSPORT | PRESS, INC., *Kingsport, Tenn. The typographic scheme* | *and the binding design are by* WARREN CHAPPELL.' [375–376]: blank.

Binding: Bound in moderate bluish green (164) cloth lettered in gold across the spine, all enclosed within a gold frame except the publisher's name: '[square and ornamental frames enclosing 4 stars] | [within a frame] THE | HEAT | OF | THE | DAY | ELIZABETH | BOWEN | [square and ornamental frames enclosing 4 stars] | ALFRED · A | KNOPF'. Blind-stamped on the front cover: '[within a frame] EB'. On the back cover, publisher's device blind-stamped at the lower right.

Dust jacket: The cover is dark bluish green (165) with decorations and lettering in yellowish white (92), grayish yellowish brown (80), and black (267). Front: '[rectangular design of grayish yellowish brown bordered by yellowish white rule with flower design in each of the four concave corners] | [yellowish white] THE | HEAT | OF | THE | DAY | [black] A NOVEL BY | [yellowish white] *Elizabeth Bowen*'. Spine: '[lettering across in yellowish white within a flower design at the top and bottom of the rectangular pattern of grayish yellowish brown] THE | HEAT | OF | THE | DAY | *Elizabeth Bowen* | [outside and below the design is publisher's device in black] | [yellowish white] *Knopf*. Back: '[dark bluish green] [carries a black-and-white photograph of Elizabeth Bowen by Angus McBean] [yellowish white] Elizabeth Bowen'. Front flap: '[carries blurb on the contents with the price in the upper corner] $3.00/net'. Back flap: '[dark bluish green] [within double boxed frame] *Elizabeth Bowen* | [blurb on the author] | [dark bluish green] [publisher's device]'.

The Literary Guild dust jacket deviates from the original Knopf jacket in the following ways:

The size of the jacket fits the larger trim size. The back of the jacket is yellowish white with black printing. The front flap: '[deletes the price] [at the bottom] [in dark bluish green] BOOK CLUB | EDITION'. The back flap does not include the publisher's device.

Notes: Published 21 February 1949, in an impression of 20,000 copies, at $3. in the United States and $3.25 in Canada. Of this impression, 500 copies constitute a simultaneous issue designed for presentation prior to publication; these copies vary only in that, on p. [1] appears: 'FIVE HUNDRED COPIES | OF THE FIRST EDITION OF | *THE HEAT OF THE DAY* | HAVE BEEN SIGNED BY | THE AUTHOR | [ornament] | [rule] | [hand signed] Elizabeth Bowen | [rule] | [ornament] | *Christmas 1948*'.

Simultaneous with the publication of the Knopf first impression, the Literary Guild offered *The Heat of the Day* to its members. Printing was from plates supplied by Knopf; however, Literary Guild copies vary from those of the first impression in the following respects:

[2]: blank. [6]: 'FIRST EDITION' deleted. [374]: blank. The page size is 7¾ x 5⅜", and the binding is of vivid green (139) cloth, without the publisher's device on the back cover.

Exclusive of the Literary Guild printing, there have been four impressions of the first edition. The second impression (3,000 copies) varies from the first in that, on p. [6], 'FIRST EDITION' is replaced by 'PUBLISHED FEBRUARY 21, 1949 | SECOND PRINTING, APRIL 1949' as a printing register. The third impression (1,000 copies) varies from the second in the following respects:

[2]: list of works reset and greatly expanded.

[5]: dateline changed to '1960'.

[6]: publisher's device added above the imprint and 'THIRD PRINTING, APRIL, 1960' added to the printing register.

The fourth impression (1,181 copies) varies from the third in the following respects:

[2]: list of works expanded.

[5]: dateline changed to '1966'.

[6]: printing register modified to 'PUBLISHED FEBRUARY 21, 1949 | REPRINTED TWO TIMES | FOURTH PRINTING, OCTOBER, 1966'.

A second American edition (in paperback) was published by Popular Library, 3 February 1966 (130,387 copies), at $.60.

A third American edition (in paperback) was published by Avon Books

21 February 1979 (45,000 copies in the United States and 8,000 copies in Canada), at $1.95.

Translated, D35–40. MS, E18. Broadcast, F33. An excerpt published in anthology, G37.1.

Reviews:
unsigned, *Kirkus* 16 (15 Dec. 1948):642
Katherine Tappert Willis, *LJ* 74 (1 Jan. 1949):58
Brendan Gill, *NY* 24 (19 Feb. 1949):78, 81
Glenway Wescott, *SatRev* 32 (19 Feb. 1949):9–10
Jack Conroy, *ChiST* (20 Feb. 1949):8x
Iris Barry, *NYHTB* 25 (20 Feb. 1949):3
Alice S. Morris, *NYTBR* 54 (20 Feb. 1949):1, 25
Gustav Davidson, *PIBR* (20 Feb. 1949):1
Theodore Kalem, *ChScM* (24 Feb. 1949):11
Diana Trilling, *Nation* 168 (26 Feb. 1949):254, 256
Jane Voiles, *SFChron* (27 Feb. 1949):17
John Farrelly, *New Republic* 120 (28 Feb. 1949):24–25
unsigned, *Time* 53 (28 Feb. 1949):96
unsigned, *Booklist* 45 (1 Mar. 1949):225
Charles J. Rolo, *Atlantic* 183 (Apr. 1949):84–86
Marguerite Pace Corcoran, *CathW* 169 (Apr. 1949):74
Anne Fremantle, *Commonweal* 49 (1 Apr. 1949):618–19
L. S. Munn, *SpRep* (3 Apr. 1949):8c
John L. Watson, *SatN* 64 (5 Apr. 1949):77
Vernon Young, *HudR* 2 (Summer 1949):311–18
Orville Prescott, *YR* n.s. 38 (Summer 1949):766
Walter Ernest Allen, *Year's Work in Literature* (1949):33

b. *First English edition*:
THE | HEAT OF THE DAY | by | ELIZABETH BOWEN | [publisher's device] | JONATHAN CAPE | THIRTY BED-FORD SQUARE | LONDON

Collation: 7½ x 4⅞″; [A]⁸ B–U⁸; pp. [1–4] 5–319 [320].
[1]: half title. [2]: list of Bowen's works. [3]: title page. [4]: '*To* | *CHARLES RITCHIE* | [swelled rule] | FIRST PUBLISHED 1949 | PRINTED IN GREAT BRITAIN IN THE CITY OF OXFORD | AT THE ALDEN PRESS | BOUND BY A. W. BAIN & CO. LTD., LON-DON'. 5–319: text. [320]: blank.

Binding: Bound in light yellowish brown (76) cloth lettered in vivid red (11) across the spine: 'THE HEAT | OF | THE DAY | [ornamental rule] | ELIZABETH | BOWEN | [publisher's device]'. On the front cover in vivid red: 'THE HEAT OF THE DAY'.

Dust jacket: [Book Society jacket] Front and spine in yellowish gray (93) paper with a strong orange (50) band across the top. Front: '[black (267) on strong orange] ELIZABETH BOWEN | [strong orange shading on black and white lettering] *The* | *heat* | [no orange] *of the* | [orange shading] *day*'. Spine: '[on strong orange band] ELIZABETH | BOWEN | [strong orange shading behind black and white lettering] *The* | *heat* | [no orange] *of* | *the* | [orange shading] *day* | [publisher's device]'. Back carries the Uniform Works of Elizabeth Bowen, listing two books in print and two in preparation, noting that each has frontispiece and embellishments by Joan Hassell and costs 7s 6d net. Front flap carries a blurb on the contents and indicates that the book was 'CHOSEN BY | THE BOOK SOCIETY'. Back flap is blank.

Notes: Published 21 February 1949, at 9/6. Although the quantity of this impression—or of any of the subsequent impressions—has not been determined, Michael S. Howard does state in *Jonathan Cape, Publisher* (London: Jonathan Cape, 1971) that, after publication, 'forty-five thousand copies were sold almost at once' (p. 240). Since five impressions were run off within the first two months, this figure may include all or some of these impressions. However, part of the first impression, whatever its total quantity, was simultaneously issued as the February offering of The Book Society. Copies from this issue vary in that, on the title page, the publisher's device is omitted and the final three lines are replaced by 'JONATHAN CAPE | AND THE BOOK SOCIETY' and, on p. [4], 'FIRST PUBLISHED 1949' is replaced by 'THIS EDITION ISSUED ON FIRST PUBLICATION | BY THE BOOK SOCIETY IN ASSOCIATION WITH | JONATHAN CAPE LTD | FEBRUARY 1949'. W. J. Furneaux (who later that same year joined Alden Press as Works Manager) states in correspondence that, according to his best recollection, such Book Society printing 'usually ran to about 8,000 or so copies'.

The second Cape impression in February 1949 varies from the first in that, on p. [4], 'FIRST PUBLISHED 1949' is replaced by 'FIRST PUBLISHED FEBRUARY 1949 | SECOND IMPRESSION 1949' as a printing register. The third impression varies from the second in that, on p. [4] 'SECOND IMPRESSION 1949' is changed to 'SECOND IMPRESSION FEBRUARY 1949' and 'THIRD IMPRESSION MARCH 1949' is added to the printing register. The fourth impression varies from the third in that, on p. [4], 'FOURTH IMPRESSION MARCH 1949' is added to the printing register. The fifth impression varies from the fourth in that, on p. [4], 'FIFTH IMPRESSION MARCH 1949' is added to the printing register.

Between the fifth and the sixth Cape impressions appeared an impression bearing on the title page, in place of the Cape device and the final three lines, '[society's device] | THE REPRINT SOCIETY | LONDON'; and following the accumulated Cape printing register on p. [4] appears 'THIS EDITION PUBLISHED BY THE REPRINT SOCIETY LTD | BY ARRANGEMENT WITH JONATHAN CAPE, 1950', followed by the original printer's imprint but not the binder's. The pages of this Reprint Society impression are reduced in size to 7¼ and 4½ inches and gathered [A]¹⁶ B–K¹⁶. Furneaux recalls that some 80,000 to 90,000 copies were printed and estimates the publishing date to have been no earlier than March of 1950.

The sixth Cape impression appeared in the same year, its copies varying from those of earlier Cape impressions only in that, on p. [4], 'SIXTH IMPRESSION 1950' is added to the printing register. A seventh impression varies from the sixth in that, on p. [4], 'SEVENTH IMPRESSION 1951' is added to the printing register, although Cape reports that it dates from December of 1950.

The eighth Cape impression (2 December 1954), in the format of its Collected Edition, varies in the following respects:

ELIZABETH BOWEN | [ornamental swelled rule] | THE | HEAT OF THE DAY | [upon a floral background] EB | JONATHAN CAPE | THIRTY BEDFORD SQUARE | LONDON

Collation: As in the previous Cape impressions, except that the size is reduced to 7 x 4½″ and a frontispiece is inserted to face page [3]. The contents vary only as follows:

[2]: [list of Bowen's works reset] [4]: 'FIRST PUBLISHED 1949 | FIRST PUBLISHED IN THE COLLECTED EDITION 1954 | [publisher's device] | *To* | *CHARLES RITCHIE* | PRINTED IN GREAT BRITAIN IN THE CITY OF OXFORD | AT THE ALDEN PRESS | BOUND BY A. W. BAIN & CO. LTD. LONDON'.

Binding: Bound in deep blue (179) cloth, lettered across the spine in gold: 'ELIZABETH | BOWEN | [ornament] | THE HEAT | OF THE | DAY | [publisher's device]'. Blind-stamped on the front cover: '[upon a floral background] EB'.

The ninth impression (March 1964) varies from the eighth in the following respects:

(1) It is gathered [A]¹⁶ B–K¹⁶.

(2) On p. [4], above the publisher's device is added 'REPRINTED 1964'.

(3) Binding cloth is moderate blue (182).

A tenth impression of November 1969 has not been seen by the compilers.

A second English edition (in paperback) was published by Penguin Books 22 November 1962, at 5/0 (25,000 copies).

Transcribed in Braille 1949, in NLB.

Reviews:
John Hayward, *Observer* (20 Feb. 1949):3
Seán O'Faoláin, *Listener* 41 (24 Feb. 1949):331
Paul Bloomfield, *Guardian* (25 Feb. 1949):3
Olivia Manning, *Spectator* 182 (25 Feb. 1949):266, 268
Walter Allen, *New Statesman* 37 (26 Feb. 1949):208–09
Paul Bloomfield, *ManGW* (3 Mar. 1949):10
L. P. Hartley, *T&T* 30 (5 Mar. 1949):229–30
unsigned, *TLS* 48 (5 Mar. 1949):152

J. Bayley, *National Review* 132 (June 1949):652–54, 656

Lord David Cecil, *Now and Then* (Autumn 1957):31 (review reprinted from unknown source)

A19   COLLECTED IMPRESSIONS   1950

a. *First edition*:

COLLECTED | IMPRESSIONS | by | ELIZABETH BOWEN | [publisher's device] | LONGMANS GREEN AND CO | LONDON NEW YORK TORONTO

Collation: 8½ x 5⅜"; [A]^6 B–S^8; pp. [2], [i–iv] v–ix [x], [1–2] 3–269 [270–272].

[*1–2*]: blank. [i]: half title. [ii]: blank. [iii]: title page. [iv]: [publisher's imprint] | '*First Published* 1950 | PRINTED IN GREAT BRITAIN BY | SPOTTISWOODE, BALLANTYNE AND CO LTD | LONDON AND COLCHESTER'. v–vi: foreword, signed and dated '*January*, 1950.' vii–viii: contents. ix: acknowledgments. [x]: blank. [1]–269: text, 2, 56, 58, 183, 202, 232, 246, and 248 blank. [270–272]: blank.

Binding: Bound in moderate purplish blue (200) cloth lettered across the spine in gold: 'ELIZABETH | BOWEN | · | *Collected* | *Impressions* | LONGMANS'.

Dust jacket: '[large old-fashioned mirror design with a moderate purplish blue (200) center to carry the yellowish white (92) lettering, framed in pale yellow (89) on a light grayish brown (60) background] ELIZABETH | BOWEN | *Collected* | *Impressions* | [pale yellow background] [moderate purplish blue] LONGMANS'. Spine with a moderate purplish blue background: 'ELIZABETH | BOWEN | · | *Collected* | *Impressions* | [publisher's device] | LONGMANS'. Back carries blurb on the contents. Front flap credits jacket design to R. A. Maynard; back flap is blank.

Contents:

I. Prefaces [to]:

Uncle Silas. First printed in B19.

The Flaubert Omnibus. In 1947 Bowen signed contracts for this volume, which originally was to have been published in England but later was planned for publication by Pilot Press in the United States. However, no record of actual publication has been found.

The Faber Book of Modern Short [*sic*] *Stories.* First printed as 'The Short Story' in B10. Published in anthology, G15.1.

The Demon Lover (The American Edition). This edition actually is entitled *Ivy Gripped the Steps*; see A15b.

The Blaze of Noon. First printed as 'A Foreword' in B12.

II. Reviews:

'The Girls'. First printed in *New Statesman* (C93).

'Horribile Dictu'. First printed in *New Statesman* (C86).
'Virginia Woolf I'. First printed in *New Statesman* (C114), where it is
'Manners'. First printed in *New Statesman* (C58).
    entitled 'Between the Acts'.
'Virginia Woolf II'. First printed in *Observer* (C128), where it is en-
    titled 'She Liked Writing'.
'The Achievement of Virginia Woolf'. First printed in *NYTBR* (C351).
    Published in anthology, G38.
'Ivy Compton-Burnett I'. First printed in *New Statesman* (C112), where
    it is entitled 'Parents and Children'.
'Ivy Compton-Burnett II'. First printed in *Cornhill* (C138), where it is
    entitled 'Post-Victorian'.
'Success Story'. First printed in *Observer* (C125).
'Anne Douglas Sedgwick'. First printed in *New Statesman* (C32).
'Fanny Burney'. First printed in *New Statesman* (C71).
'Lady Burton'. First printed in *Observer* (C127), where it is entitled
    'Being Only a Woman'.
'Myself When Young'. First printed in *TLS* (C295), where it is entitled
    'The Evolution of a Novelist'.
'Blind Alleys'. First printed in *New Statesman* (C77).
'Kindness to Women'. First printed in *New Statesman* (C56).
'Dress'. First printed in *New Statesman* (C66).
'Ben Jonson'. First printed in *New Statesman* (C42).
'E. M. Forster I'. First printed in *Spectator* (C23), where it is entitled
    'Abinger Harvest'.
'E. M. Forster II'. First printed in *New Statesman* (C74), where it is
    entitled 'Mr. Forster'.
'Manchester'. First printed in *New Statesman* (C38).
'Grace'. First printed in *New Statesman* (C79).
'A Straight Novel'. First printed in *New Statesman* (C40).
'The Shadow Across the Page'. First printed in *New Statesman* (C39).
'Van Doren on Shakespeare'. First printed in *New Statesman* (C111),
    where it is entitled 'Shakespeare'.
'Open to the Public'. First printed in *New Statesman* (C63).
'Children's Play'. First printed in *Spectator* (C119).
'Mr. Huxley's Essays'. First printed in *Spectator* (C37).
'Barrie'. First printed in *Spectator* (C109).
'Conrad'. First printed in *Spectator* (C26), where it is entitled 'Joseph
    Conrad'.
'Gorki Stories'. First printed in *New Statesman* (C91).
    Published in anthology, G20.
'D. H. Lawrence'. First printed in *NYTBR* (C220), where it is entitled
    'D. H. Lawrence: Reappraising his Literary Influence'.
'The Moores'. First printed in *New Statesman* (C95).
'Hamilton Rowan'. First printed in *New Statesman* (C132).
'Weeping Earl'. First printed in *New Statesman* (C131).
'One Ireland'. First printed in *New Statesman* (C43).
'Doubtful Subject'. First printed in *New Statesman* (C88).
'Dublin I'. First printed in *New Statesman* (C29), where it is part of

a review entitled 'Two Cities'.

'Dublin II'. First printed in *New Statesman* (C34), where it is entitled 'Portrait of a City'.

'Dublin III'. First printed in *New Statesman* (C76), where it is entitled 'Bouquet'.

III. Two Pieces:

'The Mulberry Tree'. First printed, simultaneously, in B7 and in *Life and Letters* (C15.1), where it is entitled 'A Wartime Schooling'.

'The Big House'. First printed in *The Bell* (C101).

IV. Plays, Pictures, Places:

' "King Lear" at Cambridge'. First printed in *New Statesman* (C72).

'Island Life'. First printed in *New Statesman* (C70).

'Royal Academy'. First printed in *New Statesman* (C27).

'Salzburg, 1937'. First printed in *Night and Day* (C50), where it is entitled 'Salzburg in the Distance'.

'London, 1940'. This and the following item are indicated in the text to have been prepared for the Ministry of Information. However, the Ministry was dissolved after the war; and its present counterpart, the Central Office of Information, has no information on either title. MS, E76.

'Dover: 1 June 1944'. See above.

'Folkestone: July, 1945'. First printed in *Contact* (C160), where it is entitled 'Facade at Folkestone'. MS, E60.

V. A Broadcast:

'Anthony Trollope—A New Judgment'. See A16.

VI. Two Pieces from *Orion*:

'Notes on Writing a Novel'. First printed in *Orion* (C144) and reprinted in A32. Translated into Danish and sent by Det Schønbergske Förlag as their Christmas greeting in 1947. Published in anthology, G33.

'Out of a Book'. First printed in Orion (C195). Published in anthology, G36.

Notes: Published 24 April 1950, in an impression of 1,250 copies, at 16/o in the United Kingdom and $3.50 in Canada. Two states of this single impression are known: in the first, p. ix is misnumbered 'x'; in the second, the numbering is correct. It is, of course, quite possible that the priority of states is reversed, the 'i' having fallen out during printing. However, as noted below, all copies seen of the American issue, as well as the second impression copies run off only for Knopf four months later, contain the correct pagination. The compilers suggest tentatively, then, that copies with the correct pagination be considered as in the second state.

Reviews:
Michael Swan, *Spectator* 184 (5 May 1950):618

C. V. Wedgwood, *T&T* 31 (6 May 1950):446
unsigned, *Listener* 43 (18 May 1950):887
A. M. P., *Guardian* (26 May 1950):4
Naomi Lewis, *New Statesman* 39 (27 May 1950):610, 612
unsigned, *TLS* 49 (9 June 1950):352
unsigned, *Dublin Magazine* n.s. 25 #3 (July-Sept. 1950):75
Carlyle King, *CanF* 31 (Apr. 1951):23

b. *First edition (American issue)*:
The title page is identical to that of the first edition, except that below Bowen's name is substituted the following: '[publisher's device] | NEW YORK: ALFRED A KNOPF | 1950'.

Collation: As in the first impression, second state, of the English edition, except that p. [iv] contains only the printer's imprint.

Binding: Two different bindings have been noted: black (267) cloth or grayish purplish blue (204) cloth, lettered in either case across the spine in silver: '[square and ornamental frames enclosing 4 stars] | [title within a frame] *COLLECT-* | *-ED* | *IMPRES-* | *-SIONS* | [unframed] ELIZABETH | BOWEN | [square and ornamental frames enclosing 4 stars] | ALFRED A. | KNOPF'. Blind-stamped on the front cover, within a frame: 'EB'. On the back cover, the publisher's device is blind-stamped at the lower right.

Dust jacket: Front and spine in deep purplish pink (248) with rectangular box of brownish gray (64). Front: '[rectangular design of brownish gray bordered by yellowish white (92) rule with flower design in the four concave corners as in A18a] [yellowish white] COLLECTED | IMPRESSIONS | [black] [five-line blurb on contents] [yellowish white] [outside rectangular design] *Elizabeth Bowen*'. Spine: '[rectangular design enclosing lettering] COLLECTED | IMPRES- | -SIONS | [diamond ornament] | *Elizabeth* | *Bowen* | [publisher's device] | *Knopf*'. Back carries titles of six fiction and two non-fiction books by Elizabeth Bowen. Front flap carries blurb on the contents; back flap carries a photograph by Elliot Erwitt and a blurb on Elizabeth Bowen.

Contents: As in the first edition.

Notes: Published 24 July 1950, in an issue of 2,600 copies, at $3.50, and reprinted November 1950 (1,205 copies). In each instance, sewn copies were imported from Longmans. In 1973, the edition was reprinted under the imprint of Richard West, Haverton, Pennsylvania, at $15.

Reviews:
unsigned, *Kirkus* 18 (15 June 1950):344
K. T. Willis, *LJ* 75 (July 1950):1177

Robert Gorham Davis, *NYTBR* 45 (23 July 1950):5
unsigned, *ChiST* (25 July 1950):5
unsigned, *Time* 56 (31 July 1950):70–71
Charles J. Rolo, *Atlantic* 186 (Aug. 1950):85–86
unsigned, *COS* (Aug. 1950):14
Fanny Butcher, *CTribMB* (6 Aug. 1950):3
Milton Rugoff, *NYHTB* 26 (6 Aug. 1950):5
unsigned, *Newsweek* 36 (7 Aug. 1950):79
unsigned, *NY* 26 (12 Aug. 1950):66
Joseph Kraft, *Nation* 171 (26 Aug. 1950):190–91
Ben Ray Redman, *SatRev* 33 (2 Sept. 1950):11
Kate Simon, *New Republic* 123 (11 Sept. 1950):20–21
Florence Boochever, *Bookmark* 10 (Oct. 1950):3
J. V., *SFChron* (22 Oct. 1950):24
Francis J. Thompson, *HopR* 4 (Winter 1950):69
unsigned, *NCF* 5 (1950):246–47

A20   EARLY STORIES [ENCOUNTERS & ANN LEE'S]   1951

[all within a double frame, with decorative borders at top and bottom] *Early Stories* | *[ENCOUNTERS & ANN LEE'S]* | *Elizabeth Bowen* | 19 [publisher's device] 51 | *NEW YORK* · ALFRED · A · KNOPF

Collation: 7¼ x 3¾″; [1–10]¹⁶ [11]¹⁸ [12]¹⁶; pp. [2], [i–iv] v–xx [1–2] 3–364 [365–366].
[*1*]: blank. [2]: list of Bowen's works. [i]: half title. [ii]: blank. [iii]: title page. [iv]: [publisher's imprint and copyright notice] | 'FIRST EDITION'. v–xviii: preface. xix–xx: contents. [1]–364: text, 2 and 156 blank. [365]: blank. [366]: colophon, concluding, '*Composed, printed, and bound by* | *Kingsport Press, Inc., Kingsport, Tennessee.*'

Binding: Bound in dark purplish red (259) cloth lettered across the spine in silver: '[all within a frame, except the publisher's name] [square and decorative frames enclosing 4 stars] | [within a frame] *EARLY* | *STORIES* | ELIZABETH | BOWEN | [square and ornamental frames enclosing 4 stars] | ALFRED · A | KNOPF'. Blind-stamped on the front cover: '[within a frame] EB'. On the back cover, publisher's device blind-stamped at the lower right.

Dust jacket: In three background and lettering colors with ruled borders and design. Front: '[top to bottom: background moderate reddish orange (37)] [black (267) rule] [yellowish white (92)] EARLY | STORIES | [black double rule frames horizontal center design] [background stripe of yellowish white] [moderate reddish orange] *by* [black] *ELIZABETH BOWEN* | [black background, moderate reddish orange border rule]'.

73

Spine has colors reversed, black, yellowish white, and moderate reddish orange: '[moderate reddish orange rule] *EARLY* | *STORIES* [design and moderate reddish orange rule] *Elizabeth* | *Bowen* | [publisher's device] *Alfred · A ·* | *Knopf'*. Back cover lists ten fiction and two nonfiction books by Elizabeth Bowen. Front flap has blurb on contents; back flap has a photograph by Elliott Erwitt and a blurb on Elizabeth Bowen.

Contents: Collected are all the stories from *Encounters* (see A1a) and *Ann Lee's* (see A2a), to which is added a 'Preface,' consisting of the preface to the second edition of *Encounters* (A1c), revised and combined with new prefatory observations concerning *Ann Lee's*, first published in this edition. This joint preface was again revised and printed in A25 and A26.

Notes: Published 8 January 1951, in an impression of 5,000 copies, at $3. in the United States and $3.50 in Canada. The edition is available in xerographic reproduction through University Microfilm, at $19.40.

Reviews:
unsigned, *Kirkus* 18 (15 Nov. 1950):680
K. T. Willis, *LJ* 75 (15 Dec. 1950):2149
unsigned, *NY* 26 (6 Jan. 1951):78
Richard Sullivan, *ChiSTrib* (7 Jan. 1951):3
Alice Morris, *NYTBR* 56 (7 Jan. 1951):5
William Peden, *SatRev* 34 (3 Feb. 1951):15
James Stern, *New Republic* 124 (5 Feb. 1951):20–21
Ernest Jones, *Nation* 172 (17 Feb. 1951):158–59
George F. Whicher, *NYHTB* 27 (4 Mar. 1951):20
C. S., *SFChron* (11 Mar. 1951):18
unsigned, *Booklist* 47 (15 Mar. 1951):256
Anne Fremantle, *Commonweal* 53 (23 Mar. 1951):593–94
D. M. S., *CanF* 31 (Sept. 1951):143

A21   THE SHELBOURNE HOTEL   1951

a. *First edition*:
THE | [in strong yellowish green (131)] *SHELBOURNE* | [in strong yellowish green] HOTEL | BY | *ELIZABETH BOWEN* | [in strong yellowish green: publisher's device] | *NEW YORK* : ALFRED A. KNOPF | MCMLI

Collation: 8⅜ x 5⅝"; [1–8]¹⁶; [10], [1–2] 3–240 [241–246]; plates I–XVI (in pairs between pp. 22 and 23, 54 and 55, 62 and 63, 78 and 79, 86 and 87, 118 and 119, 182 and 183, 214 and 215).
[1]: blank [2]: list of Bowen's works. [3]: half title. [4]: blank. [5]: title page. [6]: [LC number] | [publisher's imprint and copyright notice] |

'FIRST AMERICAN EDITION'. [7]: contents. [8]: blank. [9]: illustrations. [10]: blank. 1–240: text, 2 blank. [241]: blank. [242]: colophon, concluding, 'The book was composed, printed, and bound by Kings- | port Press, Inc., Kingsport, Tennessee. | Typography and binding designs are based on origi- | nals by W. A. Dwiggins.' [243–246]: blank.

Binding: Quarter-bound in vivid green (139) cloth, with boards covered in strong yellow green (117) paper bearing circular designs. The spine is lettered across in gold: '[ornamental border] | THE | SHELBOURNE | HOTEL | [ornamental border] | ELIZABETH | BOWEN | [ornamental border] | [ornamental border] | ALFRED A. | KNOPF | [ornamental border]'. At the top of the front cloth hinge, in gold: 'THE | SHEL-BOURNE | HOTEL'. The publisher's device is blind-stamped at the foot of the back cloth hinge.

Dust jacket: The cover is dark green (146) and lettered in two colors. Front: '[brilliant yellow green (116)] Elizabeth Bowen | [green white (153)] THE | SHELBOURNE | HOTEL | [brilliant yellow green] [early advertisement of the Shelbourne Hotel] | [three lines describing contents] | ALFRED A · KNOPF PUBLISHER NEW YORK'. Spine: '[vertically] [green white] Elizabeth Bowen [brilliant yellow green] THE SHELBOURNE HOTEL | [across] [publisher's device] [green white] ALFRED A | KNOPF'. Back: photograph by Elliott Erwitt of Elizabeth Bowen, with blurb below. Front flap has blurb about the book; back flap lists nine fiction and nonfiction books by Elizabeth Bowen.

Notes: Published 15 October 1951, in an impression of 3,500 copies, at $4. MS, E19.

Reviews:
unsigned, Kirkus 19 (Sept. 1951):550
Leo Lerman, NYTBR 56 (28 Oct. 1951):4
Rod Nordell, ChScM (1 Nov. 1951):7
K. T. Willis, LJ 76 (1 Nov. 1951):1805
unsigned, NY 27 (3 Nov. 1951):141
James Hilton, NYHTB 28 (11 Nov. 1951):4
unsigned, Bookmark 11 (Dec. 1951):55
L. S. Munn, SpRep (2 Dec. 1951):30a
unsigned, Booklist 48 (15 Dec. 1951):139
Francis J. Thompson, HopR 5 (Spring 1952):103–06
Marvin Magalaner, ArQ 8 (1952):286–87

b.   *First English edition*: THE SHELBOURNE
[all within an ornamental double frame] *The Shelbourne* | *A Centre in Dublin Life* | *for more than a Century* | BY | ELIZA-BETH BOWEN | *George C. Harrap & Co. Ltd.* | LONDON TORONTO WELLINGTON SYDNEY

Collation: 7¾ x 5¼"; [A]⁸ B–M⁸ N⁴; pp. [1–9] 10–200; plates: *Front.* and fourteen others (in pairs between pp. 14 and 15, 64 and 65, 80 and 81, 96 and 97, 112, and 113, 160 and 161, 176 and 177).
[1]: half title. [2]: blank. [3]: title page. [4]: *'First published* 1951' | [publisher's imprint] | [copyright notice] | [Dewey decimal number] | *'Composed in Bembo type and printed by Western Printing Services, Ltd.,* | *Bristol. Made in Great Britain'*. [5]: preface. [6]: blank. [7]: contents. [8]: blank. [9]–10: illustrations. [11]–193: text. [194]–200: index.

Binding: Bound in grayish yellowish green (122) cloth, lettered across the spine in deep olive green (126): '[ornamental border] | The | Shelbourne | [circle] | ELIZABETH | BOWEN | [ornamental border] | HARRAP'.

Dust jacket: The front cover and spine have a background color of yellowish white (92). Front: '[dominating the front cover is a black line-drawing over grayish reddish orange (39) and very light green (143) of the hotel with a couple on a staircase, a maid or two, and a butler, with the artist's insignia ('G' enclosing 'Mc') in the lower right-hand corner] [superimposed on background color is grayish reddish orange] [very light green edged in black] *THE SHELBOURNE* | [artist's rendering] [black (267)] *Elizabeth Bowen'*. Spine: '[black] *The* | *SHELBOURNE* | *ELIZABETH* | *BOWEN* | [artist's rendering of street scene] | *HARRAP'*. Back: '[very light green border on yellowish white] [black] THE SHELBOURNE | [blurb on book's contents]'. Front flap gives credit to Norah McGuinness, who created the drawings in the book and designed the jacket; back flap carries a blurb from *The Listener*.

Contents: As in the first edition, to which is added a preface and index.

Notes: From the initial proposal in 1946 through the reprinting of 1955, the publishing history of *The Shelbourne* is marked by uncertainty. Adprint, which at the time was publishing a second edition of Bowen's *English Novelists* after the first edition run of over 35,000 copies, proposed in 1946 a rather lavish volume on the Shelbourne with 48 black-and-white pictures and 8 pages in color. Plans were to print initially 10,000 copies, at 12/6, with publication expected in 1948. These plans were never carried out, however; and when the volume finally did appear five years later, published not by Adprint but by Harrap, it was much less elaborately conceived (only 15 black-and-white plates) yet even more expensive (15/0); and the first impression consisted of a more conservative 5,000 copies. The precise date of publication remains unclear. Harrap records indicate that the month was October of 1951; but *The Bookseller* lists publication during the week of 1 December, and the deposit stamp in the British Library copy is dated 12 November. Known reviews tend to confirm the later dating.
    A second impression of 2,200 copies four years later varies from the first on p. [4] by the addition of *'Reprinted* 1955' between the publisher's imprint and the copyright notice, and by the modification of the printer's

imprint to '*Composed in Bembo type by Western Printing Services, Ltd., Bristol,* | *and reproduced by photo-lithography by Novello & Co, Ltd., London, W.1* | *Made in Great Britain*'. This second impression was arranged because a number of sheets, apparently unbound from the first impression, had been destroyed.

Transcribed in Braille 1951, in NLB.

Reviews:
Harold Nicolson, *Observer* (2 Dec. 1951):7
unsigned, *Spectator* 187 (21 Dec. 1951):868
John Bryson, *New Statesman* 42 (22 Dec. 1951):737
The Earl of Longford, *T&T* 33 (5 Jan. 1952):18
unsigned, *TLS* 51 (11 Jan. 1952):22
unsigned, *The Dublin Magazine* n.s. 27:2 (Apr.-June 1952):66

A22   **A WORLD OF LOVE**   **1955**

a. *First edition*:
[title in script] A World | of Love | Elizabeth Bowen | [rule] | [publisher's device] 1955 | *Alfred A. Knopf*   NEW YORK

Collation: 8½ x 5½"; [1–8]¹⁶; pp. [8], [1–2] 3–244 [245–248].
[1]: blank. [2]: list of Bowen's works. [3]: half title. [4]: blank. [5]: title page. [6]: LC number, publisher's imprint, and copyright notice concluding, '*Published simultaneously in Canada by McClelland* | *& Stewart Limited.* | FIRST EDITION'. [7]: 'TO | *CATHERINE POMEROY COLLINS*'. [8]: six-line quotation from Traherne. [1]–244: text, 2 blank [245]: blank. [246]: colophon, concluding, '*The book was composed, printed, and bound by* | KINGSPORT PRESS, INC., *Kingsport, Tenn.* | *Typography and binding design by* GEORGE SALTER'. [247–248]: blank.

Binding: Bound in light green (144) cloth, with lettering and script in dark blue (183) and frames and borders in very deep red (14). On the spine: '[ornamental frame] | [in script, across] A World | of Love | [ornamental frame] | [in script, across] Elizabeth | Bowen | [lettered down, within an ornamental frame] KNOPF'. On the front cover: '[ornamental bordering fragment] [in script] EB'. On the back cover, at the lower right: publisher's device in very deep red.

Dust jacket: Front includes a drawing of a four-leaf clover, a packet of letters tied by a ribbon, and an obelisk-shaped structure signed by Salter. Background is a swirl pattern in moderate reddish orange (37) and deep green (142): '[white] *A* [black] *World* [white] *of Love* | *A NOVEL BY* | *Elizabeth Bowen*'. Spine: '[background moderate reddish orange] [black] *A World* | *of Love* | [background light green (144)] [black] *Elizabeth* | *Bowen* | [publisher's device] | [background yellowish white] [light green] *Alfred A · Knopf*. Back carries a photograph of Elizabeth Bowen by Angus McBean. Front flap carries blurb on the author and the contents; back flap carries a blurb on Elizabeth Bowen.

Notes: Published 17 January 1955, in an impression of 7,500 copies, at $3.50. The second impression (3,500 copies) varies in the substitution, on p. [6], of 'PUBLISHED JANUARY 17, 1955 | SECOND PRINTING, JANUARY 1955' for 'FIRST EDITION'. The third impression (5,000 copies) is paginated [*10*], [1–2] 3–244 [*245–246*] and varies otherwise from the second impression in the following respects:

[6]: 'THIRD PRINTING, FEBRUARY 1955' added to the printing register. [8]: blank. [9]: six-line quotation from Traherne. [*10*]: blank. The fourth impression (1,000 copies) varies from the third in the following respects:

[2]: list of works expanded. [5]: dateline changed to '1962'. [6]: 'FOURTH PRINTING, FEBRUARY 1962' added to the printing register.

The fifth impression (1,000 copies) varies from the fourth in the following respects:

[5]: dateline changed to '1965'. [6]: '*Random | House of Canada Limited*,' substituted for '*McClelland | & Stewart Limited*' in the copyright notice, and the printing register modified to 'PUBLISHED JANUARY 17, 1955 | REPRINTED THREE TIMES | FIFTH PRINTING, AUGUST 1966'.

Fifth-impression copies are bound in vivid green (139) cloth.

A second American edition (in paperback) was published by Avon Books 21 December 1978 (45,000 copies in the United States, and 10,000 copies in Canada) at $1.95.

Chapter five of *A World of Love* was first printed as 'The Dinner Party' in *London Magazine* (C413). Translated, D41–44. MS, E20. Broadcast, F31.

Reviews:
unsigned, *Kirkus* 22 (15 Nov. 1954):756
K. T. Willis, *LJ* 80 (1 Jan. 1955):67
Charles A. Brady, *BuffEN* (15 Jan. 1955):25
Walter Havighurst, *SatRev* 38 (15 Jan. 1955):16
Fanny Butcher, *ChiSTrib* (16 Jan. 1955):3
Virgilia Peterson, *NYHTB* 31 (16 Jan. 1955):3
Alice S. Morris, *NYTBR* 60 (16 Jan. 1955):1
unsigned, *Time* 65 (17 Jan. 1955):96–97
unsigned, *Newsweek* 45 (24 Jan. 1955):102–3
Jane Voiles, *SFChron* (30 Jan. 1955):17
J. B. Ludwig, *New Republic* 132 (31 Jan. 1955):18–19
unsigned, *Booklist* 51 (1 Feb. 1955):247
Charles J. Rolo, *Atlantic* 195 (Feb. 1955):84
Carlos Baker, *Nation* 180 (5 Feb. 1955):123–24
Richard McLaughlin, *SpRep* (6 Feb. 1955):6

Edwin Kennebeck, *Commonweal* 61 (18 Feb. 1955):532–33

Herbert Gold, *HudR* (Spring 1955):153–54

T. Fitzsimmons, *SR* 63 (Spring 1955):323–25

Paul Pickrel, *YR* n.s. 44 (Spring 1955):476–80

Douglas Grant, *Bookmark* 14 (Mar. 1955):137

Riley Hughes, *CathW* 18 (Mar. 1955):470

B. E. N., *SatN* 70 #30 (30 Apr. 1955):13

Douglas Grant, *CanF* 35 (May 1955):47 (review of 'McClelland & Stewart' issue)

unsigned, *WiscLB* 51 (May 1955):17

Patricia Broadhurst, *Queen's Quarterly* 62 (Summer 1955):296–97

unsigned, *Newsweek* 46 (26 Dec. 1955):69–70

b. *First English edition*:
ELIZABETH BOWEN | [ornamental swelled rule] | A WORLD OF LOVE | [publisher's device] | [Traherne quotation, six lines] | JONATHAN CAPE | THIRTY BEDFORD SQUARE | LONDON

Collation: 8 x 4⅞″; [A]⁸ B–O⁸: pp. [1–8] 9–224.
[1]: half title. [2]: list of Bowen's works. [3]: title page. [4]: 'FIRST PUBLISHED 1955 | PRINTED IN GREAT BRITAIN IN THE CITY OF OXFORD | AT THE ALDEN PRESS | BOUND BY A. W. BAIN & CO. LTD., LONDON'. [5]: '*To* | *CATHERINE POMEROY COLLINS*'. [6]: blank. [7]–224: text, 8 blank.

Binding: Bound in pale green (149) cloth, with a design of vivid greenish blue (158) leaves across the front onto the spine. On the spine: '[lettered upward in vivid bluish green, at the top] ELIZABETH | BOWEN | [below, lettered in silver across each of four leaves] *A* | *WORLD* | *OF* | *LOVE* | [publisher's device]'.

Dust jacket: [Book Society jacket] Cover is deep yellowish pink (27) with the identical design in black as on the binding across front, spine and back. Front: '[yellowish white (92)] ELIZABETH | BOWEN | [yellowish white and black shading] *A WORLD* | *OF LOVE*'. Spine: '[yellowish white] ELIZABETH | BOWEN | [black] *A* | *WORLD* | *OF* | *LOVE* | [publisher's device]'. Back: '[design only with yellowish white tips on five leaves]'. Front flap. '[blurb about the novel] | [deep yellowish pink (27)] [double frame design] THE BOOK SOCIETY'S | CHOICE | [black] 10s 6d net'. Back flap is blank.

Notes: Published 1 March 1955, at 10/6. As indicated by the dust jacket described above, The Book Society offered the volume as one of its choices. However, no copy seen bears the kind of modified title page noted in Book Society copies of *The Heat of the Day* (see A18b); nor have copies been seen with Book Society bookplates, as in the case of *The Death of the Heart* (see A10a). Without such indicators, it is now impossible to tell whether the Book Society drew its copies from the first impression or from another impression whose printing, according to the records of Jonathan Cape, also antedated the actual date of publication. This second impression varies from the first by the substitution on p. [4] of 'FIRST PUBLISHED MARCH 1955 | SECOND IMPRESSION 1955' for the original 'FIRST PUBLISHED 1955'. A third impression, in the format of the Cape Collected Edition, was printed in September 1968, at 25/0.

A second English edition was published by Readers Union in cooperation with Cape in 1957, at 5/6. Although it is unrecorded in *The British National Bibliography, The English Catalogue of Books,* or *Cumulative Book Index,* and no depository copy exists at the British Library, it is completely reset and thus an edition distinct from the Cape family of impressions. The quantity of printings is unknown; but, according to James Moore, current Director of Readers Union, Ltd., it would have been offered to a club membership of 30,000—40,000 at the time.

A third English edition (in paperback) was published 11 August 1966, by Panther Books, in an impression of 27,000 copies, at 3/6.

Transcribed in Braile 1955, in NLB.

Reviews:
Margery Allingham, *Tatler* 215 (2 Mar. 1955):399
unsigned, *Times* (London) (3 Mar. 1955):11
unsigned, *TLS* 54 (4 Mar. 1955):132; see also letter to editor (20 May 1955):269 concerning review
Maurice Richardson, *New Statesman* 49 (5 Mar. 1955):332; see also note of correction of error (19 Mar. 1955):411
Helen McGivering, *T&T* 36 (5 Mar. 1955):308
Stevie Smith, *Observer* (6 Mar. 1955):8
Norman Shrapnel, *Guardian* (8 Mar. 1955):4
A. P., *Punch* 228 (9 Mar. 1955):327
L. P. Hartley, *Spectator* 194 (11 Mar. 1955):293–94
Hilary Corke, *Listener* 53 (31 Mar. 1955):585
Francis Wyndham, *London Magazine* 2 (June 1955):86–89
unsigned, *Observer* (11 Sept. 1966):22 (review of Panther edition)

Stories | *by* | *Elizabeth* | *Bowen* | [swelled rule] | *NEW YORK*: *VINTAGE BOOKS* | 1959

Collation: 7¼ x 4¼″; [160 single leaves]; pp. [i–v] vi–x [xi–xii], [1] 2–305 [306–308].
[i]: half title. [ii]: blank. [iii]: title page. [iv]: [LC number, publisher's

imprint and copyright notice] | 'FIRST VINTAGE EDITION'. [v]–x: preface. [xi]: contents. [xii]: blank. [1]–305: text. [306]: biographical note and colophon, concluding, 'Composed, | printed, and bound by THE COLONIAL PRESS INC., Clinton, | Massachusetts. Paper manufactured by S. D. WARREN COMPANY, | Boston, Massachusetts. Cover design by ALFRED ZALON.' [307–308]: publisher's advertisements.

Binding: A perfect binding in greenish gray (155) card cover decorated by random geometric designs in yellowish white (92) lettered down the spine: '[in vivid orangish red (34)] STORIES BY [in yellowish white] ELIZABETH BOWEN [across the spine] [in vivid orangish red] VINTAGE | [in yellowish white] K–79'. On the front cover: '[in vivid orangish red] STORIES BY | [in yellowish white] ELIZABETH BOWEN | [in vivid orangish red] A | VINTAGE | BOOK | [in yellowish white] K–79 | [in vivid orangish red] $1.25'. On the back cover: '[in vivid orangish red] STORIES BY | [in yellowish white] ELIZABETH BOWEN | Eighteen short stories from | IVY GRIPPED THE STEPS | LOOK AT ALL THOSE ROSES | and EARLY STORIES | with a Preface by Elizabeth Bowen | [excerpts from Preface and a review] | A VINTAGE BOOK | COVER DESIGN BY ALFRED ZALON'.

Dust jacket: None.

Contents:
'Preface'. Reprinted, in revised version, in A25 and A26.
'Coming Home'. See A1a.
'The Storm'. See A2a.
'The Tommy Crans'. See A8.
'Her Table Spread'. See A8.
'The Disinherited'. See A8.
'The Easter Egg Party'. See A11a.
'No. 16'. See A11a.
'Reduced'. See A11a.
'Look at All Those Roses'. See A11a.
'A Love Story'. See A11a.
'Summer Night'. See A11a.
'Songs My Father Sang Me'. See 15a.
'The Inherited Clock'. See A15a.
'Sunday Afternoon'. See A15a.
'The Demon Lover'. See A15a.
'Ivy Gripped the Steps'. See A15a.
'The Happy Autumn Fields'. See A15a.
'Mysterious Kôr'. See A15a.

Notes: Published 14 September 1959, in an unknown number of copies, at $1.25. A second impression of unknown date and quantity varies in the following respects:
    [iii]: 'VINTAGE BOOKS | A DIVISION OF RANDOM HOUSE /

NEW YORK' substituted for 'NEW YORK: VINTAGE BOOKS |
1959'.
[iv]: publisher's imprint and copyright notice reset and 'FIRST VIN-
TAGE EDITION' deleted.
[306]: statements on paper manufacture and cover design deleted
from the colophon.
[307–308]: publisher's advertisements revised.

Reviews:
H. Strickhausen, *SR* 73 (Winter 1965):158

A24   **A TIME IN ROME**   **1960**

a. *First edition*:
A | TIME | IN | ROME | BY | ELIZABETH BOWEN | [rule] |
[publisher's device] | *New York* : Alfred · A · Knopf | 1960

Collation: 8¼ x 5½"; [1–8]¹⁶; pp. [10], [1–2] 3–241 [242–246].
[1]: blank. [2]: list of Bowen's works. [3]: half title. [4]: blank. [5]:
title page. [6]: [LC number, publisher's imprint and copyright notice] |
'FIRST EDITION'. [7]: 'TO | MY FRIENDS IN ROME | AND TO |
KIRK AND CONSTANCE ASKEW | UNDER WHOSE ROOF | IN
NEW YORK | THIS BOOK WAS FINISHED'. [8]: blank. [9]: contents.
[10]: blank. [1]–[242]: text, 2 blank. [243]: bibliography. [244]: blank.
[245]: biographical note. [246]: colophon, concluding, '*composed, printed,
and bound by Kingsport Press, Inc.,* | *Kingsport, Tenn. Paper manufac-
tured by S. D. Warren* | *Company, Boston. Designed by* | WARREN
[monogram] CHAPPELL'.

Binding: Bound in dark red (16) cloth lettered across the spine in gold:
'A | TIME | IN | ROME | [drawing: a column] | Elizabeth | Bowen |
KNOPF'. On the front, stamped in gold: [drawing: Roman on horse-
back]. On the back cover, blind-stamped: 'BORZOI | [publisher's device]
| BOOKS'.

Dust jacket: Yellowish white paper (92) with three other colors used for
artist's rendering. Front: '[moderate red (15)] A TIME IN | ROME |
[dark grayish brown (62) and light greenish blue (172)] [artist's render-
ing of a fountain and a building in Rome] | by Elizabeth Bowen | [a two-
line commentary on contents]'. Spine: '[five alternate light greenish blue
and dark grayish brown rules] | [moderate red (15)] A | TIME | IN |
ROME | [dark grayish brown and light greenish blue] [artist's rendering
of a tower] | Elizabeth | Bowen | [twenty alternate light greenish blue
and dark grayish brown broad rules to the bottom of the spine, which
includes] [publisher's device] | KNOPF'. Back carries photograph of
Elizabeth Bowen by Alfred A · Knopf. Front flap carries a blurb on the

contents; back flap completes contents' blurb and carries blurb on Elizabeth Bowen.

Notes: Published 15 February 1960, in an impression of 5,000 copies, at $4. The second impression (2,500 copies) varies in that, on p. [6], the publisher's device is added above the LC number and 'FIRST EDITION' is replaced by 'PUBLISHED FEBRUARY 15, 1960 | SECOND PRINTING, MARCH 1960' as the printing register. The third impression (3,500 copies) contains the additional line: 'THIRD PRINTING, MARCH 1960'; the fourth impression (2,500 copies) contains in addition: 'FOURTH PRINTING, MAY 1960'; and the fifth impression (1,100 copies) contains further: 'FIFTH PRINTING, OCTOBER 1965'.

Portions of *A Time in Rome* were first printed as part of 'The Virgins and the Empress' in *Harper's* (C646); different excerpts appeared as 'A Time in Rome' in *Gentlemen's Quarterly* (C646.1); another excerpt appeared in *Vogue* (C649), and yet another was reprinted as 'Eternal Lure of the Eternal City' in the *New York Times Magazine* (C652). Translated, D45. MS, E21.

Reviews:
unsigned, *Booklist* 56 (1 Feb. 1960):312, 324
Robert Donahugh, *LJ* 85 (1 Feb. 1960):656
J. H. Harrison, *ChScM* (8 Feb. 1960):5
Fanny Butcher, *CTribMB* (14 Feb. 1960):6
D. B. Bagg, *SpRep* (14 Feb. 1960):4d
John K. Hutchens, *NYHTB* 36 (15 Feb. 1960):15
George Steiner, *Newsweek* 55 (15 Feb. 1960):107
William Hagan, *SFChron* (16 Feb. 1960):27
Orville Prescott, *NYTimes* (17 Feb. 1960):33
Carlo Beuf, *NYTBR* 65 Pt. 2 (21 Feb. 1960):10
unsigned, *Bookmark* 19 (Mar. 1960):147
unsigned, *EJ* 49 (Mar. 1960):210
Francis X. Murphy, *Best Sellers,* 19 (1 Mar. 1960):418
M. Cosman, *Commonweal* 71 (4 Mar. 1960):631–32
Gilbert Highet, *BOMCNews* (12 Mar. 1960):12
George Steiner, *Reporter* 22 (17 Mar. 1960):47–49
unsigned, *NY* 36 (26 Mar. 1960):156
Ned Calmer, *SatRev* 43 (26 Mar. 1960):30
unsigned, *Current History* 38 (May 1960):291
Gene Baro, *NYHTB* 36 (1 May 1960):10
unsigned, *VQR* 36 #5 (Summer 1960):xcii
unsigned, *WiscLB* 56 (Sept. 1960):284
D. P., *ChCent* 77 (7 Sept. 1960):1023
E. F. Mengel, *ItalQ* 4 #4 (Winter 1961):62–65

b.   *First English edition*:
A Time in | [in strong reddish brown (40) block letters] ROME | *Elizabeth Bowen* | [publisher's device] | *Longmans*

Collation: 8½ x 5½"; [A–B]⁸ C–K⁸ [L]¹⁰; pp. [8], 1–169 [170–172].
[1]: half title. [2]: list of Bowen's works. [3]: title page. [4]: [publisher's imprint and copyright notice] | 'FIRST PUBLISHED 1960 | *Printed in Great Britain by* | *W. & J. Mackay & Co Ltd, Chatham'*. [5]: 'TO | MY FRIENDS IN ROME | *also to* | KIRK & CONSTANCE ASKEW | *under whose roof in New York* | *this book was finished'*. [6]: acknowledgments. [7]: contents. [8]: blank 1–168: text. 169: bibliography. [170–172]: blank.

Binding: Bound in dark reddish orange (38) cloth lettered down the spine in gold: *'Elizabeth Bowen A Time in Rome Longmans'*.

Dust jacket: Cover is strong orange (50) and yellowish white (92) with silhouetted letters in black. Front: '[front and spine contain, in the background colors, a photograph of a building in Rome] A TIME | IN | ROME | ELIZABETH | BOWEN'. Spine: '[vertically down] A TIME IN ROME Elizabeth Bowen [across] LONGMANS'. Back: '[yellowish white] [photograph of Elizabeth Bowen] [strong orange silhouetted lettering] A TIME IN | ROME | [black] Elizabeth Bowen'. Front flap contains a blurb on the book and the price 21/- net; back flap contains a blurb on Elizabeth Bowen and acknowledgments for jacket photographs (J. Allan Cash, front; Angus McBean, back), 'Printed in Great Britain, P.P. (L) Ltd.'.

Notes: Throughout this English edition, Bowen corrected a number of Italian phrases inaccurately recorded in the American edition (A24a) and its subsequent impressions. So corrected, the English edition was published 4 July 1960, at 21/0, and reprinted at least twice during that year. The compilers have seen copies of only the second of the reprints, which varies from the first impression in that, on p. [4], following the copyright notice, appears 'FIRST PUBLISHED 1960 | SECOND IMPRESSION BY PHOTOLITHOGRAPHY 1960 | THIRD IMPRESSION BY PHOTOLITHOGRAPHY 1960 | *Printed in Great Britain by* | *Lowe and Brydone* (Printers) *Limited* | *London · NW* 10'.
Transcribed in Braille 1960, in NLB.

Reviews:
Harold Nicolson, *Observer* (3 July 1960):27
Simon Raven, *Spectator* 205 (8 July 1960):70–71
unsigned, *TLS* 59 (8 July 1960):436
unsigned, *Times* (London) (14 July 1960):15
Honor Tracy, *ManG&EN* (15 July 1960):6
unsigned, *Times Weekly Review* (London) (21 July 1960):10
Peter D. Smith, *Punch* 239 Pt. 1 (10 Aug. 1960):213
unsigned, *Economist* 196 Pt. 2 (13 Aug. 1960):638
Richard Mayne, *New Statesman* 60 (27 Aug. 1960):278–79
W. A. Purdy, *Tablet* (27 Aug. 1960):785–86
Elizabeth Jennings, *London Magazine* 7 (Sept. 1960):77–79

Henry Reed, *Listener* 65 (12 Jan. 1961):91
Roger Henks, *ArchR* 129 (Mar. 1961):155

A25   SEVEN WINTERS & AFTERTHOUGHTS   1962

SEVEN WINTERS | *Memories of a Dublin Childhood* | & | AFTERTHOUGHTS | *Pieces on Writing* | BY | ELIZABETH BOWEN | [swelled rule] | [publisher's device] | *New York*: Alfred · A · Knopf | 1962

Collation: 8⅛ x 5½"; [1–4¹⁶ 5⁸ 6–7¹⁶ 8¹⁰ 9–10¹⁶]; pp. [2], [i–vi] vii–[xii], [1–2] 3–272 [273–278].
[1]: blank. [2]: list of Bowen's works. [i]: half title. [ii]: blank. [iii]: title page. [iv]: [publisher's imprint and copyright notice] | 'FIRST EDITION' | [prior publication note]. [v]: 'TO | DEREK HILL'. [vi]: blank. vii–[ix]: foreword. [x]: blank. xi–[xii]: contents. [1]–[273]: text. [274]: blank. [275]: biographical note. [276]: colophon. [277–278]: blank.

Binding: Bound in moderate bluish green (164) cloth, lettered across the spine in gold: '[all within a frame, except the publisher's imprint] [square and ornamental frames enclosing 4 stars] | SEVEN | WINTERS | AND | AFTER- | THOUGHTS | ELIZABETH | BOWEN | [square and ornamental frames enclosing 4 stars] | ALFRED · A | KNOPF'. On the front cover: '[blind-stamped, within a frame] EB'.

Dust jacket: Not seen.

Contents:
'Foreword'. Reprinted in A26, omitting paragraphs on *Seven Winters*.
Seven Winters
Afterthoughts

    Reflections:
       'The Roving Eye'. First printed as 'The Search for a Story to Tell' in *NYTBR* (C399) and reprinted in *Harper's Bazaar* (C399). Published in anthology, G43.
       'Disloyalties'. First printed as 'The Writer's Peculiar World' in *NYTBR* (C381). Published in anthology, G39.
       'Autobiography'. First printed as 'Autobiography as an Art' in *SatRev* (C387).
       'Sources of Influence'. First printed as 'The Sponge of the Present' in *SatRev* (C403). MS, E91.
       'Exclusion'. MS, E102.
       'Advice'. First printed as 'Elizabeth Bowen Talks about Writing' in *Mademoiselle* (C651).

Prefaces [to]:

Doctor Thorne. First printed, unrevised, as 'Introduction' to B31.

Orlando. First printed, unrevised, as 'Afterword' to B32.

North and South. First printed as 'Introduction' to B26. MS, E81.

Stories by Katherine Mansfield. First printed as 'Introduction' to B29, reprinted as 'A Living Writer' in *Cornhill* (C568). Published in anthology, G49.

Stories by Elizabeth Bowen. First printed, unrevised, in A23.

Encounters. See A1c.

Ann Lee's. See A20.

The Last September. See A4c.

The Second Ghost Book. First printed as 'Introduction' to B28. MS, E89.

Reviews [of]:

A Writer's Diary. First printed as 'The Principle of Art was Joy' in *NYTBR* (C417). MS, E94.

The Golden Apples. First printed in *Books of Today* (C380).

The Echoing Grove. First printed as 'The Modern Novel and the Theme of Love' in *New Republic* (C401).

Alexandria. First printed as 'Where the Pharos Stood' in *Reporter* (C653).

Broadcasts:

'She'. First printed as 'The Power in the Cave' in *Listener* (C225). MS, E64. Broadcast, F68.

'Truth and Fiction'. First printed in *Listener* (C562). Radio script, E98. Broadcast, F86–88.

Notes: Published 11 June 1962, in an impression of 5,250 copies, at $5.

Reviews:

unsigned, *Bookmark* 21 (June 1962):255

George Cloyne, *NYHTB* 38 (10 June 1962):16

Charles Poore, *NYTimes* (14 June 1962):31

Arthur MacGillivray, *Best Sellers* 22 (15 June 1962):137

Fanny Butcher, *CTribMB* (17 June 1962):Section 9, 3

Gene Baro, *NYTBR* 67 (17 June 1962):6

Horace Reynolds, *ChScM* (21 June 1962):7

Katherine G. Jackson, *Harper's* (July 1962):94

Katherine T. Willis, *LJ* 87 (July 1962):2549

unsigned, *Booklist* 58 (1 July 1962):748

Marghanita Laski, *SatRev* 45 (28 July 1962):42–43

Richard McLaughlin, *SpRep* (29 July 1962):4d

Winifred Houser, *BOMCNews* (Aug. 1962):9

Robert Norton, *Show* 2 (Aug. 1962):95

unsigned, *NY* 38 (4 Aug. 1962):72

unsigned, *WiscLB* 58 (Sept. 1962):342

unsigned, *LJ* 87 (15 Nov. 1962):4293

Francis Murphy, *BA* 37 (Winter 1964):80
H. Strickhausen, *SR* 73 (Winter 1965):158

A26　　　**AFTERTHOUGHT: PIECES ABOUT WRITING**　　　**1962**

[In vivid red (11)] AFTER- | THOUGHT | [a line of ornamental circles, in black (267)] | [in vivid red] *Pieces about Writing* | [a line of ornamental circles, in black] | [in vivid red] ELIZABETH BOWEN | [publisher's device, in black] | [in vivid red] *Longmans*

Collation: 8½ x 5½"; [A]⁸ B–M⁸ N⁶ O⁸; pp. [1–8] 9–220.
[1]: half title. [2]: list of Bowen's works. [3]: title page. [4]: [publisher's imprint and copyright notice] | 'First published 1962 | *Printed in Great Britain by* | W. & J. Mackay & Co Ltd, Chatham, Kent'. [5]: 'To Derek Hill'. [6]: blank. [7]: contents. [8]: acknowledgments. [9]: foreword. [10]: blank. [11]–220: text, 12, 106, 144, 164, and 190 blank.

Binding: Bound in dark red (16) cloth lettered down the spine in gold: 'Afterthought · Elizabeth Bowen LONGMANS'.

Dust jacket: Cover front and back in grayish blue (186) with a brick design in black on the front only. Flaps are white. Front: '[white] Elizabeth | Bowen | [rule] | Afterthought | [vertically down in black] Afterthought'. Spine: '[lettered down] [white] Elizabeth Bowen [black] Afterthought [horizontal] [white rule] [black] LONGMANS'. Back carries picture of Elizabeth Bowen by Angus McBean and a biographical blurb on the author. Front flap describes contents; back flap includes excerpts from reviews on *A Time in Rome*.

Contents:
'Foreword'. As in A25, omitting paragraphs on *Seven Winters*.
　I Prefaces: as in A25.
　II Broadcasts: as in A25.
　III Reviews: as in A25.
　IV Travel: 'A Ride South'. First printed as 'Ride Through the Deep South' in *Holiday* (C648).
　V Reflections: as in A25, except that 'Advice' precedes 'Exclusion'.

Notes: Published 5 November 1962, at 30/0. The publisher declines to reveal the number of copies printed.

Reviews:
Donald Davie, *New Statesman* 64 (9 Nov. 1962):672–74
unsigned, *TLS* 61 (9 Nov. 1962):855
William Plomer, *Punch* 243 (21 Nov. 1962):765

William Plomer, *Listener* 68 (6 Dec. 1962):975
unsigned, *Times* (London) (27 Dec. 1962):9
William Plomer, *Economist* 205 (29 Dec. 1962):1273
William Plomer, (London) *Times Weekly Review* (3 Jan. 1963):13
Jeremy Brooks, *Spectator* 210 (11 Jan. 1963):49

A27   THE LITTLE GIRLS   1964

a. *First edition*:

THE LITTLE GIRLS | [ornamental device] *By Elizabeth Bowen*
[ornamental device] | NEW YORK : ALFRED · A · KNOPF |
[publisher's device] | [double rule] | 1964

Collation: 8¾ x 5⅝"; [1–10]¹⁶; pp. [8], [1–2] 3–306 [307–312].
[1]: blank. [2]: list of Bowen's works. [3]: half title. [4]: blank. [5]:
title page. [6]: [acknowledgment, publisher's device, LC number, publish-
er's imprint, and copyright notice] | 'FIRST EDITION'. [7]: '*To Ursula
Vernon*'. [8]: blank. [1]–[307]: text, 2, 78, 170, and 172 blank. [308]:
colophon, concluding, '*Composed, printed, and bound by* | The Haddon
Craftsmen, Inc., Scranton, Pa. | *Typography and binding design by* |
WARREN CHAPPELL'. [309–312]: blank.

Binding: Bound in strong blue (178) cloth. Across the spine: '[in very
deep red (17)] [thick rule | thin rule | circular ornament | thin rule] |
[in gold] THE | Little | Girls | [short rule] | Elizabeth | Bowen | [in very
deep red] [thin rule | circular ornament | thin rule | circular ornament |
thin rule | circular ornament | thin rule] | [in gold] ALFRED A. |
KNOPF | [in very deep red] [thin rule | thick rule]'. On the front:
'[within a circle, expressed upon a gold circular background] EB'. On the
back: [in very deep red, at lower right] [publisher's device].

Dust jacket: Cover has a background of strong orange yellow (68) with
a symmetrical flower design of strong reddish brown (40) and moderate
green (145). Front: '[dark greenish blue (174) rectangular background
behind printing] [yellowish white (92)] THE LITTLE | GIRLS |
[light orange yellow (70)] A NOVEL BY | [yellowish white] ELIZA-
BETH | BOWEN'. Spine: '[dark greenish blue background stripe] [yellow-
ish white] THE | LITTLE | GIRLS | [yellowish white rule] | ELIZABETH
| BOWEN | [light orange yellow] [publisher's device] | [yellowish white]
Alfred · A · Knopf'. Back carries photograph of Elizabeth Bowen by
Angus McBean. Front flap carries a blurb on contents; back flap carries
a blurb on Elizabeth Bowen. The jacket design, typography and binding
design are by Warren Chappell.

Notes: Published 13 January 1964, in an impression of 15,238 copies,
at $4.95. The second impression (3,500 copies) varies in that, on p. [6],

'FIRST EDITION' is replaced by 'PUBLISHED JANUARY 13, 1964 | SECOND PRINTING, JANUARY 1964' as a printing register; and the third impression (1,500 copies) contains the additional line: 'THIRD PRINTING, APRIL 1964'.

A second American edition (in paperback) was published by Avon Books 21 October 1978 (50,000 copies in the United States, and 10,000 copies in Canada), at $1.95.

Translated, D46–51. MS, E22, E145. Radio script, E23. Broadcast, F55, F94.

Reviews:

Genevieve M. Casey, *LJ* 88 (1 Dec. 1963):4661–62
G. C. Hedge, *BOMCNews* (Jan. 1964):12
Shirley Ann Grau, *Cosmopolitan* 157 (Jan. 1964):28
Marghanita Laski, *SatRev* 47 (11 Jan. 1964):63
E. Fuller, *CTribMB* (12 Jan. 1964):4
Gene Baro, *NYTBR* 69 (12 Jan. 1964):4
C. Poore, *NYTimes* (14 Jan. 1964):29
Alan Pryce-Jones, *NYHTB* 1 (16 Jan. 1964):17
Ernest Cady, *ColD* (19 Jan. 1964):18
unsigned, *Time* 83 (24 Jan. 1964):70
Lewis Nichols, *NYTBR* 69 (26 Jan. 1964):8
unsigned, *SFChronTWM* (26 Jan. 1964):38
W. A. McBrien, *Critic* 22 (Feb. 1964):79
Benjamin De Mott, *Harper's* 228 (Feb. 1964):116
J. E. Oppenheim, *Best Sellers* 23 (1 Feb. 1964):373
Virgilia Peterson, *Book Week* 1 #21 (2 Feb. 1964):18
Melvin Maddoch, *ChScM* (6 Feb. 1964):11
H. C. Gardiner, *America* 110 (8 Feb. 1964):196
Frederick P. W. McDowell, *Critique* 7 (Spring 1964):139
Marvin Mudrick, *HudR* 17 (Spring 1964):114
Nancy Hale, *VQR* 40 (Spring 1964):316–20
Phoebe Adams, *Atlantic* 213 (Mar. 1964):187–88
Honor Tracy, *New Republic* 150 (7 Mar. 1964):26–27
Lucy Johnson, *Progressive* 28 (Apr. 1964):42
Frederick T. Wood, *English Studies* (Aug. 1965):360
H. Strickhausen, *SR* 73 (Winter 1965):158
Jay L. Halio, *Southern Review* n.s. 2 (Autumn 1966):952

b. *First English edition*:

THE | LITTLE GIRLS | ELIZABETH BOWEN | [publisher's device] | JONATHAN CAPE | THIRTY BEDFORD SQUARE · LONDON

Collation: 7½ x 4⅞"; [A]¹⁶ B–I¹⁶; pp. [6], [1–2] 3–277 [278–282].
[1]: half title. [2]: list of Bowen's works. [3]: title page. [4]: 'First published 1964' | [copyright notice and note of acknowledgment] |

'Printed in Great Britain | by Ebenezer Baylis and Son Limited | The Trinity Press, Worcester, and London | on paper made by John Dickinson and Co. Ltd | Bound by A. W. Bain and Co., Ltd, London'. [5]: 'To URSULA VERNON'. [6]: blank. [1]–277: text, 2, 70, 72, 154 and 156 blank. [278–282]: blank.

Binding: Bound in brilliant yellow (83) cloth, lettered across the spine in silver: 'ELIZABETH | BOWEN | THE | LITTLE | GIRLS | [publisher's device]'.

Dust jacket: Entire jacket is light gray (264). Front: '[black (267)] ELIZABETH | [dark grayish yellow (91)] BOWEN | [black] THE LITTLE GIRLS | [artist's rendering of three little girls, in four colors, by Lacey Everett]'. Spine: '[black] ELIZABETH | [dark grayish yellow] BOWEN | [black] THE | LITTLE | GIRLS | [a rendering of one of the little girls] | [publisher's device]'. Back carries a thirteen-line commentary on Bowen's writings by V. S. Pritchett, a six-line review of *A World of Love* by Lord David Cecil from *Sunday Times* and a listing of eleven other books in the Uniform Edition of the works of Elizabeth Bowen. Front flap carries a blurb on the contents including price 2/5 net; back flap carries note, 'Jacket design by Lacey Everett © Jonathan Cape 1964'.

Notes: Published 17 February 1964, at 21/0. Transcribed in Braille 1964, in NLB.
   A second edition was published by The Reprint Society in 1966; and on 11 August of that year Panther Books published a paperback edition of 25,000 copies, at 5/0.

Reviews:
Philip Toynbee, *Observer* (16 Feb. 1964):26
unsigned, *Times* (London) (20 Feb. 1964):17
unsigned, *TLS* (20 Feb. 1964):146
Anthony Burgess, *Spectator* 212 (21 Feb. 1964):254. Reprinted in *Urgent Copy: Literary Studies* (London: Jonathan Cape, 1968; New York: W. W. Norton & Co., 1969), 149–53
Nancy Mitchell, *Tablet* 223 (22 Feb. 1964):214–16
Guy Davenport, *National Review* 16 (25 Feb. 1964):162
Maggie Ross, *Listener* 71 (27 Feb. 1964):367
Anne Duchene, *ManGW* 90 #9 (27 Feb. 1964):11
Brigid Brophy, *New Statesman* 67 (28 Feb. 1964):335–36
W. A. McBrien, *Critic* 22 (Mar. 1964):79–80
Venetia Pollock, *Punch* 246 (18 Mar. 1964):430
Christine Brooke-Rose, *London Magazine* 4 (May 1964):83–86
unsigned, *Observer* (11 Sept. 1966):22 (review of Panther edition)
unsigned, *Radio Times* (London) 183 #2371 (17 Apr. 1969):41
David Wade, *Times* (London) (10 May 1969):19 (review of radio adaptation) See F55.

A DAY IN THE DARK | AND OTHER STORIES | ELIZA-
BETH BOWEN [publisher's device] | JONATHAN CAPE |
THIRTY BEDFORD SQUARE | LONDON

Collation: 7⅜ x 4⅞"; [1]¹⁶ 2–10¹⁶; pp. [1–6] 7–320.
[1]: half title. [2]: list of Bowen's works. [3]: title page. [4]: [copyright
notice] | [notice of previous appearances] | 'PRINTED IN GREAT
BRITAIN | BY EBENEZER BAYLIS AND SON, LIMITED | THE
TRINITY PRESS, WORCESTER, AND LONDON | ON PAPER MADE
BY JOHN DICKINSON AND CO. LTD | BOUND BY A. W. BAIN
AND CO. LTD. LONDON'. [5]: contents. [6]: blank. 7–9: preface.
[10]: blank. 11–320: text.

Binding: Two different bindings have been noted: grayish violet (215)
cloth with gold lettering and bluish black (193) cloth with silver lettering.
Across the spine in each case: 'A | DAY | IN THE | DARK | [orna-
mental device] | ELIZABETH | BOWEN | [publisher's device]'.

Dust jacket: Cover in strong violet (207) with inside background rectangular panels on front and spine of dark grayish blue (187). Front:
'[white] ELIZABETH | BOWEN | [horizontal rule] | [strong violet] *A
DAY IN THE DARK*'. Spine: '[white] ELIZABETH | BOWEN |
[strong violet band] | [strong violet] *A | DAY | IN | THE | DARK* |
[publisher's device]'. Back carries two review commentaries on other
novels and a list of eleven other titles carried in the Uniform Edition of
the works of Elizabeth Bowen. Front flap discusses contents and lists price
as 21s net; back flap notes jacket design is by Leigh Taylor.

Contents:
'Preface'. MS, E24.
'A Day in the Dark'. First printed in *Botteghe Oscure* (C506), then in
    Mademoiselle (C506) and *Argosy* (C506). Reprinted in A33. Published
    in anthology, G45.
'The Disinherited'. See A8.
'Breakfast'. See A1a.
'Reduced'. See A11a.
'Her Table Spread'. See A8.
'I Hear You Say So'. First printed in *New Writing and Daylight* (C146).
    Translated, D72.
'Summer Night'. See A11a.
'Gone Away'. First printed in *Listener* (C162).
'Mysterious Kôr'. See A15a.
'A Love Story'. See A11a.
'The Dancing-Mistress'. See A5a.

'Look at All Those Roses'. See A11a.
'Hand in Glove'. First printed in B28 and reprinted in A33. Translated, D72. MS, E88. Published in anthology, G42.
'The Demon Lover'. See A15a.
'No. 16'. See A11a.
'The Cheery Soul'. See A15a.
'The Happy Autumn Fields'. See A15a.
'The Dolt's Tale'.
'The Cat Jumps'. See A8.
'Ivy Gripped the Steps'. See A15a.

Notes: Published 24 June 1965, at 21/0, and reprinted August 1966. Second impression copies vary, on p. [4], with the addition of the lines, 'First published June, 1965 | Second impression, 1966'.

An abridged edition, in English, was published by Asahi Press of Tokyo in 1965. Edited with notes and Japanese glossary by Naomitsu Kumabe and Satoko Endo, the edition includes only the following stories: 'A Day in the Dark', 'Hand in Glove', 'Gone Away', 'I Hear You Say So', 'The Dolt's Tale'.

Transcribed in Braille 1965, in NLB.

Reviews:
Angus Wilson, *Observer* (27 June 1965):22
Olivia Manning, *Spectator* 215 (2 July 1965):20
B. A. Young, *Punch* 249 (7 July 1965):30
Hilary Corke, *Listener* 74 (8 July 1965):64
unsigned, *TLS* 64 (8 July 1965):573
Anastasia Leech, *Tablet* 219 (31 July 1965):858
Edwin Morgan, *New Statesman* 70 (6 Aug. 1965):191
Alex Hamilton, *B&B* 10 (Sept. 1965):27–28

A29 **THE GOOD TIGER** **1965**

a. *First edition*:
[left-hand title page] BY | *Elizabeth Bowen* | ILLUSTRATED BY | *M. Nebel* [right-hand title page] The Good Tiger | *Alfred A. Knopf* [publisher's device] *New York* [across both title pages, a drawing in medium gray (265), very light to brilliant blue (180, 177), and strong orange (50) of traffic disrupted by a tiger flanked by a boy and a girl]

Collation: 8¼ x 6¾"; [1–2]⁸; pp. [1–32].
[1]: illustration. [2–3]: title page. [4]: LC number, publisher's imprint, and copyright notice concluding, 'Manufactured in the United States of America, | and distributed by Random House, Inc. Published simultaneously in | Toronto, Canada, by Random House of Canada, Limited.'

[5]: illustration and half title. [6]: illustration. [7–30]: text, 13, 15, 22, and 28 contain full-page illustrations. [31–32]: illustrations.

Binding: Two different bindings have been noted:

(1) *Trade*: Bound in brilliant orange yellow (67) cloth, lettered down the spine in black (267): 'The Good Tiger ELIZABETH BOWEN / M. NEBEL KNOPF'. On the front cover in black, a drawing of a tiger. On the back cover, lower right, the publisher's device in black.

(2) *Library*: Bound in white (263) cloth, lettered down the spine in black (267): 'THE GOOD TIGER *Elizabeth Bowen* / M. *Nebel* [publisher's device, across] *Knopf*'. On the front cover: '[against a superimposed background of vivid orange yellow (66), covering the whole except for the drawing] [in black] The Good Tiger | *Elizabeth Bowen* / *Illustrated by M. Nebel* | [against the background of white cloth, a drawing in brilliant greenish blue (168), black, and vivid orange yellow, of a tiger and two children in the rain] | [against the vivid orange yellow background, in black] A READ ALONE BOOK | *What happens when a not-so-ferocious tiger leaves the zoo*'. On the back cover: [against a wash-colored background of brilliant greenish blue, covering the whole except for the drawing] [in black, at the upper right: the binder's device] | [a drawing of a caged tiger in vivid orange yellow, against the background of white cloth].

Dust jacket: Not seen.

Notes: Collier Publishing Company initially contracted to publish the volume but withdrew. Then Knopf, on 5 October 1965, published an impression of 6,085 copies, 1,974 of which were bound for trade, at $3.25, and 4,111 of which were library-bound, at $2.99. All reprintings were library-bound: October 1966 (4,500 copies), May 1970 (2,780 copies), October 1971 (3,239 copies), and April 1973 (2,751 copies). See MS, E25, E145.

Reviews:
unsigned, *Kirkus* 33 (15 Sept. 1965):980
Alan Pryce-Jones, *Book Week* (Fall Children's Issue) 3 #8 (31 Oct. 1965):7
Cynthia Parsons, *ChScM* 57 (4 Nov. 1965):B2
I. S. Black, *NYTBR* 70 (7 Nov. 1965):Pt. 2, 56
Charlotte Jackson, *Atlantic* 216 (Dec. 1965):155
Alison Lurie, *New York Review of Books* 5 (9 Dec. 1965):38
H. H. McGrady, *LJ* 90 (15 Dec. 1965):5508

b. *First English edition*:
[left-hand title page] Elizabeth Bowen | ILLUSTRATED BY | Quentin Blake [right-hand title page] [title in block letters] THE | GOOD | TIGER | Jonathan Cape | THIRTY BEDFORD

SQUARE | LONDON [across both title pages, a drawing in light gray (264) and deep orange (51) of a boy, a tiger, and fleeing adults]

Collation: 9 x 6⅜"; [1–4]⁴; [2], [1–4] 5–27 [28–32].
[*1–2*]: blank. [1]: half title. [*2–3*]: title pages. [*4*]: 'First Published in the U.S.A. 1965 | This edition first published 1970' | copyright notice and publisher's imprint | 'Printed in Great Britain | by Lowe & Brydone (Printers) Ltd, London | bound by G & J Kitcat Ltd, London'. 5–[31]: text. [*32*]: blank.

Binding: Bound in pale yellow green (121) cloth lettered down the spine in gold: '*ELIZABETH BOWEN THE GOOD TIGER* [publisher's device, across the spine]'.

Dust jacket: Cover has a white background with black (267) lettering and a drawing of a large vivid orange (48) tiger on the front and back. Front: '[black] *ELIZABETH* | *BOWEN* | *THE* | *GOOD* | *TIGER* | Illustrated by | QUENTIN BLAKE'. Spine: '[vertically down in black] *ELIZABETH BOWEN THE GOOD TIGER* [across] [publisher's insignia]'. Front flap contains blurb on contents and price, '16s net | in UK only | 80 op net'. Back flap contains biographical blurb on Elizabeth Bowen and Quentin Blake.

Notes: Published 22 October 1970, at 16/0.

Reviews:
John Coleman, *New Statesman* 80 (6 Nov. 1970):612
unsigned, *TLS* #3588 (11 Dec. 1970):1462

A30   **EVA TROUT, OR CHANGING SCENES**   **1968**

a. *First edition*:
Eva Trout | *or* | *Changing Scenes* | [ornamental rule] | *by* *Elizabeth Bowen* | ALFRED · A · KNOPF | NEW YORK | [at right margin] 1968 | [publisher's device]

Collation: 8⅜ x 5½"; [1–10]¹⁶; pp. [*12*], [1–3] 4–302 [303–308].
[*1–3*]: blank. [*4*]: list of Bowen's works. [*5*]: half title. [*6*]: blank. [*7*]: title page. [*8*]: [publisher's imprint] | 'First Edition' | [copyright notice]. [*9*]: 'To Charles Ritchie'. [*10*]: blank. [*11*]: contents. [*12*]: blank. [1]–302: text, 2, 156, and 158 blank. [*303–304*]: blank. [*305*]: biographical note. [*306*]: colophon, concluding, 'Composed, printed, and bound by | KINGSPORT PRESS, INC., KINGSPORT, TENNESSEE | Typography and Binding Design by Golda Fishbein'. [*307–308*]: blank.

Binding: Bound in dark bluish green (165) cloth lettered across the spine in gold: '*Eva Trout* | [ornamental design] | *Elizabeth* | *Bowen* | [ornamental design] | ALFRED · A · | KNOPF. On the front cover, in a monogram design: 'EB'. Blind-stamped on the back cover: [publisher's device].

Dust jacket: A dark yellow (88) band frames the artist's rendering of a very yellow (82) castle with white clouds drifting across the moderate blue (182) background. Front: '[white (263)] ELIZABETH | BOWEN | [black (267)] Eva Trout | [bluish gray (191)] *or* | *Changing* | *Scenes* | [black] *A NOVEL'*. Spine: '[vertically down] [black] Eva Trout [white] ELIZABETH BOWEN | [horizontal white on yellow] [publisher's device] | [black] *KNOPF'*. Back includes a large photograph of Elizabeth Bowen by Angus McBean. Front flap describes the novel and indicates the jacket was designed by Muriel Nasser; back flap carries a blurb on Elizabeth Bowen.

Notes: Published 14 October 1968, in an impression of 20,198 copies, at $5.95. A second impression (4,502 copies) varies in that, on p. [8], 'First Edition' is replaced by 'Published October 14, 1968 | Second Printing, November 1968'.

A second American edition (in paperback) was published by Avon Books 21 August 1978 (60,000 copies in the United States, and 10,000 copies in Canada), at $1.95.

Translated, D52–55. MS, E26.

Transcribed in Braille 1969, in NLB.

Reviews:

unsigned, *Kirkus* 36 (1 Sept. 1968):999

unsigned, *Publisher's Weekly* 194 (2 Sept. 1968):57

Howard Moss, *NYTBR* 73 (13 Oct. 1968):1, 28, 30. Reprinted in *Writing Against Time: Critical Essays and Reviews* (New York: William Morrow and Co., Inc., 1969), 214–19

C. Poore, *NYTimes* (17 Oct. 1968):49

Pamela Marsh, *ChScM* (24 Oct. 1968):7

Mary Ellmann, *Atlantic* 222 (Nov. 1968):124–26

K. G. Jackson, *Harper's* 237 (Nov. 1968):159

Patricia Stiles, *LJ* 93 (1 Nov. 1968):4164

unsigned, *Time* 92 (1 Nov. 1968):102–3

R. K. Morris, *Nation* 207 (18 Nov. 1968):538–39

R. Freedman, *Life* 65 (22 Nov. 1968):R2

Patrick Cruttwell, *Book World* 2 #47 (24 Nov. 1968):19

Walter Guzzardi, *SatRev* 51 (7 Dec. 1968):53

T. O'Hara, *Best Sellers* 28 (15 Dec. 1968):392–93

Bernard Bergonzi, *NYRB* 11 (2 Jan. 1969):40–41

S. Cunneen, *CathW* 206 (Feb. 1969):236

unsigned, *VQR* 45 #2 (Spring 1969):xlviii

F. P. W. McDowell, *Contemporary Literature* 11 (Summer 1970):401–04

W. Sullivan, *SR* 78 #4 (Autumn 1970):657–58
Jay L. Halio, *Southern Review* n.s. 7 (Spring 1971):635

b. *First English edition*:
ELIZABETH BOWEN | [ornamental device] | [block letters]
EVA TROUT | *or* | *Changing Scenes* | [ornamental device] |
[publisher's device] | JONATHAN CAPE | THIRTY BED-
FORD SQUARE | LONDON

Collation: 7⅜ x 5"; [A]⁸ B–P⁸ R⁸ 17–20⁸; pp. [1–10] 11–318 [319–320].
[1]: half title. [2]: list of Bowen's works. [3]: title page. [4]: 'FIRST
PUBLISHED IN GREAT BRITAIN 1969' | [copyright notice and pub-
lisher's imprint] | 'PRINTED IN GREAT BRITAIN BY | EBENEZER
BAYLIS AND SON, LIMITED | THE TRINITY PRESS, WORCESTER,
AND LONDON | ON PAPER MADE BY JOHN DICKINSON AND
CO. LTD | BOUND BY A. W. BAIN AND CO. LTD, LONDON'.
[5]: contents. [6]: blank. [7]: 'TO | CHARLES RITCHIE'. [8]: blank.
[9]–318: text, 10, 168, and 170 blank. [319–320]: blank.

Binding: Bound in vivid dark green (147) cloth, lettered across the spine
in gold: 'EVA | TROUT | [rule] | ELIZABETH | BOWEN | [publisher's
device]'.

Dust jacket: Covering the entire jacket is a black (267) line drawing
signed by Philippe Jullian of a large English manor house and landscape on
a white background with pale purplish pink (252) accents. Front: '[black]
Elizabeth | Bowen | EVA | TROUT | [publisher's device]'. Back continues
the artist's drawing. Front flap carries a blurb on the novel and some
comments about the author with price 25s net in UK only; back flap
carries a picture of Elizabeth Bowen by Angus McBean and lists fourteen
novels and short stories written by Elizabeth Bowen and published by
Jonathan Cape.

Notes: Published 23 January 1969, at 25/0, and that year awarded the
James Tait Black Memorial Prize and short-listed (honorable mention)
for the Booker Award. Advance proof copy for this edition at the Hu-
manities Research Center is gathered [A]⁸ B–M⁸ 13–20⁸.
 A second edition (in paperback) was published by Panther Books in
March 1971 (20, 000 copies), at £0.35.

Reviews:
M. Capitanchik, *Spectator* 222 (24 Jan. 1969):112
Elizabeth Taylor, *New Statesman* 77 (24 Jan. 1969):119
P. N. Furbank, *Times* (London) (25 Jan. 1969):22
Angus Wilson, *Observer* (26 Jan. 1969):27
Christopher Wordsworth, *ManGW* 10 (30. Jan. 1969):15
unsigned, *TLS* #3492 (30 Jan. 1969):101
R. G. G. Price, *Punch* 256 (5 Feb. 1969):214

Margaret Drabble, *Listener* 81 (13 Feb. 1969):214, 216
I. Quigly, *Tablet* (15 Feb. 1969):160
Francis Wyndham, *London Magazine* n.s. 8 (Mar. 1969):89–91
Roger Baker, *B&B* 14 #7 (April 1969):34

A31   **NATIVITY PLAY**   **1974**

[ornamental border] | A Christmas Musical | NATIVITY PLAY
| by | ELIZABETH BOWEN | [publisher's device] | THE
DRAMATIC PUBLISHING COMPANY | CHICAGO | [orna-
mental border]

Collation: 7 x 5″; [1–2¹⁶]; pp. [1–2] 3–63 [64].
[1]: title page. [2]: copyright notice. 3–61: text, 2 blank. 62: properties.
63: synopsis of songs. [64]: director's notes.

Binding: Internally stapled and perfect bound in light olive (106) paper,
lettered down the spine in black (267): 'NATIVITY PLAY [dash]
Bowen'. On the front cover, in black, against a background sketch of
one major radiating star and lesser stars: 'NATIVITY PLAY | A Christ-
mas Musical | by | ELIZABETH BOWEN | [double rule] [publisher's
device] [double rule] | THE DRAMATIC PUBLISHING COMPANY'.

Dust jacket: None.

Notes: Published 14 October 1974, in an impression of 1,000 copies, at
$0.85. Reprinted in A32.

A32   **PICTURES AND CONVERSATIONS**   **1975**

a. *First edition*:
[flower bouquet imposed over a swelled rule] | PICTURES AND
| CONVERSATIONS | by Elizabeth Bowen | WITH A FORE-
WORD BY | SPENCER CURTIS BROWN | [swelled rule] |
NEW YORK: ALFRED · A · KNOPF | [publisher's device] |
1975

Collation: 8⅜ x 5½″; [1–6¹⁶ 7⁸ 8¹⁶]; pp. [2], [i–vi] vii–xlii, [1–2] 3–193
[194–196].
[1]: blank. [2]: list of Bowen's works. [i]: half title. [ii]: blank. [iii]:
title page. [iv]: [publisher's imprint] | [copyright notices] | [acknowledg-
ments] | [LC data] | *'Manufactured in the United States of America* |

FIRST EDITION'. [v]: contents. [vi]: blank. vii–xlii; 'Foreword', signed 'SPENCER CURTIS BROWN' and dated 'Suffolk | September 1973'. [1]–193: text, 2, 64, 66, 78, 110, 112, 168 blank. [194]: blank. [195]: biographical note. [196]: colophon, concluding, 'Composed, printed, and bound by Kingsport Press, Inc., | Kingsport, Tennessee. Typography and binding design by | WARREN [monogram design] CHAPPELL'.

Binding: Quarter-bound in dark brown (59) cloth, with front and back covers in deep red (13) cloth. On the spine in gold: '[lettered down, within an ornamental frame] PICTURES AND CONVERSATIONS · ELIZABETH BOWEN [at the foot, lettered across] ALFRED | · A · | KNOPF'. Blind-stamped on the front cover: '[a flower bouquet] | Elizabeth Bowen'. Blind-stamped on the back cover: [the publisher's device].

Dust jacket: On yellowish white (92) paper, a ruled frame including a geometric flower design in three printed colors—dark grayish reddish brown (47), deep red (13), and dark olive green (126)—borders the front: '[deep red] Elizabeth | BOWEN | [dark grayish reddish brown] Pictures and | Conversations | [deep red] E · [deep red and dark olive green] [a flower bouquet] [deep red] B · | [dark grayish reddish brown] *Chapters of an Autobiography* | WITH OTHER COLLECTED WRITINGS'. Spine has the same geometric flower frame lettered down, which contains: '[dark grayish reddish brown] Pictures and Conversations [dark olive green] · [deep red] *Elizabeth Bowen* | [outside frame across] Alfred | · A · | Knopf | [ruled flower frame]'. On the back a photograph of Elizabeth Bowen taken by Alfred A. Knopf in 1946. Front flap has a blurb about the book and the back flap a blurb about Elizabeth Bowen.

Contents:
'Pictures and Conversations'.
'The Move-In'.
'The Art of Bergotte'. First printed in B38.
'Nativity Play'. See A31.
'Notes on Writing a Novel'. See A19.

Notes: Published 7 January 1975, in an impression of 5,000 copies, at $7.95, and reprinted (1,500 copies) in March 1975. MS, E27.

Reviews:
Albert H. Johnson, *Publisher's Weekly* 206 (16 Dec. 1974):46
Inge Judd, *LJ* 100 (1 Jan. 1975):52
Eudora Welty, *NYTBR* 80 (5 Jan. 1975):4, 20
Dorothy Rabinowitz, *SatRev* 2 #8 (11 Jan. 1975):26
Kelly Cherry, *CTribBW* (12 Jan. 1975):3
Robert Nye, *ChScM* 67 (20 Jan. 1975):15
unsigned, *NY* 50 (20 Jan. 1975):99

William Abrahams, *Atlantic* 235 (Mar. 1975):133–34, 136
unsigned, *Booklist* 71 (1 Mar. 1975):665
Gerald Weales, *Commonweal* 102 (18 July 1975):282–83

b. *First edition (English issue)*:
(The title page is identical with that of the first edition, except that the following is substituted for the original publisher's imprint and date: 'ALLEN LANE'.)

Collation: 8⅜ x 5¼"; [1–5¹⁶ 6⁸ 7–8¹⁶]; pagination as in the first edition. Contents remain as in the first edition, except in the following respects: [1]: publisher's device. [2]: list of Bowen's works (reset). [iv]: [copyright notice] | 'This edition first published in 1975' | [publisher's imprint] | [ISBN number] | [copyright notice for *Nativity Play*] | [acknowledgments] | 'Printed in Great Britain | by Lowe & Brydone (Printers) Ltd | Thetford, Norfolk'. [195–196]: blank.

Binding: Bound in very dark green (147) cloth, lettered down the spine in gold: 'ELIZABETH BOWEN | PICTURES AND CONVERSATIONS [at the foot of the spine, across in gold] [the publisher's device]'.

Dust jacket: Top portion of front, back, and spine in grayish yellow (90) and remaining portions in light grayish olive (109). An artist's sketch of trees divides the bottom portion from the top and the sketch covers the entire jacket except for the flaps. The jacket design is by Gerald Cinamon. Front: '[white] PICTURES AND CONVERSATIONS | ELIZABETH BOWEN | [grayish yellow] CHAPTERS OF AN AUTOBIOGRAPHY | WITH OTHER COLLECTED WRITINGS'. Spine: '[vertically down in white] ELIZABETH BOWEN | PICTURES AND CONVERSATIONS [across the bottom is the publisher's device in grayish yellow]'. Back: repeats front exactly. Front flap carries a blurb on the contents and lists the price as £4.50 net. The back flap provides a biographical blurb on Elizabeth Bowen and the name of the jacket designer.

Contents: As in the first edition.

Notes: Published 2 October 1975, in an unknown number of copies, at £4.50.

Reviews:
Rosamond Lehmann, *New Statesman* 90 (10 Oct. 1975):445
Raymond Mortimer, *Sunday Times* (12 Oct. 1975):39
Francis Wyndham, *TLS* (24 Oct. 1975):1254
Gabriele Annan, *Listener* 94 (30 Oct. 1975):580
unsigned, *British Book News* (Mar. 1976):222

Elizabeth Bowen's | Irish Stories | POOLBEG PRESS: DUBLIN

Collation: 7⅛ x 4⅞"; 68 single leaves; pp. [1–4] 5–135 [136].
[1]: title page. [2]: [publisher's imprint] | [copyright notices] | [acknowl-
edgments] | 'Printed by Cahill Printers Limited, | East Wall Road, Dublin
3.' [3]: contents. [4]: blank. 5–8: 'Introduction', signed 'Victoria Glendinning'. 9–135: text. [136]: blank.

Binding: Perfect binding in strong greenish blue (169) paper. On the
spine: '[lettered down] [white (263)] ELIZABETH BOWEN'S [black
(267)] IRISH STORIES [across] [publisher's device]'. On the front,
printed over the G. M. B. Holland portrait of Bowen: [publisher's device,
in white] | [in strong greenish blue] ELIZABETH | BOWEN'S [thick
rule | thin rule under the letters "OWEN'S"] | IRISH STORIES | [black]
With an introduction by | VICTORIA GLENDINNING'.

Contents:
'Sunday Afternoon'. See A15.
'Her Table Spread'. See A8.
'The Tommy Crans'. See A8.
'A Love Story'. See A11.
'Unwelcome Idea'. See A11.
'Summer Night'. See A11.
'The Happy Autumn Fields'. See A15.
'Hand in Glove'. See A28.
'A Day in the Dark'. See A28.

Notes: Published 16 August 1978, in an impression of 5,000 copies, at
£1.50.

a. *First edition*:
The | BLACK CAP | [woodcut: man with a knife at a darkened corner] | NEW STORIES of MURDER & MYSTERY | COM-PILED BY | CYNTHIA · ASQUITH | HUTCHINSON & CO. (Publishers), LTD. | Paternoster Row [rule] LONDON, E.C.4.

Collation: 9¼ x 6"; [A]⁸ B–U⁸; pp. [i–vi] vii, [8] 9–318 [319–320].

Binding: Bound in deep purplish blue (197) cloth, lettered in light bluish gray (190) across the spine: 'The | BLACK | CAP | NEW STORIES | OF | MURDER & MYSTERY | COMPILED BY | CYNTHIA | ASQUITH | HUTCHINSON'. On the front cover: 'The | BLACK CAP | [a broken circle, blackjack, lamp, handcuffs, and pistol] | NEW STORIES of MURDER & MYSTERY | COMPILED BY | CYNTHIA · ASQUITH.'

Contents: 'Telling' [pp. 250–258]. Reprinted in A5 (q.v.).

Notes: Published October 1927, at 7/6 and reprinted September 1929, at 3/6. A third impression in 1930 includes a line on the title page, above the publisher's imprint: '*THIRD EDITION*'. Publishing records as to printing quantities and exact dating were destroyed during World War II.

b. *First American edition*:
[within a frame] The | BLACK CAP | NEW STORIES OF | MURDER AND MYSTERY | COMPILED BY | CYNTHIA ASQUITH | [ornament] | NEW YORK | CHARLES SCRIB-NER'S SONS | 1928

Collation: 7¾ x 5¼"; [1–21⁸ 22⁴]; pp. [8], 1–344 [345–346].

Binding: Bound in strong orange (50) cloth, lettered in black (267) across the spine: '[thick rule] | The | BLACK | CAP | SCRIBNERS | [thick rule]'. On the front cover, within a thick frame: 'The | BLACK CAP | [picture of a man with a knife at a darkened corner] | NEW STORIES of MURDER & MYSTERY | COMPILED BY | CYNTHIA ASQUITH'.

Contents: 'Telling' [pp. 259–268]. Reprinted in A5 (q.v.).

Notes: Published 2 March 1928, in an unknown number of copies, at $2.

a. *First edition*:
THE FUNNY BONE | NEW | HUMOROUS STORIES |
COMPILED BY | LADY CYNTHIA ASQUITH | JARROLDS
Publishers LONDON | *Limited* 34 *Paternoster Row, E.C.*4

Collation: 7⅞ x 4⅞"; [A]⁸ B–S⁸; pp. [1–8] 9–287 [288].

Binding: Bound in dark purple (224) cloth, lettered in dark reddish
orange (38) across the spine: '[ornamental border] | THE | FUNNY |
BONE | [rule] | COMPILED BY | LADY CYNTHIA | ASQUITH |
JARROLDS | [ornamental border]'. On the front cover, all within an or-
namental frame: 'THE | FUNNY BONE | COMPILED BY | LADY
CYNTHIA ASQUITH'.

Contents: 'Maria' [pp. 152–165]. Reprinted in A8 (q.v.).

Notes: Published 28 September 1928, at 7/6, and reprinted in 1929, at
3/6.
    A second edition was published by Jarrolds under the title, *New Tales
of Humor*, in May 1935, at 2/6; and was reprinted in 1941. Publishing
records as to printing quantities and exact dating were destroyed during
World War II.

b. *First American edition*:
[all within a frame] *The* | FUNNY BONE | NEW HUMOROUS
STORIES BY | [authors listed in two parallel columns] | DE-
SIGNED BY CYNTHIA ASQUITH | [ornament] | NEW YORK
| CHARLES SCRIBNER'S SONS | 1928

Collation: 7¾ x 5⅛"; [1–19⁸ 20⁴]; pp. [8], 1–303 [304].

Binding: Bound in strong orange (50) cloth, lettered in black (267)
across the spine: '[thick rule] | *The* | FUNNY | BONE | SCRIBNERS |
[thick rule]'. On the front: '[all within a frame] *The* | FUNNY BONE |
[thick rule] | NEW | HUMOROUS STORIES | DESIGNED BY |
CYNTHIA ASQUITH'.

Contents: 'Maria' [pp. 157–172]. Reprinted in A8 (q.v.).

Notes: Published 2 November 1928, in an unknown number of copies,
at $2.

B3   **SHUDDERS: A COLLECTION**   **1929**
            OF NEW NIGHTMARE TALES

a. *First edition*:

SHUDDERS | *A Collection of new Nightmare Tales* | COM-
PILED BY | CYNTHIA ASQUITH | HUTCHINSON & CO.
(Publishers), LTD. | Paternoster Row [rule] LONDON, E.C.4

Collation: 9¼ x 6"; [A]⁸ B–S⁸; pp. [i–vi] vii, [8] 9–287 [288].

Binding: Bound in light blue (181) cloth, lettered in black (267) across
the spine: '[a gibbet] | SHUDDERS | CYNTHIA | ASQUITH | HUTCH-
INSON'. On the front: '[a woman's head] | SHUDDERS'.

Contents: 'The Cat Jumps' [pp. 119–132]. Reprinted in A8 (q.v.).

Notes: Published 3 September 1929, at 7/6, and reprinted June 1931, at
3/6. Publishing records as to printing quantities were destroyed in World
War II.

b. *First American edition*:
[all within a frame] SHUDDERS | [authors listed in two parallel
columns] | DESIGNED BY | CYNTHIA ASQUITH | [orna-
ment] | NEW YORK | CHARLES SCRIBNER'S SONS | 1929

Collation: 7⅜ x 5¼"; [1–17]⁸ [18]²; pp. [8], 1–268.

Binding: Bound in strong orange (50) cloth, lettered in black (267)
across the spine: '[two thick rules] | SHUDDERS | [wavy rule] | [wavy
rule] | SCRIBNERS | [two thick rules]'. On the front: '[all within a
frame, within which flying bats are depicted] [title in alternately slant-
ing letters] SHUDDERS | DESIGNED BY | CYNTHIA | ASQUITH'.

Contents: 'The Cat Jumps' [pp. 138–150]. Reprinted in A8 (q.v.).

Notes: Published 25 October 1929, in an unknown number of copies,
at $2.

B4   **WHEN CHURCHYARDS YAWN**   **1931**

WHEN | CHURCHYARDS | YAWN | *Fifteen New Ghost
Stories* | A COLLECTION OF GHOST STORIES MADE BY |
CYNTHIA ASQUITH | London: | HUTCHINSON & CO.
(Publishers), LTD.

Collation: 9¼ x 5⅞"; [A]⁸ B–S⁸; pp. [1–6] 7–287 [288].

Binding: Bound in black (267) cloth, lettered in silver across the spine:
'[thick and thin rules] WHEN | CHURCHYARDS | YAWN | *A Collec-
tion of* | *Ghost Stories* | *made by* | Cynthia Asquith | HUTCHINSON |

[thin and thick rules]'. Blind-stamped on the front cover, a frame.

Contents: 'The Apple Tree' [pp. 7–23]. Reprinted in A8 (q.v.).

Notes: Published 24 September 1931, at 7/6. Publishing records as to printing quantities were destroyed during World War II.
   A second edition (in paperback) was published by Arrow Books, Ltd., 4 November 1963, in an impression of 29,000 copies, at 2/6.

B5   **MR. FOTHERGILL'S PLOT**   1931

a. *First edition*:
[title in block letters] MR. FOTHERGILL'S | PLOT | HIS CONSPIRATORS | [eight-line list of contributing authors] | [ornament] | NEW YORK | OXFORD UNIVERSITY PRESS

Collation: $7\frac{7}{8}$ x $5\frac{1}{4}$"; $[1-22^8\ 23^4\ 24-25^8]$; pp. [2], [i–iv] v–xxi, [1–2] 3–363 [364–368].

Binding: Two different bindings have been noted: one in light greenish blue (172) cloth and the other in brilliant green (140) cloth. Both are lettered across the spine in black (267): 'Mr. | Fothergill's | Plot | Oxford'. On the front in black, in each case: '[silhouette of a stagecoach scene] | [thick rule] | Mr. Fothergill's | Plot'.

Contents: 'Flavia' [pp. 33–36].

Notes: Published 19 November 1931, in an unknown number of copies, at $2.50.

b. *First English edition*: THE FOTHERGILL OMNIBUS
[title in block letters] THE | FOTHERGILL OMNIBUS | for which | SEVENTEEN EMINENT AUTHORS | have written | SHORT STORIES | upon | ONE AND THE SAME PLOT | With introductions by | JOHN FOTHERGILL | R. G. COLLINGWOOD & GERALD GOULD | MCMXXXI | EYRE AND SPOTTISWOODE | PUBLISHERS.   LONDON

Collation: $7\frac{3}{4}$ x $5\frac{1}{4}$"; $[1]^8\ 2-25^8$; pp. [i–iv] v–xxiv, [25–26] 27–398 [399–400].

Binding: Copies of the autographed issue are bound in deep green (142) leather, lettered across the spine in gold: '[ornamental border] | *The* | *Fothergill* | *Omnibus* | *Eyre* | *and* | *Spottiswoode* | [ornamental border]'. Housed in a slipcase of pale yellow green (121) with a silver geometric print.

Copies of the trade edition are bound in vivid green (139) boards, lettered across the spine in black (267): 'The | Fothergill | Omnibus | [swelled rule] | Stories by | G. K. Chesterton | A. E. Coppard | E. M. Delafield | Storm Jameson | Sheila Kaye Smith | Margaret Kennedy | J. C. Squire | Frank Swinnerton | L. A. G. Strong | Rebecca West | Etc. Etc. | [swelled rule] | Eyre & | Spottiswoode'.

Contents: 'Flavia' [pp. 57–70].

Notes: Published 31 November 1931, in two issues. An autographed issue of 250 copies was offered at 30/0; and the trade issue of an unknown number of copies was offered at 8/6.

B5.1   **THE SILVER SHIP**   **1932**

"The Silver Ship. . ." | [encircled drawing of galleon, signed 'A. H. Watson'] | New Stories, Poems, & Pictures | for Children. | Collected by | Lady Cynthia Asquith. | Putnam. | London. & New York.

Collation: $9\frac{5}{8}$ x $7\frac{1}{4}''$; [A]^6 B–P^8 Q^4; pp. [i–iv] v–x [xi–xii], 1–232.

Binding: Bound in light greenish blue (172) cloth, lettered in very dark bluish green (166) across the spine: '[title only in ornamented letters] THE | SILVER | SHIP | LADY | CYNTHIA | ASQUITH | PUTNAM'. On the front cover: '[title only in ornamental letters] THE | SILVER | SHIP | LADY CYNTHIA | ASQUITH | [ornament: a sea shell]'.

Contents: 'Brigands' [pp. 183–200].

Notes: Published in November 1932, according to *The English Catalogue of Books*, although the verso of the volume's title page (p. [iv]) bears the statement 'First Published October 1932'. *Cumulative Book Index* records the United Kingdom price as 6s and the United States price as $2.50.

B6   **CONSEQUENCES**   **1932**

a. *First edition*:
CONSEQUENCES | A COMPLETE STORY | IN THE MANNER OF | THE OLD PARLOUR GAME | IN NINE CHAPTERS | EACH BY A DIFFERENT AUTHOR | [publisher's device] | PRINTED & MADE IN GREAT BRITAIN BY | THE GOLDEN COCKEREL PRESS | WALTHAM SAINT LAWRENCE | BERKSHIRE

Collation: 9⅜ x 6⅛"; [A]⁴ B–E⁸ F⁴ [$1 (+B2, C2, D2, E2) signed]; pp. [8], 1–66 [67–72].

Binding:
(1) Copies of the signed issue are bound in boards covered in grayish reddish orange (39) paper with an ornamental geometric pattern whose background is grayish reddish brown (46). The spine is covered with dark blue (183) leather, lettered down in gold: 'CONSEQUENCES'.
(2) Copies of the unsigned issue are bound in moderate red (15) cloth, lettered across the spine in bluish black (193):
'C | O | N | S | E | Q | U | E | N | C | E | S'.

Contents: 'She Gave Him' [pp. 46–51]. MS, E33.

Notes: Published 15 November 1932. The colophon on p. [69] indicates that the book was *'completed on the 14th day of October, 1932'* and that *'this first edition consists of 200 numbered copies on hand made paper signed by the authors, and 1,000 unsigned copies on machine made paper'*. Since 520 copies from the unsigned issue are known to have borne the Houghton Mifflin imprint (see B6b), probably 480 copies were actually published in England. The signed copies were priced at 42/0 and the unsigned copies at 6/0.

b. *First edition (American issue)*:
The title page is identical to that of the first edition, except that the following is substituted for the original publisher's imprint: 'BOSTON AND NEW YORK | HOUGHTON MIFFLIN COMPANY | 1933'.

Collation: As in the first edition.

Binding: As the unsigned issue of the first edition.

Contents: As in the first edition.

Notes: Published 26 July 1933, at $2., in an issue of 520 copies, as part of the 1,000 unsigned copies described in the colophon (see B6a).

B7   **THE OLD SCHOOL**   **1934**

The | OLD SCHOOL | Essays | by Divers Hands | Edited by | GRAHAM GREENE | [publisher's device] | Jonathan Cape | Thirty Bedford Square | London

Collation: 7⅞ x 5⅜"; [A]⁸ B–Q⁸; pp. [1–4] 5–256.

Binding: Bound in black (267) cloth, lettered in light blue (181) across the spine: 'THE OLD | SCHOOL | GRAHAM | GREENE | JONA-

THAN | CAPE'. On the front cover: 'THE OLD SCHOOL'. On the back cover: [publisher's device].

Contents: 'The Mulberry Tree [Downe House]' [pp. 45–59]. See A19.

Notes: Published 23 July 1934, in an impression of 1,500 copies, at 7/6 in the United Kingdom and $2.75 in Canada. It was reprinted August 1934 (1,000 copies), at 3/6.

B8 **THE PRINCESS ELIZABETH GIFT BOOK** **1935**

THE | PRINCESS ELIZABETH | GIFT BOOK | [thin and thick rules] | *In aid of* | *The Princess Elizabeth of York* | *Hospital for Children* | [rule] | [sketch of horse-drawn coach] | [rule] | Edited by | *Cynthia Asquith & Eileen Bigland* | [thick and thin rules] | Hodder & Stoughton

Collation: 9⅝ x 7¼"; [A]⁸ B–O⁸; pp. [1–6] 7–224; plates [10].

Binding: Bound in yellowish white (92) cloth, lettered in deep blue (179) across the spine: '[silver crown] | *The* | PRINCESS | ELIZABETH | GIFT BOOK | [wreath with silver 'E' in center] | [ornament: flower] | HODDER & | STOUGHTON'. On the front: '[silver crown] | [wreath with silver 'E' in center] | *The* | PRINCESS | ELIZABETH | GIFT BOOK | IN AID OF THE PRINCESS ELIZABETH | OF YORK HOSPITAL FOR CHILDREN'.

Contents: 'The Unromantic Princess' [pp. 83–99].

Notes: The publisher lacks informaton on either the date of publication or the number of copies printed, and neither *The English Catalogue* nor *Whitaker's Cumulative Book List* records publication.

B9 **THE ENGLISH NOVELISTS** **1936**

a. *First edition*:
THE | ENGLISH NOVELISTS | A SURVEY OF THE NOVEL | BY TWENTY CONTEMPORARY NOVELISTS | *Edited by* | Derek Verschoyle | 1936 | CHATTO & WINDUS | LONDON

Collation: 8¼ x 5¼"; [A]⁶ B–T⁸ U⁴; pp. [i–iv] v–xii, [1–2] 3–293 [294–296].

Binding: Bound in moderate green (145) cloth, lettered in gold across the spine: 'THE | ENGLISH | NOVELISTS | Edited | by | DEREK | VERSCHOYLE | CHATTO & WINDUS'.

Contents: 'Jane Austen' [pp. (97)–110]. Reprinted as 'Jane Austen: Artist on Ivory' in *SatRev* (C30). The essay was to have been included in *Collected Impressions* (A19), but shortly before publication Bowen decided to exclude it. MS, E42. Published in anthology as 'Elizabeth Bowen on Jane Austen' in G14.

Notes: Published 30 April 1936, in an impression of 2,100 copies, at 8/6.

b. *First American edition*:
THE | English Novelists | A SURVEY OF THE NOVEL | BY TWENTY CONTEMPORARY NOVELISTS | *Edited by Derek Verschoyle* | HARCOURT, BRACE AND COMPANY | NEW YORK

Collation: 8 x 5¼"; [1–21]⁸; pp. [i–iv] v–x, [1–2] 3–324 [325–326].

Binding: Bound in dark grayish blue (187) cloth, lettered in gold across the spine: 'THE | English | Novelists | *Verschoyle* | HARCOURT, BRACE | AND COMPANY'.

Contents: 'Jane Austen' [pp. (99)–113]. See B9a.

Notes: Published 15 October 1936, at $2.50, in an impression of 1,500 copies, 1,000 of which were bound.

B10   **THE FABER BOOK OF MODERN STORIES**   **1937**

The Faber Book | of Modern Stories | [rule] | edited | with an introduction by | Elizabeth Bowen | Faber and Faber Limited | 24 Russell Square | London

Collation: 7⅜ x 4¾"; [A]⁸ B–2M⁸; pp. [1–4] 5–554 [555–560].

Binding: Bound in deep yellowish pink (27) cloth, lettered in gold across the spine: 'THE | FABER | BOOK | OF | MODERN | STORIES | *edited by* | ELIZABETH | BOWEN | FABER AND | FABER'.

Contents:
'The Short Story' [pp. 7–19]. Reprinted in A19 (q.v.).
'The Disinherited' [pp. 36–90]. See A8.

Notes: Published October 1937, in an impression of 5,000 copies, at 8/6; and reprinted 26 June 1941, in what is described as a 'cheap edition' (2,530 copies), at 5/0. However, the impression of November 1941 (3,000 copies) is described on its copyright page as the 'second impression', apparently because it was priced equivalent to the first impression. A final impression (3,000 copies) was imprinted in 1942 and went out of print on 16 May 1945. In 1943 (probably in May, according to Faber and Faber) A/B Lujus had reprinted the Faber edition by photoduplication, with its own imprint substituted on the title page. The number of copies is unknown, but it remained in print until 1950.

B11   **NO ONE TO BLAME (by H. M. Taylor)**   **1939**

NO ONE TO BLAME | by | H. M. TAYLOR | [publisher's device] | *With an introduction by* | ELIZABETH BOWEN | JONATHAN CAPE | THIRTY BEDFORD SQUARE | LONDON

Collation: 5 x 7¼"; [A]⁸ B–N⁸; pp. [1–4] 5–208.

Binding: Bound in strong blue (178) cloth, lettered across the spine in gold: 'NO | ONE | TO | BLAME | [ornamental rule] | H. M. | TAYLOR | [publisher's device]'.

Contents: 'Introduction' [pp. 7–12].

Notes: Published 16 June 1939, at 7/6 in the United Kingdom and $2.50 in Canada. The publisher declines to reveal the number of copies printed.

B12   **THE BLAZE OF NOON (by Rayner Heppenstall)**   **1939**

a.   *First edition*:
RAYNER HEPPENSTALL | [swelled rule] | The Blaze of Noon | [four-line quotation from Milton] | 1939 | [swelled rule] | SECKER AND WARBURG

Collation: 7¼ x 4¾"; [A]⁸ B–U⁸ X⁴; pp. [i–iv] v–xi [xii], [1–2] 3–313 [314–316].

Binding: Bound in bluish black (193) cloth, lettered across the spine in deep reddish orange (36): 'RAYNER | HEPPENSTALL | [swelled rule] | *The* | *Blaze* | *of* | *Noon* | [swelled rule] | *Secker &* | *Warburg*'.

Contents: 'Foreword' [pp. vii–xii].

Notes: Published 9 November 1939, in an impression of 1,278 copies, at 7/6, and reprinted 16 November (2,439 copies), 29 November (3,000 copies), 13 December (3,000 copies). A 'cheap edition' at 3/6 is recorded on November 1940 by *Whitaker's Cumulative Book List*; however, the publisher's records fail to indicate any printing at that time, although they do indicate that such a cheaper version was contemplated. David Farrer at Secker & Warburg suggests in correspondence that, because of the wartime paper shortage, possibly a portion of the fourth impression was remaindered to constitute this cheaper version.

An edition of Heppenstall's novel by Barrie and Rockliff in 1962 does not contain the Bowen foreword but does contain the following statement by Heppenstall: 'The original edition contained a flattering and (to my mind) extremely perceptive foreword by Elizabeth Bowen, whom I had not met at that time (and was not to meet until four or five years later). It carried no dedication. I hope that Miss Bowen will now accept the dedication of this reprint.'

Translated, D56.

b. First American edition:

[left-hand title page] *WITH A FOREWORD BY ELIZABETH BOWEN*

[right-hand title page] RAYNER HEPPENSTALL | [title in white upon a vivid purplish blue (194) rectangular background, flanked to left and right by clusters of three sunbursts in black] THE BLAZE | OF NOON | NEW YORK AND TORONTO | ALLIANCE BOOK CORPORATION

Collation: 8⅜ x 5¼"; [1–20]⁸; pp. [2], [i–iv] v–xi [xii], [1–2] 3–303 [304–306].

Binding: Bound in medium gray (265) cloth, lettered in gold across the spine: '[sunburst with deep blue (185) center] | [title upon a deep blue background] THE | BLAZE | OF | NOON | [sunburst with deep blue center] | BY RAYNER | HEPPENSTALL | [deep blue sunburst with gold center] ALLIANCE'. On the front cover upon a deep blue rectangular background: 'THE BLAZE OF NOON'.

Contents: 'Foreword' [pp. v–xi].

Notes: Published during the week of 20 April 1940, in an unknown number of copies, at $2.50, and reprinted twice during the same month.

B13   **ENGLISH STORY: THIRD SERIES**   **1942**

ENGLISH STORY | *Third Series* | *Edited by* | WOODROW WYATT | [publisher's device] | COLLINS | 48 PALL MALL LONDON | 1942

Collation: 7½ x 5"; [A]⁸ B–M⁸; pp [1–5] 6–192.

Binding: Bound in light olive gray (112) cloth, lettered in dark olive green (126) across the spine: '*English* | *Story* | *3rd Series* | *Edited by* | *Woodrow* | *Wyatt* | *Collins*'.

Contents: 'Pink May' [pp. 184–192]. Reprinted in A15 (q.v.).

Notes: Published 26 October 1942, at 7/6. The exact printing quantity is now unknown; however, the publisher states in correspondence that, combined, the printings of this *Third Series* and the *Fifth Series* (B14) amounted to 6,500 copies.

B14   **ENGLISH STORY: FIFTH SERIES**   **1944**

ENGLISH STORY | *Fifth Series* | *Edited by* | WOODROW WYATT | [publisher's device] | COLLINS | 48 PALL MALL LONDON | 1944

Collation: 7½ x 5"; [A]⁸ B–K⁸; pp. [1–4] 5–160.

Binding: Bound in light olive gray (112) cloth, lettered in deep red (13) across the spine: '*English* | *Story* | *5th Series* | *Woodrow* | *Wyatt* | *Collins*'.

Contents: 'Songs My Father Sang Me' [pp. 11–23]. Reprinted in A15 (q.v.).

Notes: Published 27 November 1944, at 7/6. The exact printing quantity is now unknown; however, the publisher states in correspondence that, combined, the printing of this *Fifth Series* and the *Third Series* (B13) amounted to 6,500 copies.

B15   **SOHO CENTENARY**   **1944**

SOHO CENTENARY | A Gift from | Artists, Writers and Musicians | to the | Soho Hospital for Women | HUTCHIN-SON & CO. (Publishers) LTD. | LONDON : NEW YORK : MELBOURNE

Collation: 9¾ x 7½"; [A]¹⁰ (+A₂) B–C⁸ [D]⁴ E–G⁸; pp. [1–3] 4–107 [108]; seventeen plates.

Binding: Trade copies are bound in moderate yellow (87) cloth, the autographed copies in deep red (16) cloth, lettered in each case down the spine in gold: '*Soho Centenary* [across] *Hutchinson*'. On the front, within an ornate frame: '*Soho Centenary*'.

Contents: 'Calico Windows' [pp. 19–20].

Notes: Published 30 November 1944, in an unknown number of copies. Two hundred and fifty copies out of the total impression represent a simultaneous signed issue. These copies vary only in that, on the recto of a sheet pasted to the front end-paper, appears 'THIS EDITION IS LIMITED TO | 250 SIGNED COPIES, OF WHICH | THIS IS NUMBER . . . . . ', followed by the signatures of twenty-seven contributors. The signed copies were offered at 105/0, and the trade copies at 21/0.

B16   **DIVERSION**   **1946**

DIVERSION | EDITED BY | HESTER W. CHAPMAN | and | PRINCESS ROMANOVSKY-PAVLOVSKY | *Published for the benefit of* | *the Yugoslav Relief Society* | [publisher's device] | COLLINS | 14 ST. JAMES'S PLACE LONDON | 1946

Collation: 7½ x 5⅜"; [A]⁸ B–K⁸; pp. [1–4] 5–160.

Binding: Bound in bluish black (193) cloth, lettered in gold across the spine: 'DIVERSION | COLLINS'.

Contents: 'The Good Earl' [pp. 133–146]. MS, E62.

Notes: Published 23 September 1946, in an impression of 4,000 copies, at 7/6.

B17   **CHOICE: SOME NEW STORIES AND PROSE**   **1946**

CHOICE | SOME NEW STORIES AND PROSE | *edited by William Sansom* | *decorations by Leonard Rosoman* | [ornament] | PROGRESS PUBLISHING [publisher's device] I, DOUGHTY ST., W.C.I

Collation: 7¼ x 4¾"; [A]⁸ B–I⁸ J⁸ K⁸ L⁴ M⁸; pp. [i–iv] v–viii, 1–191 [192].

Binding: Bound in moderate orange (53) cloth, lettered in vivid purplish blue (194) on the spine: '[across] WILLIAM | SANSOM | [down] *Choice* | [across] [publisher's device]'.

Contents: 'I Died of Love' [pp. 129–137]. MS, E63.

Notes: Published in an unknown number of copies, at 8/6 in the United Kingdom and $3.50 in the United States. The exact date of publication is unclear: *The English Catalogue* indicates the week of 5 December 1946; and the deposit receipt stamp in the British Library copy is dated 20 November 1946.

B18   **PRIDE AND PREJUDICE**   **1948**
                              (by Jane Austen)

Pride and Prejudice | By | Jane Austen | With an Introduction by | Elizabeth Bowen | London | Williams & Norgate Ltd. | Great Russell Street

Collation: 7¼ x 4¾″; [A]¹⁶ B–M¹⁶; pp. [i–iv] v–xv [xvi], 1–368.

Binding: Bound in deep green (142) cloth, lettered in gold across the spine: '[rule] | Pride and | Prejudice | Jane | Austen | Williams | and | Norgate | [rule]'. On the front cover, within an impressed rectangle: 'Pride and | Prejudice | Jane Austen'.

Contents: 'Introduction' [pp. vii–xv].

Notes: Published 21 April 1948, in an unknown number of copies, at 8/6.

B19   **UNCLE SILAS: A TALE OF BARTRAM-HAUGH**   **1948**
                              (by J. S. Le Fanu)

UNCLE SILAS | *A tale of* | Bartram-Haugh | *by* | J. S. LE FANU | WITH | AN INTRODUCTION BY | ELIZABETH BOWEN | THE CRESSET PRESS | MCMXLVII

Collation: 7¾ x 4⅞″; [A]¹⁶ B–P¹⁶; pp. [1–6] 7–480. (Page numbers appear within brackets.)

Binding: Bound in dark blue (183) cloth, lettered in gold across the spine: 'UNCLE | SILAS | [ornamental border] | SHERIDAN | LE FANU | THE | CRESSET | PRESS'. On the front cover, within a frame with ornamental borders above and below: 'UNCLE SILAS'.

Contents: 'Introduction' [pp. 7–23]. Reprinted in A19.

Notes: Although on the title page appears 'MCMXLVII' and on its verso '*Published in Great Britain in 1947*', actual publication was not until 30 June 1948, at 8/6. The number of copies involved in this lone impression is unknown; however, according to the publisher, remaindered copies from it probably were sold to both the Chanticleer Press of New York and Dufour Editions of Chester Springs, Pa. *CBI* records the Chanticleer issue in 1949, at $2. Copies of this issue are identical to the Cresset copies except that, pasted over the original publisher's imprint on the title page, is a label printed 'CHANTICLEER PRESS | *NEW YORK*', and at the foot of the *verso* is rubber stamped 'PRINTED IN GREAT BRITAIN'. The Dufour copies, on the other hand, are identifiable only by a deep green (142) label pasted on the front end-paper and lettered in white: '[within a frame] PUBLISHED IN THE UNITED STATES BY | DUFOUR EDITIONS | CHESTER SPRINGS, PENNSYLVANIA'.

B20 **HOW I WRITE MY NOVELS** **1948**

HOW I WRITE MY | NOVELS | *by* | ELIZABETH BOWEN | PETER CHEYNEY | NORMAN COLLINS | RICHMAL CROMPTON | MONICA DICKENS | LOUIS GOLDING | MARGARET KENNEDY | JOHN PUDNEY | *Collected and produced for the* | *B.B.C. Television Magazine Programme* | *"Kaleidoscope" by* | JOHN IRWIN | *Edited by* TED JONES | [publisher's device] | spearman publishers limited | 50 Old Brompton Road, London, S.W.7

Collation: 7¼ x 4¾"; [A–B]⁸ C⁸ D⁴; pp. [1–5] 6–52 [53–56].

Binding: Bound in yellowish white (92), heavy paper, lettered in black (267) down the spine: 'HOW I WRITE MY NOVELS'. On the front: 'HOW I WRITE MY NOVELS'.

Contents:
' "Always Welcome Criticism" ' [pp. 9–10]. Questions and answers on process of writing. First broadcast as 'Meet Your Favourite Authors No. 6' (F70). Re-broadcast on radio as 'How I Write' (E68 and F78). 'Two Way Passage . . . ' [p. 11]. Excerpt from *The House in Paris* (A9).

Notes: Published 21 September 1948, in an unknown number of copies, at 3/6.

B21 **WHY DO I WRITE? AN EXCHANGE OF** **1948**
VIEWS BETWEEN ELIZABETH BOWEN,
GRAHAM GREENE & V. S. PRITCHETT

Why Do I Write? | AN EXCHANGE OF VIEWS | BETWEEN

114

| *Elizabeth Bowen* | *Graham Greene* | & | *V. S. Pritchett* | WITH
A PREFACE BY | V. S. PRITCHETT | [ornamental rule] |
LONDON | *Percival Marshall*

Collation: 8½ x 4⅞″; [1–3]⁸ [4]⁶; pp. [1–6] 7–57 [58–60].

Binding: Bound with boards, covered in yellowish white (92) paper with
a pattern of pink vertical designs, lettered in deep red (13) down the
spine: '*Why Do I Write?* ELIZABETH BOWEN * GRAHAM GREENE *
V. S. PRITCHETT PERCIVAL MARSHALL'.

Contents:
'Elizabeth Bowen to V. S. Pritchett' [pp. 20–26]. First printed in *Contact:
World of Neighbours* (C268); revised and broadcast over BBC on 10
July 1948; modified further and reprinted simultaneously in the present
form as 'The Creative Life in Our Time: An Exchange of Letters' in
Partisan Review (C312). MS, E67. Published in anthology, G37.
'Elizabeth Bowen to Graham Greene' [pp. 53–58]. Revised and broadcast
over BBC on 10 July 1948. Published in anthology, G37.

Notes: Published November 1948, in an unknown number of copies, at
6/0 in the United Kingdom and $1.50 in the United States.
Translated, D57. Radio script, E69. Broadcast, F74.

Reviews:
Robert Kee, *Spectator* 181 (31 Dec. 1948):876
unsigned, *TLS* (15 Jan. 1949):41, 46
Walter Allen, *New Statesman* 37 (5 Feb. 1949):133–34

B22   **FROST IN MAY (by Antonia White)**   **1948**

ANTONIA WHITE | FROST IN MAY | LONDON | EYRE
& SPOTTISWOODE

Collation: 6⅞ x 4½″; [A]⁸ B–O⁸; pp. [i–iv] v–x [xi–xii], 13–220 [221–222].

Binding: Bound in deep red (13) cloth, lettered in gold across the spine:
'[rule] | [rule] | [title and author's name upon a black background]
FROST | IN | MAY | · | ANTONIA | WHITE | [rule] | E & S |
[rule]'.

Contents: 'Introduction' [pp. v–x].

Notes: Published 10 December 1948, in an unknown number of copies,
at 6/0 in the United Kingdom and $1.50 in Canada, and reprinted 2
May 1957.

(by Nigel Kneale)

a. *First edition*:
Tomato Cain | AND OTHER STORIES | *By* | NIGEL
KNEALE | *With a Foreword by* | ELIZABETH BOWEN |
COLLINS | ST. JAMES'S PLACE LONDON | 1949

Collation: 7¼ x 5¼"; [A]⁸ B–Q⁸; pp. [1–14] 15–256.

Binding: Two different bindings have been noted: strong bluish green
(160) or deep yellowish pink (27) cloth, lettered in each case across the
spine in gold: '[double wavy rule | star | double wavy rule] | TOMATO
| CAIN | & | OTHER | STORIES | NIGEL | KNEALE | [double wavy
rule | star | double wavy rule] | COLLINS'.

Contents: 'Foreword' [pp. 9–12]. MS, E71.

Notes: Published 10 November 1949, in an impression of 3,750 copies,
at 8/6. Collins published a second edition (in paperback) 31 July 1961,
in a single impression of 13,000 copies, at 2/6.

b. *First American edition*:
TOMATO CAIN | *and Other Stories* | by NIGEL KNEALE |
[rule] | WITH A FOREWORD BY | ELIZABETH BOWEN |
[rule] | 1950 | [publisher's device] | *NEW YORK* ALFRED A.
KNOPF.

Collation: 7½ x 5¼"; [1–10]¹⁶; pp. [2], [i–vi] vii–xvi, [1–2] 3–300 [301–
302]. The following pages have bracketed numberings: vii, xv, 3.

Binding: Bound in dark yellow (88) cloth, lettered across the spine:
'[ornamental design, in moderate reddish purple (241)] | [black] TO-
MATO | CAIN | AND OTHER | STORIES | [ornamental design, in
moderate reddish purple] | [black] *Nigel Kneale* | *Knopf*'. On the front
cover, in moderate reddish purple: '[ornamental design] | [black] *Nigel
Kneale*'. On the back cover, at the lower right, in moderate reddish purple:
[publisher's device].

Contents: 'Foreword' [pp. vii–xi]'.

Notes: Published 6 November 1950, in an unknown number of copies,
at $3.

a. *First edition*:
    Flower of Cities | A BOOK OF | LONDON | STUDIES AND
    SKETCHES | illustrated with original drawings | twenty-four
    plates in monochrome | twelve plates in colour | and two maps |
    in colour | 1949 | MAX PARRISH LONDON

    Collation: 8⅝ x 6⅜"; A–B^8 C^6 D^{12} E^6 F^8 G^4 H^6 K–M^8 [N]^8 O–Q^8
    [R]^8 S^6 T^8 U^6 W^{12} X^8 [\$1 (−C$_1$, E$_1$, H$_1$, O$_1$, S$_1$, U$_1$; +C$_2$, E$_2$, H$_2$, O$_3$,
    S$_2$, U$_2$) signed]; pp. [1–8] 9–324.

    Binding: Bound in brilliant yellow (83) cloth, lettered down the spine
    in black (267): 'FLOWER OF CITIES · A Book of London PARRISH'.

    Contents: 'Regent's Park and St. John's Wood' [pp. 149–158]. MS, E70.1.

    Notes: Published during the week of 26 November 1949, in an unknown
    number of copies, at 18/6.

b. *First edition (American issue)*:
    The title page is identical to that of the first edition, except that
    the following is substituted for the original date and publisher's
    imprint: 'HARPER & BROTHERS · PUBLISHERS | NEW
    YORK | 1950'.

    Collation: As in the first edition, except that the size is 8¾ x 6¼".

    Binding: Bound in black (267) cloth, lettered across the spine in brilliant
    yellow (83): '[title within a frame of leaves] FLOWER | *of* | CITIES |
    [subtitle below the frame] *A BOOK OF* | LONDON | HARPER'. Pub-
    lisher's device is blind-stamped on the front, at the lower right.

    Contents: As in the first edition.

    Notes: Published 19 July 1950, at \$4. The publisher states that records
    are unclear as to the number of copies involved but that probably no
    more than 2,000 to 2,500 copies were imported, bound, from England.

ELIZABETH BIBESCO | [swelled rule] | HAVEN | Short

Stories Poems and | Aphorisms | *Foreword by* | ELIZABETH BOWEN | LONDON | JAMES BARRIE | 1951

Collation: 7¼ x 4¾"; [A–2A]⁸; pp. [i–iv] v–vi, 7–381 [382–384].

Binding: Two different bindings have been noted: black (267) cloth and moderate blue (182) cloth. Both are lettered in gold across the spine: '[title and author within a triple frame] HAVEN | [short rule] | Elizabeth | Bibesco | *James* | *Barrie*'.

Contents: 'Foreword' [pp. 7–12]. Dated 'September 1950' and signed 'Elizabeth Bowen'. MS, E78.

Notes: Published, at 10/6, during the week of 28 April 1951 (British Library deposit: 27 April). The printing quantity is unknown.

B26   NORTH AND SOUTH (by Elizabeth Cleghorn Gaskell)   1952

[all within an ornamented frame] NORTH | AND SOUTH | [star] | MRS GASKELL | WITH AN INTRODUCTION BY | ELIZABETH BOWEN | JOHN LEHMANN | MCMLI

Collation: 7¼ x 4¾"; [A]¹⁶ B–M¹⁶ N⁸ O¹⁶; pp. [i–v] vi–viii [ix–x], 11–432.

Binding: Bound in deep red (13) cloth, lettered in gold across the spine: 'NORTH | AND | SOUTH | MRS. GASKELL | [five groups of thin, thick, and thin rules] | *THE* | *CHILTERN* | *LIBRARY*'.

Contents: 'Introduction' [pp. (v)–viii]. Reprinted in A25 (q.v.) and A26.

Notes: Although the title page indicates 1951, the deposit receipt stamp in the British Library copy is dated 25 February 1952, and *The English Catalogue of Books* records publication on 13 March 1952, at 10/6. The printing quantity is unknown.

B27   THE CINQUE PORTS (by Ronald and Frank Jessup)   1952

[all within five concentric frames] THE | CINQUE PORTS | [swelled rule] | Ronald and Frank | Jessup | WITH A FORE-WORD | BY | ELIZABETH BOWEN | B. T. BATSFORD LTD | LONDON *and* NEW YORK

Collation: 7¼ x 4⅞"; [A]⁶ B–K⁴ L⁶; pp. [1–10] 11–128; plates 1–52 (opp. [A2] and between [A5]ᵛ and [A6], C4ᵛ and D1, D4ᵛ and E1, E1ᵛ and

E2, E3^v and E4, G1^v and G2, G3^v and G4, G4^v and H1, H4^v and I1, I1^v and I2, I3^v and I4, I4^v and K1, K1^v and K2, K3^v and K4, K4^v and L1). The sixteen leaves of plates are incorporated into the pagination sequence as pp. [3-4], 13-14, 33-34, 43-44, 47-48, 53-54, 67-68, 73-74, 77-78, 87-88, 91-92, 97-98, 101-102, 105-106, 111-112, and 115-116.

Binding: Bound in moderate blue (182) cloth, lettered in gold across the spine: '[triple rule] | THE | CINQUE | PORTS | [rule] | R. & F. | Jessup | [double rule] | [double rule] | Batsford | [triple rule]'.

Contents: 'Foreword' [pp. 11-15].

Notes: Published 27 March 1952, at 9/6, in an impression estimated by the publisher to have been between 5,000 and 6,000 copies.

B28   **THE SECOND GHOST BOOK**   **1952**

a. *First edition*:
[title in block letters] THE | SECOND | GHOST BOOK | *Edited by* | CYNTHIA ASQUITH | LONDON | JAMES BARRIE | 1952

Collation: 7$\frac{7}{8}$ x 5$\frac{1}{8}$″; [1]^8 2-15^8 16^4; pp. [i-vi] vii-x, 1-236 [237-238].

Binding: Two different bindings have been noted: black (267) cloth with grayish yellow green (122) lettering and black cloth with gold lettering. Across the spine, in each case: '*The* | *Second* | *Ghost* | *Book* | *Edited by* | CYNTHIA | ASQUITH | *James* | *Barrie*'.

Contents:
'Introduction' [pp. vii-x]. Reprinted in A25 (q.v.) and A26.
'Hand in Glove' [pp. 191-202]. Reprinted in A28 (q.v.).

Notes: Published 27 October 1952, in an unknown number of copies, at 12/6. The publisher states that the title was reprinted but is uncertain of the date.
    A second edition (in paperback) was published by Pan Books, 16 November 1956, at 2/0.

b. *First American edition*: A BOOK OF MODERN GHOSTS
A BOOK | OF | [in block letters] Modern Ghosts | *Edited by* | CYNTHIA ASQUITH | NEW YORK | *Charles Scribner's Sons* | 1953

Collation: 7$\frac{3}{4}$ x 5$\frac{1}{2}$″ [1]^{14} χ'[2-8]^{16}; pp. [i-vi] vii-x, 1-236 [237-244].

Binding: Bound in olive gray (112) cloth lettered in deep red (13) on the spine: '[across] Asquith | A BOOK OF | [down, in block letters] MODERN GHOSTS | [across] SCRIBNERS'.

Contents: As in the English edition.

Notes: Published 26 January 1953, in an impression of 5,000 copies, at $3.

B28.1   **THE OBSERVER PRIZE STORIES**   **1952**

THE OBSERVER | PRIZE STORIES | *THE SERAPH AND THE ZAMBESI* | AND TWENTY OTHERS | [thick and thin rules] | WITH AN INTRODUCTION BY | ELIZABETH BOWEN | [publisher's device] | WILLIAM HEINEMANN LTD | MELBOURNE :: LONDON :: TORONTO

Collation: 7¾ x 5"; [A]⁸ B–O⁸ P⁶; pp. [i–vi] vii–xi [xii], 1–221 [222].

Binding: Bound in vivid red (11) cloth, lettered in gold across the spine: '[rule] | THE | OBSERVER | PRIZE | STORIES | [rule] | HEINE-MANN'.

Contents: 'Introduction' [pp. vii–xi].

Notes: Published 17 November 1952, in an impression of 4,000 copies, at 10/6.

B29   **STORIES (by Katherine Mansfield)**   **1956**

a. *First edition*:
STORIES | *BY* | KATHERINE | MANSFIELD | [device: flower] | *SELECTED, AND WITH* | *AN INTRODUCTION, BY* | ELIZABETH BOWEN | [publisher's device] | *NEW YORK* | VINTAGE BOOKS | *1956*

Collation: 7¼ x 4¼"; 192 single leaves; pp. [2], [i–v] vi–xxiv [xxv–xxvi], [1–3] 4–348 [349–356].

Binding: A perfect binding glued in a white card cover, lettered down the spine in strong blue (178), strong reddish brown (40), and black (267): '[in strong blue] *STORIES* [in strong reddish brown] *KATHERINE MANSFIELD* [in black, across] [publisher's device] | *VINTAGE* | V–36'. On the front: '[in strong blue] *STORIES* | [in black] [rule] | *KATH-*

ERINE MANSFIELD | [a silhouette of the author in strong blue, black, and strong reddish brown, signed "Lionni"] | [in black] *Selected, and with an introduction, by* [in strong blue] *Elizabeth Bowen* | [in black] *K36 A VINTAGE BOOK'*. On the back, in black: '[on a strong reddish brown panel] *STORIES* | *KATHERINE MANSFIELD* | [on a strong blue panel] [an excerpt from the preface] | A Vintage Book Cover design by Leo Lionni'.

Contents: 'Introduction' [pp. v–xxiv]. Reprinted as 'Preface' to *Stories* by Katherine Mansfield in A25 (q.v.).

Notes: Published 10 September 1956, in an unknown number of copies, at $.95, and reprinted August 1958 and August 1960. Subsequent reprintings: May 1962 (3,943 copies), April 1963 (5,871 copies), August 1964 (7,000 copies, 1,000 of which were library-bound), February 1966 (7,099 copies), June 1967 (7,313 copies), December 1969 (4,957 copies), and October 1971 (2,988 copies).

b. *First English edition*:

34 SHORT STORIES | KATHERINE MANSFIELD | [swelled rule] | *Selected and with an Introduction by* | ELIZABETH BOWEN | [publisher's device] | COLLINS | LONDON AND GLASGOW

Collation: 7 x $4\frac{3}{8}''$; [1]^{16} 2–12^{16}; pp. [1–4] 5–384.

Binding: Bound in vivid deep purplish red (257) buckram, lettered in gold across the spine: '[title and author's name within an impressed rectangle] 34 | SHORT | STORIES | [circle] | KATHERINE | MANSFIELD | COLLINS'.

Contents: 'Introduction' [pp. 9–26]. Reprinted as described in B29a above.

Notes: Published 25 October 1957, in an unknown number of copies, at 7/6, and reprinted ca. 1962, ca. 1965, and in 1970 and 1972. Although the number of copies printed in each impression is unknown, the publisher states that some 23,000 copies had been sold by 1973.

B30   **DOWNE HOUSE SCRAP-BOOK**   [1957]

DOWNE HOUSE | SCRAP-BOOK

Collation: $9\frac{3}{4}$ x $7\frac{1}{8}''$; [A]^8 B–D^8 E^{10} [$1 (+E$_2$) signed]; pp. [1] 2–83 [84]; plate opp. p. 2.

Binding: Bound in greenish white (153) paper. On the front cover in

deep green (142): '[within thin and thick frames] DOWNE | HOUSE |
SCRAP- | BOOK | [ornament] | 1907–1957'.

Contents: 'Elizabeth Bowen (Cameron), 1917' [pp. 35–37]. (A memoir of
Downe House.) MS, E99.

Notes: Only by inference from the title can the date of publication be
estimated as around 1957. The volume was privately printed, as indicated
by the imprint on p. [84]: 'Printed in Great Britain at the University
Press Oxford by Charles Batey printer to the University'.

B31   **DOCTOR THORNE (by Anthony Trollope)**   **1959**

Anthony Trollope | DOCTOR THORNE | [triple rule] | WITH
AN INTRODUCTION BY | ELIZABETH BOWEN | [rule] |
HOUGHTON MIFFLIN COMPANY | *Boston* · [in Gothic]
The Riverside Press Cambridge

Collation: 8¼ x 5¼"; 256 single leaves; pp. [i–v] vi–xxv [xxvi], [1–5] 6–
484 [485–486].

Binding: Perfect binding in dark bluish green (165) paper, with a shaded
triangular label of yellowish white (92) extending across back, spine, and
front. Printed down the spine: '[in yellowish white] *Trollope* [in dark
bluish green, and in yellowish white] DOCTOR THORNE [across, in
yellowish white] HM Co. | B43'. On the front: '[in yellowish white]
EDITED BY *Elizabeth Bowen* $1.15 | [in dark bluish green] DOCTOR |
THORNE | *Anthony Trollope* | [in yellowish white] RIVERSIDE EDI-
TIONS B43 | [publisher's device] | HOUGHTON MIFFLIN COM-
PANY'. On the back, in yellowish white: '[publisher's device] B43'.

Contents: 'Introduction' [pp. v-xxv]. Revised and reprinted as 'Preface'
in A25 and A26.

Notes: Published 2 June 1959, in an impression of 15,000 copies, at $1.15.
A copy in the Humanities Research Center contains the author's holograph revisions that served as the basis for the reprinted version in A25
and A26.

B32   **ORLANDO (by Virginia Woolf)**   **1960**

[in script] Virginia Woolf | ORLANDO | A BIOGRAPHY |
With an Afterword by | [in script] Elizabeth Bowen | [publisher's
device] A SIGNET CLASSIC | *Published by* | THE NEW
AMERICAN LIBRARY

Collation: 7⅛ x 4¼″; 112 single leaves; pp. [1–6] 7–222 [223–224].

Binding: Perfect binding in pale yellow (89) paper. On the spine: [lettered across] '[publisher's device, in pale yellow against a black background] | [in black (267)] CP | 156 | [down] ORLANDO *Virginia Woolf*'. On the front, within a greenish yellow olive (110) border: '[in black] CD18 [publisher's device, in black and greenish yellow olive] [in black] 50¢ | [in greenish yellow olive] *Virginia Woolf* | [in black] ORLANDO | [in color, three renaissance figures iceskating] | [in black] A SIGNET CLASSIC'.

Contents: 'Afterword' [pp. 216–222]. Revised and reprinted as 'Preface' in A25 and A26.

Notes: Published 18 February 1960, in an impression of 61,903 copies, at $.50; and reprinted in March 1963 (16,181 copies), March 1965 (15,885 copies), October 1966 (15,220 copies), June 1969 (16,415 copies), and November 1971 (21,420 copies).
A copy in the Humanities Research Center contains the author's holograph revisions that served as the basis for the reprinted versions in A25 and A26.

B33   **THE KING OF THE GOLDEN RIVER**   **1962**
(by John Ruskin)

THE | KING | OF THE | GOLDEN RIVER | *OR* THE BLACK BROTHERS | BY JOHN RUSKIN | INTRODUCED BY ELIZABETH BOWEN | [color print: running stream in a flowered field] | ILLUSTRATED BY SANDRO NARDINI | THE MACMILLAN COMPANY, NEW YORK MACMILLAN NEW YORK, LONDON 1962

Collation: 13 x 9½″; [3]⁸; pp. [i–ii] iii–v [vi], 1–42.

Binding: Three different bindings have been noted:
Trade copies are bound in boards covered with glazed paper lettered down the spine: '[in vivid red (11)] RUSKIN [in black (267)] THE KING OF THE GOLDEN RIVER [in vivid red] MACMILLAN'. On the front cover: '[title in vivid red] THE | King of the Golden River | [in black] A FAIRY TALE BY JOHN RUSKIN | INTRODUCED BY [in vivid red] ELIZABETH BOWEN | [color illustration: boy walking past a scrub tree toward mountains]'. On the back cover in vivid red and black, notice of titles in the series.
Library copies are bound in brilliant greenish blue (168) cloth, lettered down the spine: '[in greenish white (153)] RUSKIN [in moderate orange

yellow (71)] THE KING OF THE GOLDEN RIVER [in greenish white] MACMILLAN'. On the front: '[in greenish white] THE KING OF THE | GOLDEN RIVER | [in moderate orange yellow, a head-shaped mug] | [in greenish white] A FAIRY TALE BY JOHN RUSKIN'. On the back, in greenish white, at the upper left: 'MACMILLAN | MASTER LIBRARY | EDITION'.

Copies of the Italian issue are bound in dark grayish brown (62) cloth, lettered down the spine in gold: 'RUSKIN THE KING OF THE GOLDEN RIVER'.

Contents: 'Ruskin's Tale: An Introduction' [pp. iii–v].

Notes: Published 24 October 1962, at $1.95, and simultaneously published in an Italian issue in which, on the title page, the publisher's imprint is changed to 'FRATELLI FABBRI EDITORI'.

B34   **THE STORIES OF WILLIAM SANSOM**   **1963**

a.   *First edition*:
THE | STORIES | OF | WILLIAM | SANSOM | [ornamental swelled rule] | *With an Introduction by* | Elizabeth Bowen | THE HOGARTH PRESS

Collation: 8½ x 5⅜"; [A]^{16} B–M^{16} N^{20}; pp. [1–6] 7–421 [422–424].

Binding: Bound in black (267) cloth, lettered in gold across the spine: '[ornamental border and double rule] | [title and author's name upon a dark grayish reddish brown (47) background] The Stories | OF | WIL-LIAM | SANSOM | [double rule and ornamental border] | THE | HOGARTH | PRESS'.

Contents: 'Introduction' [pp. 7–12].

Notes: Published 9 May 1963, at 25/0, in an issue of 4,000 copies (out of a total impression of 8,000). A second impression (750 copies) was printed in May 1969.

b.   *First edition (American issue)*:
The title page is identical to that of the first edition, except that the following is substituted for the original publisher's imprint: '[ornamental swelled rule] | [publisher's device] | *An Atlantic Monthly Press Book* | LITTLE, BROWN AND COMPANY | BOSTON TORONTO'.

Collation: As in the first edition.

Binding: Bound in light greenish blue (172) cloth, lettered across the spine in gold: 'THE STORIES | OF | WILLIAM | SANSOM | *Atlantic* | Little, Brown'. On the front cover: '[blind-stamped] [publisher's device]'.

Notes: Published 10 June 1963, at $6., in an issue of 4,000 copies (from a total impression of 8,000 copies). Books for Libraries, Inc., photo-lithographically reprinted 300 copies of the title under its own imprint 14 January 1971.

B35   **CRITICS WHO HAVE INFLUENCED TASTE**   **1965**

CRITICS WHO HAVE | INFLUENCED TASTE | (*From "The Times"*) | [twelve-line double column list of critics' names] | Preface by Elizabeth Bowen | Edited by A. P. Ryan | GEOFFREY BLES LIMITED | PUBLISHERS

Collation: 8½ x 6⅜"; [A]⁸ B–G⁸; pp. [2], [i–vi] vii–xii, [1–2] 3–97 [98].

Binding: Bound in grayish olive (110) cloth, lettered across the spine in gold: '*Critics | who have | influenced | Taste | Editor | A. P. Ryan | Bles*'. On the front cover, in script: '*Critics | who have | influenced | Taste*'.

Contents: 'Preface' [pp. vii–x].

Notes: Published 18 October 1965, at 16/0, and reprinted October 1967, at 6/0.

B35.1   **AN ANGELA THIRKELL OMNIBUS**   **1966**

An | Angela | Thirkell | Omnibus | [ornamented rule] | WITH AN INTRODUCTION BY | ELIZABETH BOWEN | [publisher's device] | HAMISH HAMILTON | LONDON

Collation: 8⅜ x 5⅜"; [1]¹⁶ 2–15¹⁶; [i–vi] vii–ix [x], [1–2] 3–467 [468–470].

Binding: Bound in brilliant greenish blue (168) cloth, lettered across the spine in silver: '[line of ornaments] | [title only, stamped upon a pale greenish yellow (104) background] AN | ANGELA | THIRKELL | OMNIBUS | [line of ornaments] | [publisher's device]'.

Contents: 'Introduction' [pp. vii–ix].

Notes: Published 14 July 1966, at 30/0.

a. *First edition*:
THE HOUSE | BY THE CHURCH-YARD | *By* | J. SHERI-DAN LE FANU | *Introduction by* | *Elizabeth Bowen* | [publisher's device] | ANTHONY BLOND

Collation: 8¼ x 5⅜″; [A]⁶ B–P¹⁶ Q⁸ R¹⁶; pp. [i–v] vi–xi [xii], 1–496.

Binding: Bound in strong pink (2) cloth, lettered in gold across the spine: 'Sheridan | Le Fanu | The House | by the | Churchyard | *Doughty* | *Library* | *No* 12 | [within a laurel device] BLOND'.

Contents: 'Introduction' [pp. vii–xi].

Notes: Published 24 June 1968, at 30s. From an impression of 5,000 copies, 3,000 copies were issued in England with the Blond imprint; and, according to the publisher, 2,000 copies were issued for American publication. However, as indicated in B36b, the figure reported by the American publisher for the American issue is at variance.

b. *First edition (American issue)*:
The title page is identical to that of the first edition, except that the following is substituted for the original publisher's imprint: '[publisher's device] | STEIN AND DAY | Publishers | New York'.

Collation: As in the first edition.

Binding: As in the first edition, except that across the spine the following is substituted for the original publisher's imprint: '*Stein* | *and* | *Day*'.

Contents: As in the first edition.

Notes: Published in September of 1968, at $6.95, in an issue of 2,500 copies drawn from the first impression.

B37   **ASPECTS OF E. M. FORSTER**   **1969**

a. *First edition*:
Aspects of E. M. Forster | Essays and Recollections written for | his Ninetieth Birthday 1st January 1969 by | JOHN ARLOTT

ELIZABETH BOWEN   MALCOLM BRADBURY | BENJA-
MIN BRITTEN   B. W. FAGAN   DAVID GARNETT | K.
NATWAR-SINGH WILLIAM PLOMER ALEC RANDALL |
WILLIAM ROERICK W. J. H. SPROTT | OLIVER STAL-
LYBRASS (editor)   WILFRED STONE | GEORGE H.
THOMSON   PATRICK WILKINSON | [publisher's device]
EDWARD ARNOLD

Collation: 8¼ x 5⅜″; [1–12]⁸ [13]⁶; pp. [i–vii] viii, [1] 2–195 [196]; frontispiece opp. p. [iii].

Binding: Bound in dark brown (59) cloth, lettered in gold down the
spine: 'STALLYBRASS [title within an ornamental frame] Aspects of E.
M. Forster   Arnold'. A frame is blind-stamped on the front and the back
covers.

Contents: 'A Passage to E. M. Forster' [pp. (1)–12].

Notes: Published 1 January 1969, in an impression of 2,000 copies, at
42/0.

b.   *First American edition*:
The title page is identical to that of the first edition, except that
the following is substituted for the original publisher's imprint:
'[publisher's device] Harcourt, Brace & World, Inc., New York'.

Collation: 8¼ x 5⅜″; [1–5]¹⁶ [6]⁸ [7]¹⁶; pp. [i–vii] viii [ix–xii], [1] 2–195
[196]; frontispiece opp. p. [iii].

Binding: Bound in moderate blue (182) cloth, lettered in gold down the
spine: 'OLIVER STALLYBRASS, Editor   Aspects of E. M. Forster [pub-
lisher's device] | HARCOURT, BRACE & WORLD'.

Contents: As in the first edition.

Notes: Published 15 January 1969, by offsetting 3,000 copies from the
Arnold edition, at $5.95.

B38   **MARCEL PROUST, 1871–1922**   **1971**

a.   *First edition*:
A Centenary Volume | Edited by Peter Quennell | MARCEL
PROUST | 1871–1922 | WEIDENFELD AND NICOLSON |
5 Winsley Street   London W1

Collation: 9⅝ x 7¼"; [A]⁸ B–O⁸; pp [8], [1–2] 3–216; seventy-one plates (sixty-four in black and white, gathered in fours between pp. 8 and 9, 32 and 33, 48 and 49, 72 and 73, 120 and 121, 152 and 153, 168 and 169, 200 and 201; seven in color tipped in opposite pp. 16, 42, 64, 112, 144, 170, and 180).

Binding: Bound in strong purplish red (255) cloth, lettered in gold. On the spine: '[vertically down] *Marcel Proust* | [across] Edited by | Peter | Quennell | Weidenfeld | & Nicolson'. On the front cover, in script: 'Marcel Proust'.

Contents: 'Bergotte' [pp. 59–75]. Reprinted as 'The Art of Bergotte' in A32.

Notes: Published 21 August 1971, at £4.25. The publisher declines to reveal the print quantity; but see, below, the note for the American issue (B38b).

b. *First edition (American issue)*:

The title page is identical to that of the first edition, except that the following is substituted for the original publisher's imprint: '[publisher's device] | SIMON AND SCHUSTER | New York'.

Collation: As in the first edition.

Binding: As in the first edition, except that on the spine below the editor's name the following is substituted for the original publisher's imprint: '[publisher's device] | [across] Simon and Schuster'.

Contents: As in the first edition.

Notes: Published 21 September 1971, at $12.95. The publisher states that 10,000 copies, printed and bound, were ordered from Weidenfeld & Nicolson, and that 'slightly over 9,800 copies' were received.

C CONTRIBUTIONS BY ELIZABETH
BOWEN TO PERIODICALS

C1 'Salon des Dames'. *WWGaz* (7 Apr. 1923):16–17. Short story. Signed: E. D. Bowen.

C2 'Moses'. *WWGaz* (30 June 1923):16. Short story. Signed: E. D. Bowen.

C3 'Making Arrangements'. *Everybody's Magazine* 50 #6 (June 1924): 45–50; *Eve* (London) 23 (20 Nov. 1925): 4–5, 7, 19, 88. Short story.

C4 'Ann Lee's'. *Spectator* 133 (5 July 1924):10–12. Short story. Revised and reprinted in A2 (q.v.).

C5 'The Contessina'. *Queen* (London) (12 Nov. 1924):24–26. Short story. Reprinted in A2 (q.v.).

C6 'The Parrot'. *Everybody's Magazine* 52 #4 (Apr. 1925):135–42; *London Mercury* 12 #69 (July 1925):242–52. Short story. Reprinted in A2 (q.v.).

C7 'The White House'. *The Royal Magazine* (London) (Nov. 1926): 45–52. Revised and reprinted as 'Joining Charles' *Harper's Bazaar* 73 (1 Sept. 1939):90–91, 133–35. Short story. See A5.

C8 'Just Imagine'. *Eve* (London) 27 (Oct.–Dec. 1926):27, 37–39, 72, 74, 78, 80. Short story. Published in anthology, G3

C9 'Aunt Tatty'. *Queen* (London) (Christmas 1926):28–31. Short story. Reprinted in A5 (q.v.).

C10 'Modern Lighting.' *SatRev* 5 (27 Oct. 1928):294. Essay.

C11 'Pink Biscuit'. *Eve* (London) (22 Nov. 1928):34–35, 76, 78, 80. Short story.

C12 'The Tommy Crans'. *The Broadsheet Press* (London) #1 (Feb. 1930); *Listener* 9 (29 Mar. 1933):511–12. Short story. Reprinted in A8 (q.v.).

C13 'A Conversation Picture'. *The Broadsheet Press* (London) #4 (May 1930):1–10. This story entitled 'A Conversation Picture', while the cover entitles it 'A Conversation Piece', later appeared as 'Her Table Spread' in *Listener* 11 (7 Mar. 1934):419–21. Reprinted in A8 (q.v.).

C14 'The Good Girl'. *Time and Tide* 25 (11 Feb. 1933):143–46. Short story. Reprinted in A8.

C15 'The Little Girl's Room'. *London Mercury* 28 #165 (July 1933): 213–21. Short story. Reprinted in A8.

C15.1 'A Wartime Schooling'. *Life and Letters* 10 (June 1934):361–68. Essay. See 'The Mulberry Tree' in A19.

C16 'Reduced'. *Listener* 13 (12 June 1935):1022–24. Short story. Reprinted in A11 (q.v.).

C17 'New Novels'. *NewSt* (rev) 10 (17 Aug. 1935):225–26. *Follow the Furies*, Eleanor C. Chilton; *The Transients,* Mark Van Doren; *Not in a Day*, George Albee.

C18 'New Novels'. *NewSt* (rev) 10 (31 Aug. 1935):282, 284. *The Inquisitor*, Hugh Walpole; *Honey in the Horn*, H. L. Davis; *The Mountain and the Tree,* Helen Beauclerk; *A Fawn in the Field,* Rosalind Wade.

C19 'New Novels'. *NewSt* (rev) 10 (14 Sept. 1935):345. *Paths of Glory*, Humphrey Cobb; *Woman of Glenshiels,* Lennox Kerr; *Four Gardens*, Margery Sharp; *In Search of Love*, Francis Stuart; *The House of the Spaniard*, Arthur Behrend.

C20 'New Novels'. *NewSt* (rev) 10 (28 Sept. 1935):416, 418. *Dead Centre,* Arthur Calder-Marshall; *Fool's Quarter Day,* Louis Marlow; *The Whole of the Story,* Phyllis Bentley; *Victory to the Vanquished,* Barbara Goolden; *He Sent Forth a Raven,* E. M. Roberts; *Go Home Unicorn*, Donald Macpherson.

C21 'New Novels'. *NewSt* (rev) 10 (12 Oct. 1935):532–33. *Hungry Men*, E. Anderson; *Conveyor*, James Steele; *Act of Darkness,* John Peale Bishop; *The Royal Way*, André Malraux; *Flower Pot End*, R. H. Mottram; *Events in the Early Life of Anthony Price*, P. Henderson.

C22 'New Novels'. *NewSt* (rev) 10 (26 Oct. 1935):604, 606. *Virgin Soil Upturned*, M. Sholokhov; *Rachel Rosing*, Howard Spring; *I Let

Him Go, John Brophy; *The Frozen Heart*, Mrs. St. Loe Strachey; *River Niger*, Simon Jetty; *Beyond Sing the Woods*, Trygve Gulbranssen.

C23 'Abinger Harvest'. *Spectator* 156 (20 Mar. 1936):521. Review of *Abinger Harvest*, E. M. Forster. Reprinted as 'E. M. Forster I' in A19.

C24 'New Novels'. *NewSt* (rev) 11 (11 Apr. 1936):571–72. *The Thinking Reed*, Rebecca West; *I'll Mourn You Later*, Catharine Whitcomb; *Lucasta's Wedding*, Hans Dufy; *A Mirror for Skylarks*, Martin Hare; *Young Men in Spats*, P. G. Wodehouse.

C25 'Attractive Modern Homes'. *Listener* 15 (15 Apr. 1936):742–44; *Listener* 51 #1298 (14 Jan. 1954):87, 89, 91. Short story. Reprinted in A11a (q.v.).

C26 'Joseph Conrad'. *Spectator* 156 (24 Apr. 1936):758. Review of *Joseph Conrad: Some Aspects of the Art of the Novel*, Edward Crankshaw. Reprinted as 'Conrad' in A19.

C27 'Royal Academy'. *New Statesman* 12 (9 May 1936):702–03. Essay. Reprinted in A19.

C28 'The Weather in the Streets'. *NewSt* (rev) 12 (11 July 1936):54. Rosamond Lehmann's book of the same title.

C29 'Two Cities'. *NewSt* (rev) 12 (25 July 1936):128. *Dublin under the Georges, 1714–1830*, Constantia Maxwell; *Londoner's New York*, E. Stewart Fay. First review reprinted as 'Dublin I' in A19.

C30 'Jane Austen: Artist on Ivory'. *SatRev* 14 (15 Aug. 1936):3–4, 13–14. Essay. First printed in B9 (q.v.).

C31 'Tears, Idle Tears'. *Listener* 16 (2 Sept. 1936):447–49; *The Blarney Magazine* 7 (1954):15–21. Short story. Reprinted in A11 (q.v.).

C32 'Anne Douglas Sedgwick'. *NewSt* (rev) 12 (10 Oct. 1936):516. *Anne Douglas Sedgwick: A Portrait in Letters*, ed. Basil de Selincourt. Reprinted in A19.

C33 'This Freedom'. *NewSt* (rev) 12 (31 Oct. 1936):678. *Our Freedom and Its Results*, ed. Ray Strachey.

C34 'Portrait of a City'. *NewSt* (rev) 12 (7 Nov. 1936):722. *A Biography of Dublin*, Christine Longford. Reprinted as 'Dublin II' in A19.

C35 'What We Need in Writing'. *Spectator* 157 (20 Nov. 1936):901–02. Essay.

C36 'Short Stories'. *NewSt* (rev) 12 (5 Dec. 1936):938–39. *Collected Short Stories*, Stella Benson; *Best Short Stories of 1936: English and American*, ed. Edward J. O'Brien.

C37 'Mr. Huxley's Essays'. *Spectator* 157 (11 Dec. 1936):1046. Review of *The Olive Tree and Other Essays*, Aldous Huxley. Reprinted in A19.

C38 'Manchester'. *NewSt* (rev) 13 (20 Feb. 1937):292. *Manchester*, Rachel Ryan. Reprinted in A19.

C39 'The Shadow Across the Page'. *NewSt* (rev) 13 (13 March 1937): 418. *The Shadow Across the Page*, G. W. Stonier. Reprinted in A19.

C40 'A Straight Novel'. *NewSt* (rev) 13 (27 Mar. 1937):525. *Theatre*, Somerset Maugham. Reprinted in A19.

C41 'An Unknown Society'. *Listener* 17 (28 Apr. 1937) Supp. X–XI. *The Irish Countryman, An Anthropological Study*, Conrad M. Arensberg.

C42 'Ben Jonson'. *NewSt* (rev) 13 (8 May 1937):775. *Ben Jonson* 5, C. H. Herford and Percy Simpson eds; *Drama and Society in the Age of Ben Jonson*, L. C. Knights. The first of the reviews was reprinted in A19.

C43 'One Ireland'. *NewSt* (rev) 13 (26 June 1937):1050, 1052. *My Ireland*, Lord Dunsany. Reprinted in A19.

C44 'The Theatre'. *N&D* 1 (1 July 1937):37. Drama review of *Victoria Regina* and *The Great Romancer*.

C45 'The Theatre'. *N&D* 1 (8 July 1937):29. Drama review of *No Sleep for the Wicked* and *Floodlight*.

C46 'The Theatre'. *N&D* 1 (15 July 1937):29. Drama review of *Hamlet* and *Women of Property*.

C47 'The Theatre'. *N&D* 1 (22 July 1937):29. Drama review of *The Ice Show: St. Moritz.*

C48 'The Theatre'. *N&D* 1 (29 July 1937):29. Drama review of *Comus* and *Revudeville.*

C49 'The Theatre'. *N&D* 1 (5 Aug. 1937):30. Drama review of *The First Legion, Bulldog Drummond Hits Out,* and *The Cotton Club Revue.*

C50 'Salzburg in the Distance'. *N&D* 1 (9 Sept. 1937):22–23. Travel essay. Reprinted in A19.

C51 'Agreeable Reading'. *NewSt* (rev) 14 (9 Oct. 1937):542, 544. *The Farm by Lough Gur,* Lady Carbery; *A Plain Tale from the Bogs,* Reardon Conner.

C52 'Two Ways to Travel'. *Listener* 18 (13 Oct. 1937) Supp. XII. *Sinabada,* Elinor Mordaunt; *Three Ways Home,* Sheila Kaye-Smith.

C53 'At the Theatre'. *N&D* 1 (14 Oct. 1937): 37–38. Drama review of *Mr. Gladstone* and *Youth's the Season . . . ?*

C54 'At the Theatre'. *N&D* 1 (21 Oct. 1937):37–38. Drama review of *Measure for Measure.*

C55 'At the Theatre'. *N&D* 1 (28 Oct. 1937):29–30. Drama review of *Autumn, Blondie White* and *Punch and Judy.*

C56 'Kindness to Women'. *NewSt* (rev) 14 (30 Oct. 1937):688. *Pity for Women* and *The Young Girls,* Henri de Montherlant; both trans. Thomas McGrewy and John Radker. Reprinted in A19.

C57 'At the Theatre'. *N&D* 1 (4 Nov. 1937):29–30. Drama review of *Yes and No* and *The Laughing Cavalier.*

C58 'Manners'. *NewSt* (rev) 14 (6 Nov. 1937):727–28. *Can I Help You?,* Viola Tree. Reprinted in A19.

C59 'Look At All Those Roses'. *Listener* 18 (10 and 17 Nov. 1937): 1026–27, 1092–93. Short story. Reprinted in A11 (q.v.).

C60 'At the Theatre'. *N&D* 1 (11 Nov. 1937):29–30. Drama review of *Goodbye to Yesterday, The Unquiet Spirit,* and *It's You I Want.*

C61 'At the Theatre'. *N&D* 1 (18 Nov. 1937):37–38. Drama review of *Richard III, Ghosts,* and *It's in the Bag.*

C62 'At the Theatre'. *N&D* 1 (25 Nov. 1937):30. Drama review of The Hambima Players: *The Dybbuk, Cymbeline,* and *Mourning Becomes Electra.*

C63 'Open to the Public'. *NewSt* (rev) 14 (27 Nov. 1937):882, 884. *Helen's Tower,* Harold Nicolson. Reprinted in A19.

C64 'A Walk in the Woods'. *London Mercury* 37 #218 (Dec. 1937): 161–69. Short story. Reprinted in A11 (q.v.).

C65 'At the Theatre'. *N&D* 1 (2 Dec. 1937):29–30. Drama review of *It's a Wise Child, The School for Scandal* and *People at Sea;* discussion of the Unity Theatre.

C66 'Dress'. *NewSt* (rev) 14 (4 Dec. 1937):930, 932. *English Women's Clothing in the Nineteenth Century.* C. Willett Cunnington. Reprinted in A19.

C67 'At the Theatre'. *N&D* 1 (9 Dec. 1937):30. Drama review of *Macbeth, Thank you, Mr. Pepys,* and *Distant Point.*

C68 'At the Theatre'. *N&D* 1 (16 Dec. 1937):29–30. Drama review of *Oh! You Letty, Aristocrats,* and *Out of the Picture.*

C69 'At the Theatre'. *N&D* 1 (23 Dec. 1937):29–30. Drama review of *Room Service.*

C70 'Island Life'. *NewSt* (rev) 15 (5 Mar. 1938):367–68. Drama review of *Land's End* and *No More Music.* Reprinted in A19.

C71 'Fanny Burney'. *NewSt* (rev) 15 (12 Mar. 1938):415–16. *Be Loved No More: The Life and Environment of Fanny Burney,* A. B. Tourtellot. Reprinted in A19.

C72 '*King Lear* at Cambridge'. *NewSt* (rev) 15 (19 Mar. 1938): 478. Review of the Cambridge production of *King Lear.* Reprinted in A19.

C73 'The Easter Egg Party'. *London Mercury* 38 #222 (Apr. 1938): 611–20. Short story. Reprinted in A11 (q.v.).

C74 'Mr. Forster'. *NewSt* (rev) 15 (2 Apr. 1938):572–74. *The Writings of E. M. Forster,* Rose Macaulay. Reprinted as 'E. M. Forster II' in A19.

C75 'The 1938 Academy: An Unprofessional View'. *Listener* 19 (4 May 1938):952–53. Essay.

C76 'Bouquet'. *NewSt* (rev) 15 (7 May 1938): 782. *Dublin Old and New,* Stephen Gwynn. Reprinted as 'Dublin III' in A19.

C77 'Blind Alleys'. *NewSt* (rev) 16 (23 July 1938):162–63. *Brought Up and Brought Out,* Mary Pakenham. Reprinted in A19.

C78 'Then and Now'. *NewSt* (rev) 16 (17 Sept. 1938):424, 426. *Three Homes,* Lennox Robinson, T. Robinson, Nora Dorman; *Irish Holiday,* Dorothy Hartley.

C79 'Grace'. *NewSt* (rev) 16 (12 Nov. 1938):778, 780. *Unforgotten Years,* Logan Pearsall Smith. Reprinted in A19.

C80 'Overtures to Death'. *Now and Then* #61 (Winter 1938):32–33; excerpt reprinted in *Now and Then* #100 (Autumn 1957) 23. Review of *Overtures to Death,* Cecil Day Lewis.

C81 'The Same Way Home'. *London Mercury* 39 #230 (Dec. 1938): 156–64. Short story, later revised and entitled 'A Queer Heart' *Living Age* 355 (Feb. 1939):517–23. Reprinted in A11 (q.v.).

C82 'The Girl with the Stoop'. *JO'LW* 40 (23 Dec. 1938):493–94. Short story. Reprinted in A11.

C83 'Number 16'. *Listener* 21 (19 Jan. 1939):157–59; *Living Age* 357 (Sept. 1939):36–42. Short story. Reprinted in A11 (q.v.).

C84 'Fiction'. *Purpose* 11 #1 (Jan.-Mar. 1939):51–55. Review of *Amerika,* Franz Kafka; *USA,* John Dos Passos; *Entanglement,* George Buchanan; *A Character in Distress,* Luigi Pirandello; and *People are Curious,* James Hanley.

C85 'Gusto'. *NewSt* (rev) 17 (25 Feb. 1939):298, 300. *Dr. Quicksilver: The Life of Charles Lever,* Lionel Stevenson.

C86 'Horribile Dictu'. *NewSt* (rev) 17 (11 Mar. 1939):367–68. *A Housewife in Kensington,* Mary Wylde. Reprinted in A19.

C87 'Fiction'. *Purpose* 11 #2 (Apr.-June 1939):116–19. Review of *The Black Book,* Lawrence Durrell; *Hawk Among the Sparrows,* Desmond Hawkins; *The Long Valley,* John Steinbeck; and *Uncle Arthur,* John Pudney.

C88 'Doubtful Subject'. *NewSt* (rev) 17 (6 May 1939):689. *Irish Life in the Seventeenth Century: After Cromwell,* Edward MacLysaght; *The Sword of Light,* Desmond Ryan; and *Irish Cavalcade,* M. J. MacManus. Reprinted in A19.

C89 'The Needlecase'. *Harper's Bazaar* 73 (May 1939):72, 132–33, 141. Short story. Reprinted in the London edition of *Harper's Bazaar* (June 1939):40, 95–96. First printed in A8 (q.v.).

C90 'Fiction'. *Purpose* 11 #3 (July-Sept. 1939):177–80. Review of *Finnegan's Wake,* James Joyce; *At Swim-Two Birds,* Flann O'Brien; *Hope of Heaven,* John O'Hara.

C91 'Gorki Stories'. *NewSt* (rev) 18 (5 Aug. 1939):220, 222. *A Book of Short Stories,* Maxim Gorki, eds. Avrahm Yarmolinsky and Moura Budberg, foreword Aldous Huxley. Reprinted in A19 (q.v.).

C92 'Fiction'. *Purpose* 11 #4 (Oct.-Dec. 1939):238–41. Review of *Child of Misfortune,* Cecil Day Lewis; *Coming Up For Air,* George Orwell; *Pale Horse, Pale Rider,* Katherine Anne Porter; *No Orchids for Miss Blandish,* James Hadley Chase.

C93 'The Girls'. *NewSt* (rev) 18 (21 Oct. 1939):559–60. *The Daughters of George III,* Dorothy Margaret Stewart. Reprinted in A19.

C94 'Love'. *Listener* 22 #563 (26 Oct. 1939):826–28. Short story. Reprinted in A11.

C95 'The Moores'. *NewSt* (rev) 18 (25 Nov. 1939):759–60. *The Moores of Moore Hall,* Joseph Hone. Reprinted in A19.

C96 'Fiction'. *Purpose* 12 #1 (Jan.-Mar. 1940):37–41. Review of *The Grapes of Wrath,* John Steinbeck; *To Town,* Randal Swingler; *The Blaze of Noon,* Rayner Heppenstall; and *Mrs. Miniver,* Jan Struther.

C97 'Fiction'. *Purpose* 12 #2 (Apr.-June 1940):92–95. Review of *The Power and the Glory*, Graham Greene; *Our Time is Gone*, James Hanley; *Portrait of the Artist as a Young Dog*, Dylan Thomas; and *Tomorrow Started Yesterday*, Robert Westerby.

C98 'A Love Story'. *Horizon* 1 #7 (July 1940):481–98. Short story, also entitled 'A Love Story, 1939'. Reprinted in A11 (q.v.).

C99 'Fiction'. *Purpose* 12 #3 & #4 (July-Dec. 1940):145–49. Review of *The Lepers*, Henri de Montherlant; *Lighter than Day*, Desmond Hawkins; *The Backward Son*, Stephen Spender; *Dutch Interior*, Frank O'Connor; and *Country Tales*, H. E. Bates.

C100 'Unwelcome Idea'. *New Statesman* 20 (10 Aug. 1940):133–34. Short story. Reprinted in A11a (q.v.).

C101 'The Big House'. *The Bell* (Dublin) 1 #1 (Oct. 1940):71–77. Essay. Reprinted in A19.

C102 Review of *Come Back to Erin*, Seán O'Faoláin. *The Bell* (Dublin) 1 #3 (Dec. 1940):87, 89.

C103 'Oh, MADAM . . .'. *Listener* 24 #621 (5 Dec. 1940):815–16; *Living Age* 359 (Feb. 1941):556–60. Short story. Reprinted in A11.

C104 'The Perfect Theatre-Goer'. *Spectator* 166 (3 Jan. 1941):18, 20. Review of *Drama*, Desmond MacCarthy.

C105 'Advance in Formation'. *Spectator* 166 (17 Jan. 1941):65. Review of *New Writing in Europe*, ed. John Lehmann.

C106 'Portrait of the Artist'. *Spectator* 166 (14 Mar. 1941):286. Review of *James Joyce: A Definitive Biography*, Herbert Gorman.

C107 'James Joyce'. *The Bell* (Dublin) 1 #6 (Mar. 1941):40–49.

C108 'New Writers'. *The Bell* (Dublin) 2 #1 (Apr. 1941):54.

C109 'Barrie'. *Spectator* 166 (4 Apr. 1941):374. Review of *The Story of JMB, Sir James Barrie Bart*, O. M. Denis Mackail. Reprinted in A19.

C110 'Eire'. *New Statesman* 21 (12 Apr. 1941):382–83. Essay on the neutrality of Ireland.

C111 'Shakespeare'. *NewSt* (rev) 21 (19 Apr. 1941):413–14. *Shakespeare*, Mark Van Doren. Reprinted as 'Van Doren on Shakespeare' in A19.

C112 'Parents and Children'. *NewSt* (rev) 21 (24 May 1941):536, 538. *Parents and Children*, Ivy Compton-Burnett. Reprinted as 'Ivy Compton-Burnett I' in A19.

C113 'Sunday Afternoon'. *Life and Letters Today* 30 #47 (July 1941):45–55; *The Bell* (Dublin) 5 #1 (Oct. 1942):19–27. Short story. Reprinted in A15 (q.v.).

C114 'Between the Acts'. *NewSt* (rev) 22 (19 July 1941):63–64. *Between the Acts*, Virginia Woolf. Reprinted as 'Virginia Woolf I' in A19.

C115 'An Invitation to Think'. *Spectator* 167 (25 July 1941):86, 88. Review of *Ideals and Illusions*, L. Susan Stebbing.

C116 "Flaubert Translated'. *Spectator* 167 (15 Aug. 1941):161. Review of *Sentimental Education*, Gustave Flaubert (trans. Anthony Goldsmith).

C117 'In the Square'. *Horizon* 4 (Sept. 1941):192–99. Short story. Reprinted in A15 (q.v.).

C118 'Truths about Ireland'. *Spectator* 167 (5 Sept. 1941):240. Review of *Ireland—Atlantic Gateway,* Jim Phelan.

C119 'Children's Play'. *Spectator* 167 (19 Sept. 1941):286. Review of *The Brontës' Web of Childhood*, Fannie Elizabeth Ratchford. Reprinted in A19.

C120 'Everything's Frightfully Interesting'. *New Yorker* 17 (11 Oct. 1941):58–59. Short story. Reprinted as 'Careless Talk' in A15.

C121 'Strength of Mind—Do Women Think Like Men?'. *Listener* 26 #668 (30 Oct. 1941):593–94. Part of a discussion between G. M. Young, John Mabbott, Phyllis Vallance, and Elizabeth Bowen broadcast on BBC radio (F59). Radio script, E48.

C122 'The Demon Lover'. *Listener* 26 #669 (6 Nov. 1941):631–32; *Selected Writing* 181 #2 ed. Reginald Moore (London: Nicholson &

Watson, n.d. [1942–43]), 104–12; *BD* 2 #6 (Feb. 1946):19–24. Short story. Reprinted in A15 (q.v.).

C123 'Strength of Mind—Do Conventions Matter?'. *Listener* 26 #675 (18 Dec. 1941):823–24. Part of a discussion between John Mabbott, Lt. Commander J. Noad, Captain Alan Pryce-Jones, and Elizabeth Bowen broadcast on BBC radio (F61). Radio script, E50.

C123.1 Review of *Open the Door* and *A Place of One's Own,* Sir Osbert Sitwell, *Life and Letters* 32 (Jan. 1942):76–80.

C124 'Dubliner'. *Spectator* 168 (1 May 1942):423. Review of *Pictures in the Hallway,* Sean O'Casey.

C125 'Success Story'. *Observer* (10 May 1942):3. Review of *Crusader in Crinoline: The Life of Harriet Beecher Stowe,* Forrest Wilson. Reprinted in A19.

C126 'Contemporary'. *NewSt* (rev) 23 (23 May 1942):340. Review of *In My Good Books,* V. S. Pritchett.

C127 ' "Being Only a Woman" '. *Observer* (31 May 1942):3. Review of *Sir Richard Burton's Wife,* Jean Burton. Reprinted as 'Lady Burton' in A19.

C128 'She Liked Writing'. *Observer* (14 June 1942):3. Review of *The Death of the Moth,* Virginia Woolf, and *Virginia Woolf,* E. M. Forster. Reprinted as 'Virginia Woolf II' in A19.

C129 'Dancing in Daylight'. *The Bell* (Dublin) 5 #2 (Nov. 1942): 90–98. Essay on Miss Bowen's personal experiences in a children's dancing class. An extract from *Seven Winters* (A14).

C130 'The Cheery Soul'. *Listener* 28 #728 (24 Dec. 1942):821–23; *Magazine of Fantasy and Science Fiction* (Apr. 1952):57–65. Short story. Reprinted in A15 (q.v.).

C131 'Weeping Earl'. *NewSt* (rev) 25 (6 Mar. 1943):160–61. *The Great O'Neill: A Biography of Hugh O'Neill, Earl of Tyrone, 1550–1616,* Seán O'Faoláin. Reprinted in A19.

C132 'Hamilton Rowan'. *NewSt* (rev) 25 (22 May 1943):340. *The Desire to Please,* Harold Nicolson. Reprinted in A19.

C133 'Panorama du Roman'. *Fontaine* 37–40 Special Number (1944): 33–177 to 43–187, trans. Pier Ponti. 'Der englische Roman von 1918 bis 1939'. *Die Neue Zürcher Zeitung: Literatur und Kunst*, 168 #1933 (4 Oct. 1947):1–2, trans. E. and H. R. Conrad. The French version is published in anthology, G29.

C134 'Tipperary Woman'. *The Windmill*, 1 #1 (1944):39–47; *Synopsis* 6 (Spring 1945):15–20. Short story. MS, E52.

C135 'Inherited Clock'. *Cornhill* #961 (Jan. 1944):36–53. Short story. Reprinted in A15 (q.v.).

C136 'Mysterious Kôr'. *Penguin New Writing* #20 (Jan. 1944):53–67. Short story. Reprinted in A15 (q.v.).

C137 'By the Unapproachable Sea'. *ChScMM* (5 Feb. 1944):10. Essay.

C138 'Post-Victorian'. *Cornhill* #962 (May 1944):92–96. Review of *Elders and Betters*, Ivy Compton-Burnett. Reprinted as 'Ivy Compton-Burnett II' in A19.

C139 'The Happy Autumn Fields'. *Cornhill* #963 (Nov. 1944):238–51. Short story. Reprinted in A15 (q.v.).

C140 'Mainie Jellett'. *The Bell* (Dublin) 9 #3 (Dec. 1944):250–56. Essay. MS, E57.

C141 'Green Holly'. *Listener* 32 #832 (21 Dec. 1944):684–85, 688. Short story. Reprinted in A15.

C141.1 'With Silent Friends'. *T* (rev) 175 (28 Feb. 1945):278, 280. *The Naval Heritage*, David Mathew; *The Blinds Are Down*, Pamela Kellino; *Ladies May Now Leave Their Machines*, Diana Murray Hill; *Transatlantic Jazz*, Peter Noble; *You Under the Magnifying Glass*, Jack Bilbo.

C142 'The Short Story in England'. *Britain Today* #109 (May 1945): 11–16; *BD* 1 #12 (Aug. 1945):39–43. Essay. MS, E58.

C143 'Opening Up the House'. *Vogue* (English edition) (Aug. 1945): 38, 75, 82. Essay. MS, E59.

C144 'Notes on Writing a Novel'. *Orion* 2 (Autumn 1945):18–29. Essay. Reprinted in A19 (q.v.).

C145 'Comfort and Joy'. *Modern Reading* 11–12 (1945):10–16. Short story.

C146 'I Hear You Say So'. *New Writing and Daylight* #6 (Sept. 1945):23–29. Short story. Reprinted in A28 (q.v.).

C147 'Ivy Gripped The Steps'. *Horizon* 12 #69 (Sept. 1945): 179–208. Short story. Reprinted in A15 (q.v.).

C148 'With Silent Friends'. *T* (rev) 178 (3 Oct. 1945):22, 24. *Final Score*, Warren Beck; *Education To-Day and Tomorrow*, ed. R. W. Moore; *Secondary Schools for Girls*, Miss E. Strudwick; *British Journalists and Newspapers*, Derek Hudson.

C149 'With Silent Friends'. *T* (rev) 178 (10 Oct. 1945):54, 56. *Charles Dickens*, Dame Una Pope-Hennessy; *Marching Soldier*, Joyce Cary.

C150 'With Silent Friends'. *T* (rev) 178 (17 Oct. 1945):86, 88. *The English Teacher*, R. K. Narayan; *Worlds Beginning*, Robert Ardrey; *Thursday Afternoon*, Monica Dickens.

C151 'With Silent Friends'. *T* (rev) 178 (24 Oct. 1945):118, 120. *In Search of Two Characters*, Dormer Creston; *At Mrs. Leppincote's*, Elizabeth Taylor; *One Minute, Please*, Robert Benchley.

C152 'With Silent Friends'. *T* (rev) 178 (31 Oct. 1945):150, 152. *Mine Own Executioner*, Nigel Balchin; *Rudyard Kipling: A New Appreciation*, Hilton Brown; *The Moderns: Past-Present-Future*, Jack Bilbo; *The Case of the Smoking Chimney*, Erle Stanley Gardner.

C153 'EB's Book of the Week'. *T* (rev) 178 (7 Nov. 1945):182. *Novels of Mystery*, ed. Maurice Richardson.

C154 EB Reviews. 178 (14 Nov. 1945):214, 222. *The House in Clewe Street*, Mary Lavin; *Early Britain*, Jacquetta Hawkes; *Stories of the Forties*, ed. Reginald Moore and Woodrow Wyatt; *Early Morning Murder*, Miles Burton. See G23.

C155   EB Reviews. 178 (28 Nov. 1945):280, 284. *Cannery Row*, John Steinbeck; *The Film and the Future*, Andrew Buchanan.

C156   EB Reviews. 178 (5 Dec. 1945):311, 316. *Ego 7*, James Agate; *Curious Relations*, William D'Arfey, ed. William Plomer; *Peony*, Keith West.

C157   EB Reviews. 178 (12 Dec. 1945):342, 348. *The Gazebo*, D. A. Ponsonby; *Farewell Campo 12*, Brigadier James Hargest; *First Impressions*, Isobel Strachey; *I'll Say She Does*, Peter Cheyney.

C158   EB Reviews. 178 (19 Dec. 1945):375, 380. *West Country Stories*, A. L. Rowse; *Only Ghosts Can Live*, Guy Morgan; *The Only Paradise*, Kathleen Hewitt.

C159   EB Reviews. 178 (26 Dec. 1945):406, 412. *The Readiness Is All*, G. P. Griggs; *Flemish Painting*, ed. Emile Cammaerts; *The Weak and the Strong*, Gerald Kirsh; *Marshmallow*, Clare Turlay.

C160   'Façade at Folkestone'. *Contact: First Spring of Peace* 1 [1946]: 49–52. Essay. Elizabeth Bowen lived at Folkestone as a child. Reprinted in A19.

C161   EB Reviews. 179 (2 Jan. 1946):23, 28. *London Belongs to Me*, Norman Collins; *Bedelia*, Vera Caspary; *The Guilds of the City of London*, Sir Ernst Pealey.

C162   'Gone Away'. *Listener* 35 #886 (3 Jan. 1946):13–15. Short story. Reprinted in A28.

C163   EB Reviews. 179 (9 Jan. 1946):55, 60. *Livingstone's Last Journey*, Sir Reginald Coupland; *Transit Visa*, Anna Seghers; *In These Five Years*, Daphne Nixon.

C164   EB Reviews. 179 (16 Jan. 1946):87, 92. *Another World Than This*, comps. V. Sackville-West and Harold Nicolson; *The Battle of the Narrow Seas*, Lt. Cdr. Peter Scott; *Flemish Painting*, pref. J. B. Manson.

C165   EB Reviews. 179 (23 Jan. 1946): 116, 124. *The Condemned Playground*, Cyril Connolly; *Miss Bunting*, Angela Thirkell.

C166   EB Reviews. 179 (30 Jan. 1946):152, 156. *The Pursuit of Love*,

Nancy Mitford; *The Leaning Tower*, Katherine Anne Porter; *Madame Sarah*, May Agate.

C167   EB Reviews. 179 (13 March 1946):343, 348. *B.B.C. War Report*, Desmond Hawkins and Donald Boyd; *Carp Country*, Elisabeth Kyle; *The Way to Cook*, Philip Harben.

C168   EB Reviews. 179 (20 March 1946):374–75. *The Harp and the Oak*, Hugh Massingham; *Critical Essays*, George Orwell; *The Clock Strikes Twelve*, Patricia Wentworth; *The Beauty of Women*, Clifford Bax.

C169   EB Reviews. 179 (27 March 1946):406–07, 412. *Georgian London*, John Summerson; *The Black Eye*, Conyth Little; *English Rivers and Canals*, Frank Eyre and Charles Hadfield.

C170   'Elizabeth Bowen Introduces Guy De Maupassant'. *Literary Digest* 3 #1 (Apr. 1946):26. Introduction to his short story 'The Little Soldier'.

C171   EB Reviews. 180 (3 Apr. 1946):22–23, 28. *The Umbrella Thorn*, Peter De Polnay; *Titus Groan*, Mervyn Peake; *Sallypark*, Margaret Hasset.

C172   EB Reviews. 180 (10 Apr. 1946):55, 60. *An Indian Album* and *Chinese Album*, intro. Cecil Beaton; *Three*, William Sansom; *The Innocents of Paris*, Gilbert Cesbron.

C173   EB Reviews. 180 (17 Apr. 1946):87, 92. *The Gipsy's Baby*, Rosamond Lehmann; *Cass Timberlane*, Sinclair Lewis.

C174   EB Reviews. 180 (24 Apr. 1946):122, 124. *A Woman of the Pharisees*, François Mauriac; *So Few Got Through: The Diary of an Infantry Officer*, Lt. Col. Martin Lindsay; *Towards an Appreciation of Literature*, Frank O'Connor.

C175   EB Reviews. 180 (1 May 1946):151, 156. *Shelley: A Life Story*, Edmund Blunden.

C176   EB Reviews. 180 (7 May 1946):183, 188. *Lost Moorings*, G. Simenon (trans. Stuart Gilbert); *The New School Tie*, G. C. T. Giles; *Be Beautiful*, Jean Cleland; *Death and the Dear Girls*, Jonathan Stagge.

C177 EB Reviews. 180 (15 May 1946):215, 220. *La Princesse de Clèves*, Madame de Lafayette; *Manon Lescaut*, Abbe Prévost; *Les Liaisons Dangereuses*, Choderlos de Laclos; *La Duchesse de Langeais*, Honoré de Balzac.

C178 EB Reviews. 180 (22 May 1946):247, 252. *Then and Now*, Somerset Maugham; *None Shall Know*, Martha Albrand; *The Wolf at the Door*, Michael Barsley; *Houses: Permanence and Prefabrication*, Hugh Anthony.

C179 EB Reviews. 180 (29 May 1946):278–79. *A Star Danced*, Gertrude Lawrence; *How Small a Part of Time*, Magdalen King-Hall; *Merchant Airmen*, Ministry of Information; *With a Bare Bodkin*, Cyril Hare.

C180 EB Reviews. 180 (5 June 1946):310–11, 316. *The Moonlight*, Joyce Cary; *Henry Ford: A Biography*, William Adams Simonds; *Village Affairs*, Roger Armfelt.

C181 EB Reviews. 180 (12 June 1946):342–43. *Marjory Fleming*, Oriel Malet; *Penguin New Writing*, ed. John Lehmann; *The Garden*, Vita Sackville-West; *Trees in Britain*, Alexander L. Howard. EB's review of John Lehmann's volume was reprinted in *Penguin New Writing* #28 (July 1946):191–92.

C182 EB Reviews. 180 (19 June 1946):374–75. *That Lady*, Kate O'-Brien; *Four Quartets Rehearsed*, Raymond Preston; *Mrs. Privett*, Lionel Bonsey.

C183 EB Reviews. 180 (26 June 1946):406–07. *Around Cinemas*, James Agate; *Peggy Windsor and the American Soldier*, Frank Tilsley; *Anna Collett*, Barbara Lucas.

C184 EB Reviews. 181 (3 July 1946):22–23. *A History of Trinity College, Dublin*, Constantia Maxwell; *My Life Line*, Phyllis Bottome; *Oak Leaves and Lavender*, Sean O'Casey; *Flowing Water*, Patrick Stevenson.

C185 EB Reviews. 181 (10 July 1946):54–55. *The Patchwork Book: an Omnibus for Children*, Marghanita Laski; *Winter Meeting*, Ethel Vance; *Auto-da-Fé*, Elias Cavetti; *British Garden Flowers*, George M. Taylor.

C186   EB Reviews. 181 (17 July 1946):86–87. *The Cruise of the Breadwinner*, H. E. Bates; *China Servant*, C. S. Archer; *Detour*, ed. J. E. R. Wood.

C187   EB Reviews. 181 (24 July 1946):118–19. *The Outsider*, Albert Camus (trans. Stuart Gilbert); *The Road of Excess*, Terence De Vere White; *The Late Mrs. Prisleau*, Peter Davies; *The Pen is Mightier*, ed. J. J. Lynx.

C188   EB Reviews. 181 (31 July 1946):150–51. *The Merry Wives of Westminster*, Mrs. Belloc Lowndes; *Pro*, Bruce Hamilton: *Time Exposure*, Cecil Beaton; *Toulouse-Lautrec and Steinlen*, Jack Bilbo.

C189   [EB's reply to a questionnaire in] 'Questionnaire: The Cost of Letters', ed. Cyril Connolly, *Horizon* 14 #81 (Sept. 1946):141–42. MS, E61. Published in anthology, G35.

C190   'Irish Country Life'. *Vogue* (English edition) (Aug. 1946):45–46; reprinted in the American edition as 'Ireland Makes Irish' 108 (15 Aug. 1946):180–81, 214–17.

C191   EB Reviews. 181 (7 Aug. 1946):182–83. *The Pilgrim Hawk*, Glenway Westcott; *Return to Cottington*, Francis Bamford; *The Tale of Beatrix Potter*, Margaret Lane.

C192   EB Reviews. 181 (14 Aug. 1946):214–15. *Bright Day*, J. B. Priestley; *Myrmyda*, John Lodwick; *The American People*, ed. B. A. Botkin; *Suitable for Framing*, Marion Holbrook.

C193   EB Reviews. 181 (21 Aug. 1946):246–47. *The Congress of Vienna*, Harold Nicolson; *Aurélien*, Louis Aragon.

C194   'A Preface'. *Cornhill* #968 (Autumn 1946): 149–53. First printed, A15b.

C195   'Out of a Book'. *Orion* 3 (Autumn 1946): 10–14. Essay. Reprinted in A19 (q.v.).

C196   EB Reviews. 181 (4 Sept. 1946):314, 316. *The Trollopes*, Lucy Poate Stebbins; *A Flask for the Journey*, F. L. Green; *Letters to Florence Farr*, ed. Clifford Bax.

C197   EB Reviews. 181 (11 Sept. 1946):342, 343. *The Scarlet Tree*,

Sir Osbert Sitwell; *The River*, Rumer Godden; *Old Marylebone and Some of Its Famous People*, comp. H. J. Mathews.

C198   EB Reviews. 181 (18 Sept. 1946):374–75, 382. *Rogue Elephant*, Walter Allen; *Collected Stories*, T. O. Beachcroft; *Thank God! I'll Take It From Here*, Jane Allen and Mary Livingstone; *The Englishman Builds*, Ralph Tubbs.

C199   EB Reviews. 181 (25 Sept. 1946):406, 412. *British Weather*, Stephen Bone; *You Forget So Quickly*, Ashley Smith; *The Moving Toy Shop*, Edmund Crispin; *He Who Whispers*, John Dickson Carr.

C200   EB Reviews. 182 (2 Oct. 1946):22–23. *The River Road*, Frances Parkinson Keyes; *Mainly on the Air*, Max Beerbohm; *Judgment in Suspense*, Gerald Bullett.

C201   EB Reviews. 182 (9 Oct. 1946):54–55. *Britannia Mews*, Margery Sharp; *Le Livre du Courage et de la Peur*, Remy; *Lord of the Sorcerers*, Carter Dickson.

C202   EB Reviews. 182 (16 Oct. 1946): 86–87. *Fanfare for Elizabeth*, Edith Sitwell; *Pipe Night*, John O'Hara; *Death and the Pleasant Voices*, Mary Fitt; *Pandora*, Clara Turlay Newberry.

C203   EB Reviews. 182 (23 Oct. 1946):118–19. *They Went to Portugal*, Rose Macaulay; *Diversion*, ed. Hester W. Chapman and Princess Romanovsky-Pavlovsky; *House Under Mars*, Norah Hoult.

C204   EB Reviews. 182 (30 Oct. 1946):150–51. *The King of Brentford*, Robert Henrey; *Indian Route March*, Louis Ragen; *The Pursuit of Happiness*, Joan Evans; *The Key*, Patricia Wentworth.

C204.1   'Pink May'. *Argosy* 7 #11 (Nov. 1946):87–93. Short story. See A15.

C205   EB Reviews. 182 (6 Nov. 1946):184–85. *The Clearing House*, John Buchan; *Children of Vienna*, Robert Neumann; *Get Away Old Man*, William Saroyan; *Here Comes A Chopper*, Gladys Mitchell.

C206   EB Reviews. 182 (13 Nov. 1946):220–21. *Four Studies in Loyalty*, Christopher Sykes; *The Campaign in Burma*, Lt. Col. Frank Owen; *To Bed With Grand Music*, Sarah Russell.

C207   EB Reviews. 182 (20 Nov. 1946):256–57. *European Witness*,

Stephen Spender; *The Storming Dawn*, Mark Freshfield; *Uneasy Terms*, Peter Cheyney; *Junior Film Annual 1946–1947*, ed. Eric Gillett.

C208 EB Reviews. 182 (27 Nov. 1946):292–93. *Back*, Henry Green; *The Becker Wives*, Mary Lavin; *Grimm's Household Tales*, illus. Mervyn Peake; *Uncle Albert's Manual of Practical Photography*, Powell Perry.

C209 EB Reviews. 182 (4 Dec. 1946):328–29. *Thieves in the Night*, Arthur Koestler; *A Rough Walk Home*, Lillian Bowes Lyon; *Velvet Studies*, C. V. Wedgwood; *The White Deer*, James Thurber.

C210 EB Reviews. 182 (11 Dec. 1946):364–65. *The Year of Stalingrad*, Alexander Werth; *Mist on the Tagus*, Tom Hopkinson; *The Blue Danube*, Ludwig Bemelmans; *Good Films and How to Appreciate Them*, Jempson Harman.

C211 EB Reviews. 182 (18 Dec. 1946):400–401. Reviews a number of children's books; *Marguerite Reilly*, Elizabeth Lake; *The Hollow*, Agatha Christie.

C211.1 'In the Days of My Youth'. *WD* 16 (Christmas 1946):19–21. Excerpted from *Seven Winters* (A14).

C212 EB Reviews. 182 (25 Dec. 1946):436–37. *Montgomery*, Alan Moorhead; *Palladian*, Elizabeth Taylor; *The Nine Men of Soho*, J. Maclaren Ross; *Don't Be Afreud*, Lionel Gamlin.

C213 'How They Live in Ireland 1. Conquest by Cheque Book'. *Contact: Points of Contact* 3 [1947]:84. Essay.

C214 EB Reviews. 183 (1 Jan. 1947):24–25. *The Sixth Heaven*, L. P. Hartley; *The Contemporary Theater 1944–1945*, comp. James Agate; *Transformation Scene*, Claude Houghton.

C215 EB Reviews. 183 (8 Jan. 1947):60–61. *The Life of the Heart*, Francis Winwar; *Westwood*, Stella Gibbons; *How to be an Alien*, George Mikes; *In the Asey Mayor Trio*, Phoebe Atwood Taylor.

C216 EB Reviews. 183 (15 Jan. 1947):96–97. *Jonathan Wild*, Henry Fielding; *The State of Mind of Mrs. Sherwood*, Naomi Royde-Smith; *6th Guards Tank Brigade; The Story of Guardsmen in Churchill Tanks*, Patrick Forbes; *The Little Kingdom*, Emyr Humphreys.

C217   EB Reviews. 183 (22 Jan. 1947):132–33. *The Hooded Hawk*, D. B. Wyndham Lewis; *Ursa Major*, C. E. Vulliamy; *Life Among the Scots*, Janet Adam Smith; *"Services Wrendered" by Sonia Snodgrass*, J. E. Broome.

C218   EB Reviews. 183 (29 Jan. 1947):168–69. *The Guiding Star*, Vercors (trans. Eric Sutton); *The Lonely Skier*, Hammond Innes; *Wildwood*, Josephine W. Johnson; *Adventure and Discovery*, preface Kenneth Lindsay; *Discovery and Romance*, preface Mary Treadgold. Latter two works are anthologies for young people.

C219   EB Reviews. 183 (5 Feb. 1947):204–5. *Lady Gregory's Journals 1916–1930*, ed. Lennox Robinson; *More Deadly Than the Male*, Ambrose Grant; *Our Bird Book*, Sydney Rogerson; *English Glass*, W. B. Honey.

C220   'D. H. Lawrence: Reappraising His Literary Influence'. *NYTBR* 52 (9 Feb. 1947):4. Review of *The Portable D. H. Lawrence*, ed. and intro. Diana Trilling. Reprinted as 'D. H. Lawrence' in A19.

C221   EB Reviews. 183 (12 Feb. 1947):240–41. *War in Val d'Orcia*, Iris Origo; *Peace Breaks Out*, Angela Thirkell; *RAAF over Europe*, ed. Frank Johnson; *Memoirs of Mipsie*, Mary Dunn.

C222   EB Reviews. 183 (5 March 1947):276–77. *The Castles on the Ground*, J. M. Richards; *Himalayan View*, Susan Gillespie; *Children of Wrath*, Edmond Bucket; *The Holiday Book*, John Singer.

C223   EB Reviews. 183 (12 March 1947):312–13. *The Life of Neville Chamberlain*, Keith Feiling; *A Pin's Fee*, Peter de Polnay; *Orion III*, ed. C. Day Lewis, D. Kelham Roberts, Rosamond Lehmann; *Cooking Quickly*, Philip Harben.

C224   EB Reviews. 183 (19 March 1947):346–47. *Young Enthusiast*, Elizabeth Jenkins; *A Distant Summer*, Edith Saunders; *States of Grace*, Francis Steegmuller; *Death's Old Sweet Song*, Jonathan Stagge.

C225   'The Power in the Cave'. *Listener* 37 #947 (20 Mar. 1947):431–32. Essay on imagination. Describes the impact on an Edwardian child of *She* by Rider Haggard. Originally a radio broadcast for BBC. Reprinted as 'She' in A25 (q.v.).

C226   EB Reviews. 183 (26 March 1947):378–79. *Manservant and Maidservant*, Ivy Compton-Burnett; *The Return to the Farm*, Robert Henrey; *The Farm Théotime*, Henri Bosco (trans. Mervyn Savill); *Sophy Valentine*, D. A. Ponsonby.

C227 'Third Programme'. *Vogue* (English edition) (Apr. 1947):76, 102, 104. Heavily revised and reprinted in the American edition as 'Britain's Wave Length for Intellectuals' 110 (15 July 1947):40, 73. Essay.

C228 EB Reviews. 184 (2 April 1947):22–23. *Ego 8*, James Agate; *Through Eastern Windows*, Winifred Peck; *The Rumor in the Forest*, Madeleine Couppey.

C229 EB Reviews. 184 (9 April 1947):54–55. *English Popular and Traditional Art*, Margaret Lambert and Enid Marx; *Peabody's Mermaid*, Guy and Constance Jones; *Dark Interlude*, Peter Cheyney; *Cats Don't Need Coffins*, D. B. Olsen.

C230 EB Reviews. 184 (19 April 1947):86–87. *The Street*, Ann Petry; *The Age of Reason*, Jean-Paul Sartre; *Dangling Man*, Saul Bellow.

C231 EB Reviews. 184 (23 April 1947):118–19. *The Traveller's Eye*, Dorothy Carrington; *The Angelic Avengers*, Pierre Andrezel; *The Dark Wood*, Christine Weston; *The Horizontal Man*, Helen Eustes.

C232 EB Reviews. 184 (30 Apr. 1947):150–51. *The Poetic Image*, Cecil Day Lewis; *Teresa and Other Stories*, Seán O'Faoláin; *The Twins*, Bernard Glemser; *Honolulu Murder Story*, Leslie Ford.

C233 EB Reviews. 184 (7 May 1947):182–83. *Dialstone Lane*, W. W. Jacobs; *The House Near Paris*, Drue Tartière; *Cleopatra in the Tide of Time*, Oliver C. deC. Ellis; *Final Curtain*, Ngaio Marsh.

C234 EB Reviews. 184 (14 May 1947):214–15. *Life of William Hazlitt*, P. P. Howe; *The Deer on the Stairs*, Louise Field Cooper; *The History of Mr. Polly*, H. G. Wells; *British Golf*, Bernard Darwin.

C235 EB Reviews. 184 (21 May 1947):246–47. *The Hunters and the Hunted*, Sacheverell Sitwell; *Genevieve*, Jacques Lemarchand (trans. Rosamond Lehmann); *Sussex*, Esther Meynell; *The Black Stocking*, Conyth Little.

C236 EB Reviews. 184 (28 May 1947):278–79. *Ciano's Diary: 1939–1945*, ed. Malcolm Muggeridge; *The Rock Pool*, Cyril Connolly.

C237 EB Reviews. 184 (4 June 1947):310–11. *Gilbert and Sullivan*, Hesketh Pearson; *Peal of Ordnance*, John Lodwick; *My One Contribution to Chess*, F. V. Morley; *The White Dress*, M. G. Eberhart.

C238   EB Reviews. 184 (11 June 1947):342–43. *PQ17*, Godfrey Winn; *An Astrologer's Day*, R. K. Narayan; *The Inn Closes for Christmas*, Cledwyn Hughes; *Cultural Forces in British Life Today*, Adult Education in Britain.

C239   EB Reviews. 184 (18 June 1947):374–75. *Agents and Witnesses*, P. H. Newby; *A Summer in Buenos Aires*, Isobel Strachey; *Beautiful Friend*, Richard Collier.

C240   EB Reviews. 184 (25 June 1947):406–7. *High Bonnet*, Idwal Jones; *George Eliot*, Gerald Bullett; *English Story: Seventh Series*, ed. Woodrow Wyatt; *Vassos the Goatherd: A Story of Cyprus*, Laurie Lee; *Sadler's Wells Ballet at Covent Garden*, Merlyn Severn.

C241   EB Reviews. 185 (2 July 1947):22–23. *Irish Miles*, Frank O'-Connor; *The Hands of Veronica*, Fannie Hurst; *The Lonely*, Paul Gallico; *The Voice of the Turtle*, John Van Druten.

C242   EB Reviews. 185 (9 July 1947):54–55. *Passengers of Destiny*, Louis Aragon; *First Love and Other Stories*, Viola Meynell; *Black Country*, Walter Allen; *A Man Called Jones*, Julian Symons.

C243   EB Reviews. 185 (16 July 1947):86–87. *Minute for Murder*, Nicholas Blake; *The Check Board*, Nevil Shute; *Castle in Denmark*, Janet Diebold.

C244   EB Reviews. 185 (23 July 1947):118–19. *Eustace and Hilda*, L. P. Hartley; *Indian Flamingo*, Charles Fabri; *A Way of Looking at Pictures*, Alan Gwynne-Jones; *The Young King and Other Stories*, Oscar Wilde.

C245   EB Reviews. 185 (30 July 1947):150–51. *Nineteen Stories*, Graham Greene; *The English at the Seaside*, Christopher Marsden; *Great Expectations*, Charles Dickens (foreword Bernard Shaw); *Twelfth-Century Paintings at Hardham and Clayton*, Helmut Gernsheim.

C246   EB Reviews. 185 (6 Aug. 1947):182–83. *People of Quality*, Collie Knox; *Delta Wedding*, Eudora Welty: *We Happy Few*, Helen Howe.

C247   EB Reviews. 185 (13 Aug. 1947):214–15. *Creatures of Circumstances*, Somerset Maugham; *Treadmill*, Michael Harrison; *Leave to Presume the Death*, Cyril Hall; *The Novel Since 1939*, Henry Reed.

C248   EB Reviews. 185 (20 Aug. 1947):246–47. *John Buchan*, by his wife and friends; *Lord, I Was Afraid*, Nigel Balchin; *The English People*, George Orwell; *Return to Night*, Mary Renault.

C249   EB Reviews. 185 (27 Aug. 1947):278–79. *Novels of High Society from the Victorian Age*, comp. Anthony Powell; *Certified*, H. G. Woodley; *So Long at the Fair*, Anthony Thorne; *Penguin Guides*, ed. L. Russell Muirhead.

C250   EB Reviews. 185 (3 Sept. 1947):310–11. *The Judge's Story*, Charles Morgan; *Twilight Stories*, Rhoda Broughton; *The Captain Comes Home*, Helen Ashton; *Now Barabbas*, William Douglas Home.

C251   EB Reviews. 185 (10 Sept. 1947):342–43. *Flaubert and Madame Bovary*, Francis Steegmuller; *Agostino*, Alberto Moravia (trans. Beryl de Zoete); *The Labours of Hercules*, Agatha Christie.

C252   EB Reviews. 185 (17 Sept. 1947):374–75. *Dandy Hart*, Hamilton Ellis; *Winning Hazard*, Noel Wynward; *The Glass of Fashion*, Ira Morris; *Early Morning Poison*, Belton Cobb.

C253   EB Reviews. 185 (24 Sept. 1947):406–7. *Browns and Chester: A Portrait of a Shop*, Mass-Observation; *A View of the Harbour*, Elizabeth Taylor; *The Brontës*, Phyllis Bentley; *Georgia Boy*, Erskine Caldwell.

C254   EB Reviews. 186 (1 Oct. 1947):22–23. *The Countryman at Work*, Thomas Hennell; *The Lowells and Their Seven Worlds*, Ferris Greenslet; *Keeping House for Jan*, Maxine Hewson.

C255   EB Reviews. 186 (8 Oct. 1947):54–55. *A Case to Answer*, Edward Lustgarten; *Portrait of Edith Wharton*, Percy Lubbock; *Dance Without Music*, Peter Cheyney; *Western Highlands*, Arthur Gardner.

C256   EB Reviews. 186 (15 Oct. 1947):86–87. *Worlds Apart*, Hester Chapman; *The Admiral's Daughter*, Betty Askwith; *This Is the Way*, Geoffrey Cotterell; *Black Goatee*, Conyth Little.

C257   EB Reviews. 186 (22 Oct. 1947):118–19. *The Building of Bath*, Bryan Little; *Private Enterprise*, Angela Thirkell; *A'Wede Away*, B. Montagu Scott; *British Universities*, S. C. Roberts.

C258   EB Reviews. 186 (29 Oct. 1947):150–51. *Addams and Evil*,

Charles Addams; *The House by the Sea,* Jon Godden; *Midnight Oil,* Peter Traill; *Come Into the Kitchen,* Alexie Gordon and Trudy Bliss.

C259   EB Reviews. 186 (5 Nov. 1947):182–83. *Novels of George du Maurier,* intro. John Masefield and Daphne du Maurier.

C260   EB Reviews. 186 (12 Nov. 1947):214–15. *A Peck of Troubles,* comp. Daniel George; *Arthur Rimbaud,* Enid Starkie; *A Will in the Way,* Miles Burton.

C261   EB Reviews. 186 (19 Nov. 1947):246–47. *The Blue Stocking Ladies,* Walter Scott; *Tea With Mrs. Goodman,* Philip Toynbee; *Sisters by a River,* Barbara Conyns; *The Snail that Climbed up the Eiffel Tower,* Odo Cross; *In the Hands of the Senecas,* Walter D. Edmonds; *English Hymns and Hymn Writers,* Adam Fox.

C262   EB Reviews. 186 (26 Nov. 1947):278–79. *Shelley in Italy,* ed. John Lehmann; *The Undertaker's Wife,* Theodora Benson; *Night Darkens the Street,* Arthur La Bern.

C263   'A Way of Life'. *Vogue* 110 (1 Dec. 1947):145, 210, 212. Essay reprinted in the English edition under the title 'Way of Life' (Jan. 1948) 44, 92, 96.

C264   EB Reviews. 186 (10 Dec. 1947):346–47. Review of a number of Christmas books, including some for children.

C265   EB Reviews. 186 (17 Dec. 1947):378–79. *The Prevalence of Witches,* Aubrey Menen; *The Common Chord,* Frank O'Connor; *Paintings of the Ballet,* Theyre Lee-Elliotts (intro. Arnold L. Haskell); *Stranger than Truth,* Vera Caspary.

C266   EB Reviews. 186 (24 Dec. 1947):410–11. *English Home-Life 1500–1800,* Christina Hole; *The Donkey Inside,* Ludwig Bemelmans; *Killer Mine,* Hammond Innes; *The Lady of Glentwith Grange,* Wilkie Collins.

C267   EB Reviews. 186 (31 Dec. 1947):442–43. *Henry Fielding,* Elizabeth Jenkins; *The Wind at My Back,* Victoria Lincoln; *The Children of Primrose Lane,* Noel Streatfield; *No Mistaking Corker,* Monica Edwards; *The Bell of the Four Evangelists,* Violet Needham. These last three are children's books.

C268   [with V. S. Pritchett and Graham Greene] 'Why Do I Write?'
Contact: World of Neighbours 8 (1947):55–64. Reprinted in B21 (q.v.).

C269   EB Reviews. 187 (7 Jan. 1948):22–23. *I Fight to Live,* Robert
Boothby, M.P.; *Roman Britain,* Ian Richardson; *A House in the Up-
lands,* Erskine Caldwell; *Daisy Miller,* Henry James.

C270   EB Reviews. 187 (14 Jan. 1948):54–55. *The Red Prussian,*
Leopold Schwarzschild; *Stranger at Home,* George Sanders; *The Woman
in Black,* Leslie Ford; *The Royal Family in Africa,* Dermott Morrah.

C271   EB Reviews 187 (21 Jan. 1948):86–87. *Samuel Pepys: The
Man Making,* Arthur Bryant; *The Reprieve,* Jean-Paul Sartre.

C272   EB Reviews. 187 (28 Jan. 1948):118–19. *The Trains We Loved,*
Hamilton Ellis; *Afterglow,* Elizabeth Wood; *These I Have Loved,* Katherine Sim; *Aspects of British Art,* intro. Michael Ayrton.

C273   EB Reviews. 187 (4 Feb. 1948):150–51. *Suddenly at His Resi-
dence,* Christianna Brand; *Land Without Heroes,* G. F. Green; *Lady
Shane's Daughter,* Magdalen Kinghall; *British Music,* comp. Russell
Palmer.

C274   EB Reviews. 187 (11 Feb. 1948):182–83. *Foundations in the
Dust,* Seton Lloyd, F.S.A.; *Another Woman's House,* M. G. Eberhart;
Rafe Granite, Bill Naughton; *Dinner for None,* Maureen Sarsfield.

C275   EB Reviews. 187 (18 Feb. 1948):214–15. *The Swan Sang Once,*
Marjorie Carleton; *The Port of London,* John Herbert; *Living Writers,*
ed. G. H. Phelps; *With Murder in Mind,* Elizabeth Ferrars.

C276   EB Reviews. 187 (17 March 1948):342–43. *The Unforgiven,*
Howard Clewes; *Thérèse,* François Mauriac; *The Loved One,* Evelyn
Waugh; *The Last of Philip Banter,* J. F. Bardin.

C277   EB Reviews. 187 (24 March 1948):374–75. *Nightmare Abbey
and Crotchet Castle,* Thomas Love Peacock; *Tempestuous Petticoat,*
Clare Leighton; *The Government Inspector,* Nikolai Gogol; *Music Tells
All,* E. R. Punshon.

C278   EB Reviews. 187 (31 March 1948):406–7. *Mariner Dances,*
P. H. Newby; *San-Sou-Ci,* André Nature; *Victorian Tales for Girls,* ed.
Marghanita Laski; *Our Dog,* Lane Norcott.

C279 'Prague Before the Coup'. *Vogue* (English edition) (Apr. 1948):
68, 103. Essay printed simultaneously in the American edition under the
title 'Prague and the Crisis' 111 (1 Apr. 1948):156, 195–6.

C280 EB Reviews. 188 (7 Apr. 1948):22–23. *Charade*, John Mortimer; *Shapton Affair*, Roger Armfelt; *Turnstile One,* ed. V. S. Pritchett;
The Voice of the Corpse, Max Murray.

C281 EB Reviews. 188 (14 Apr. 1948):54–55. *Joan of Arc and The
Recovery of France,* Alice Buchan; *A. Crowd Is Not Company,* Robert
Klee; *Prince Leopold and Anna,* Laurian Jones.

C282 EB Reviews. 188 (21 Apr. 1948):86–87. *Silver Wedding,* Louis
Wielff, M.V.O.; *The Last Pre-Raphaelite,* Douglas Goldring; *An Attic
in Jermyn Street,* Robert Henrey.

C283 EB Reviews. 188 (28 Apr. 1948):118–19. *Paris Herself Again,*
George Augustus Sala; *Something Terrible, Something Lovely,* William
Sansom; *The Military Orchid,* Jocelyn Brooke; *A Puzzle for Pilgrims,*
Patrick Quentin.

C284 EB Reviews. 188 (5 May 1948):150–51. *The Goebbels Diaries,*
ed. and trans. Louis P. Lochner; *Answer to Question 33,* Christopher
Sykes; *The Harp in the South,* Ruth Park.

C285 EB Reviews. 188 (12 May 1948):182–83. *Winged Dagger,* Ron
Farran; *Still Glides the Stream,* Flora Thompson; *The Widow's House,*
Betty de Scherbinin; *Boy Blossom Stories,* Jim Phelan.

C286 EB Reviews. 188 (19 May 1948):214, 222. *Great Morning,* Sir
Osbert Sitwell; *To Tell My Daughter,* Jean Curtis Brown; *A Wife's
Tale,* Sheila Alexander; *How to Scrape Skies,* George Mikes.

C287 EB Reviews. 188 (26 May 1948):246–47. *Monarchy and the
Chase,* Sabretache; *Growing Up,* Olivia Manning; *Caligula,* Albert
Camus; *Notes on the Verse Drama,* Christopher Hassall.

C288 EB Reviews. 188 (2 June 1948):278, 286. *The Heart of the
Matter,* Graham Greene; *Southward from Swiss Cottage,* B. Curtis
Brown; *A Hard Winter,* Raymond Queneau; *Flight Out of Fancy,* anon.

C289 EB Reviews. 188 (9 June 1948):310–11. *Two Quiet Lives,* Lord
David Cecil; *Asking For Trouble,* T. O. Bancroft; *Country Place,* Ann

Petry; *What the Countryman Wants to Know*, Fred Kitchen and Clifford Grevtorex.

C290   EB Reviews. 188 (16 June 1948):342, 350. *Jane Austen*, Elizabeth Jenkins; *Chrysantha*, Margaret Drake.

C291   EB Reviews. 188 (23 June 1948):374–75. *Dirty Eddie*, Ludwig Bemelmans; *Covent Garden*, Desmond Shawe-Taylor; *The Story of the Grand Canyon*, Edwin Corle; *George du Maurier*, Derek Pepys Whitely.

C292   EB Reviews. 188 (30 June 1948):406, 414. *The Foolish Gentlewoman*, Margery Sharp; *The Tapestry Bed*, Louise de Vilmorin; *Pay-Off in Calcutta*, Richard Collier; *Movie Review*, A. E. Wilson.

C293   EB Reviews. 189 (7 July 1948):22–23. *Who Has Seen the Wind*, W. O. Mitchell; *Wonderful Mrs. Marriott*, Josephine Bell; *British Chess*, Kenneth Mathews; *Moscow Murder*, Bernard Newman.

C294   EB Reviews. 189 (14 July 1948):54, 62. *Mount Ida*, Monk Gibbon; *Twelve Million Black Voices*, Ralph Wright; *The Woman in the Sea*, Shelley Smith.

C295   'The Evolution of a Novelist'. *TLS* 47 (17 July 1948):395. Review of *Myself When Young*, H. H. Richardson. Reprinted as 'Myself When Young' in A19.

C296   EB Reviews. 189 (21 July 1948):86–87. *Whispering Hill*, Martha Albrand; *Blood Money*, Edward Hyams; *British Hospitals*, A. G. L. Ives; *The Bedside Shakespeare*, comp. Arthur Stanley.

C297   EB Reviews. 189 (28 July 1948):118–19. *The Idea of Summer*, Marc Brandel; *Attic and Area*, Francesca Marton; *Acres and Pains*, S. J. Perelman; *The Englishman's Home*, Val Doone; *The Governess of Ashburton Hall*, Neil Bell; *Nights at the Opera*, Barbara McFadyean and Spike Hughes.

C298   EB Reviews. 189 (4 Aug. 1948):150–51. *46 Not Out*, R. C. Robertson Glasgow; *Bel Ami*, Guy de Maupassant; *Two Lovely Beasts*, Liam O'Flaherty.

C299   EB Reviews. 189 (11 Aug. 1948):182, 190. *Joy and Josephine*, Monica Dickens; *Hetty Dorval*, Ethel Wilson; *Mr. Guy's London*, A. P. Herbert.

C300　EB Reviews. 189 (18 Aug. 1948):214–15. *The Borgia Testament*, Nigel Balchin; *The Wisdom of Dr. Johnson*, comp. Constantia Maxwell; *Portrait of a House*, Mary Howard McClintock; *Devil's Reckoning*, Miles Burton.

C301　EB Reviews. 189 (25 Aug. 1948):246–47. *Mrs. Beeton and Her Husband*, Nancy Spain; *Champion Road*, Frank Tilsley; *Paper Orchid*, Arthur La Bern.

C302　EB Reviews. 189 (1 Sept. 1948):278–79. *Catalina*, Somerset Maugham; *A Candle for St. Jude*, Rumer Godden; *I Love Miss Tilli Bean*, Ilka Chase; *The Black Piano*, Conyth Little.

C303　EB Reviews. 189 (8 Sept. 1948):310, 318. *Yours Faithfully*, Leslie Henson; *Of Wives and Wiving*, John Bunch; *British Boxing*, Denzil Batchelor.

C304　EB Reviews. 189 (15 Sept. 1948):342–43. *The Blood of Others*, Simone de Beauvoir; *The Secret Thread*, Ethel Vance; *Malice Bites Back*, T. O. Beachcroft; *The Glass Room*, Edwin Rolfe and Lester Fuller.

C305　EB Reviews. 189 (22 Sept. 1948):374–75. *The Complete Short Stories of Saki*, E. M. Munro; *Bulwer-Lytton*, Earl of Lytton; *Letter to Five Wives*, John Kempner.

C306　EB Reviews. 189 (29 Sept. 1948):406–7. *Love Among the Ruins*, Angela Thirkell; *Little I Understood*, Joanna Cannan; *English Cottage and Farm Houses*, C. Henry Warren; *Bullets for the Bridegroom*, David Dodge.

C307　'The Next Book'. *Now and Then* 77 (Autumn 1948):11–12. From a broadcast by Elizabeth Bowen. See E65, F72.

C308　EB Reviews. 190 (6 Oct. 1948):22–23, 30. *That Winter*, Merle Miller; *Letters of an Economic Father*, W. S. Hill-Reid; *Tamburlaine the Great*, Christopher Marlowe, ed. Basil Ashmore; *Sorry, Wrong Number*, Allen Ullman and Lucille Fletcher.

C309　EB Reviews. 190 (13 Oct. 1948):54–55. *A Film Star in Belgrave Square*, Mrs. Robert Henrey; *Sinecure*, Michael Harrison; *The Artamonov Business*, Maxim Gorki.

C310 EB Reviews. 190 (20 Oct. 1948):86–87. *The Sky and The Forest*, C. S. Forester; *Theatre Street*, Tamara Karsavina; *A Book of Ballads*, A. P. Herbert; *Rude Health*, Dennis Rooke and Alan d'Egville.

C311 EB Reviews. 190 (27 Oct. 1948):118–19. *The Rage of the Vulture*, Alan Moorehead; *The Mask of Wisdom*, Howard Clewes; *Boys Will Be Boys*, E. S. Turner.

C312 'The Creative Life in Our Time: An Exchange of Letters'. *Partisan Review* 15 (Nov. 1948):1175–89. This is part of a longer correspondence between Elizabeth Bowen, Graham Greene, and V. S. Pritchett. See B21.

C313 EB Reviews. 190 (3 Nov. 1948):150–51. *Ego 9*, James Agate; *The Case of Mr. Crump*, Ludwig Lewisohn; *Byron*, C. E. Vulliamy; *The Dark Wheel*, Philip MacDonald.

C314 EB Reviews. 190 (17 Nov. 1948):218–19. *Miss Josephine and the Colonel*, Oriel Malet; *The Washbournes of Otterley*, Humphrey Pakington; *A Second Book of Russian Verse*, ed. C. M. Bowra; *Green Shiver*, Clyde B. Clason.

C315 EB Reviews. 190 (24 Nov. 1948):252–53. *The Conspirator*, Humphrey Slater; *Maiden's Trip*, Emma Smith; *Taken at the Flood*, Agatha Christie; *The Best of Beardsley*, Aubrey Beardsley, ed. R. A. Walker.

C316 'The Forgotten Art of Living'. *Contact: Good Living* 13 (Dec. 1948):xxvi–I; *WD* 21 (Apr. 1949):74–76. Essay. MS, E70.

C317 'Elizabeth Bowen's Choice of Children's Books for Christmas'. *T* (rev) 190 (1 Dec. 1948):286–87. *Black Ivory*, Norman Collins; *Miss Kelly*, Elizabeth Holding; *Uncle Mac's Children's Hour*, ed. Derek McCulloch; *Slippery Sam*, Enid Marx.

C318 EB Reviews. 190 (8 Dec. 1948):320–21. *Concluding*, Henry Green; *Round the Year with Lady Addle*, Mary Dunn; *Cigarette Card Cavalcade*, A. J. Cruse; *The Rape of Lucretia* [opera libretto], foreword Benjamin Britten.

C319 'Heart or Soul?' *Spectator* 181 (10 Dec. 1948):766. Review of *From the Heart of Europe*, F. O. Matthiessen.

C320   EB Reviews. 190 (15 Dec. 1948):354–55. *A Passing World*, Mrs. Belloc Lowndes; *Morning, Noon and Night in London*, Sacheverell Sitwell; *Devil Take the Blue Tail Fly*, J. F. Bardin; *The Voyage of the Luna I*, David Craigie; *The Junior Weekend Book*, comp. J. R. Evans; *The Bells of Leyden Sing*, Catherine Cate. These last three are children's books.

C321   'Salt on the Lips'. *Observer* (19 Dec. 1948):3. Review of *The Unknown Sea*, François Mauriac, trans. Gerard Hopkins.

C322   'But Once a Year'. *Tatler* 190 (22 Dec. 1948):390. Essay on Christmas.

C323   EB Reviews. 190 (29 Dec. 1948):422–23. *Four Favourites*, D. B. Wyndham Lewis; *No Highway*, Nevil Shute; *A Nineteenth Century Childhood*, Mary McCarthy.

C324   EB Reviews. 191 (5 Jan. 1949):24–25. *The Train*, Vera Panova, trans. Eve Manning and Marie Budberg; *John Keats: The Principle of Beauty*, Lord Gorell; *Rain Stopped Play*, R. C. Robertson-Glasgow; *Villain with a Smiling Cheek*, Paul Murray.

C325   EB Reviews. 191 (12 Jan. 1949):58–59. *Fifteen Years' Hard Labour*, Claud Mullins; *London*, Robert Henrey; *The Tongue-Tied Canary*, Nicolas Bentley; *Death Knocks Three Times*, Anthony Gilbert.

C326   EB Reviews. 191 (19 Jan. 1949):92, 100. *Europe Without Baedeker*, Edmund Wilson; *Georgian Lady*, Nerena Shute; *Elegies for the Dead in Cyrenaica*, Hamish Henderson.

C327   EB Reviews. 191 (26 Jan. 1949):126–27. *Kevin O'Higgins*, Terence De Vere White; *The Bachelor of Arts*, R. K. Narayan; *The Unexpected Angel*, John Watney; *The Saracen's Head*, Osbert Lancaster.

C328   EB Reviews. 191 (2 Feb. 1949):161, 168. *The Jacaranda Tree*, H. E. Bates; *Cry, the Beloved Country*, Alan Paton; *There's No Need to Shout*, Frances Warfield.

C329   EB Reviews. 191 (9 Feb. 1949):194–95. *Isabel and the Sea*, George Millar; *Men and Wives* and *More Women Than Men*, Ivy

Compton-Burnett; *The Hunting Wasp*, John Crompton; *False Beauty,*
Stephen Ransome.

C330 EB Reviews. 191 (16 Feb. 1949):229, 236. *Four Countries,*
William Plomer; *The Sickle and the Stars*, Alexander Clifford and
Jenny Nicholson; *Adolphe*, Benjamin Constant, intro. Harold Nicolson,
trans. Carl Wildman.

C331 EB Reviews. 191 (23 Feb. 1949):262–63. *More Work for the
Undertaker*, Margery Allingham; *The Strange Life of August Strind-
berg*, Elizabeth Sprigge; *The Scapegoat*, Jocelyn Brooke; *Arrest the
Bishop?*, Winifred Peck; *Printer's Devil*, James Milne.

C332 EB Reviews. 191 (2 March 1949):297, 304. *Ape and Essence,*
Aldous Huxley; *The Snow Pasture*, P. H. Newby.

C333 'Miss Bowen on Miss Bowen'. *NYTBR* 54 (6 March 1949):33.
An abridgement of a biographical account she wrote for her publisher,
A. A. Knopf, before publication of *The Heat of the Day* (A18a).

C334 EB Reviews. 191 (9 March 1949):332–33. *Nollekens and His
Times*, John Thomas Smith; *The People Opposite*, Sylvia Thompson;
Randle in Springtime, Geoffrey Cotterell; *Wisteria Cottage*, Robert M.
Coates; *Chinese Escapade*, Laurence Tipton.

C335 EB Reviews. 191 (16 March 1949):368, 376. *Poets and Story-
Tellers*, Lord David Cecil; *The Wooden Horse*, Eric Williams; *The
Oasis*, Mary McCarthy.

C336 EB Reviews. 191 (23 March 1949):404–5. *The Auction Sale,*
C. H. B. Kitchin; *The Nightingales Sing*, Elizabeth Parsons; *My Fath-
er's Son*, Richard Lumford; *The March Hare Murders*, Elizabeth
Ferrars.

C337 EB Reviews. 191 (30 March 1949):440, 448. *Rumming Park,*
John Mortimer; *Lovers Aren't Company*, Monica Stirling.

C338 EB Reviews. 192 (6 Apr. 1949):24–25. *A Wreath of Roses,*
Elizabeth Taylor; *Death of Jezebel*, Christianna Brand; *The Wrong
Set*, Angus Wilson; *Worcestershire*, L. T. C. Rolt; *Shropshire*, Edmund
Vale; *Alphabetical Order*, Daniel George.

C339 'Downfall'. *Observer* (10 Apr. 1949):3. Review of *The Best Days*, Hugh Massingham.

C340 EB Reviews. 192 (13 Apr. 1949):60, 68. *Artist Among the Missing*, Olivia Manning; *The Green Carnation*, Robert Hichens; *Children's Illustrated Books*, Janet Adam Smith.

C341 EB Reviews. 192 (20 Apr. 1949):96–97. *The Happy Yes*, comps. Margaret Crosland and Patricia Ledward; *I Capture the Castle*, Dodie Smith; *You Can Call It a Day*, Peter Cheyney; *The Squirrel Cage*, Edwin Gilbert.

C342 EB Reviews. 192 (27 Apr. 1949):132, 140. *Throw Me a Bone*, Eleanor Lothrop; *The Long Walk*, Betsey Barton; *The Beast in Me and Other Animals*, James Thurber.

C343 EB Reviews. 192 (4 May 1949):168–69. *Sarah Bernhardt: My Grandmother*, Lysianne Bernhardt; *Straw to Make Brick*, Alan Marcus; *In the Green Tree*, Alun Lewis; *The Queen's Awards: Second Series*.

C344 EB Reviews. 192 (11 May 1949):204, 212. *Fabled Shore*, Rose Macaulay; *Mrs. Gatty and Mrs. Ewing*, Christabel Maxwell; *Fairy Tales of Land and Sea*, Simonne Ratel.

C345 EB Reviews. 192 (18 May 1949):240–41. *Elephant and Castle*, R. C. Hutchinson; *The Naked and the Dead*, Norman Mailer; *Advice to a Young Poet*, Llewellyn Powys; *British Butterflies*, Vere Temple.

C346 EB Reviews. 192 (25 May 1949):277, 284. *The Buried Self*, Isobel Macdonald; *Icedrome*, Frank Tilsley.

C347 EB Reviews. 192 (1 June 1949):312–13. *Great Villiers*, Hester Chapman; *The Body*, William Sansom; *Conversation in Sicily*, Elio Vittorini, trans. Wilfrid David; *Suffolk*, Oliver Cook.

C348 EB Reviews. 192 (8 June 1949):348, 356. *Dead Souls*, Nikolai Gogol; *Redemption*, Francis Stuart; *Train to Nowhere*, Anita Leslie.

C349 EB Reviews. 192 (15 June 1949):384–85. *Broken Images*, John Guest; *Crooked House*, Agatha Christie; *The Practical Cook*, Frances Dale; *The Return of Erica*, Louise de Vilmorin, trans. Mona Andrade.

C350 EB Reviews. 192 (22 June 1949):420, 428. *Two Worlds and*

Their Ways, Ivy Compton-Burnett; *The Conservative Party*, Nigel Birch, *The Liberal Party*, R. J. Cruikshank, and *The Labor Party*, William Glenvil Hall; *Death Goes on Skis*, Nancy Spain.

C351 'The Achievement of Virginia Woolf'. *NYTBR* 54 part 1 (26 June 1949):1, 21. Review of *Virginia Woolf*, Bernard Blackstone. Reprinted in A19 (q.v.).

C352 EB Reviews. 192 (29 June 1949):456–57. *A Sort of Traitors*, Nigel Balchin; *We Follow the Roads*, Jim Phelan; *Olivia*, anon.; *The Black Coat*, Conyth Little.

C353 EB Reviews. 193 (6 July 1949):26, 34. *The Life and Times of Coventry Patmore*, Derek Patmore; *Nineteen Eighty-Four*, George Orwell; *The Little Sister*, Raymond Chandler.

C354 EB Reviews. 193 (13 July 1949):70–71. *Laughter in the Next Room*, Osbert Sitwell; *Hunting and Fairies*, Compton Mackenzie; *Orpheus II*, ed. John Lehmann; *Years of Wrath* (collection of cartoons).

C355 EB Reviews. 193 (20 July 1949):114, 122. *Emily, Duchess of Leinster*, Brian Fitzgerald; *Head of a Traveller*, Nicholas Blake; *Death Be Not Proud*, John Gunther; *In the East My Pleasure*, J. Alan Thompson.

C356 EB Reviews. 193 (29 July 1949):154–55. *The Moment of Truth*, Storm Jameson; *Condemned to Life*, Angela Jeans; *Green Grow the Rushes*, Howard Clewes; *The Rose and the Star*, Iris Morley and Phyllis Manchester.

C357 EB Reviews. 193 (3 Aug. 1949):196, 204. *Love in a Cold Climate*, Nancy Mitford; *Mrs. Gaskell*, Yvonne Ffrench; *Boys and Girls Come Out to Play*, Nigel Dennis; *Thou Shalt Not Suffer a Witch*, Dorothy K. Haynes.

C358 EB Reviews. 193 (10 Aug. 1949):236–37. *Ellen Terry and Bernard Shaw*, ed. Christopher St. John; *The River Line*, Charles Morgan; *Parson Austen's Daughter*, Helen Ashton.

C359 EB Reviews. 193 (17 Aug. 1949):276, 284. *Shakespeare*, Ivor Brown; *The Margin*, J. D. Scott; *Fontagre*, Jean Orieux; *The Casebook of Ellery Queen*, Ellery Queen.

C360 EB Reviews. 193 (24 Aug. 1949):316–17. *The Bank of Ireland: 1783–1946*, Dr. Hall, ed. George O'Brien; *Philippa*, Mrs. Robert Henrey; *The King and the Corpse*, Max Murray.

C361 EB Reviews. 193 (31 Aug. 1949):356, 364. *A Woman's Life*, Guy de Maupassant, trans. Antonia White; *Popcorn on the Ginza*, Lucy Herndon Crockett; *An American Visitor*, Joyce Cary; *Trouble in Triplicate*, Nero Wolfe.

C362 EB Reviews. 193 (7 Sept. 1949):402. *A Small Star*, James Bridie and Moray McLaren; *The Conversations of Dr. Johnson*, ed. Raymond Postgate; *The Doctor Wears Three Faces*, Mary Bard; *The Rainbow*, Andrew Shirley; *The Lovers Disturbed*, Elizabeth Lake.

C363 EB Reviews. 193 (21 Sept. 1949):504–5. *Benjamin Constant*, Harold Nicolson; *The Tormentors*, Richard Cargoe; *The Wonderful Summer*, Jocelyn Brooke.

C364 EB Reviews. 193 (28 Sept. 1949):556, 564. *Little Boy Lost*, Marghanita Laski; *The Far Cry*, Emma Smith; *The Face and Mind of Ireland*, Arland Ussher; *Question Mark*, Donald McCullough.

C365 'On Writing *The Heat of the Day*'. *Now and Then* #79 (Autumn 1949):11. Footnote indicates that part of this article appeared in the *Bookman*.

C366 'Confessions'. *Saturday Book* #9 (Oct. 1949):108–9. Answer to a questionnaire.

C367 'Bright-Plumaged Brood'. *T* (rev) 194 (5 Oct. 1949):32–33. *Call a Dog Hervey*, D. A. Ponsonby; *The Holiday*, Stevie Smith; *The Valley of St. Ives*, Arthur Herbert Bryant.

C368 'A Street in Florence'. *T* (rev) 194 (12 Oct. 1949):84, 92. *A Tale of Poor Lovers*, Vasco Pratolini; *A Mine of Serpents*, Jocelyn Brooke; *The Bats of Hell*, Bridget Chetwynd; *James Pryde: 1866–1941*, Derek Hudson; *The Wonderful Story of London*.

C369 'Proust and the Duke'. *T* (rev) 194 (19 Oct. 1949):128. *The Veiled Wanderer*, Marthe Bibesco; *In a Harbour Green*, Benedict Kiely.

C370 'The Second Sight'. *T* (rev) 194 (26 Oct. 1949):188–89. *Tele-*

vision, Maurice Gorham; *The Best of Times,* Ludwig Bemelmans; *The Distaff Muse,* comp. Clifford Bax and Meum Stewart; *One of Those Things,* Peter Cheyney.

C371 'Workshop Guide'. *T* (rev) 194 (2 Nov. 1949):240–41. *A Writer's Notebook,* Somerset Maugham; *The Old Bank House,* Angela Thirkell.

C372 'When Liberation Came'. *T* (rev) 194 (9 Nov. 1949):292–93. *The Impossible Shore,* Robert Kee; *Alice,* Elizabeth Eliot; *The World Is a Wedding,* Delmore Schwartz; *A Pictorial Gospel,* comp. Eliot Hodgkin.

C373 'A Glimpse of the Pit'. *T* (rev) 194 (16 Nov. 1949):344–45. *On a Dark Night,* Anthony West; *Ceremony of Innocence,* Elizabeth Charlotte Webster; *Some Classic Locomotives,* C. Hamilton Ellis; *Cat of Many Tails,* Ellery Queen.

C374 'The Quaker Marksmen'. *T* (rev) 194 (23 Nov. 1949):396, 398. *The Unbroken Thread,* Lord Templewood; *The Saturday Book,* ed. Leonard Russell; *Mariam,* Ennio Flaiano.

C375 'Elizabeth Bowen at Her Typewriter'. *Listener* 42 #1087 (24 Nov. 1949): 890. Excerpt from BBC radio broadcast: Overseas Service to the Pacific on ABC Women's Programme No. 7, entitled 'The Mechanics of Writing'. MS, E73.1. Broadcast, F76.

C376 'The Young May Moon'. *Now and Then* 80 (Spring 1950):16–17. Review of *The Young May Moon,* P. H. Newby.

C377 'The Books That Grow Up With One'. *London Calling* #546 (9 Mar. 1950):10. Essay. MS, E72.

C378 'Once Upon a Yesterday'. *SatRev* 33 (27 May 1950):9–10, 36–37. Reprinted as 'The Bend Back' in *Cornhill* 165 #987 (Summer 1951):221–27. Essay on the importance of the past in fiction.

C379 'New York Waiting in My Memory'. *Vogue* 116 (July 1950): 78–79. Essay. MS, E75.

C380 'The Golden Apples'. *Books of Today* n.s. 5 part 5 (Sept. 1950):2–3. Review of *The Golden Apples,* Eudora Welty. Reprinted in A25 (q.v.).

C381 'The Writer's Peculiar World'. *NYTBR* 55 part 2 (24 Sept. 1950):3, 40. Reprinted as 'Disloyalties' in A25 (q.v.).

C382 'Elizabeth Bowen of Cork and London'. *NYHTB* 27 (8 Oct. 1950):15. Autobiographical comments regarding her work and her homes in Ireland and London.

C383 'Christmas at Bowen's Court'. *Flair* 1 #11 (Dec. 1950):20–21. Essay.

C384 'The Light in the Dark'. *Vogue* 116 (Dec. 1950):89–90, 157, 158; reprinted in the English edition with the same title (Jan. 1951):25, 84. Essay about Christmas. Published in anthology, G40.

C385 'First Writing'. *Mademoiselle* 32 (Jan. 1951):57, 117–20. Essay on the difficult, creative labor of learning to write.

C385.1 'Life in the Irish Counties'. *NYHTB* 27 (11 Feb. 1951):7. Review of *The Fire in the Dust*, Francis MacManus. MS, E77.

C386 'The Writer's Predicament'. *Now and Then* 83 (Spring 1951): 17. From a conversation with Jocelyn Brooke.

C387 'Autobiography as an Art'. *SatRev* 34 (17 Mar. 1951):9–10. Essay. Reprinted as 'Autobiography' in A25 (q.v.).

C388 'The Land Behind'. *Observer* (8 July 1951) Review of *Sheridan Le Fanu*, Nelson Browne. MS, E79.

C389 'The Cult of Nostalgia'. *Listener* 46 #1171 (9 Aug. 1951):225–26. Essay. Broadcast on BBC radio. MS, E80. Broadcast, F80.

C390 'So Much Depends'. *Woman's Day* 14 (Sept. 1951):72, 149–50, 152–60. Short story.

C391 'A Matter of Inspiration'. *SatRev* 34 (13 Oct. 1951):27–28, 64. Essay.

C392 'Books in General'. *New Statesman* 42 (20 Oct. 1951):438–39. Review of *Mr. Beluncle*, V. S. Pritchett.

C392.1 'The Fear of Pleasure'. *Adult Education* 24 (Winter 1951): 167–69. Address.

C393 'The Art of Respecting Boundaries'. *Vogue* 119 (1 Apr. 1952): 116–17. Essay. MS, E82. Published in anthology, G41.

C394 'Exploring Ireland'. *Observer* (4 May 1952):7. Review of *Wait Now!*, Rachel Knappett. MS, E84.

C395 'A City Growing'. *Observer* (18 May 1952):7. Review of *Dublin 1660–1860*, Maurice Craig. MS, E85.

C396 'Introduction'. *Chance: New Writing and Art* #1 (Oct. 1952): 6–7. Introduction to the opening number of *Chance*.

C397 'Ascendancy'. *Observer* (16 Nov. 1952):8. Review of *The Anglo Irish*, Brian Fitzgerald.

C398 'A Man and His Legend'. *Spectator* 189 (5 Dec. 1952):778. Review of *Arnold Bennett*, Reginald Pound. MS, E90.

C399 'The Search for a Story to Tell'. *NYTBR* 57 (14 Dec. 1952):1; *Harper's Bazaar* (English edition) 44 #3 (June 1953). Essay. Reprinted as 'The Roving Eye' in A25 (q.v.).

C399.1 'Three Novels by an English Writer with a Keen and Sardonic Eye', *NYHTB* 29 #27 (15 Feb. 1953):1, 8. Review of *Agents and Patients, Venusberg*, and *A Buyer's Market*, Anthony Powell.

C400 'In Spite of Words'. *New Republic* 128 (9 Mar. 1953):18–19. Review of *The Laughing Matter*, William Saroyan.

C401 'The Modern Novel and the Theme of Love'. *New Republic* 128 (11 May 1953):18–19. Review of *The Echoing Grove*, Rosamond Lehmann. Reprinted as 'The Echoing Grove' in A25 (q.v.).

C402 'Mind and Temperament'. *Spectator* 190 (22 May 1953):681. Review of *Ideas and Places*, Cyril Connolly.

C403 'The Sponge of the Present'. *SatRev* 36 (20 June 1953):11, 43–44. Essay. Reprinted as 'Sources of Influence' in A25 (q.v.).

C404 'An Enormous Channel of Expectation'. *Vogue* 122 (July 1953): 54–55. Essay on the coronation of Elizabeth in England.

C405 'The Informer'. *Observer* (19 July 1953):9. Review of *Witness*, Whittaker Chambers.

C405.1 'Teen-agers'. *Punch* 225 #5890 (19 Aug. 1953):226–27. Essay.

C406 'English Fiction at Mid-Century'. *New Republic* 129 (21 Sept. 1953):15–16. Essay. MS, E92. Published in anthology, G44.

C407 'Virtue of Optimism'. *House and Garden* 104 (Oct. 1953):151, 228. Essay.

C408 'The Art of Giving'. *Mademoiselle* 38 (Nov. 1953):74, 135–38; *Spectator* 191 (18 Dec. 1953):732–33. Essay. MS, E93.

C409 'Subject and Time'. *Proceedings, Second Series, Number 4: American Academy of Arts and Letters* (New York: National Institute of Arts and Letters with the Evangeline Wilbour Blashfield Foundation, 1954), 22–28.

C410 'One Man's Verdict on a War'. *T* (rev) 211 (20 Jan. 1954): 108, 111. *Nine Rivers from Jordan*, Denis Johnston; *The Blossoming Tree*, Betty Askwith; *The Child in Fashion*, Doris Lanby Moore; *The Rosy Pastor*, Nigel Fitzgerald.

C411 'Miss Macaulay Rifles a Treasure Chest'. *T* (rev) 211 (27 Jan. 1954):148, 158. *Pleasure of Ruin*, Rose Macaulay; *A Bed of Roses*, William Sansom; *Life Among the Savages*, Shirley Jackson; *Postmarked Moscow*, Lydia Kirk.

C412 'An X-Ray Is Turned on Dean Swift'. *T* (rev) 211 (3 Feb. 1954):188, 198. *I Live Under a Black Sun*, Edith Sitwell; *The General's Summer House*, Anthony Rhodes; *The Shame of New York*, Ed Reed; *Goodbye to Bacchus*, Vernon Charles.

C413 'The Dinner Party'. *London Magazine* 1 #1 (Feb. 1954):49–63; *Irish Writing* 27 (June 1954):5–17. Chapter five from *A World of Love* (A22).

C414 'The Badge of Courage'. *Parents Magazine* 29 (Feb. 1954):35. Essay.

C415 'A Film Magician's Testament'. *T* (rev) 211 (10 Feb. 1954): 230, 239. *Reflection on the Cinema*, M. René Clair; *The Death of Kings*,

Charles Westenbaker; *Thomas Hardy*, Evelyn Hardy; *The Alderman's Son*, Gerald Bullett.

C416 'Story of a Bloom in a Hothouse'. *T* (rev) 211 (17 Feb. 1954): 276, 288. *The Crooked Wall*, Faith Compton MacKenzie; *The Venetian Bride*, Magdalen King-Hall; *The Cretan Counterfeit*, Katherine Farrer; *The Right to Marry*, A. P. Herbert.

C417 'The Principle of Art Was Joy'. *NYTBR* 59 part 1 (21 Feb. 1954):1, 26. Review of *A Writer's Diary*, Virginia Woolf, ed. Leonard Woolf. Reprinted in A25 (q.v.).

C418 'Light on Newton'. *T* (rev) 211 (24 Feb. 1954):322, 332. *Sir Isaac Newton*, E. N. Da C. Andrade; *In Love*, Alfred Hayes; *Wine Growing in England*, George Ordish.

C418.1 'Disappointment'. *Family Doctor* 4 (Mar. 1954):145–46. Essay. MS, E95.

C419 'The New Tyranny'. *T* (rev) 211 (3 Mar. 1954):363, 376. *Tomorrow is Already Here*, Robert Jungk; *Fanfare for a Witch*, Vaughan Wilkins.

C420 'High Comedy in Tokyo'. *T* (rev) 211 (10 Mar. 1954):432, 453. *The Wise Bamboo*, J. Malcolm Morris; *Spinsters in Jeopardy*, Ngaio Marsh; *Portraits of Rivers*, ed. Eileen Molony.

C421 'Miss Mitford Studies the Pompadour'. *T* (rev) 211 (17 Mar. 1954):504–5. *Madame de Pompadour*, Nancy Mitford; *Black Argosy*, Mercedes Mackay; *The Laughing Matter*, William Saroyan.

C422 'Boy Who Stopped Bump in Night'. *T* (rev) 211 (27 Mar. 1954):559, 570. *Johnny Forsaken*, G. B. Stern; *The Flaw in the Crystal*, Godfrey Smith; *Leaving Home*, Elizabeth Janeway; *Borderline*, Vercors.

C423 'Historian's Holiday'. *T* (rev) 211 (31 Mar. 1954):607, 618. *A Layman's Love of Letters*, Dr. G. M. Trevelyan; *Honey Seems Bitter*, Benedict Kiely; *Little Heyday*, Hubert Nicholson.

C424 'Britain's Lure is Her Story'. *T* (rev) 212 (7 Apr. 1954):48. *Historic Britain*, ed. Graham Fisher and intro. John Pennington; *The Wars of Love*, Mark Schorer.

C425 'An Enchantress in Tweeds'. *T* (rev) 212 (14 Apr. 1954):118, 136. *The Tortoise and the Hare*, Elizabeth Jenkins; *Friends Apart: A Memoir of the Thirties*, Philip Toynbee; *Go Tell It on the Mountain*, James Baldwin; *Consult Your Pillow*, John Coates.

C426 'A Russian Patriot'. *T* (rev) 212 (21 Apr. 1954):171, 184. *Half a Life: The Reminiscences of a Russian Gentleman*, Count Benckendorff; *The Hidden Heart*, Jane Gillespie.

C427 'The Philosophy of Good Looks'. *T* (rev) 212 (28 Apr. 1954): 228, 232. *On Fair Vanity*, Betty Page; *Persia Is My Heart*, Najmeh Najafi; *Death of an Intruder*, Nedra Tyre.

C428 'Seeing History from Below'. *T* (rev) 212 (5 May 1954):303, 313. *Footman in Powder*, Helen Ashton; *The End of an Old Song*, J. D. Scott; *For Worse*, Angela Jeans; *My Name Is Celia*, Rayne Kruger.

C428.1 'What Jane Austen Means to Me'. *Everybody's Weekly* (10 May 1954):19, 39. Essay.

C429 'An Artist of the Air'. *T* (rev) 212 (12 May 1954):358, 374. *The New Men*, C. P. Snow; *Echoes*, Compton Mackenzie; *Just So Far*, Hardy Amies.

C430 'The Rocky Hill Tragedy'. *T* (rev) 212 (19 May 1954):414, 426. *Brothers to Dragons*, Robert Penn Warren; *Lord Nelson*, Carola Omen; *Mary Anne*, Daphne du Maurier; *Return Journey*, Barbara Goolden.

C431 'Doom Lurked in His Knapsack'. *T* (rev) 212 (26 May 1954): 464, 478. *Only Fade Away*, Bruce Marshall; *The Night of the Hunter*, Davis Grubb; *A Villa in Summer*, Penelope Mortimer.

C432 'Ireland'. *House and Garden* 105 (June 1954):92, 158. Essay.

C433 'The Labyrinth of Spain'. *T* (rev) 212 (2 June 1954):528, 546. *The Spanish Temper*, V. S. Pritchett; *Royal Purple*, D. A. Ponsonby; *A Rogue with Ease*, M. Argus; *The Narrowing Circle*, Julian Symons.

C434 'Two "Musical" Giants'. *T* (rev) 212 (9 June 1954):588, 604. *Bring on the Girls*, P. G. Wodehouse and Guy Bolton; *The Charm of Hours*, Peter Skelton; *A Bewilderment of Birds*, J. K. Stanford.

C435 'When the Legions Left India'. *T* (rev) 212 (16 June 1954):642,

656. *Bhowani Junction*, John Masters; *White House*, Jefferson Young; *Old Men Have Grey Beards*, Leopold Louth.

C436 'House-Party in Apulia'. *T* (rev) 212 (23 June 1954):694, 708. *Falling Stream*, Hester W. Chapman; *Under the Net*, Iris Murdoch; *The Strange Land*, Hammond Innes; *M for Mother*, Marjorie Riddell; *The One That Got Away*, Helen McCloy.

C437 'They Were All Guests in Ireland'. *T* (rev) 212 (30 June 1954): 740, 754. *The Stranger in Ireland*, Constantia Maxwell; *The Deserters*, Honor Tracy.

C438 'The Cheetah on the Hearth'. *T* (rev) 213 (7 July 1954):32, 46. *Married to Adventure*, Jule Mannix; *The World in the Evening*, Christopher Isherwood.

C439 'The Private Life of Robinson Crusoe'. *T* (rev) 213 (14 July 1954):76, 90. *Daniel Defoe*, Brian Fitzgerald; *A Wreath for the Enemy*, Pamela Frankau; *Murder at Midyears*, Marion Mainwaring.

C440 'The Beau Ideal of Essayists'. *T* (rev) 213 (21 July 1954):122–23. *Selected Essays by E. V. Lucas*, comp. H. N. Wethered; *What Did it Mean?*, Angela Thirkell; *According to the Evidence*, Henry Cecil.

C441 'Self-Portrait of a Rebel'. *T* (rev) 213 (28 July 1954):168, 180. *Half Term Report*, William Douglas Home; *Prison and Chocolate Cake*, Nayantara Sahgal; *Love From Elizabeth*, Mary Fitt; *The Light in the Forest*, Conrad Richter; *Chateaux of the Loire*, Vivian Rowe.

C442 'Italy with a Dash of Vinegar'. *T* (rev) 213 (4 Aug. 1954):206. *The Surprise of Cremona*, Edith Templeton; *The Four Seasons Cookery Book*, Robin Adair.

C443 'A Distinguished First Novel'. *T* (rev) 213 (11 Aug. 1954):246, 260. *The Governor's Wife*, David Unwin; *Lonely Pleasures*, Daniel George; *Voices in the House*, John Sedges; *A River Full of Stars*, Elizabeth Hamilton; *Patrick Campbell's Omnibus*, Patrick Campbell.

C444 'Tapestries of Travel in the Mind's Eye'. *T* (rev) 213 (18 Aug. 1954):290, 302. *The Four Continents*, Osbert Sitwell; *The Course of Love*, Rachel Trickett; *The Riddle of Samson*, Andrew Garve.

C445 'To What Far Bourne Oh Traveller?'. *T* (rev) 213 (25 Aug.

1954):334, 346. *Flight*, Evelyn Eaton; *A Kiss Before Dying*, Ira Levin; *My Mother-In-Law*, Celeste Andrews.

C446 'The Splendours of Edinburgh'. *T* (rev) 213 (1 Sept. 1954):374–75. *Edinburgh: Picturesque Notes*, Alvin Langdon Coburn; *Spare the Rod*, Michael Croft; *Water on the Brain*, Compton Mackenzie.

C447 'In Confidence from Miss Barrett'. *T* (rev) 213 (8 Sept. 1954): 418, 434. *Elizabeth Barrett to Miss Mitford: Letters Written 1836–1846* ed. Betty Miller; *A Shower of Summer Days*, May Sarton.

C448 'The Family Found a Wreck'. *T* (rev) 213 (15 Sept. 1954):496, 528. *Treasure Diving Holidays*, Jane and Barney Crick; *The Key That Rusts*, Isobel English; *Ill Met by Moonlight*, Michael Mac Liammóir; *The Wife of Robert Sheldon*, Patrick Quentin.

C449 'The Happy Four Lost Ladies'. *T* (rev) 213 (22 Sept. 1954): 572, 586. *The Wilder Shores of Love*, Leslie Blanch; *The White Wand*, L. P. Hartley; *The People in the Garden*, Lorna Wood.

C450 'Aftermath of Scandal'. *T* (rev) 213 (29 Sept. 1954):620, 636. *Son of Oscar Wilde*, Vyvyan Holland; *The Romantic Egoists*, Louis Auchincloss; *The Party at Number 5*, Shelley Smith; *The Cobweb*, William Gibson.

C451 'The Great Khan'. *T* (rev) 214 (6 Oct. 1954):44, 52. *Memoirs of Aga Khan*, Aga Khan; *The Narrowing Stream*, John Mortimer; *Yew Hall*, Lucy M. Boston; *Love of Seven Dolls*, Paul Gallico.

C452 'Genius of the Deep South'. *T* (rev) 214 (13 Oct. 1954):108, 116. *The Ponder Heart*, Eudora Welty; *A History of Courtship*, E. S. Turner; *Bella North*, Diana Marr-Johnson.

C453 'Searchlight on a Torturer'. *T* (rev) 214 (20 Oct. 1954):172. *A Bar of Shadow*, Laurens Van der Post; *The Feast of July*, H. E. Bates; *Mr. Hobb's Holiday*, Edward Streeter.

C454 'Miss Stark Reads a Code'. *T* (rev) 214 (27 Oct. 1954):238, 256. *Iona—A Quest*, Freya Stark; *Ben Nevis Goes East*, Compton Mackenzie; *The Centre of the Stage*, Gerald Sykes.

C455 'The Civilised Lord M.'. *T* (rev) 214 (3 Nov. 1954):294, 310. *The Young Melbourne*, David Cecil; *The Nightmare*, C. S. Forester;

Admiral on Horseback, Geoffrey Willans; *An Alligator Named Daisy*, Charles Terrot.

C456 'The Glorious Unregimented Woman'. *T* (rev) 214 (10 Nov. 1954):362–63. *The Queen's Countrywomen*, Godfrey Winn; *Hester Lilly*, Elizabeth Taylor; *The Black Swan*, Thomas Mann; *The Journal of Edwin Carp*, Richard Haydn.

C457 'Maugham on Valhalla'. *T* (rev) 214 (17 Nov 1954):430, 449. *Ten Novels and Their Authors*, Somerset Maugham; *Commando Extraordinary*, Charles Foley; *With Destination Unknown*, Agatha Christie.

C458 'Emergency in the Gothic Wing'. *Tatler* 214 (18 Nov. 1954): 18–19, 52. Short story.

C459 'Mrs. Siddons Reveal'd'. *T* (rev) 214 (24 Nov. 1954):494, 514. *Mrs. Siddons: Tragic Actress*, Yvonne Ffrench; *A Summer Night*, Alan Moorehead; *Dogs in Clover*, D. A. Ponsonby; *He Never Came Back*, Helen McCloy.

C460 'Star-Crossed Heroines'. *T* (rev) 214 (1 Dec. 1954):588. *Beyond the Glass*, Antonia White; *The Candle and the Light*, Hilda Vaughan.

C461 'Ancestor of Sir Winston'. *T* (rev) 214 (8 Dec. 1954):654, 672. *The Fabulous Leonard Jerome*, Anita Leslie; *The Fourteenth of October*, Bryher [Annie Winifred Ellerman].

C462 'Amanda the Glorious'. *T* (rev) 214 (15 Dec. 1954):712, 730. *O Rare Amanda*, Jack Loudan; *After the Flood*, Prince Constantine of Bavaria.

C463 'Mr. Balchin's Sorcery'. *T* (rev) 214 (22 Dec. 1954):758, 772. *Last Recollections of My Uncle Charles*, Nigel Balchin; *Queen Anne's Son*, Hester Chapman; *The Collected Poems of C. Day Lewis*.

C464 'A Free-Lance of Total War'. *T* (rev) 214 (29 Dec. 1954): 798–99. *Popski—A Life of Lt. Col. Vladimir Peniakoff*, John Willett; *Private View*, Jocelyn Brooke.

C465 'The Cloistered Fantastic'. *T* (rev) 215 (5 Jan. 1955):28, 44. *Lewis Carroll*, Derek Hudson; *Smith*, Kate Christie.

C466 'Montezuma's Mistake'. *T* (rev) 215 (12 Jan. 1955):72–73. *Cortés and Montezuma*, Maurice Collis; *Good Morning, Miss Dove*, Frances Gray Patton; *A Grand Man*, Catherine Cookson; *The House Is Falling*, Nigel Fitzgerald.

C467 'Commonsense on Burns'. *T* (rev) 215 (19 Jan. 1955):118–19. *Robert Burns*, Maurice Lindsay; *The Eye of Heaven*, Isabel Quigly; *A Kite's Dinner: Poems, 1938–1954*, Sheila Wingfield; *Go Lovely Rose*, Jean Potts.

C468 'Peter Pan's Creator'. *T* (rev) 215 (26 Jan. 1955):162, 174. *Portrait of Barrie*, Cynthia Asquith; *Glorious Life*, Derek Barton; *The Century of the Common Peer*, Lord Kinross; *Three Men Out*, Rex Stout.

C469 'Without Coffee, Cigarettes, or Feeling'. *Mademoiselle* 40 (Feb. 1955):174–75, 211–23. Essay about the youth in Germany.

C470 'Legacy of Scorpions'. *T* (rev) 215 (2 Feb. 1955):204–5, 220. *The Hidden River*, Storm Jameson; *The Bird's Nest*, Shirley Jackson; *We Are Utopia*, Stefan Andres; *The Story of Albert Schweitzer*, Jo Manton.

C471 'The Blindfold King'. *T* (rev) 215 (9 Feb. 1955):250–51, 266. *The King's Place*, C. V. Wedgwood; *The Spoor of Spooks*, Bergen Evans; *Stone Cold Dead in the Market*, Christopher Landon.

C472 'The Dry Stones Live'. *T* (rev) 215 (16 Feb. 1955):316, 318. *Still Digging*, Mortimer Wheeler; *Mother and Son*, Ivy Compton-Burnett; *Rainbow on the Road*, Esther Forbes.

C473 'Mr. Greene in Monaco'. *T* (rev) 215 (23 Feb. 1955):350–51. *Loser Takes All*, Graham Greene; *The Lakers*, Norman Nicholson; *Poems*, John Blanfords; *The House Is Falling*, Nigel Fitzgerald.

C474 'The Problem Mother'. *T* (rev) 215 (2 March 1955):398. *The Winds of Heaven*, Monica Dickens; *A Grand Man*, Catherine Cookson.

C475 'Mischief in Canada'. *T* (rev) 215 (9 March 1955):464–65. *Leaven of Malicy*, Robertson Davies; *The Figure in the Mist*, Elizabeth Coxhead; *Details of Jeremy Stretton*, Audrey Erskine Lindop.

C476 'War Overtakes a Cynic'. *T* (rev) 215 (16 March 1955):536,

554. *We Shall March Again*, Gerhard Kramer; *The Diary of an Ugly Duckling*, Marianne Becker; *The Novels of I. Compton-Burnett*, Robert Liddell; *Manuela*, William Woods.

C477 'The Rain It Raineth'. *T* (rev) 215 (23 March 1955):598–99. *The Moving Waters*, John Stuart Collis; *Vanquish the Angel*, Diana and Meir Gillon; *The Worcester Account*, S. N. Behrman.

C478 'A Goddess of Summer'. *T* (rev) 215 (30 March 1955):666, 684. *Georgiana*, ed. Earl of Bessborough; *The Treasures of Darkness*, Cornelia Jessey; *Death Walked in Berlin*, M. M. Kaye.

C479 'The Ambitious Raccoon'. *T* (rev) 216 (6 Apr. 1955):34–35, 52. *Dearest Bess*, Dorothy Margaret Stuart; *Milow's Daughter*, Mrs. Robert Henrey; *Brothers-in-Law*, Henry Cecil.

C480 'Candid Empress'. *T* (rev) 216 (13 Apr. 1955):98–99. *The Memoirs of Catherine the Great*, intro. Dr. G. P. Gooch; *Melilot*, Naomi Royde Smith; *Murder in France*, Alester Kershaw; *Good Morning, Miss Dove*, Frances Gray Patton; *Little Mallows*, Viola Bayley; *Famous Plays of 1954*.

C481 'Knell for a Traitor'. *T* (rev) 216 (20 Apr. 1955):158–59. *Not Honour More*, Joyce Cary; *Far Morning*, Edward Grierson; *Violent Saturday*, W. L. Heath; *A Corpse of the Old School*, Jack Ians.

C482 'The Poisoned Crown'. *T* (rev) 216 (27 Apr. 1955):212, 230. *Bavarian Fantasy*, Desmond Chapman-Huston; *Requiem for a Wren*, Nevil Shute; *Little Cabbages*, George Mikes; *Invitation to Murder*, Leslie Ford.

C483 'Wink of the Sphinx'. *T* (rev) 216 (4 May 1955):286–87, 314. *The Picnic at Sakkara*, P. H. Newby; *Russian Roulette*, Anthony Bloomfield; *The Try-Out*, John Wiles; *Windows in a Vanished Time*, Gerald Bullett; *Moonraker*, Ian Fleming.

C484 'Evolution of a Warrior'. *T* (rev) 216 (11 May 1955):362–63. *Going to the Wars*, John Verney; *Enter Sir Robert*, Angela Thirkell; *I'll Cry Tomorrow*, Lillian Roth; *Rake Rochester*, Charles Norman.

C485 'Why Crime Does Not Pay'. *T* (rev) 216 (18 May 1955):416–17. *Cloak Without Dagger*, Percy Sillitoe; *A Difficult Young Man*, Martin Boyd.

C486 'Mr. Campion Rusticates'. *T* (rev) 216 (25 May 1955):468–69. *The Beckoning Lady,* Margery Allingham; *Rossano,* Gordon Lett.

C487 'Novelist with a Grand Design'. *T* (rev) 216 (1 June 1955): 532–33. *The Acceptance World,* Anthony Powell; *Scales of Justice,* Ngaio Marsh; *Bonjour Tristesse,* Françoise Sagan; *Lost Girls,* Caroline Brown.

C488 'Endurance in the Snows'. *T* (rev) 216 (8 June 1955):594–95. *We Die Alone,* David Howarth; *This Charming Pastime,* Edith Templeton; *The Gentle House,* Anna Perrott Rose; *The Case of the Six Mistresses,* Brigid Maxwell.

C489 'The Nonsense-Mongers'. *T* (rev) 216 (15 June 1955):646–47. *The Oracles,* Margaret Kennedy; *Evidence for the Crown,* Molly Lefebure; *Canal in Moonlight,* Kathleen Sully.

C490 'Twenties Treasure-Hunt'. *T* (rev) 216 (22 June 1955):694–95. *Fools of Choice,* Peter de Polnay; *Sea of Glass,* Dennis Parry; *Fatal in My Fashion,* Pat McGerr.

C491 'Swashbuckler in India'. *T* (rev) 216 (29 June 1955):743, 754. *Coromandel,* John Masters; *The Regoville Match,* David Walker; *The Basque Country,* Vivian Rowe: *The Second Miracle,* Peter Greave.

C492 'Sharp Whiff of Grapeshot'. *T* (rev) 217 (6 July 1955):30, 44. *Officers and Gentlemen,* Evelyn Waugh; *Thirty Years,* John P. Marquand; *The Singular Hope,* Elizabeth Sewell; *Grand Prix Murder,* Douglas Rutherford.

C493 'Builder of the Northern Wall'. *T* (rev) 217 (13 July 1955):76–77. *Memoirs of Hadrian,* Marguerite Yourcenar; *A Rose for Winter,* Laurie Lee; *Vamp Till Ready,* Terry Rieman.

C494 'A Master Satirist'. *T* (rev) 217 (20 July 1955):120. *Hogarth's Progress,* Peter Quennell; *By Invitation Only,* Felicien Marceau; *James By The Grace of God,* Hugh Rose Williamson.

C495 'Huxley Rides Again'. *T* (rev) 217 (27 July 1955):164–65. *The Genius and the Goddess,* Aldous Huxley; *The Temptation of Roger Heriott,* Edward Newhouse; *Thérèse Raquin,* Émile Zola, trans. Philip G. Downs.

C496 'English Lips Unsealed'. *T* (rev) 217 (3 Aug. 1955):206–7. *Exploring English Character*, Geoffrey Gorer; *The Sandwiches Are Waiting*, Jane McClure; *The Title's My Own*, David Eames.

C497 'Devil in the Pulpit'. *T* (rev) 217 (10 Aug. 1955):246–47. *Messiah*, Gore Vidal; *Danger Ahead*, Georges Simenon; *No True Life*, Miriam Blanco-Fombona; *Death of a Godmother*, John Rhode; *Change Here for Babylon*, Nina Bawden.

C498 'Conqueror of the Infidels'. *T* (rev) 217 (17 Aug. 1955):288–89, 301. *The Grand Captain*, Gerald de Gaury; *Living in the Present*, John Wain; *Come Fill the Cup*, Rosalind Wade.

C499 'A Prospect of Ireland'. *T* (rev) 217 (24 Aug. 1955):330, 343. *The Crying of the Wind*, Ithell Colquhoun; *The Capri Letters*, Mario Soldati; *Draughts in the Sun*, Richard Parker; *Maigret and the Young Girl*, Georges Simenon.

C500 'Memoirs of a Strolling Player'. *T* (rev) 217 (31 Aug. 1955): 370, 383. *Too Late to Lament*, Maurice Brown; *Trumpets Over Merriford*, Reginald Arkell; *Hell's Pavement*, Josephine Bell.

C501 'An African Boyhood'. *T* (rev) 217 (7 Sept. 1955):416, 434. *In the Dark Child*, Camara Laye; *That Uncertain Feeling*, Kingsley Amis; *Keep Him My Country*, Mary Durack; *Major Thompson Lives in France*, Pierre Daninos.

C502 'The Graf Spee's Jackal'. *T* (rev) 217 (14 Sept. 1955):494, 519. *The Navy's Here*, Willi Frischauer and Robert Jackson; *Change Here For Babylon*, Nina Bawden; *Tour de Force*, Christianna Brand.

C503 'Mental Annuity'. *Vogue* 126 (15 Sept. 1955):108–9. Essay.

C504 'The Man Who Had Everything'. *T* (rev) 217 (21 Sept. 1955): 570–71. *The Fall of the Sparrow*, Nigel Balchin; *To Whom She Will*, R. Prawer Jhabvala; *Angels and Space Ships*, Frederic Brown; *Walled City*, Mary Dunstan.

C505 'Life with Mother'. *T* (rev) 217 (28 Sept. 1955):620, 638. *To the One I Love Best*, Ludwig Bemelmans; *The Chrysalids*, John Wyndham; *Angel with a Sword*, Oriel Malet.

C506 'A Day in the Dark'. *Botteghe Oscure* 16 (Autumn 1955):85–94;

Mademoiselle 45 (July 1957):30–35; *Argosy* 18 #9 (Sept. 1957):55–62. Short story. Reprinted in A28 (q.v.).

C507 'A Vignette of Village Life'. *T* (rev) 218 (5 Oct. 1955):34–35. *Village School,* Miss Read (pseud.); *The Vicarious Years,* John Van Druten; *The Man with Two Wives,* Patrick Quentin.

C508 'Wasp Waists in Calcutta'. *T* (rev) 218 (12 Oct. 1955):102, 122. *Golden Interlude,* Janet Dunbar; *The Guardians,* J. I. M. Stewart.

C509 'Crisis at Larjuzon'. *T* (rev) 218 (19 Oct. 1955):178–79, 196. *The Lamb,* François Mauriac; *Dates and Parties,* Christopher Sykes; *The Stepmother,* R. C. Hutchinson.

C510 'A Poet's Chronicle'. *T* (rev) 218 (26 Oct. 1955):244–45. *The Whispering Gallery,* John Lehmann; *The Enormous Shadow,* Robert Harling.

C511 'The Dollar's Two Sides'. *T* (rev) 218 (2 Nov. 1955):300, 316. *Journey Down a Rainbow,* J. B. Priestley and Jacquetta Hawkes; *H. M. S. Ulysses,* Alistair MacLean; *A Song to Sing—O!,* Winifred Lawson.

C512 'A Sister Remembers'. *T* (rev) 218 (9 Nov. 1955):370–71, 392. *The Life of Kathleen Ferrier,* Winifred Ferrier; *The Threshold,* Dorothea Rutherford; *The Chelsea Rainbow,* Charles Terrot; *A Tigress on the Hearth,* Margery Sharp.

C513 'The Claimant'. *Vogue* 126 (15 Nov. 1955):122–23, 167–68; *Argosy* 17 #1 (Jan. 1956):23–29. Short story. Published in anthology, G46.

C514 'Adventure Story'. *T* (rev) 218 (16 Nov. 1955):442–43. *The Young Winston Churchhill,* John Marsh; *New Poems, 1955,* Patric Dickinson, J. C. Hall, and Erica Mark.

C515 'The Terrible Conflict'. *T* (rev) 218 (23 Nov. 1955):504–5, 524. *The Dark Eye in Africa,* Laurens Van der Post; *Roman Wall,* Bryher [Annie Winifred Ellerman]; *My Bones and My Flute,* Edgar Mittelholzer; *The Unquiet Spirit,* Marguerite Stein; *Majollika and Company,* Wolf Mankowitz.

C516 'A Master of Surprise'. *T* (rev) 218 (30 Nov. 1955):564–65,

584. *A Perfect Woman*, L. P. Hartley; *A Murder in Paradise*, Richard Gehman; *Pantomime Christmas*, Hilda Hewett.

C517 'Home for Christmas'. *Mademoiselle* 42 (Dec. 1955):57, 120–23. Essay. Published in anthology, G47.

C518 'The Gift That Speaks'. *Tatler* 218 (7 Dec. 1955):660. A listing of various opportunities for Christmas book buying.

C519 'The Dear Little Children'. *T* (rev) 218 (14 Dec. 1955):726–27. *Christmas with the Savages*, Mary Clive; *Aspects of Love*, David Garnett.

C520 'Portrait of an Innocent'. *T* (rev) 218 (21 Dec. 1955):772–73. *Deliverance*, L. A. G. Strong; *More for Your Garden*, V. Sackville-West.

C521 'Savage Masterpiece'. *T* (rev) 218 (28 Dec. 1955):812, 826. *The Quiet American*, Graham Greene; *Sincerely Willis Wade*, John P. Marquand; *Ludmila*, Paul Gallico.

C522 'Poetess of the Oceans'. *T* (rev) 219 (4 Jan. 1956):24–25. *The Sea Around Us*, Rachel Carson; *The Submarine Child*, James Kenward; *Triple Quest*, E. R. Punshon.

C523 'Criminal in the Family'. *T* (rev) 219 (11 Jan. 1956):64–65. *Thicker Than Water*, Frank Tilsey; *Good Morning, Miss Dove*, Frances Gray Patton.

C524 'The Prince of Dogdom'. *T* (rev) 219 (18 Jan. 1956):104–5. *Thurber's Days*, James Thurber; *For All We Know*, G. B. Stern.

C525 'Despatches from France'. *T* (rev) 219 (25 Jan. 1956):146–47. *Letters from Madame de Sévigné*, trans. Violet Hammersley; *Old Father Antic*, Barbara Worsley-Gough.

C526 'Antiquarian's Log'. *T* (rev) 219 (1 Feb. 1956):192–93. *Antique Dealer*, R. P. Way; *A Tangled Web*, Nicholas Blake.

C527 'The House of Hornbeam'. *T* (rev) 219 (8 Feb. 1956):232. *The Half-Crown House*, Helen Ashton.

C528 'Child of the Rectory'. *T* (rev) 219 (15 Feb. 1956):274. *Spam Tomorrow*, Verily Anderson; *The Dinner Party*, Gretch Finletter.

C529 'Coming to London . . . VI'. *London Magazine* 3 #3 (March 1956):49–53. Published in anthology. G48.

C530 'For the Feminine Shopper'. *Holiday* 19 (Apr. 1956):90–91, 129, 131–32. Essay.

C531 'Essence of Ireland'. *T* (rev) 220 (11 Apr. 1956):70–71. *The Patriot Son*, Mary Lavin; *Rox Hall Illuminated*, Phyllis Paul; *Harold in London*, Kate Christie.

C532 'Small Island—Big Novel'. *T* (rev) 220 (18 Apr. 1956):140–41. *Island in the Sun*, Alec Waugh; *No Coward Soul*, Noël Adeney; *Old Hall, New Hall*, Michael Innes; *Collins Pocket Guide to Wild Flowers*, David McClintock and R. S. R. Fitter; *The Long Body*, Helen McCloy; *Fair Haven*, E. M. Almedinger.

C533 'The Prisoner of Chilben'. *T* (rev) 220 (25 Apr. 1956):220. *The Summer House*, Rosemary Harris; *A Contest of Ladies*, William Sansom.

C534 'The Niece of Bonaparte'. *T* (rev) 220 (2 May 1956):280. *Princess Mathilde*, Marguerite Castillon du Perron; *The Paradise Garden*, Michael Swan; *Beauty Belongs to You*, Jean Grey.

C535 'Mr. Llewellyn Examines a Traitor'. *T* (rev) 220 (9 May 1956): 328–29. *Mr. Hamish Gleave*, Richard Llewellyn; *Enchanted Bellamy*, Cyril Hughes Hartmann; *Minerva*, intro. A. W. P. Robertson.

C536 'The Respectable at Bay'. *T* (rev) 220 (16 May 1956):380–81. *A View of the Heath*, David Unwin; *Beyond the Black Stump*, Nevil Shute; *Noblesse Oblige*, ed. Nancy Mitford; *The Megstone Plot*, Andrew Garve; *A High-Pitched Buzz*, Roger Longrigg.

C536.1 'Out of the World of Dickens Comes This Memoir of a Bitter Childhood'. *NYHTB* 32 #41 (20 May 1956):3. Review of *A Cornish Waif's Story: An Autobiography*, Emma Smith.

C537 'An Odyssey of the Footlights'. *T* (rev) 220 (23 May 1956): 432–33. *Les Girls*, Constance Tomkinson; *The Five Fathers of Pepi*, Ira Avaery; *The Prince and Petronella*, John Brophy.

C538 'Master of the Sardonic'. *T* (rev) 220 (30 May 1956):484. *Anglo-Saxon Attitudes*, Angus Wilson; *Collected Stories*, V. S. Pritchett.

C539 'A Powerful Study in Destiny'. *T* (rev) 220 (6 June 1956):538. *Band of Angels*, Robert Penn Warren; *She, the Accused*, Maurice Moiseiwitsch.

C540 'Mankowitz Rings the Bell'. *T* (rev) 220 (13 June 1956):597. *My Old Man's a Dustman*, Wolf Mankowitz; *The Sleepless Moon*, H. E. Bates.

C541 'A Caustic Comedy of the Highlands'. *T* (rev) 220 (20 June 1956):648–49, 662. *Marching with April*, Hugho Charteris; *Eighteenth Century Story*, Magdalen King-Hall; *The Second Man*, Edward Grierson; *Where the Turk Trod*, Anthony Rhodes; *Never Too Late*, Angela Thirkell.

C542 'Dwellers in the Wilderness'. *T* (rev) 220 (27 June 1956):696–97. *The Outsider*, Colin Wilson; *The Mermaids*, Eva Boros.

C543 'How to Be Yourself, But Not Eccentric'. *Vogue* 128 (July 1956):54–55. Essay with a brief biographical sketch appended.

C544 'Suspense in the Air'. *T* (rev) 221 (4 July 1956):32–33. *The Proving Flight*, David Beaty; *Roman Mornings,* James Lees-Milne; *Trick of the Sun*, John St. John; *Unhallowed House*, D. A. Ponsonby.

C545 'The Laird Who Went to War'. *T* (rev) 221 (11 July 1956):82, 97. *Freshly Remembered*, Cecil Aspinall-Oglander; *A Single Pebble*, John Hersey.

C546 'A Stranger in the Midst'. *T* (rev) 221 (18 July 1956):132–33. *Thin Ice*, Sir Compton Mackenzie; *Six Feet of the Country*, Nadine Gordimer; *Collins Guide to Roses*, Bertram Park.

C547 'The Silver Cord That Strangles'. *T* (rev) 221 (25 July 1956): 178, 199. *The Secret River*, C. H. B. Kitchin; *Letters From a Portuguese Nun*, trans. Lucy Norton; *Time Right Deadly*, Sarah Grainham.

C548 'Some Horrors of Childhood II: On Not Rising to the Occasion'. *Listener* 56 (26 July 1956):121–22; *Vogue* 129 (15 Feb. 1957):124–25. Essay on the introspective questionings of childhood. MS, E97. Broadcast, F85.

C549 'A Notebook for Posterity'. *T* (rev) 221 (1 Aug. 1956):222, 237. *My Aunt's Rhinoceros*, Peter Fleming; *Comfort Me With Apples*, Peter De Vries; *The Solitary Child*, Nina Bawden; *The Sleeping Partner*, Winston Graham; *Maalish*, Jean Cocteau.

C550 'A Tragedy of Sensibility'. *T* (rev) 221 (8 Aug. 1956):266–67. *Schumann and The Romantic Age*, Marcel Brion; *The Night-Comers*, Eric Ambler; *Peter Perry*, Michael Campbell.

C551 'The Impossible Happened'. *T* (rev) 221 (15 Aug. 1956):310–11, 325. *A Night to Remember*, Walter Lord; *The Truth Will Not Help Us*, John Bowen; *A Young Girl's Touch*, Barbara Skelton.

C552 'Suspense on Three Levels'. *T* (rev) 221 (22 Aug. 1956):352. *Three Winters*, John Mortimer; *Sunk Island*, Hubert Nicholson; *The October Country*, Ray Bradbury.

C553 'Testing Ground for Schoolmasters'. *T* (rev) 221 (29 Aug. 1956):394–95. *The New Headmaster*, Alan Ker; *And the Rain My Drink*, Hans Suyin; *A Certain Smile*, Françoise Sagan.

C554 'Childhood through a Magnifying Glass'. *T* (rev) 221 (5 Sept. 1956):440–41. *Morning*, Julian Fane; *The State of Mind*, Mark Schorer; *The Nightwalkers*, B. Cross.

C555 'A Virtuoso Novelist'. *T* (rev) 221 (12 Sept. 1956):492–93. *The Towers of Trebizond*, Rose Macaulay; *The Little Laundress and the Fearful Knight*, Bertram Bloch and George Shanks; *The Diehard*, Jean Potts.

C556 'Mr. Snow Anatomizes Matrimony'. *T* (rev) 221 (19 Sept. 1956):546–47. *Homecomings*, C. P. Snow; *Some Darling Folly*, Monica Sterling.

C557 'The Unraveling of an Ancient Knot'. *T* (rev) 221 (26 Sept. 1956):622–23, 655. *The Dark of Summer*, Erik Linklater; *G. M.: Memories of George Moore*, Nancy Cunard; *The Penguin Story*, Sir William Emrys Williams; *Drum*, Anthony Sampson.

C558 'Twilight of the Air Gods'. *T* (rev) 222 (3 Oct. 1956):30–31. *Falling Leaves*, Gird Gaiser; *The Haunted Land*, Randolph Snow; *The Bright Prison*, Penelope Mortimer.

C559   'The Byronic Legend'. *T* (rev) 222 (10 Oct. 1956):94–95. *Byron,* Eileen Bigland; *His Saving Face,* Pierre Boulle; *Remember the House,* Santha Rama Rau.

C560   'A Bundle of Letters'. *T* (rev) 222 (17 Oct. 1956):164–65. *The Hungry Leopard,* Mary Borden; *T'Other Miss Austen,* Kathleen Freeman.

C561   'The Mouse Who Succeeded a Mountain'. *T* (rev) 222 (24 Oct. 1956):226–27. *Louis XV,* G. P. Gooch; *Here Be Dragons,* Stella Gibbon; *The Man in the Net,* Patrick Quentin.

C562   'Truth and Fiction'. *Listener* 56 #1439, #1440, #1441 (25 Oct., 1 Nov., 8 Nov. 1956):651–52, 704–6, 751–52. Three-part essay on the novel: 1 'Story, Theme, and Situation'; 2 'People: the Creation of Character'; 3 'Time, Period, and Reality'. Originally a series of radio talks on BBC. Reprinted in A25 (q.v.).

C563   'Off the Map in Spain'. *T* (rev) 222 (31 Oct. 1956):278, 294. *Descent from Burgos,* Peter de Polnay; *Eldorado Jane,* Phyllis Bottome; *Cartoon Treasury,* ed. Lucy Black Johnson and Pike Johnson Jr.; *Sweetbread and Other Stories,* Michelle Maurois.

C564   'The New Dickens' London'. *T* (rev) 222 (7 Nov. 1956):338. *The Angel in the Corner,* Monica Dickens.

C565   'Lord Gorell's Own Story'. *T* (rev) 222 (14 Nov. 1956):400. *One Man. . . Many Parts,* Lord Gorell; *Breakfast with a Corpse,* Max Murray.

C566   'Inside the Vicarage'. *T* (rev) 222 (21 Nov. 1956):456–57. *Picture A Country Vicarage,* Anthony Brode; *The One That Got Away,* Kendal Burt and James Leasor; *Springtime,* H. B. Morton; *Twelve Horses and the Hangman's Noose,* Gladys Mitchell.

C567   'Mr. Sansom's New Novel'. *T* (rev) 222 (28 Nov. 1956):508. *The Loving Eye,* William Sansom.

C568   'A Living Writer'. *Cornhill* 169 #1010 (Winter 1956–1957): 120–34. This article is from an Introduction to Katherine Mansfield's stories (B29). Reprinted as Preface to *'Stories by Katherine Mansfield'* in A25 (q.v.).

C569 'Trio of Mysteries'. *T* (rev) 222 (5 Dec. 1956):597. *Madame Solario*, anon.; *Dead Man's Folly*, Agatha Christie; *The China Roundabout*, Jan Austen.

C569.1 'A Haunting, Enchanting Story Set in Budapest', *NYHTB* 33 #18 (9 Dec. 1956):1, 16. Review of *The Mermaids*, Eva Boros.

C570 'The Highway Story'. *T* (rev) 222 (12 Dec. 1956):652–53. *The Rolling Road*, L. A. G. Strong; *The Intruder*, Storm Jameson.

C571 'Conquerors in the Hardest Battle'. *T* (rev) 222 (19 Dec. 1956): 702–3. *Conquest of Disability*, ed. Ian Fraser; *Les Belles Amours*, Louise de Vilmorin, trans. Francis Wyndham.

C572 'Cousin-Hunt in Africa'. *T* (rev) 222 (26 Dec. 1956):744–45. *The Lighthearted Quest*, Ann Bridge; *Out of Season*, Spike Hughes.

C573 "Guide to the Future, for Those Setting Out'. *T* (rev) 223 (2 Jan. 1957): 24–25. *Jobs and Careers*, Tony Gibson; *A Sky-Blue Life*, Maurice Moiseiwitsch; *Pleasure Garden*, Brian Hill; *The Bright Blue Sky*, John Symonds.

C574 'Turgenev the Master'. *T* (rev) 223 (9 Jan. 1957):66–67. *First Love*, Ivan Turgenev, trans. Isaiah Berlin; *The Compassionate Lady*, H. Joyce Blackley; *Potter on America*, Stephen Potter; *Did It Happen*, anonymous collection of short stories.

C575 'A Scent of Red Roses in the By-Street'. *T* (rev) 223 (16 Jan. 1957):108–9. *The Eye of Love*, Margery Sharp; *Merry Christmas, Mr. Baxter*, Edward Streeter.

C576 'Knavery at Essex'. *T* (rev) 223 (23 Jan. 1957):150–51. *Country Copper*, G. H. Totterdell; *Lines of Life*, François Mauriac, trans. Gerard Hopkins.

C577 'Source of Greatness'. *T* (rev) 223 (30 Jan. 1957):198–99. *The Early Churchills*, A. L. Rowse; *Off with His Head*, Ngaio Marsh; *Baby Doll*, Tennessee Williams.

C578 'Novel That Handsomely Repays a Long Wait'. *T* (rev) 223 (6 Feb. 1957):246–47. *The Fountain Overflows*, Rebecca West; *The Sacrifice*, Georges Simenon.

C579 'Dreyfus Revisited'. *T* (rev) 223 (13 Feb. 1957):290–91. *My Secret Diary of the Dreyfus Case*, Maurice Paléologue.

C580 'A Gale-Force Talent'. *T* (rev) 223 (20 Feb. 1957):334–35. *The Other Traveller*, N. Brysson Morrison; *Good Relations*, Derek Barton; *The Talented Mr. Ripley*, Patricia Highsmith.

C581 'Belloc to the Life'. *T* (rev) 223 (27 Feb. 1957):380–81. *The Life of Hilaire Belloc*, Robert Speaight; *The Happy Ones*, Maurice Edelman.

C582 'Secret of a Poetess'. *T* (rev) 223 (6 March 1957):440–41. *The Heroes of Clove*, Margaret Kennedy; *Gulf Coast Stories*, Erskine Caldwell; *Borrow the Night*, Helen Nielsen.

C583 'Mr. Morgan's New Novel'. *T* (rev) 223 (13 March 1957):500–1. *Challenge to Venus*, Charles Morgan; *Difficult to Die*, Jean Matheson.

C584 'Light on the Dark Ladies of History'. *T* (rev) 223 (20 March 1957):550–51. *Dark Ladies*, Ivor Brown; *The Ram in the Thicket*, Anthony Glyn.

C585 'An Artist-Watcher Sends in His Report'. *T* (rev) 223 (27 March 1957):602–3. *From Renoir to Picasso*, Michel Georges-Michel; *All a Nonsense*, Mark Bence-Jones.

C586 'Persuasion'. *London Magazine* 4 #4 (Apr. 1957):47–51. Essay about Jane Austen and her novel *Persuasion*. MS, E100.

C587 'Whirlwind Tour with Clare Sheridan'. *T* (rev) 224 (3 Apr. 1957):28–29. *To the Four Winds*, Clare Sheridan; *The Friend in Need*, Elizabeth Coxhead.

C588 'Baron the Unforgettable'. *T* (rev) 224 (10 Apr. 1957):88, 102. *Baron*, Baron [Baron Stirling Henry Nahum]; *Room at the Top*, John Braine; *The Lady and the Unicorn*, Rumer Godden.

C589 'Novelists of Gaul'. *T* (rev) 224 (17 Apr. 1957):155. *Jacob*, Jean Cabriés; *The Last Detachment*, Maurice Druon; *Beau Clown*, Berthe Grimault; *First Poems*, Minori Drouet.

C590 'Countryside of Poets'. *T* (rev) 224 (24 Apr. 1957):214–15.

Poets in a Landscape, Gilbert Highet; *The Day the Money Stopped*, Brendan Gill.

C591 'Bright Young Days'. *T* (rev) 224 (1 May 1957):272–73. *The Twenties*, John Montgomery; *Without Love*, Gerald Hanley.

C592 'An English Master of the Novella'. *T* (rev) 224 (8 May 1957): 328–29. *Death of a Huntsman*, H. E. Bates; *James Joyce's World*, Patricia Hutchins; *From Russia with Love*, Ian Fleming.

C593 'Haunting Variation on an Ageless Theme'. *T* (rev) 224 (15 May 1957):378–79. *The Sandcastle*, Iris Murdoch; *Complete and Free*, Eric Williams.

C594 'Return to Africa'. *T* (rev) 224 (22 May 1957):430–31. *Going Home*, Doris Lessing; *Morgan*, Kate Christie; *Two-Thirds of a Ghost*, Helen McCloy.

C595 'The Dynamic Abbess Was No Saint'. *T* (rev) 224 (29 May 1957):480–81. *The Reluctant Abbess*, Margaret Trouncer; *The Gilded Fly*, Hamilton Macallister; *How to be a Deb's Mum*, Petronella Portobello.

C596 'The Hiss of the Sword'. *T* (rev) 224 (5 June 1957):538–39. *Invasion 1940*, Peter Fleming; *A Time to Keep Silence*, Patrick Leigh Fermor.

C597 'Literary Evil Genius'. *T* (rev) 224 (12 June 1957):592–3. *The Thing Desired*, Lalage Pulvertoft; *The Prodigy*, Hermann Hesse, trans. W. J. Strachan.

C598 'Outspoken Grief'. *T* (rev) 224 (19 June 1957):640–41. 656. *Leftover Life to Kill*, Caitlin Thomas; *The Great World and Timothy Colt*, Louis Auchincloss; *Collected Stories*, Viola Meynell.

C599 'Edwardian Lioness'. *T* (rev) 224 (26 June 1957):688. *Angel*, Elizabeth Taylor; *Our Square*, Verily Anderson.

C600 'A Writer Remembers'. *T* (rev) 225 (3 July 1957):26–27. *The Widening Circle*, John Van Druten; *Seven Times Seven*, G. B. Stern; *End Without Glory*, Richard Viner.

C601 'Five Star Thriller'. *T* (rev) 225 (10 July 1957):72–73. *Stop-over: Tokyo*, John P. Marquand; *The Bystander*, Randolph Stow.

C602 EB Reviews. 225 (17 July 1957):118–19. *Testament of Experience*, Vera Brittain; *The Innocent Gunman*, Jean Paul Lacroix; *Furnished for Murder*, Elizabeth Ferrars.

C603 'Leadbitter's Folly'. *T* (rev) 225 (24 July 1957):162–63. *The Hireling*, L. P. Hartley; *The Mendelman Fire*, Wolf Mankowitz; *The Claimant*, Michael Gilbert.

C604 'Mr. Waugh's Ordeal'. *T* (rev) 225 (31 July 1957):208–9. *The Ordeal of Gilbert Pinfold*, Evelyn Waugh; *Far, Far the Mountain Peak*, John Masters; *Churchill: The Statesman and Writer*, Joaquim Paço; *Independent Education: In Defense of the Public Schools*, A. N. Gilkes.

C605 'The Uncommon Reader'. *T* (rev) 225 (7 Aug. 1957):252–53. *The Fine Art of Reading*, David Cecil; *The Called and the Chosen*, Monica Baldwin; *The Short Reign of Pippin IV*, John Steinbeck.

C606 'With the Theosophists'. *T* (rev) 225 (14 Aug. 1957):294–95. *Candles in the Sun*, Emily Luytens; *My Husband Cartwright*, Olivia Manning.

C607 'Interlude in Paris'. *T* (rev) 225 (21 Aug. 1957):338–39. *Jam Today*, Oriel Malet; *The Success of Margot Masters*, Helen Howe; *Paper Dolls*, Laura Beheler.

C608 'Millionaire Queen of New York'. *T* (rev) 225 (28 Aug. 1957): 382–83. *The Vanderbilt Feud*, Grace Wilson Vanderbilt; *A Father and His Fate*, I. Compton-Burnett.

C609 'The Candid Friend'. *T* (rev) 225 (4 Sept. 1957):432–33. *A Regency Visitor*, Prince Puckler-Muskau; *Strange Evil*, Jane Gaskell.

C610 'Savoury Strategems'. *T* (rev) 225 (11 Sept. 1957):482–83. *Thoughts for Food*, Cecily Finn and Joan O'Connor; *The Double*, F. Dostoevsky, trans. George Bird; *The Soft Talkers*, Margaret Millar.

C611 'Knife That Reprieves the Condemned'. *T* (rev) 225 (18 Sept. 1957):534–35. *Surgery and Crime*, George Sava; *Rockets Galore*, Compton Mackenzie.

C612 'From Brighton to Beauregard'. *T* (rev) 225 (25 Sept. 1957): 604–5. *Miss Howard and Her Emperor*, Simone Maurois; *City of Spades*, Colin MacInness.

C613 'The Waxen Image'. *T* (rev) 226 (2 Oct. 1957):32–33. *I, Madame Tussaud*, Sylvia Martin; *A Daughter for a Fortnight*, Mrs. Robert Henrey; *The Sky Above the Roof*, Paul Verlaine (trans. Brian Hill).

C614 'A Persian Journey'. *T* (rev) 226 (9 Oct. 1957):86–87. *A Persian Spring*, Wilfrid Blunt; *The Rich Die Hard*, Beverley Nichols; *Actress*, Yvonne Mitchell.

C615 'A Lifelong Attachment'. *T* (rev) 226 (16 Oct. 1957):150–51. *George Moore: Letters 1895–1933 to Lady Cunard*, ed. Rupert Hart-Davis; *Search Me*, Patrick Anderson.

C616 'Cracks across the Victorian Facade'. *T* (rev) 226 (23 Oct. 1957):210–11. *Cousin Harriet*, Susan Tweedsmuir; *The Elegant Edwardian*, Ursula Bloom; *Aubade*, Kenneth Martin.

C617 'Invitation to Dance'. *T* (rev) 226 (30 Oct. 1957):262, 276. *Come Dance with Me*, Ninette de Valois; *Minku and Curdy*, Antonia White.

C618 'Tarnished Youth'. *T* (rev) 226 (6 Nov. 1957):328–29. *Those without Shadows*, Françoise Sagan; *The Lonely Woman*, Gerda Rhoads; *The Twenty-Third Man*, Gladys Mitchell.

C619 'A Romance of the Past'. *T* (rev) 226 (13 Nov. 1957):398–99. *Voltaire in Love*, Nancy Mitford; *Victorian Days*, Clodah Anson; *Love Story*, Louise de Vilmorin; *The Golden Impala*, Pamela Ropner.

C620 'Tumult in Mississippi'. *T* (rev) 226 (20 Nov. 1957): 458–59. *The Voice at the Back Door*, Elizabeth Spencer; *Over Seventy*, P. G. Wodehouse; *In Sugar for the Horse*, H. E. Bates; *Rachel Weeping*, Shelley Smith.

C621 'The Temperament of Genius'. *T* (rev) 226 (27 Nov. 1957): 510–11. *Gilbert: His Life and Strife*, Hesketh Pearson; *Alfred Hitchcock Presents*, Alfred Hitchcock; *Dublin Phoenix*, Olivia Robertson; *Say Darling*, Richard Bissell.

C622 'The Virtuoso Touch'. *T* (rev) 226 (5 Dec. 1957):598, 600. *At Lady Molly's,* Anthony Powell; *A Measure of Love,* Iris Origo; *Among the Dahlias,* William Sansom; *From Paddington,* Agatha Christie; *You Can't Get There From Here,* Ogden Nash.

C623 'Oxford Seen Darkly'. *T* (rev) 226 (11 Dec. 1957):652–53. *A Cup of Tea For Mr. Thorgell,* Storm Jameson; *The Blitz,* Constantine FitzGibbon; *Village Diary,* Miss Read; *The Main Chance,* Peter Wildeblood.

C624 'The Decay of Comfort'. *T* (rev) 226 (18 Dec. 1957):702–3. *Ten Pollett Place,* C. H. B. Kitchin; *Roman Candle,* Letitia Baldridge; *A Cage for the Nightingale,* Phyllis Paul.

C625 'A Child Sees Truth'. *T* (rev) 226 (25 Dec. 1957):744–45. *This Side of the Truth,* Elizabeth Montagu; *Windsor Castle,* Owen Morshead; *The Habit of Loving,* Doris Lessing; *The Devil by the Sea,* Nina Bawden; *Then There Was Fire,* Minori Drouet, trans. Margaret Crosland.

C626 'From Saddle to Pen'. *T* (rev) 227 (1 Jan. 1958):24–25. *The Sport of Queens,* Dick Francis; *The Fine and the Wicked,* Monica Sterling; *The Spy's Bedside Book,* comps. Graham Greene and Hugh Greene.

C627 'A Winter Journey to the Spice Islands'. *T* (rev) 227 (8 Jan. 1958):64–65. *Journey to Java.* Harold Nicolson; *Intimate Letters of England's Queens,* comp. Margaret Sanders; *Mainly on the Air,* Max Beerbohm.

C628 'The Most Bewitching of Meddlers'. *T* (rev) 227 (15 Jan. 1958): 104–5. *Arch Intriguer,* Priscilla Zamoyska; *The Seductive Mirror,* Leonard Mosley; *So Deadly My Love,* Stephen Ransome; *Double Affair,* Angela Thirkell; *Five Modern No Plays,* Yukio Mishima.

C629 'Satiric Story of the Englishman Abroad'. *T* (rev) 227 (22 Jan. 1958):148–49. *I Like It Here,* Kingsley Amis; *The Late George Apley,* John P. Marquand; *Claudine in Paris,* Colette, trans. Antonia White; *The Adopted Child,* Mary Ellison.

C630 'The Hero's Sideline was Villainy'. *T* (rev) 227 (29 Jan. 1958): 194–95. *The Man on the Rock,* Francis King; *The Meddlesome Friar,*

Michael de la Bedoyere; *With Lions by My Side,* Paulette Lloyd Greame; *Doubting Thomas,* Wilson Bribner.

C631 'Flemish Interior by a New Painter'. *T* (rev) 227 (5 Feb. 1958): 238–39. *The House of Lies,* Françoise Mallet-Joris; *Engaged in Writing,* Stephen Spender; *Suspicious Circumstances,* Patrick Quentin.

C632 'Northern Pilgrimage to the Midnight Sun'. *T* (rev) 227 (12 Feb. 1958):282–83. *The Icicle in the Sun,* William Sansom; *Certain Women,* Erskine Caldwell; *Unreasonable Doubt,* Elizabeth Ferrars.

C633 'When the Primitive Cracks the Shell of Manners'. *T* (rev) 227 (19 Feb. 1958):334–35. *A Letter to Elizabeth,* Bettina Linn; *The Assize of the Dying,* Elizabeth Pargeter; *Born in Wedlock,* Margaret Echard; *Second Class Taxi,* Sylvester Stein.

C634 'Magic in the Middle Distance'. *T* (rev) 227 (26 Feb. 1958): 388–89. *Georgian Afternoon,* Laurence Jones; *The Dud Avocado,* Elaine Dundy; *After the Rain,* John Bowen; *A Furnished Room,* Janet McNeill.

C635 'Inspired Amateurs Won the Atlantic Wall Game'. *T* (rev) 227 (5 March 1958):436–37. *Ten Thousand Eyes,* Richard Collier; *My Face for the World to See,* Alfred Hayes; *The Seeing Eye,* Josephine Bell; *Merrily to the Grave,* Kathleen Scully.

C636 'Texas beyond the Oil Wells'. *T* (rev) 227 (13 March 1958): 506–7. *Home From the Hill,* William Humphrey; *Henry James and H. G. Wells,* ed. Leon Edel and Gordon N. Ray; *How Still My Love,* Doris Siegel.

C637 'The Change from Amber'. *T* (rev) 227 (19 March 1958):580–81. *America, with Love,* Kathleen Winsor; *A Grain of Wheat,* Margaret Trouncer; *The Miscreant,* Jean Cocteau, trans. Dorothy Williams.

C638 'A Psychic Autobiography'. *T* (rev) 227 (26 March 1958):638–39, 654. *Look Towards the Sea,* Frank Baines; *The Quick Years,* Jean Ariss; *My Great-Aunt Appearing Day,* John Prebble; *See Rome and Die,* Louisa Revell.

C639 'A Blind Author's Novel with a Blind Hero'. *T* (rev) 228 (2 Apr. 1958):29. *The Stars Grow Pale,* Karl Barnhof; *The Birth of a*

Grandfather, May Sarton; *Lord Chatham and America*, O. A. Sherrard.

C640 'Mr. Faulkner Raises a Laugh'. *T* (rev) 228 (23 Apr. 1958): 197. *Uncle Wllly and Other Stories*, William Faulkner; *Siamese Counterpart*, Elizabeth Lake; *Blanche*, Nicolas de Croster.

C641 'A Jack-of-All-Trades Tries Fiction'. *T* (rev) 228 (30 Apr. 1958):250–51. *Black Midas*, Jan Carew; *Dr. No*, Ian Fleming; *I Watch and Listen*, Nancy Price.

C642 'Rx for a Story Worth the Telling'. *NYTBR* 58 (31 Aug. 1958): 1, 13; reprinted in *Writer* 71 (Dec. 1958):14–15, 36. Essay. Published in anthology, G50.

C643 'Candles in the Window'. *Woman's Day* 22 (Dec. 1958):32, 81–83. Short story.

C644 'Bowen's Court'. *Holiday* 24 (Dec. 1958):86–87, 190–93. Reminiscent essay on her family home, with a photograph of Elizabeth Bowen beside a horse and cart.

C644.1 'Welsh, and Quite Explosive', *NYHTB* 35 #35 (26 April 1959):8. Review of *The Rape of the Fair Country*, Alexander Cordell.

C644.2 'The Long Arm of Chance in Life's Tangle'. *NYTBR* (17 May 1959):4–5, 20. Review of *The Third Choice*, Elizabeth Janeway.

C645 'Enemies of Charm in Women, in Men'. *Vogue* 134 (15 Sept. 1959):158–59, 201. Essay.

C646 'The Virgins and the Empress'. *Harper's* 219 (Nov. 1959):50–55. Essay incorporating excerpts from chapters 'On Such a Night' and 'The Smile' from *A Time in Rome* (A24).

C646.1 'A Time in Rome'. *Gentlemen's Quarterly* 29 #8 (Dec. 1959): 107, 160, 162, 165, 181–82. Essay excerpted from the opening chapters of *A Time in Rome* (A24).

C647 'Happiness'. *Woman's Day* 23 (Dec. 1959):58, 122–24. Short story.

C648 'Ride Through the Deep South'. *Holiday* 27 (Feb. 1960):72–

73, 105, 107, 110–11, 113. Essay on Bowen's trip through the American South. Reprinted as 'A Ride South' in A26.

C649 'The Best of the Best'. *Vogue* 135 (15 Feb. 1960):152. Excerpts from recent books by Garrett Mattingly, Father Teilhard, Joyce Cary, Donald Keene, Van Wyck Brooks, and Elizabeth Bowen. Includes a brief excerpt from *A Time in Rome* (A24).

C650 'The Case for Summer Romance'. *Glamour* 43 (June 1960):94–95, 180. Essay on summer love.

C651 'Elizabeth Bowen Talks about Writing'. *Mademoiselle* 51 (July 1960):89, 6, 20–21. Reprinted as 'Advice' in A25 (q.v.).

C652 'Eternal Lure of the Eternal City'. *New York Times Magazine* (31 July 1960):28–29, 43. Essay. Excerpt from *A Time in Rome* (A24).

C653 'Where the Pharos Stood'. *Reporter* 24 (27 Apr. 1961):49–51. Review of *Alexandria*, E. M. Forster. Reprinted as 'Alexandria' in A25 (q.v.).

C653.1 'Second Home'. *Reporter* 24 (25 May 1961):54–55. Review of *The Chateau*, William Maxwell.

C654 'Wonders of a Traveler's World'. *NYTBR* 66 part 2 (18 June 1961):1. Review of *Blue Skies, Brown Studies*, William Sansom.

C655 'The Beauty of Being Your Age'. *Harper's Bazaar* (English edition) 64 #4 (July 1961). Essay. MS, E101.

C656 'Comeback of Goldilocks et al'. *New York Times Magazine* (26 Aug. 1962):18–19, 74–75. Essay.

C657 'Lawrence of Arabia'. *Show* II #12 (Dec. 1962):66–67. Review of the film.

C658 'The Teakettle'. *House and Garden* 123 (Jan. 1963):70–71. Essay. Published in anthology, G51.

C659 'Enchanted Centenary of the Brothers Grimm'. *New York Times Magazine* (8 Sept. 1963):28–29, 112–13.

C659.1 'Holroyd's Strachey', *TLS* #3447 (21 Mar. 1968):293. A letter by Bowen, David Cecil, L. P. Hartley, and Julian Huxley to the editor. In defense of Ottoline Morrell.

C660 'Portrait of a Man Reading Elizabeth Bowen'. *CTribBW* (10 Nov. 1968):6. Interview with Miss Bowen.

C661 'Ecstasy of the Eye'. *Vogue* 152 (Dec. 1968):189–90. Essay.

C662 'The Thread of Dreams'. *Réalités* (American edition) #219 (Feb. 1969):56–59. Essay.

C662.1 'All People Great and Small'. *Spectator* 223 (20 Sept. 1969): 367–68. Review of *The People's War*, Angus Calder.

C663 'New Waves of the Future'. *American Home* (California home edition) 72 (Oct. 1969):70–71. Essay.

C664 'A Novelist and His Characters'. *Essays by Divers Hands: Being the Transactions of the Royal Society of Literature*, ed. Mary Stocks, n.s. 36 (1970):19–23. Paper was read by Elizabeth Bowen C.B.E., C. Lit., D. Litt., F.R.S.L. on 6 May 1969.

C665 'Kindred and Affinity'. *Spectator* 224 (31 Jan. 1970):151. Review of *The Irish Cousins*, Violet Powell.

C666 'Gift for the Gaffe'. *Spectator* 224 (21 Mar. 1970):382–84. Review of *Making Conversation*, Christine Longford.

C667 'Dickens and the Demon Toy Box'. *Spectator* 224 (30 May 1970):713. Review of *The World of Charles Dickens*, Angus Wilson.

The difficulty of locating foreign editions of Elizabeth Bowen's work prevents a complete bibliography of translations at this time. There is a list of contracts signed, but in some cases these translations have not been seen or have not been published. The compilers have been aided greatly by Bowen's collection of her translations and her contracts. For the contracts, see Appendix A. The books which have not been seen are starred (*).

A3 THE HOTEL 1927

D1 *El Hotel (Barcelona: Luis de Caralt). Contract noted in Appendix A.

A4 THE LAST SEPTEMBER 1929

D2 L'ultimo settembre (Milan: Arnoldo Mondadori, 1948), trans. Laura Merlatto.

D3 Aldrig mer september (Stockholm: P. A. Norstedt & Söners Förlag, 1960), trans. Cilla Johnson. Hardbound edition is bound paper edition with cover of paper edition bound in. Dust jacket matches paper cover.

A5 JOINING CHARLES AND OTHER STORIES 1929

D4 *Ein Abschied (Munich: Nymphenburger Verlagshandlung, 1958), trans. Siegfried Schmitz, ed. Elisabeth Schnack. Contains only six stories from the above collection. No list of the six stories has been seen by the compilers.

A7 TO THE NORTH 1932

D5 Gen Norden (Cologne: Schaffrath, 1948), trans. Margarete Rauchenberger.

D6 Emmeline (Paris: Éditions du Seuil, 'Pierre Vives', 1949), trans. Georges Globa.

D6.1 Na północ (Warsaw: Czytelnik, 1974), trans. Aldona Szpakowska.

D7 Hacia el Norte (Buenos Aires: Emecé Editores, 'Grandes Novelistas' series, 1951), trans. María Antonia Oyuela.

D8　*Kohti Pohjoista* (Porvoo & Helsinki: Werner Söderström Osa-keyhtiö Kirjainossa, 'Euroopa-Sarja' series, 1951), trans. Ville Repo.

A9　THE HOUSE IN PARIS　1935

D9　*La maison à Paris* (Paris: Nouvelle Revue Française, Éditions Gallimard, 1941), trans. Marie Tadié.

D10　*Et Hus i Paris* (Copenhagen: Det Schønbergske Förlag, 1947), trans. Jørgen L. Engberg.

D11　*Das Haus in Paris* (Berlin: Hera Verlag, 1947), trans. Ruth Weiland.

D12　*Huset i Paris* (Oslo: Ernest G. Mortensen, 1947), trans. Liv Malling.

D13　*Das Haus in Paris* (Vienna: Verlag Ernst Pelda & Sohn, 1948), trans. Ruth Weiland.

D14　*Talo Pariisissa* (Porvoo & Helsinki: Werner Söderström Osa-keyhtiö Kirjainossa, 1949), trans. Liisa Vesikansa-Saarinen.

D15　*Huset i Paris* (Stockholm: P. A. Norstedt & Söners Förlag, 1958), trans. Cilla Johnson.

D16　*Kucá u Parizu* (Belgrade: Narodna Knjiga, 1962), trans. into Serbo-Croatian by Vasilija Djukanovic, afterword by Lubitsa Bayer-Protich, pp. 329–32.

D17　*La casa en Paris* (Santiago: Editorial Zig-Zag, 'Narradores Europeos' series, 1969), trans. Cecilia Boisier and Antonio Skármeta.

A10　THE DEATH OF THE HEART　1938

D18　*Les coeurs détruits* (Paris: Librairie Plon, 'Feux Croisés' series, 1941), trans. and intro. (pp. i-iii) by Jean Talva.

D19　*Hjärtats död* (Stockholm: Albert Bonnier Förlag, 1941), trans. Viveka Starfelt, intro. (pp. 3–4) Anders Österling.

D20　*Hjertets død* (Copenhagen: Det Schønbergske Förlag, 1942), trans. Hedda Syberg.

D21 *Ha muerto un corazón* (Barcelona: Luis de Caralt, 'Novelistas Grandes' series, 1945), trans. Emilia Bertel.

D22 *Crepuscolo* (Verona: Arnoldo Mondadori, 1948), trans. Beata della Frattina.

D23 **Der Tod des Herzens* (Germany: 1949).

D24 *smrt srca* (Novi Sad, Yugoslavia: Bratsvo-Jedinstvo, 1952), trans. Darinka Stevanovic.

D25 *Les coeurs détruits* (Paris: Librairie Générale Française, 1954), trans. Jean Talva.

D26 *skon srdce* (Prague: Odeon, 1966), trans. Jarmila Fastrova.

D27 *A morte do coração* (Lisbon: Portugália Editôra, 'Contemporânea' series, June 1966), trans. Marília Guerra de Vasconcelos, biographical statement on Bowen by Jorge de Sena.

D28 *strta srca* (Ljubljani, Yugoslavia: Cankarjeva Založba, Zbirka 'Mozaik' series, 1966), trans. into Slovene by Tita Janež, postscript by Radoslav Nenadál, pp. 359–368.

A12 ENGLISH NOVELISTS 1942

D29 *Romancistas ingleses* (Rio de Janeiro: Livraria José Olympio, n.d.), 8 gravuras, 18 illustrations, trans. Geraldo Cavalcanti. First Brazilian edition, printed in Great Britain.

D30 *Romançiers anglais* (Paris: Éditions du Seuil, 1946).

A15 THE DEMON LOVER AND OTHER STORIES 1945

D31 *Pacte avec le diable* (Paris: La Jeune Parque, 1947), trans. Hélène Robin (includes preface).

D32 *Der dämonische Liebhaber u.a. Geschichten* (Cologne: Josef Schaffrath Verlag, 1947), trans. Prof. H. Hussmann, preface pp. 5–12.

D33 *Älskaren som var demon, och andra noveller* (Stockholm: Albert Bonnier Förlag, 'Panache' series, 1947), trans. Viveka Starfelt.

D34 *Lykken og de høstlige jordene* (Oslo: Ernest G. Mortensen, 1949), trans. Peter Magnus.

A18 THE HEAT OF THE DAY 1949

D35 *De Hitte Des Daags* (Amsterdam: J. M. Meulenhoff, 1950), trans. N. Brunt.

D36 *Middagshöjd* (Stockholm: Albert Bonnier Förlag, 1950), trans. Sonja Bergvall.

D37 *L'ardeur du jour* (Paris: Éditions du Seuil, Collection 'Pierre Vives', 1952), trans. Georges Globa, preface by Claude-Edmonde Magny, pp. 7–14.

D38 *Hizakari* (Tokyo: Shincho-Sha, 1952), trans. Ken'ichi Yoshida.

D39 *Žega* (Belgrade: Omladina, 1955), trans. Kaliopa Nikolajević.

D40 *L'ora decisiva* (Milan and Verona: Arnoldo Mondadori, 1956), trans. Maria Jung.

A22 A WORLD OF LOVE 1955

D41 *En verden åbner sig* (Copenhagen: Det Schønbergske Förlag, 1956), trans. Aase Hansen, printed by Nordlundes Bogtrykkeri.

D42 *En värld av kärlek* (Stockholm: P. A. Norstedt & Söners Förlag, 1956), trans. Jane Lundblad. Reprinted in paper: Bokklubben Var bok, 1963.

D43 *Eine Welt der Liebe* (Cologne and Berlin: Kiepenheuer and Witsch, 1958), trans. Hilde Spiel.

D44 *Un monde d'amour* (Paris: Plon, 1966), trans. Henrietta de Sarbois.

A24 A TIME IN ROME 1960

D45 *En Tid I Rom* (Stockholm: P. A. Norstedt & Söners Förlag, 1962), trans. Brita Björkbom. Reprinted in paper: Bokförlaget Pan, P. A. Norstedt & Söners Förlag, 1967.

D46   *Småpigerne* (Copenhagen: Gyldendal Norsk, 1965), trans. Aase Hansen.

D47   *Die kleinen Mädchen* (Cologne and Berlin: Kiepenheuer & Witsch, 1965), trans. Helmut Winter.

D48   *Devojčice* (Belgrade: Srpska Književna Zadruga Izdanja Kolo, 1965), trans. Milenko Popovič and Milica Popovič.

D49   *Ikuiset tytöt* (Porvoo and Helsinki: Werner Söderström Osakeyhtiö Kirjainossa, 1966), trans. Anja Samooja Gersov.

D50   *Flickorna* (Stockholm: P. A. Norstedt & Söners Förlag, 1966), trans. Aida Törnell. Simultaneously released in paper.

D51   *Les petites filles* (Paris: Plon, 1967), trans. Amelia Audiberti.

D51.1   *Dziewczynki* (Warsaw: Pánstwowy Instytut Wydawniczy, 1975), trans. Urszula Lada-Zablocka.

D52   *Eva, Eller Scenförändringar* (Stockholm: P. A. Norstedt & Söners Förlag, 1970), trans. Brita Dahlman.

D53   *Eva* (Schildt and Helsingfors, Finland: Findlandskt Förlag, 1970), trans. Brita Dahlman.

D54   *Eva Trout* (Rio de Janeiro: Editôra Expressão e Cultura, December 1971), trans. Aurea Weissenberg.

D55   *Seine einzige Tochter* (Freiberg: Walter-Verlag, 1973), trans. Elisabeth Schnack.

D56   *L'embrasement de Midi* (Paris: Éditions Albin Michel, 1947), trans. Alexandre Ralli, intro. Elizabeth Bowen, pp. 9–14.

D57   *Pourquois j'écris* (Paris: Éditions du Seuil, Collection 'Pierre Vives', 1950), trans. Marcelle Sibon.

196

Contributions to Books and Periodicals

D58 'Tante Tatty'. (Paris: *Mercure de France* 306, June 1949):283–300, trans. René Leplat. 'Aunt Tatty'. See A5.

D59 *Katten springer* (Copenhagen: Det Schønbergske Förlag, 1952), trans. and postscript (pp. 264–67) Jørgen Engberg. Includes 'Recent Photograph', first printed in A2 (q.v.); 'Shoes: An International Episode', first printed in A5; 'Telling', see A5; 'The Good Girl', see A8; 'The Cat Jumps', see A8; 'Maria', see A8; 'The Needlecase', first printed in A8 (q.v.); 'Tears, Idle Tears', see A11; 'Look At All Those Roses', see A11; 'The Demon Lover', see A15; 'In the Square', see A15; 'Ivy Gripped the Steps', see A15; 'Mysterious Kôr', see A15.

D60 *Nitten moderne irske noveller* (Copenhagen: Thaning & Appels, 1947), ed. and trans. Ove Brusendorff. A collection of Irish short stories including Elizabeth Bowen's 'Katten springer' ('The Cat Jumps'), pp. 25–36. See A8 and E257.

D61 *Spookverhalen* (Utrecht and Antwerp: Het Spectrum Prisma-boeken, 1964), trans. C. A. G. van den Broek. A collection of ghost narratives including Elizabeth Bowen's 'Kat in Hetnauw' ('The Cat Jumps'), pp. 17–28, reprinted from *Spine Chillers,* Elek Books, 1961. See A8.

D62 *Deset Anglických Novel* (Prague: Československý spisovatel, 1967), trans. Aloys Skoumal. A collection of short stories by twentieth century English novelists including Elizabeth Bowen's 'Šitíčko' ('The Needlecase'), pp. 145–56. See A8.

D63 *Irland erzählt* (Frankfurt am Main and Hamburg: der Fischer Bücherei, May 1968), ed. and trans. Elisabeth Schnack. A collection of seventeen stories by Irish authors, including Elizabeth Bowen's 'Das Nadelkästchen' ('The Needlecase'), pp. 75–84. See A8.

D64 'Reduction' (*La Table Ronde* #47, Nov. 1951): 109–21, trans. René Leplat. 'Reduced'. See A11.

D65 'Realisationsvara' (*Vecko-Journalen* 43 #37 18 Sept. 1952):38–39, 42, trans. Stig Dahlstedt. 'Reduced'. See A11.

D66 *Tanpen Bungaku Zenshu v. 2: Igirisu Bungaku Nijuseiki* [Collections of World Short Story Literature, v. 2: Twentieth-Century English Literature] (Tokyo: Shuei-Sha, 1962), ed. Yoshio Nakano, trans. Tatsuo Matsumura. Includes Elizabeth Bowen's 'Summer Night', pp. 67–99. First printed in A11.

D67 *Natsu no yoru* (Tokyo: Kenkyusha, 1967), trans. Osamu Doi. 'Summer Night'. First printed in A11.

D67.1 *Aikamme parhaita rakkauskertomuksia* [Best love stories of our time] (Helsinki: Otava, 1954), ed. Erkki Reenpää. Includes Elizabeth Bowen's 'Aaverakastaja' ('The Demon Lover'), trans. Elsa Vuorinen, pp. 77–84. See A15.

D68 *Samlingen* (Copenhagen: Det Schønbergske Förlag, 1946), trans. Jørgen L. Engberg. A collection of short stories including 'En plads i London' ('In the Square'). The publisher used this story for his Christmas greeting of 1946. See A15.

D69 *Englisch Novellen der Gegenwart* (Cologne: Schaffrath, 1947), trans. Margarete Rauchenberger and Harry Rohmann. A translation of *English Stories from New Writing,* ed. John Lehmann, including Elizabeth Bowen's 'Mysterious Kôr'. See A15.

D70 'Kor (*Atlantis: Länder, Völker, Reisen* #20, Jan. 1948):33–39, trans. Harry Kahn. 'Mysterious Kor'. See A15.

D71 *Irische Erzähler* (Zürich: Manesse Verlag, 1952), ed. and trans. Elisabeth Schnack. A collection of twenty stories by Irish authors, including Elizabeth Bowen's 'Geheimnisvolles Khôr' ('Mysterious Kôr'), pp. 271–95. See A15.

D72 *Schody zarostlé brect'anem* (Prague: Odeon, 1972), trans. Hana Skoumalová; intro. (pp. 7–13) by Aloys Skoumal. Includes: 'Ivy Gripped the Steps', see A15; 'Mysterious Kôr', see A15; 'The Demon Lover', see A15; 'The Happy Autumn Fields', see A15; 'I Hear You Say So', see A28; 'Tears, Idle Tears', see A11; 'Look At All Those Roses', see A11; 'Hand in Glove', see A28; 'Reduced', see A11; 'A Walk in the Woods', see A11; 'The Cat Jumps', see A8; 'The Disinherited', first printed in A8 (q.v.).

This section does not pretend to be complete; it lists manuscripts that have been made available during the compilation of the bibliography. Consistent with the overall design, this section is arranged according to works by or about the author. Manuscripts by Bowen are listed under Books and Pamphlets, Contributions to Books and Periodicals, Miscellaneous and Unpublished Items, and Letters from Elizabeth Bowen. Manuscripts about Bowen are listed under Miscellaneous Items and under Letters to Elizabeth Bowen. All divisions are arranged in chronological order of first publication with the exception of letters, which are first arranged alphabetically by recipient or sender. Where no date is available on the manuscript, the date of publication appears within brackets. The term 'final version' indicates a manuscript in which the text is essentially the same as that of the first printed edition. With regard to Bowen's manuscripts, it is not uncommon to find a typescript draft and one or more carbons; Bowen corrected not the original but the carbon. As a result, the Tccms became the later version and often became the printed version after heavy revision. In complicated situations where numerous versions, revisions, or variants of a story or novel exist, P is used to designate the printed version, and P1 according to emendations is one revision away from the printed version. P2 would, by logical extension, be two complete revisions away from the printed version.

The location of manuscript or typescript is given in parentheses within each entry. The following abbreviations are used:

ALS	autograph letter signed
ANS	autograph note signed
APC	autograph postcard
BBC	BBC Written Archives Centre
NYPL-B	Berg Collection, The New York Public Library
TccL	typed carbon copy letter
Tccms	typed carbon copy manuscript
TccmsAN	typed carbon copy manuscript with autograph note
TccmsS	typed carbon copy manuscript signed
TccN	typed carbon copy with note in unidentified hand
Texas	Humanities Research Center, The University of Texas at Austin
TLS	typed letter signed

Books and Pamphlets

E1   Preface to *Encounters* n.d. [Apr. 1949]
Lightly revised in pencil, black and red ink typescript of 9 numbered

sheets. As emended, this copy is identical to the published version. Holograph notes: 'Duplicate'. Also includes notes for typesetting. (Texas) See A1c.

E2 *Ann Lee's and Other Stories* n.d. [1926]
Signed manuscript, with holograph revisions; 179 pages. Incomplete, this manuscript includes only nine stories: 'Ann Lee's', 'The Parrot', 'The Visitor', 'Human Habitation', 'The Secession', 'Making Arrangements', 'The Storm', 'Charity', and 'The Back Drawing-Room'.

This manuscript and E3, E4, E6, E7, E9, and E10 have been bound in different covers of the same size ($8\frac{1}{2}$ x 11") and general appearance. Each of these volumes is quarter-bound on the spine in one fabric or leather, with a different fabric on the front and back covers. Probably the volumes were bound at the author's request. The size of the paper within each volume varies: some of the paper is $8\frac{1}{2}$ x 10" and other sheets interspersed within the same volume are $8\frac{1}{2}$ x 13", with the bottom part of the page turned up to fit the bound volume. Some sheets are of colors and quality comparable to a woman's stationery. Thus the stories most likely were written at different places, and the bindings bring together those stories Elizabeth Bowen selected for inclusion in these particular volumes. After *The House in Paris* Bowen used the typewriter almost exclusively for first drafts.

The manuscript of '*Ann Lee*'s [*and Other Stories*]' is bound in covers which have a red and white geometric print design on the outside front and back, and a red linen spine containing a cream leather insert on which the title is stamped in gold. There is no title page and the stories are on different-sized paper, as noted above. They are bound in the order listed. (Texas) See A2.

E3 *The Hotel* (novel) n.d. [1927]
Signed manuscript with holograph revisions; 339 pages. Chapter headings are not included in this draft. This volume is bound in covers of a yellow and white print design on the outside front and back, with a black spine containing a brown leather insert on which the title is stamped in black. The ink, handwriting, and paper differ throughout the volume. (Texas) See A3.

E4 *The Last September* (novel) n.d. [1929]
Signed manuscript with holograph revisions; 385 pages. Chapter headings are included. The title page and epigraph are on $8\frac{1}{2}$ x 11" onionskin similar to that used in 'The Hotel'. The volume is bound in covers of a pale blue and yellow small print design on the outside front and

back, with a red spine containing a black leather insert on which the title is stamped in gold. The size of the paper differs throughout the volume. (Texas) See A4.

E5 Preface to *The Last September* n.d. [22 Sept. 1952]
Typescript of 7 sheets heavily revised in blue ink. This is very close to the final version. (Texas) See A4c.

E6 *Joining Charles and Other Stories* n.d. [1929]
Manuscript with holograph revisions; 254 pages. Incomplete, the manuscript contains only ten stories, bound in the order listed: 'Joining Charles', 'The Jungle', 'The Shoes', 'The Dancing Mistress', 'Dead Mabelle', 'The Working Party', 'Foothold', 'The Cassowary', 'Telling', 'Mrs. Moysey'.
   There is no title page. The volume is bound in covers of avocado and blue print design on the outside front and back, with a yellow spine containing a black leather insert on which the title is stamped in gold. The size and quality of the paper vary. 'Joining Charles' has two titles: 'The White House' is cancelled. 'Foothold' also has two titles, with 'Houseroom' deleted. (Texas) See A5.

E7 *Friends and Relations* (novel) n.d. [1931]
Manuscript with holograph revisions; 345 pages. There is no title page. The volume is quarter-bound with a white linen spine and a green and white print design on the front and back outside covers. The title is stamped in gold on green leather and inserted in the spine. The ink is badly faded throughout most of the manuscript, and the revisions are quite light. The size and quality of the paper vary. (Texas) See A6.

E8 *Friends and Relations* (radio typescript) April-July 1957
Series of twelve readings by Alice Laudene, edited for broadcasting by Mary Hope Allen. Pencil revisions on each typescript. 8 x 13" mimeograph paper. The readings number 19, 14, 14, 18, 20, 17, 21, 22, 21, 19, 23, and 18 pages in order of presentation. (BBC) See F36.

E9 *To the North* (novel) n.d. [1932]
Manuscript with holograph revisions; 461 pages. There is no title page. The volume is bound in covers bearing a green, blue, and beige surrealistic design on the front and back, and a beige linen spine containing a black leather insert on which the title is stamped in gold. The size of the paper differs, but here, at variance with the preceding volumes, some of the sheets are smaller as if cut. Revisions are slight compared to the earlier novels. (Texas) See A7.

E10   *The House in Paris* (novel) n.d. [1935]
Manuscript with holograph revisions; 365 pages. The title is signed. The volume is quarter-bound in blue fabric on the spine, with a blue and white geometric print design on the front and back covers. Inserted in the spine is a black leather label with the title stamped in gold. Bowen revises more freely than in E9 *To the North,* and appears to use the same ink and paper throughout, which is unusual. Her handwriting is tight and larger than in her early work. Some parts of the first section of the novel are heavily revised. Considering later work which includes a number of drafts and which shows her method of composition, this manuscript appears to be a revised final version. The parts are marked, but the chapter headings within the parts are not clearly noted. (Texas) See A9.

E10.1   *The House in Paris* (radio manuscript) 21 May 1950
Holograph statement about the value of the novel from Bowen's point of view. She calls it a 'mysterious book'. Accordingly, she rates this novel above other novels she has written. The image of the two children came to her as 'out of a dream'. She began the novel shortly after leaving New York in 1933. (NBC)

E11   *The House in Paris* (radio typescript) 18 Sept. 1955
'Chapter One' as read by Mary Wimbush. T.74 on microfilm. (BBC) See F32.

E12   *The Death of the Heart* (novel) n.d. [1938]
(NYPL–B) See A10.

   a.) Incomplete holograph drafts of part I on $8\frac{1}{2}$ x 10″ paper: three drafts of chapter 1, one each of chapters 2 and 3. Unsigned, undated; 69 pages. 'Draft (1)' is written in blue pencil across the top of a page [1] entitled 'Part I Ch. I.' The holograph drafts are in a purple case with gold lettering.
   b.) Incomplete typescript, an early draft of the novel, with holograph revisions. Unsigned and undated; 336 pages. Chapters 2, 4, 5, and 6 are missing from Part III. From the chapter headings that have been typed in and emended, it seems that the organization of the novel has been altered in the direction of the first edition.
   c.) Incomplete typescript of the novel as a whole, with holograph revisions, undated; 411 pages. Later than E12b, although Part II, chapter 8 is similar to that chapter in E12b. The manuscript heading at the top reads: 'Richly Corrected Typescript with much holograph material ELIZABETH BOWEN.' Laid in, after the first page: signed manuscript

note on Elizabeth Bowen by David Daiches (see E175), 2 pp. (see E212). Kept in the case with the holograph drafts of Part I (E12a, above).

E13 *The Death of the Heart* (radio typescript) 9 Sept. 1957
Adapted for broadcasting by Anne Allan and Julian Amyes. 53 pages, 8 x 13″. (BBC) See F37.

E14 *English Novelists* (literary history) n.d. [1942]
Signed typescript with extensive holograph revision; 63 pages. Each typescript page is mounted on a larger sheet and contained in a blue case with a red leather mounting. The title is printed in gold. On the title page is typed: 'The English Novel' with 'Novel' cancelled and 'Novelists' written in ink and signed by Elizabeth Bowen. On page 2 not one typed line remains unrevised, and seven lines have been completely obliterated or changed. Such heavy emendation is not found throughout the typescript, but most pages bear typewritten or manuscript revisions. (Texas) See A12.

E15 *Bowen's Court* (family history) n.d. [1942]
Signed typescript with extensive holograph revision; 588 pages. The typescript is contained in a brown case with the title printed in gold on purple leather. The typescript includes nine of the ten chapters (the third is missing); there are two versions of chapter 1, three versions of chapter 10. There are two versions of the afterword. A holograph note on the first page states: 'Corrected typescript corrections in my hand Elizabeth Bowen.' The genealogical chart of the Bowen family is among the papers in the case. (Texas) See A13.

E16 Preface to *The Demon Lover* n.d. [Apr. 1946]
Clean typescript of 7 sheets at the end of which in type is noted: 'Elizabeth Bowen / October 1945.' The typescript is identical to the version first printed in *Ivy Gripped the Steps*, the first American edition of this collection. (Texas) See A15b.

E17 *New Judgement: Elizabeth Bowen on Anthony Trollope* (radio typescript) 4 May 1945
New Judgement Series for BBC with pencilled revisions; 20 pages, 8 x 13″ cream paper. Transmission on 4 May 1945, 8:30–9:00 PM. Play form with narrator, William, Uncle Jasper, Anthony Trollope, two ladies and two men. Produced by Stephen Potter and Peter Watts. (BBC) See A16.

Manuscript and typescript, with author's holograph revisions and holograph and typed inserts; 685 pages. Different typewriters, ink, pencils, and kinds of paper have been used in the earlier versions and in the emendations. (Texas) See A18.

Chapter 1: one version, 19 pages.

Chapter 2: three versions: the final typescript of 31 pages, and two earlier and partial drafts. On the earliest version, the title of the novel is in manuscript with the author's signature beneath it.

Chapter 3: the final version, part in manuscript and part in typescript, 26 pages; and an earlier draft of 24 pages.

Chapter 4: the final version, part in manuscript and part in typescript, 34 pages; and an earlier typescript draft of 23 pages.

Chapter 5: the final version, a typescript of 17 pages, with few manuscript revisions. There are two earlier typescripts, a rejected version of 9 pages and a typescript of 19 pages.

Chapter 6: the final version, a typescript of 36 pages on three colors of paper—white, pink, and blue. Though the same typewriter appears to have been used, the ribbon ink is alternately black and blue. There is an earlier version of 12 pages of black type on white paper with substantial manuscript revision in black and blue ink. The third, earliest, version, 28 pages, is cut and pasted on white paper, with revisions both handwritten in black ink and typed in a different size type from the original.

Chapter 7: the final version, a typescript (black ribbon) on white and on blue paper, 24 pages, heavily revised in pencil and ink; and an earlier version, a typescript of 22 pages, only slightly revised.

Chapter 8: the final version, a typescript of 22 pages, heavily revised, including three smaller sized sheets, two typewritten and one in manuscript. There is also an earlier version, typescript of 24 pages on white and on pink paper, with revisions in blue ink and pages numbered in pencil.

Chapter 9: the final version, a typescript of 28 pages on white paper, heavily revised; and an earlier version, 31 pages on pink and on white paper, not heavily revised.

Chapter 10: one version only, a typescript of 29 pages on white and on blue paper, heavily revised. In general, the blue sheets appear to be retyped portions of the white pages which were probably too heavily revised to read.

Chapter 11: one version, 25 pages, on blue paper except for the last two pages, which are white. This chapter is heavily revised in black ink. Includes ANS.

Chapter 12: one version, a typescript of 34 pages on blue, pink, and white paper, cut, pasted, and heavily revised in black ink.

Chapter 13: one version, a typescript of 12 pages on white paper except for page 11 which is blue. This final version, as is the case with most of the final versions, is heavily revised.

Chapter 14: one version, a typescript of 23 pages on white and on blue paper, heavily revised in black ink. There are some partial pages. Although there is only one version of this chapter, it does not accord with the chapter printed but instead with the beginning of the printed version of chapter 15.

Chapter 15: one version, a typescript of 30 pages on white paper with manuscript revisions in black ink and pencil. This draft, which is not the final version, is heavily revised. In some cases the ink revisions are superimposed upon the pencilled manuscript revisions, indicating the order in which revision was made.

Chapter 16: one version, a typescript of 13 pages. The first page is in manuscript on stationery, and the other sheets are typed on blue or white paper with few revisions.

Chapter 17: 34 pages, all fragments of early versions. They may be divided in the following way: a.) Numbered pages 1–9 on white, blue, and grey paper in typescript and revised in ink. b.) Eight sheets numbered 1, 2, 3, 4a, 4b, 5, and two unnumbered sheets. The first four sheets are in manuscript in black ink. The next two sheets are in typescript and heavily revised; the next two sheets are in typescript, on heavier paper and hardly revised. c.) Four pages typed on white paper, lightly revised in pencil. d.) Pages 1–4 are in typescript on blue paper with pencil revision. These sheets correspond roughly with pp. 364ff of the Knopf edition. e.) Pages 1–2 are in typescript and heavily revised. Page numbers are in ink in the right corner. f.) Pages 1–6 and the last page, unnumbered, are in typescript on white paper with ink revisions. These pages correspond to the Knopf edition, p. 367 to the end.

E19　*The Shelbourne* (history) n.d. [1951]
Heavily revised typescript in accord with printed version of chapter 1. The typescript title reads: 'I. / *TODAY.*' 8 pages, one shortened sheet. (Texas) See A21.

E20　*A World of Love* (novel) n.d. [1955]

Signed typescript, with holograph and typewritten revision and holograph and typewritten inserts; 318 pages. The paper is of various colors; more than one typewriter has been used; and the holograph revisions· appear in a number of different inks. The typescript is heavily revised. (Texas) See A22.

Chapter 1: one version, 24 pages. This draft, in which the protagonist is named George rather than Guy, is not the final version.

Chapter 2: of the four versions, the final typescript is 10 pages; the progressively earlier versions are 5, 13, and 13 pages respectively.

Chapter 3: the final version is 15 pages; two earlier versions are 14 and 11 pages. Paper and color of ink and size of type vary within each version as well as from one version to the other.

Chapter 4: the typescript of the final version is 18 pages on yellow and on pink paper; an earlier version is 19 pages on yellow paper.

Chapter 5: a typescript of 22 pages on pink paper. It is a fair copy with no revisions, but the printed text has minor variations.

Chapter 6: of the two versions, the final typescript is 20 pages on yellow paper; the earlier is 16 pages on pink paper.

Chapter 7: both on pink paper, the final version of 17 pages, and an earlier version of 20 pages. A different typewriter was used for the two versions, and both typescripts are revised, some pages heavily.

Chapter 8: of the two versions, the final typescript is 15 pages; and the earlier, 18 pages. Within the final version there is inserted a loose page, heavily revised.

Chapter 9: one version only, of 20 typescript pages on pink paper in a large type size.

Chapter 10: missing.

Chapter 11: one version only, a typescript of 27 pages on apricot paper. Some of the pages, apparently retyped, are identical with the first printed edition and are fair copy. Other pages, more heavily revised, do not correspond to the printed text.

E21   *A Time in Rome* (history and travel) n.d. [1960]
Manuscript and typescript versions of chapters 1 and 2 and layout preliminaries. (Texas) See A24.

a.) Chapter 1: 21 sheets, one half-sheet, typescript and Tccms and three holograph sheets heavily corrected. Sheets 1–10 are carbon of E21d, sheets 10a–12 are typescripts, sheets 13 and 14 are carbons of E21d, and sheets 15ff are different typescripts. This version lacks the final two sections of the printed chapter from pages 21–35, but otherwise is the printed version.

b.) Chapter 1: 23 sheets, one half-sheet, one typescript page, others manuscript in blue ink and heavily revised. Corresponds closely to final printed version from pp. 21 to the end of the chapter and completes E21a. Pages 30–35, originally numbered 1–6, are renumbered and inserted at this point. They are revised in blue and gray inks.

c.) Chapter 1: heavily revised earlier typescript of 13 sheets, some cut, beginning 'The passions of Roman . . .', on p. 24 of the printed edition.

d.) Chapter 1: 17 sheets, typescript with few emendations whose carbon copy was revised for the printed version in E21a. Often Bowen has corrected the Tccms rather than the typescript. (P1)

e.) Chapter 1: 16 sheets of heavily corrected Tccms and typescript, from two different typewriters. Pp. 1–5 Tccms; pp. 5–15b typescript. This version lacks the final two sections from pp. 21–35 of the printed edition. (P2)

f.) Chapter 1: 28 sheets with two copies of page 3. Typescript with no revisions. This version differs in numerous paragraphs from the chapter as published, but is complete.

g.) Chapter 1: the earliest version, a heavily revised typescript entitled 'The Confusion'. 10 unnumbered sheets with revisions in blue ink.

h.) Chapter 2: manuscript version of printed edition entitled 'Mists of Antiquity' (changed to 'A Long Day' in the published version); 52 pages, numbered in blue at the right-hand top corner. There are some revisions also in blue ink and others in different ink and on different kinds of paper.

i.) Chapter 2: two earlier typescript versions (P1) and (P2), the early one of 4 pages and the later of 6 pages with half-sheets. Both versions, heavily revised, are also entitled 'Mists of Antiquity'.

j.) Chapter 2: 9 sheets, some cut, beginning mid-sentence, '. . . staying the way it was', on p. 39 of the printed version. This is an earlier version as the sentence in the revised typescript begins, '. . . remaining the way it was'.

k.) Chapter 2: 4 sheets, one cut, beginning, 'Work now going on on the Palatine . . .', on p. 47 of the printed version. This too is an earlier revised typescript beginning, 'The uncovering of the Palatine. . .'.

l.) 8 sheets, heavily revised typescript beginning, 'The point from which to start round the Forum is . . .', p. 51 of the printed version; and 10 sheets, one cut, lightly revised typescript, beginning and ending at the same place.

m.) 6 sheets, heavily revised typescript, beginning, 'All said and done. . .', p. 66 of the printed version.

n.) 5 typescript pages with blue ink and pencil revisions. They appear to be miscellaneous pages which have been taken out of other sections. 4 page typescript with manuscript revisions sketching chronology of Rome.

o.) Layout preliminaries for Longmans edition. 7 sheets. Includes: Title page, copyright and imprints, acknowledgments, contents, and dedication.

E22 *The Little Girls* (novel) n.d. [1964]
(Texas) See A27.

a.) Typescript (originals interspersed with some carbon copies) with holograph revisions; not all chapters are complete; 466 pages. The folder indicates, 'original) *The Little Girls* | From Curtis Brown Ltd | 13 King Street, Covent Garden | London'.
 Part I: includes four chapters of 34, 11, 32, and 47 pages respectively. Moderate revisions in ink are made on white, yellow, goldenrod, blue, and pink paper. Each page is numbered, and the chapters are numbered consecutively.
 Part II: includes seven chapters of 20, 19, 16, 21, 17, 6, and 35 pages respectively that are moderately to heavily revised. Again a mixture of colored sheets is included.
 Part III: includes seven chapters of 31, 3, 32, 15, 9, 37, and 81 pages respectively with light to moderate revisions. There are TccmsS on white paper. Each chapter is numbered but the internal numbering of the individual chapters is not consistent with the printed version in chapters 3 and 7.

b.) Incomplete typescript of miscellaneous sections of the novel; 120 pages.
 Part I: an early version of chapter 3, 22 sheets on yellow and blue paper with holograph revisions.
 Part II: (i.) a version of chapter 5, on 13 yellow and blue sheets,

not always sequential as some pages are reworked versions of earlier pages.

(ii.) A numbered version of chapter 6, typescript of 6 pages on white paper with manuscript revisions.

(iii.) The last half of chapter 7, typescript of 9 sheets on blue paper with pencil and ink revisions. Some pages, not rewritten, are completely marked out.

Part III: (i.) typescript of chapter 1; black ribbon on white paper; moderately to heavily revised in blue ink; 31 sheets.

(ii.) an earlier version of the first half of chapter 1 (corresponding to pp. 157–67 Cape edition); 17 sheets on yellow paper with holograph revisions.

(iii.) a portion of the middle of chapter 1 (corresponding to pp. 161–65 Cape edition); 5 sheets of yellow paper.

(iv.) two fair typescript sheets from chapter 6 (corresponding to pp. 244–45 in the Knopf edition).

(v.) 15 miscellaneous typescript sheets which, except for the first 8, do not follow sequentially. 5 of the pages, although not heavily emended, have been marked out as rejected.

c.) Parts II and III: Incomplete typescript of miscellaneous versions of a few pages from chapter 7, Part II, and chapters 6 and 7 of Part III.

Part II: Typescript with holograph corrections. 6 disconnected yellow sheets from the first half of chapter 7 (corresponding to pp. 152–60 of Knopf edition).

Part III: (i.) chapter 6, blue and pink paper typescript partially numbered in hand; 19 sheets (corresponds to pp. 232–44 of Knopf edition). Holograph emendations in blue and black ink.

(ii.) chapter 6, orange paper typescript two versions of p. 238 (2 sheets) of Knopf edition, both richly revised in blue ink. Typescript with holograph revisions in blue ink of p. 233 (1 sheet) of Knopf edition, of p. 235 (1 sheet) of Knopf edition, and 3 such versions of p. 236 (3 sheets) of Knopf edition.

(iii.) chapter 6, white paper versions of different pages: Tccms of p. 238 (1 sheet) of Knopf edition, typescript and Tccms of pp. 245–47 (4 sheets) of Knopf edition, Tccms of pp. 245–46 (2 sheets) of Knopf edition, and Tccms of pp. 246–47 (2 sheets) of Knopf edition. These sheets overlap the previous version.

(iv.) chapter 7, white paper typescript (3 sheets) with blue ink emendations (corresponding to pp. 275–77 of Knopf edition).

(v.) chapter 7 typescript of last page of book, crossed out and numbered in hand. p. 390 (corresponds to p. 307 of Knopf edition).

E23   *The Little Girls* (radio typescript) 25 Apr. 1969
Prepared for BBC performance. 94 pages, 8 x 13" mimeograph. Produced by Anthony Cornish. Adapted by Norman Painting. Recorded 19 Oct. 1968 (BBC) See F55.

E24   Preface to *A Day in the Dark* n.d. [1965]
Typescript of 5 sheets with a few manuscript revisions in blue ink. With the exception of one adjective, comparable with the printed version. (Texas) See A28.

E25   *The Good Tiger* (children's story) 28 Oct. 1964
(Texas) See A29.

a.) On an envelope in holograph, Bowen writes: '[deleted] M.S | Eva's Future | To take with me | [in blue ink] M.S.S. | of | *THE GOOD TIGER* | by | *Elizabeth Bowen*'. [Underlining is Bowen's.] Manuscript includes no pages from *Eva Trout*, even though the title refers to a draft of Part III, Chapter 3 of that novel. Typescript of printed version with very few holograph corrections dated in ink at the top right 'Oct 28 1964'; 10 pages. An earlier typescript on onionskin and heavily corrected with red and blue ink; 25 pages.

b.) On an envelope in holograph, Bowen writes: '[deleted] [in blue ink] Letters | 16th Oct '61 | *Personal* | [in pencil] 'THE GOOD TIGER | (My original M.S. | plus a re-type'. Typescript with holograph corrections in blue and black ink and numbered in hand at the top of the page; 33 sheets with one short sheet. Tccms with holograph corrections of the above typescript. Mimeographed 'Vocabulary List for Beginning Readers' by Collier Books, 5 sheets.

E26   *Eva Trout* (novel) n.d. [1968]
(Texas) See A30.

a.) Typescript and Tccms with author's manuscript revisions. Different typewriters, inks and various kinds of colored paper. Novel is printed in two parts. The typescript contains twelve chapters from Part I and four chapters from Part II; 497 pages.

Part I:
   Chapter 1: One version of 10 sheets with moderate corrections.
   Chapter 2: The title of the chapter is hand-printed in ink. Moderate to heavy revisions are made in blue and red ink; 22 sheets.

Chapter 3: Red and blue ink are used for the moderate revisions on the 10 sheets; again title of chapter printed by hand.

Chapter 4: Moderate to heavy revisions on 28 sheets in red and blue ink; chapter's title printed by hand.

Chapter 5: Moderate to heavy revisions; 43 sheets on yellow paper.

Chapter 6: Title changed in holograph from 'A Conspiracy' to 'Saturday Afternoon', which coincides with printed version. 13 pages heavily revised with deleted paragraphs.

Chapter 7: 30 pages of moderate to heavy revisions on white and yellow paper.

Chapter 8: 8 pages with moderate revisions on yellow paper.

Chapter 9: 24 pages with light revisions on yellow paper.

Chapter 10: 20 pages with moderate revisions.

Chapter 11: 12 pages Tccms with light to moderate revisions.

Chapter 12: 29 pages with moderate to heavy revisions on Tccms.

Part II:

Chapter 1: Originally numbered in holograph 'XIII', then crossed out and marked '1' to signify the beginning of Part II. 25 pages with light to moderate revisions on Tccms.

Chapter 2: 'Part II' printed in hand and lined through. Interior pagination of pp. 246–76. 31 pages of moderate to heavy corrections on Tccms. Different typewriters used.

Chapter 3: The title of this chapter is typed and underlined, but no chapter number is designated. This chapter contains 62 sheets, as follows: sheets 1–25 are Tccms; sheet 26 is ½ Tccms; sheets 27–62, more heavily revised throughout, are Ts. Various styles of pica and elite type appear throughout the chapter.

Chapter 4: 130 pages typescript moderately to heavily revised containing inconsistent internal numbering indicating considerable changes and rearranged mss.

b.) Incomplete Tccms with a few pages in typescript. Chapter 12 of Part I and chapters 2 and 4 of Part II are missing. A mixture of white and yellow paper, different typewriters and colors of ink. One miscellaneous page. 313 sheets.

Part I:

Chapters 1–5: Tccms corresponding to the same chapters in version E26a above.

Chapter 6: Tccms of version E26a except that the title has not been changed.

211

Chapter 7: Tccms of version E26a except that pp. 2–6 are missing.
Chapters 8–9: Tccms corresponding to same chapters in version E26a.

Chapter 10: Incomplete typescript with duplicate paragraphs in some instances; 16 sheets. 8 sheets representing pp. 115–28 of printed version.

Chapter 11: Three earlier versions of chapter on typescript and Tccms consisting of 10, 7, and 10 sheets respectively.

Part II:

Chapter 1: Typescript and Tccms of earlier version than E26a; 19 sheets.

Chapter 3: Typescript of 26 pages of which E26a is Tccms; typescript of 17 sheets representing pp. 199–208 of printed edition; typescript of 5 sheets representing pp. 217–19 of printed edition.

c.) Incomplete typescript and Tccms utilizing different typewriters, different colors and kinds of paper and ink. Only 4 of 16 chapters are represented, but in multiple versions; 139 sheets..

Part I:

Chapter 12: Complete version of chapter heavily corrected in blue and black ink; 29 sheets. An incomplete version of the chapter, heavily corrected and utilizing multiple ribbons and different kinds of white paper; corrections in blue and black ink; 17 sheets.

Part II:

Chapter 1: Complete typescript of chapter and identical to Tccms version in E26b above; the corrections are not as advanced as on E26a; 25 sheets.

Chapter 2: Incomplete typescript on white paper with blue holograph emendations; 16 sheets.

Chapter 3: Heavily corrected Tccms of first half of chapter in blue and red ink; 11 sheets. Typescript of the former with fewer corrections in blue ink; 11 sheets. Tccms dealing with the middle portion of the chapter representing pp. 207–13 of printed edition; lightly corrected 17 sheets. Tccms dealing with middle portion of the chapter representing pp. 216–23; moderately corrected 13 sheets.

d.) An early manuscript with most chapters marked in pen 'Rejected Draft'. Some chapters are missing and some bear no titles. Different typewriters, inks, and various kinds of white paper; corrections moderate to heavy; 186 sheets.

Part I:

Chapter 1: Heavily corrected typescript; 9 sheets.

Chapter 2: Heavily corrected typescript; 16 sheets.

Chapter 3: Typescript and Tccms, the latter more heavily corrected in blue ink; 8 sheets each.

Chapter 5: Typescript, titled and numbered; light to moderate corrections; 45 sheets.

Chapter 6: Typescript, titled and numbered; heavily corrected; 12 sheets.

Chapter 7: Incomplete Tccms, titled, numbered, and lightly corrected; 6 sheets.

Chapter 8: Typescript, titled, numbered, and moderately corrected; 9 sheets.

Chapter 9: Typescript, titled 'A Nocturnal Call' rather than 'A Late Call', numbered and heavily corrected; 27 sheets.

Part II:

Chapter 2: Typescript, titled, numbered and heavily corrected in blue ink; 31 sheets.

Chapter 3: Incomplete Tccms covering middle portion of the chapter; heavily corrected in red and blue ink; 15 sheets.

e.) An incomplete typescript and Tccms; chapters are numbered but not all are titled. Some chapters bear the note 'Rejected Draft'. Corrections are moderate to heavy; 92 sheets.

Part I:

Chapter 1: Typescript, titled, numbered, and heavily corrected, 11 sheets.

Chapter 2: Tccms with no title, but chapter and pages numbered; heavily corrected in blue ink, 16 sheets.

Chapter 3: Typescript, heavily corrected in blue and black ink, 8 sheets.

Chapter 5: Typescript corrected in blue and black ink with chapter and pages numbered, 34 sheets.

Chapter 7: Typescript, titled in ink and marked 'Draft' with pages numbered; corrected in blue and black ink, pages 17–19 missing; 23 sheets.

f.) Incomplete typescript and Tccms on pink, yellow, and white paper with holograph revisions; 343 pages.

Part I:

Chapter 1: Chapter numbered 'one (1)' but not titled. Only pages 1 and 2 numbered. 9 sheets (including two half-sheets) with two colors of type with moderate to heavy revisions on pink, yellow, and white paper.

Chapter 4: There are four versions of this chapter:

Chapter numbered IV in type, no title, in holograph at the top of the first page appears: 'Chap. 4. Part II (Conference) Rejected Draft'. All pages are numbered. The last three sheets are on odd over-size paper. Corrections are light except for crossing out the entire face of page 1. 15 sheets.

This draft begins, as does the published version, with a letter to Mrs. Arble, but contains only 5 sheets, though each is numbered and the first page has been crossed out.

Though the first page of this version of the typescript has also been crossed out, and though the pages are not numbered, this chapter has greater development than the former chapter. On the 12 sheets, there are light to moderate corrections.

This version begins midway into the chapter as compared to the published version and thus appears to be a version of the second half of the chapter. Again the first page is crossed out. Regular-sized and over-sized paper is used. One page is holograph. Corrections are moderate to heavy on the 10 sheets.

Chapter 8: Entitled: 'At Larkins'. With 'rejected draft' noted on first page. 13 heavily revised sheets.

Chapter 9: 28 partially numbered pages with moderate revisions. 'Original Draft' in ink at top of first page.

Chapter 10: 20 pages lightly revised.

Chapter 11: 12 pages with light to moderate revisions and numbered in ink.

Part II:

Chapter 3: 2 pages which constitute an insert to a draft of this chapter entitled: Part II. Chapter 3: 'Eva's Future'. 21 heavily corrected and partially numbered sheets. The final sheet compares with p. 211 of the published version. 8 unnumbered but heavily revised sequential sheets. The first sheet compares with p. 218 of the published version.

Chapter 4: 54 pages comparing with the Knopf version from pp. 224–58. 40 partially numbered pages whose first page bears the title of the chapter, but other characteristics show this version to be earlier than the above version. 6 partially numbered sheets comparing with pp. 241–45 which are heavily corrected. 6 sheets comparing with pp. 250–54 which are heavily corrected. 6 sheets comparing with pp. 254–58 and are heavily corrected. 3 sheets of same pages and different version. 17 sheets comparing with pp. 259–68 and lightly corrected. 5 sheets comparing with pp. 254–58 with no corrections. 3 sheets which compare with pp. 259–62 with no corrections. 11 pages comparing with pp. 269–75 moderately corrected. 11 non-sequentially numbered sheets comparing with pp. 275–82 and heavily corrected. 12 pages comparing with pp. 282–89 and heavily corrected. 13 very lightly revised pages numbered sequentially and comparing with pp. 289–97 of the published version.

E27 *Pictures and Conversations* (autobiographical fragment) n.d.
[1975]
(Texas) See A32.

a.) Typescript with holograph revisions. Different papers. The autobiography is printed in three parts. The typescript contains three parts and rejected pages; synopsis of projected book; and three work notebooks.
    1. In green folder: final typescript with holograph corrections. 'Origins', 34 sheets; 'Places', 23 sheets; 'People', 2 photocopies of final typescript with note in another hand indicating the space and inclusion as represented of synopsis material; 7 sheets each set.
    2. 'Origins': same as printed version. Heavily corrected 36 sheets, one loose sheet. 'Places': lightly corrected typescript of 8 sheets covering material from pp. 34–41, to end of quote from *The House in Paris*. Heavily corrected typescript of 21 pages which compares with the published version and continues from the above section. Another version of second part of 'Places', beginning in text on p. 42 and continuing to the end of the section; moderately corrected typescript of 15 pages. 6 loose sheets belonging to internal rewrites of Part II. 'People': 3-page lightly corrected typescript of published version; 3-sheet heavily corrected typescript of earlier version; 5-sheet rewritten versions of p. 59 in published version; 3-sheet lightly corrected typescript of earlier version; trial conclusions not printed of Part III, consisting of lightly corrected typescript of 3 loose pages and 2 sets of photocopies of these pages. On one set of photocopies in another hand are notes found in italics on p. 61 of published version. Synopsis of 4 typescript pages published as pp. 61–63 in Part III.
    3. In yellow envelope, in Jetline notebook of airmail stationery, lined paper, original holograph of chapter 1, 9 sheets. Holograph and heavily corrected typescript of 'Places' II comparing with pp. 34–41 of published version; 12 sheets.
    4. Spiral notebook containing quotes from *Jonah Barrington,* vol. I, 3 pages; vol. II, $1\frac{1}{2}$ pages; vol. III, $2\frac{1}{2}$ pages. *Dead Souls,* vol. I and vol II, 2 pages.
    5. Spiral notebook containing quotes from *On the Art of the Novel,*

and from *The Tale of Genji* by The Lady Murasaki, 2 pages.
6. Shorthand notebook containing trivia and jottings, 5 pages.

b.) 'The Move-In', lightly revised typescript, 9 pages.
c.) 'Bergotte', n.d. [21 Aug. 1971]
Near final holograph corrected typescript with single carbons, and duplicate carbons of some pages. In some cases the carbons are corrected as well. A brief comparison of the corrections indicates an earlier version. Typescript 36 pages; Tccms 36 pages, but some pages are duplicates and others are missing.

Contributions to Books and Periodicals

Often Bowen's short stories were adapted for radio or television after first publication. On the other hand, some broadcasts were commissioned especially for radio or television. In all cases, the date following the item in this section is the date of first performance, first airing, etc., while the bracketed date that follows is the date of first publication.

E28   TELLING (radio typescript) 5 June 1948 [Oct. 1927]
Prepared from short story for BBC broadcast. Produced by Henry Bentinck and read by Alan Blair. 8 x 13″ mimeo format with few emendations, 10 pages. T.49 on microfilm. (BBC) See A5a.

E29   THE CAT JUMPS (radio typescript) 27 Dec. 1956 [Sept. 1929]
Prepared from short story for BBC broadcast, 'A Book at Bedtime: The Cat Jumps'. Produced by Michael Wharton and read by Olive Gregg. 8 x 13″ mimeo format heavily revised, 11 pages. (BBC) See A8.

E30   THE TOMMY CRANS (radio typescript) 6 Nov. 1946 [Feb. 1930]
Prepared from short story for BBC broadcast. Producer not listed. Written and arranged for broadcasting by Elizabeth Bowen and read by Beatrice Curtis Brown. 6 pages. T.49 microfilm. Adapted for Radio 4 from Northern Ireland. 22 Nov. 1973, 11 pages. (BBC) See A8.

E31   HER TABLE SPREAD (short story) n.d. [May 1930]
Holograph with revisions, in black ink on light-weight paper. The titles 'The Heroes' and 'Hospitality' have been deleted in favor of 'Her Table Spread', originally published as 'A Conversation Picture'. 15 pages. (Texas) See A8.

E32 THE APPLE TREE (radio typescript) 14 Aug. 1962
[24 Sept. 1931]
Adapted short story, 7 pages. SS27 on microfilm. (BBC) See A8.

E33 SHE GAVE HIM (short story) n.d. [15 Nov. 1932]
Signed typescript, with few manuscript emendations. The title typed on
the manuscript, 'What She Gave Him', is signed by the author in black
ink. This story is one of nine in *Consequences,* initiated by A. E. Coppard. The manuscripts for all nine stories are contained in the same
case. 8 pages. (Texas) See B6.

E34 THE LITTLE GIRL'S ROOM (short story) n.d. [July 1933]
Manuscript, heavily revised. 20 sheets. (Texas) See A8.

E35 THE DISINHERITED (short story) n.d. [6 July 1934]
Signed manuscript, with revisions, 10 sheets. (Texas) See A8.

E36 FIRELIGHT IN THE FLAT (short story) n.d. [6 July 1934]
Manuscript with author's revisions, 12 pages. (Texas) See A8.

E37 FIRELIGHT IN THE FLAT (radio typescript) 24 Mar. 1971
Adapted from short story for BBC broadcast, 10 pages. (BBC) See A8.

E38 REDUCED (short story) n.d. [12 June 1935]
Signed manuscript, with authorial revisions. The title 'Marked Down' is
deleted for the present title. 16 sheets. (Texas) See A11.

E39 REDUCED (radio typescript) 8 May 1962
Adapted short story 9 pages, SS26 on microfilm. Produced 4 Apr. 1974
for Radio 4 from Bristol, 14 pages. (BBC) See A11.

E40 ATTRACTIVE MODERN HOMES (short story) n.d.
[15 Apr. 1936]
Signed manuscript, with revisions, 18 sheets. (Texas) See A11a.

E41 ATTRACTIVE MODERN HOMES (radio typescript) 12 Dec.
1963
Prepared from short story for BBC broadcast. Recorded for Future
Home Service. Produced by Michael Bukht. 8 x 13″ mimeo format, 12
pages. (BBC) See A11a.

E42 JANE AUSTEN (essay) n.d. [30 Apr. 1936]
Signed manuscript, with extensive revisions, in a case. 17 pages. (Texas)
First printed in B9 (q.v.).

E43 TEARS, IDLE TEARS (radio typescript) 15 Sept. 1964
[2 Sept. 1936]
Adapted short story, 10 pages. SS30 on microfilm (BBC) See A11.

E44 LOOK AT ALL THOSE ROSES (short story) n.d. [10 and 17
Nov. 1937]
Typescript, with considerable manuscript revision, 14 sheets. (Texas)
See A11.

E45 LOOK AT ALL THOSE ROSES (radio typescript) 25 and 26
May 1964
Prepared from short story for BBC broadcast and recorded for repeat
performance. Selected and edited by Eric Ewens. Produced by Cynthia
Pughe and read by Nicolette Bernard. 8 x 13″ mimeo format with
emendations in blue pencil, 12 pages. (BBC) See A11.

E46 THE EASTER EGG PARTY (radio typescript) 29 June 1964
[Apr. 1938]
Prepared from short story for BBC broadcast and recorded for repeat
performance. Selected and edited by Eric Ewens. Produced by Cynthia
Pughe and read by Hilda Schroder, 14 pages. (BBC) See A11.

E47 IN THE SQUARE (short story) n.d. [Sept. 1941]
Signed typescript, with manuscript and typed revisions. The title is in
manuscript, and Bowen has written 'Horizon' in pencil beneath her
name. 11 pages numbered in pencil in her hand. (Texas) See A15.

E48 STRENGTH OF MIND SERIES: DO WOMEN THINK LIKE
MEN? (radio typescript) 17 Oct. 1941 [30 Oct. 1941]
T.306 on microfilm (BBC) See C121.

E49 THE DEMON LOVER (radio typescript) 27 Aug. 1946 [6
Nov. 1941]
Adapted short story read by Evelyn Russell. 10 pages. SS8 on micro-
film. Produced 6 Apr. 1951 by Paul Stephenson and read by Catherine
Salkeld, 8 pages, W.H.18 on microfilm. Read on 17 Dec. 1956 by
Catherine Salkeld, 9 pages, T.49 on microfilm. Produced 10 Jan. 1974
for Radio 4 from Bristol, 10 pages. (BBC) See A15.

E50 STRENGTH OF MIND SERIES: CONVENTION AND VAL-
UE (radio typescript) 5 Dec. 1941 [18 Dec. 1941]
T.306 on microfilm (BBC) See C123.

E51 PINK MAY (radio typescript) 21 Nov. 1960 [Oct. 1942]
Adapted short story, 9 pages, SS24 on microfilm. Produced on 8 Nov. 1973 for Radio 4 from Bristol, 9 pages. (BBC) See A15.

E52 THE MOST UNFORGETTABLE CHARACTER I'VE MET (essay) n.d. [1944]
Typescript, with manuscript revision. In a case, with 'A MEMOIR' on the cover of the case. Each sheet on 8½ x 11" paper is mounted on a larger sheet. This is an autobiographical essay about Bowen's Court and Sarah Barry, the housekeeper when Elizabeth's father Henry took over Bowen's Court. The deleted title is: "Sarah Barry (or? 'Tipperary Woman')." 18 pp. (Texas) See C134.

E53 THE INHERITED CLOCK (short story) n.d. [Jan. 1944]
Typescript, with heavy manuscript and typed revisions, 29 pages. An address is pencilled at top of the typescript: 2 Clarence Terrace Regent's Park NW1. There is also an earlier typescript with pencil, ink, and typed revisions, 22 pages. (Texas) See A15.

E54 MYSTERIOUS KÔR (short story) n.d. [Jan. 1944]
Signed typescript, with manuscript revisions. Title is printed by hand in pencil, 10 pages. (Texas) See A15.

E55 SONGS MY FATHER SANG ME (short story) n.d. [Nov. 1944]
Typescript, with manuscript and typed revisions, 14 sheets. (Texas) See A15.

E56 SONGS MY FATHER SANG ME (radio typescript) 8 Aug. 1948
Prepared from short story for BBC broadcast. Produced by James Langham and read by Ara Calder-Marshall. 8 x 13" mimeo format with some authorial emendations referring primarily to tone or quality of delivery. 15 pages. T.49 on microfilm. (BBC) See A15.

E57 MAINIE JELLETT (essay) n.d. [Dec. 1944]
Typescript with few black ink revisions, 7 sheets. (Texas) See C140.

E58 THE SHORT STORY IN ENGLAND (essay) 6 Mar. 1945 [May 1945]
Two copies, Tccms. One copy contains minor blue ink revisions and says: '(*Corrected*)'. In pencil at the top of both copies: 'For Britain To day'. 8 pages. (Texas) See C142.

E59   OPENING UP THE HOUSE (essay) n.d. [Aug. 1945]
Tccms with few black ink revisions, 5 sheets. (Texas) See C143.

E60   FOLKESTONE 1945 (essay) [1946]
Tccms with few blue ink revisions. In hand at the top of the first page
is the title underlined twice; 9 sheets. (Texas) See A19.

E61   [ANSWER TO CYRIL CONNOLLY QUESTIONNAIRE FOR
HORIZON SYMPOSIUM] 15 Mar. 1945 [Aug. 1946]
Signed typescript to Cyril Connolly, in the form of a letter, with the first
sentence crossed out. In a case, with answers to the same questionnaire
by E. M. Forster, Osbert Sitwell, Lord David Cecil, Kathleen Raine,
Clive Bell, Maurice Baring, Graham Greene, David Gascoyne, Philip
Toynbee, Charles Morgan, C. V. Wedgwood, Enid Starkie, A. L. Rouse,
John Lehmann, and V. S. Pritchett. (Texas) See C189.

E62   THE GOOD EARL (short story) n.d. [23 Sept. 1946]
Typescript, on white paper with few emendations in black ink, of final
printed version, 18 sheets. Typescript on pink paper and heavily
emended in black ink; 17 sheets, some cut. (Texas) See B16.

E63   I DIED OF LOVE (short story) n.d. [ca. 5 Dec. 1946]
Typescript on white paper and richly emended in blue ink, compares
closely with printed version, 10 pages. (Texas) See B17.

E64   CRISIS (radio broadcast) 28 Feb. 1947 [20 Mar. 1947]
Tccms dated on the last page, 9 pages. First printed as 'The Power in
the Cave' (C225). (Texas) See 'She' in A25. Broadcast, F68.

E65   BOOKS AND AUTHORS: THE NEXT BOOK (radio typescript) 13 July 1947
T.66 on microfilm. (BBC) See C307.

E66   IMPRESSIONS OF CZECHOSLOVAKIA (radio broadcast) 15
Mar. 1948 [16 Mar. 1948]
Typescript and Tccms, 3 pages each. Tccms is a clean copy made from
the corrected typescript. (Texas) See F17.

E67   ELIZABETH BOWEN TO V. S. PRITCHETT (letters) n.d.
[July 1948]
Clean final typescript and Tccms notes on front page 'Copy'; each 6
pages. (Texas) See B21.

E68   ARTS MAGAZINE: HOW I WRITE (radio typescript) 10 May 1950 [21 Sept. 1948]
Interview with Glyn Jones. This appears to be a radio re-broadcast derived from the Television Magazine Programme 'Kaleidoscope'. T.13 on microfilm. (BBC) Mimeo-script, 9 pages. (Texas) See B20. Broadcast, F78.

E69   THE ARTIST IN SOCIETY (radio typescript) 10 July 1948 [Nov. 1948]
Scripted discussion between Graham Greene, Elizabeth Bowen and V. S. Pritchett. T.416 on microfilm. (BBC) See B21.

E70   LOST ART OF LIVING (essay) Oct. 1948 [Dec. 1948]
Tccms with holograph note at top of first page: "For: 'Contact' Oct 1948". 8 sheets. (Texas) See C316.

E70.1   REGENT'S PARK AND ST JOHN'S WOOD 1 Mar. 1949
Four versions: (Texas).
a.) Tccms on same typewriter and paper as version c, but a revised b version. The first page, and the first paragraph in particular, has been heavily revised in blue ink. Pages 2–8 are clean.
b.) Typescript on bond with black ink revisions, 8 sheets. In pencil at the top of the page, '2,350 words'.
c.) Tccms onionskin large type and marked on the front sheet in hand: '(Duplicate)'. Emendations in blue ink.
d.) Typescript on blue paper which is marked at the top: 'Duplicate'. Heavily emended in black ink. 6 pages. See B24.

E71   FOREWORD BY ELIZABETH BOWEN (essay) 9 Aug. 1949 [Nov. 1949]
Tccms (2 copies), one marked in black '(Corrected)' and the other '(Uncorrected)', which is crossed out. 'Foreword By Elizabeth Bowen to TOMATO CAIN By Nigel Kneale'. The first is corrected in black ink and the second in blue ink. The carbons are identical in their corrections and compare exactly with the printed version, 4 sheets. (Texas) See B23.

E72   BOOKS THAT GROW UP WITH ONE (radio essay) 26 Sept. 1949 [9 Mar. 1950]
Tccms, 7 sheets. (Texas) See C377.

E73   IMMORTAL CITY (book review) [1950]

Tccms with one emendation. Review of *James Joyce's Dublin*, by Patricia Hutchins, 5 sheets. (Texas)

E73.1 FAMOUS WOMEN NO. 7: THE MECHANICS OF WRITING (talk) 14 Nov. 1949 [24 Nov. 1949]
Talk by Elizabeth Bowen. T.139 on microfilm. (BBC) See C375, F76.

E74 D. H. LAWRENCE (book review) Apr. 1950
Tccms book review of *Portrait of a Genius, But . . .* , a life of D. H. Lawrence, by Richard Aldington. Numerous holograph corrections in blue ink and a few typed carbon corrections. 5 sheets. (Texas)

E75 THOUGHTS IN NEW YORK (essay) n.d. [July 1950]
Typescript on blue paper with blue ink and pencil emendations; one page a re-drafting of another. Each numbered in hand separately. Pages of the first draft contain the title: 'Thoughts in America. By Elizabeth Bowen'. America is crossed out and in holograph, in blue ink, is inserted 'New York', underlined twice. 9 sheets, 2 cut. (Texas) See C379.

E76 BRITAIN IN AUTUMN BY ELIZABETH BOWEN (essay) n.d. [24 Apr. 1950]
Clean typescript on onionskin. Page 6 has been cut in two places and pasted on a firmer sheet. Note on page: 'CUT BY CENSOR'. Names were cut out on the 5th page. This is a longer version of 'London 1940', published in *Collected Impressions*, 10 sheets. (Texas) See A19a.

E77 FIRE AND WATER (book review) n.d. [1950–1951]
Tccms with few emendations; review of *The Fire in the Dust,* by Francis MacManus, 2 sheets. (Texas) See C385.1.

E78 FOREWORD TO THE STORIES AND POEMS OF ELIZABETH BIBESCU (essay) n.d. [Apr. 1951]
Clean Tccms. On front sheet in Bowen's hand, 'Foreword'. Differs only in a few sentences and phrases from the printed version, 6 sheets. (Texas) See B25.

E79 THE LAND BEHIND (book review) n.d. [8 July 1951]
Tccms with few corrections in black ink. Review of *Sheridan Le Fanu,* by Nelson Browne, 3 sheets. (Texas) See C388.

E80 WRITING AND WRITER'S REMINISCENCES: THE CULT OF NOSTALGIA (radio typescript) n.d. [4 Aug. 1951]

Mimeo-script with authorial emendations. Elizabeth Bowen recorded the broadcast for later transmission. Produced by B. C. Horton, 7 pages. T.49 on microfilm. (BBC) Tccms 7 pages. (Texas) See C389.

E81 INTRODUCTION (essay) n.d. [ca. Feb. 1952]
Typescript with one page holograph, greatly revised in blue ink. Introduction to *North and South* by Elizabeth Cleghorn Gaskell, 7 pages, some cut. (Texas) See A25.

E82 THE ART OF RESERVE OR, THE ART OF RESPECTING BOUNDARIES (essay) n.d. [1 Apr. 1952]
Typescript with moderate to heavy blue ink revisions, 5 sheets. (Texas) See C393.

E83 E. M. ALMEDINGEN (book review) 18 Apr. 1952
Tccms with few emendations. Review of E. M. Almedingen's autobiography, 2 sheets. (Texas)

E84 EXPLORER (book review) 18 Apr. 1952 [4 May 1952]
Tccms. Review of *Wait Now!*, by Rachel Knappett, 2 sheets. (Texas) See C394.

E85 DUBLIN: 1660–1860 (book review) 18 Apr. 1952 [18 May 1952]
Tccms with few ink emendations. Review of *Dublin: 1660–1860*, by Maurice Craig, 3 sheets. (Texas) See C395.

E86 THE BIG MASTER (book review) 22 May 1952
Tccms. Review of *Dr. E. De Somerville: A Biography,* by Geraldine Cummins. Preface by Lennox Robinson, 4 sheets. (Texas)

E87 COME TO IRELAND (book review) 30 May 1952
Tccms. Review of *Ireland and the Irish*, by Charles Duff, 4 sheets. (Texas)

E88 HAND IN GLOVE (short story) 23 June 1952 [27 Oct. 1952]
Two Tccms copies on yellow paper with minor ink emendations. Date in pencil at the top of the first page. These Tccmss compare with the printed edition, 14 sheets each. (Texas) See A28.

E89 PREFACE TO THE SECOND GHOST BOOK (essay) 28 July 1952 [27 Oct. 1952]
Typescript and Tccms in white and yellow paper respectively. The date

is noted in black ink at the top of the first page of the carbon. Both copies are only lightly emended. On the first page of the typescript, notes are made for setting the Ts in type, 4 sheets each. (Texas) See A25.

E90   CELEBRITY (book review) 27 Nov. 1952 [5 Dec. 1952]
Two Tccms copies with few emendations. Review of *Arnold Bennett*, by Reginald Pound, 4 sheets. (Texas) See C398.

E91   SOURCES OF INFLUENCE (essay) n.d. [29 June 1953]
Tccms on pink second sheets with only one emendation, 5 pages. (Texas) See A25, A26.

E92   ENGLISH FICTION AT MID-CENTURY (essay) 21 Aug. 1953 [21 Sept. 1953]
Tccms. In hand on top of first page: 'New Republic | (21 | 8 | 53)'. 4 pages. (Texas) See C406.

E93   ON GIVING A PRESENT (essay) n.d. [18 Dec. 1953]
Typescript with few holograph emendations. Housed with 'Eva Trout' manuscript, 8 sheets. (Texas) See C408.

E94   WHAT I WANT NOW TO DO . . . (book review) n.d. [21 Feb. 1954]
Tccms with few corrections. Review of *A Writer's Diary*, by Virginia Woolf, ed. Leonard Woolf, 5 sheets. (Texas) See A25, A26.

E95   DISAPPOINTMENT (essay) n.d. [Mar. 1954]
Tccms on yellow paper with black ink emendations. In pencil on the top right hand of the first page: 'Reader's Digest | (30 | 9 | 1953)'. 8 pages. Tccms on pink second sheets without emendations or date. Discusses the same issue as does the Tccms on yellow paper, but is not a draft of the former article, 3 pages. (Texas) See C418.1.

E96   OUTRAGEOUS LADIES (essay) n.d. [after June 1956]
Tccms clean copy, 7 pages. Typescript heavily revised with blue ink on pink paper. Pages 2 and 5 are cut sheets. The revisions on this typescript are reproduced in the clean Tccms above, 6 pages. (Texas)

E97   SOME HORRORS OF CHILDHOOD SERIES: RISING TO THE OCCASION (radio typescript) 19 July 1956 [26 July 1956]
Produced by B. C. Horton. 8 x 13" mimeo-script heavily revised. Re-

fers to occasions in Bowen's Edwardian childhood which provoked responses of gratitude, sympathy, interest, and enthusiasm. 6 pages. T.49 on microfilm. (BBC) See C548.

E98 TRUTH AND FICTION SERIES (radio typescript) 26 Sept. | 3 Oct. | 10 Oct. 1956
Produced by B. C. Horton. (BBC) See A25.
 a.) 'Story, Theme and Situation', read by Elizabeth Bowen. *Vanity Fair,* by W. M. Thackeray, excerpt read by Arthur Ridley. *Brighton Rock,* by Graham Greene, excerpt read by Robert Sansom. *Jane Eyre,* by Charlotte Brontë, excerpt read by Marjorie Mars. 8 x 13" mimeo format, 9 pages.
 b.) 'People: The Creation of Character', read by Elizabeth Bowen. *Portrait of a Lady,* by Henry James, excerpt read by Arthur Ridley. *The Tunnel,* by Dorothy Richardson, excerpt read by Marjorie Mars. *Mansfield Park,* by Jane Austen, excerpt read by Arthur Ridley. *Howard's End,* by E. M. Forster, excerpt read by Robert Sansom. *Elders and Betters,* by Ivy Compton-Burnett, excerpt read by Robert Sansom. 8 x 13" mimeo format and a clean copy, 10 pages.
 c.) 'Time, Period and Reality', read by Elizabeth Bowen. *Mrs. Dalloway,* by Virginia Woolf, excerpt read by Marjorie Mars. *Bleak House,* by Charles Dickens, excerpt read by Robert Sansom. 8 x 13" mimeo format and a clean copy, 9 pages. T.49 on microfilm.

E99 MISS WILLIS (essay) 11 July 1952 [1957]
Tccms on onionskin paper with few blue ink revisions. Miss Willis was Bowen's headmistress at Downe House. Early version of printed essay, 3 sheets. (Texas) See B30.

E100 PERSUASION (essay) n.d. [Apr. 1957]
Clean Tccms on Jane Austen, 9 pages. Typescript on pink paper, some cut and most greatly revised in blue ink, 9 pages. (Texas) See C586.

E101 THE BEAUTY OF BEING YOUR AGE n.d. [July 1961].
Typescript, with holograph emendations. The essay was received from Mrs. Sewell Haggard of Curtis Brown, Ltd. 5 pages. (Texas) See C655.

E102 EXCLUSION (essay) n.d. [1962]
Typescript with revisions in blue ink on pink second sheets, 6 pages. (Texas) See A25, A26.

Miscellaneous, Unfinished, and Unpublished Items

This section is arranged alphabetically as follows: Address, Autobiography, Broadcast or Dramatic Production, Essay, Notebook, Novel, Short Story, Translation. Within each section, items whose dating is unknown or unclear precede those listed chronologically.

Address

E103   LANGUAGE n.d.
Manuscript 9 x 11" white bond, 6 pages; manuscript, 8 x 10" white paper, earlier outline, 5 pages. (Texas)

E104   THE POETIC ELEMENT IN FICTION n.d. [22 Dec. 1950]
Typescript heavily emended in blue ink on first two pages; 14 pages; Tccms, 14 sheets. Included with the two copies is a letter from Mrs. Sewell Haggard, of Curtis Brown, Ltd. in New York. (Texas)

Autobiography

E105   *BIOGRAPHICAL NOTE* | ELIZABETH BOWEN June 1948
Tccms, 1 sheet. (Texas)

E106   BIOGRAPHICAL NOTE ELIZABETH BOWEN 3 June 1948
Tccms, 2 sheets. (Texas)

E107   MATERIAL FOR *THE BROADSHEET* FROM ELIZABETH BOWEN | *THE HEAT OF THE DAY* n.d. [refers to finishing *The Shelbourne*: therefore after 1949 and before 1951]
Tccms, 3 pages. (Texas)

E108   ELIZABETH BOWEN | AUTOBIOGRAPHICAL NOTE n.d.
[holograph note in another hand refers to the retirement of Bowen's husband in January 1952 and to his death on 26 August 1952]
Two identical copies 6 sheets each; Tccms copy with fewer emendations and lacking note on husband, 6 pages. (Texas)

E109   AUTOBIOGRAPHICAL NOTE | FOR *EVERYWOMAN* | ELIZABETH BOWEN n.d.
Typescript with a few emendations, 2 sheets. (Texas)

E110   ELIZABETH BOWEN 17 Aug. 1953
Tccms written for and sent to *Mademoiselle*, New York, 2 sheets. Type-script of above with emendations, earlier version, 2 sheets. (Texas)

E111   THE LITTLE GIRLS n.d. [1963]
Biographical material for dust jacket, sent to publishers. The piece itself was written by William Plomer. Tccms and photocopy on 8 x 10" paper with few manuscript revisions. Each 2 pages. (Texas) See E187.

Broadcast or Dramatic Production

E112   KINSALE | SON ET LUMIÈRE n.d.
Mimeo-script, 35 pages; Tccms, onionskin, 8 x 10" script, 48 pages; historical notes for mimeo-script, 8 x 13", 1 sheet; poem 'After Aughrim', by Hon. Emily Lawless, 8 x 13", 1 sheet; Tccms, historical notes on 17th-century Kinsale Co., Cork, 8 x 13", 5 sheets. (Texas)

E113   THE LIVING IMAGE SERIES 4 Dec. 1941
T.416 on microfilm. (BBC) See F60.

E114   THE LIVING IMAGE SERIES 23 Jan. 1942
T.416 on microfilm. (BBC) See F62.

E115   NEW JUDGEMENT: ELIZABETH BOWEN ON JANE AUS-TEN 8 Mar. 1942
Typescript with manuscript revision. Play format with narrator, charac-ters from Jane Austen's novels, and Austen's sisters and brothers. Produced by Stephen Potter, 13 pages. 16 August 1948. 2 copies mimeo-script of revised version recorded for new production. Jane Austen spoken by Celia Johnson, reader Carleton Hobbs. 24 pages. (BBC) and (Texas) See F1.

E116   LONDON REVISITED | AS SEEN BY FANNY BURNEY n.d. [14 Nov. 1942]
Incomplete draft, 8 x 13", radio typescript with pencil revisions. Play format with six characters, 7 pages. (Texas) See F2.

E117   THE CONFIDANTE n.d. [9 Sept. 1943]
Typescript of a play, heavily corrected in pencil, 17 pages. Accompany-ing draft is ALS (9 Sept. 1943) from Edward Charles Sackville-West suggesting improvements to be made on radio script. 3 pages. (Texas)

E118   BOOK TALK—NEW AND RECENT FICTION 25 June 1945
Book reviews on the radio by Elizabeth Bowen. Reviews of Hester
Chapman, *I Will be Good*, Rumer Godden, *A Fugue in Time*, and L. F.
Loveday, *The Horse of the Sun*. 8 x 13" mimeo-typescript format with
holograph emendations. T.49 on microfilm. 6 pages. (BBC) See F63.

E119   BOOK TALK—NEW AND RECENT FICTION 16 July 1945
Book reviews on the radio by Elizabeth Bowen. Reviews of Frank
Tilsley, *Jim Comes Home*, Louis Bromfield, *What Became of Ann
Bolton,* and Hilda Vaughan, *Pardon and Peace*. 8 x 13", mimeo-type-
script, format heavily revised. T.49 on microfilm. 7 pages. (BBC) See
F64.

E120   SANDITON COMPETITION 21 Oct. 1948
Report by judges, one of whom was Elizabeth Bowen. T.455 on microfilm
(BBC) See F21.

E121   A YEAR I REMEMBER 1918   10 Mar. 1949
Two copies of typescript, produced by R. D. Smith with a cast of
thirteen. 8 x 13" mimeo-typescript, 20 pages. (BBC) and (Texas) See
F23.

E122   IN MY LIBRARY 2 Nov. 1949
Prerecorded 'talk' for broadcast, about the books to which one is at-
tached and comes back. Bowen includes Mrs. Gaskell's *Cranford,*
Louisa May Alcott's juvenile novels, and Dickens' *David Copperfield*.
There are four critical criteria, the last of which is the most important.
The novel must have the power to expand. As examples she mentions
Jane Austen's *Emma*, Flaubert's *Sentimental Education* and Tolstoi's
War and Peace. Produced by Kay Fuller. 8 x 10" mimeo-typescript,
heavily revised. T.49 on microfilm. 8 pages. (BBC) See F75.

E123   ELIZABETH BOWEN AND JOCELYN BROOKE 15 Dec.
1950
Two copies of mimeo-script 8 x 13", transcribed from telediphone recording 3 Oct. 1950. Subject: Elizabeth Bowen as novelist. Suggests her
emphasis is on landscape or place and not on plot and character. She
has least feeling for *Friends and Relations* and most for *The Last September*, which is an example of a novel of place. She is surprised that
critics refer to *The Death of the Heart* as a novel about adolescence.
15 pages. T.58 on microfilm. (BBC) Accompanying the script is ALS
(11 Oct. 1950) from Howard Newby. Typescript of early version with

holograph emendations by Bowen and Brooke. Outline of ideas to be covered in broadcast, 8 pages. (Texas) See F79.

E124 CONVERSATION ON TRAITORS 21 Aug. 1952
Unscripted discussion with three other speakers. T.10 on microfilm. (BBC) See F81.

E125 CORONATION—RECOLLECTIONS 31 May 1953
Some thoughts on the Coronation, by C. V. Wedgwood and Elizabeth Bowen. T.634 on microfilm. (BBC) See F82.

E126 CONTEMPORARY BRITISH NOVELISTS 2 June 1955
Unscripted discussion with Walter Allen. T.632 on microfilm. (BBC) See F84.

E127 WRITING ABOUT ROME 14 Oct. 1959
Elizabeth Bowen discusses writing *A Time in Rome*. Produced by B. C. Horton. Transcribed from telediphone recording, 8 x 13″ mimeo-script. T.49 on microfilm. 3 pages. (BBC) See F90.

E128 FRANKLY SPEAKING 16 Mar. 1960
Two copies of interview of Elizabeth Bowen by John Bowen, William Craig, and W. N. Ewer. 1: original uncut transcript with pencil and blue ink corrections, 8 x 13″ white sheets dated at the top of the first page, '11th September, 1959'. (Texas) 2:T.167 on microfilm. (BBC) See F91.

E129 THE WORLD OF BOOKS 14 Mar. 1964
Interview of Elizabeth Bowen by Robert Waller. Also included, a review of *The Little Girls*. T.673 on microfilm. (BBC) See F96.

E130 THE WORLD OF BOOKS 26 June 1965
Elizabeth Bowen reviews Elizabeth Coxhead's *Daughters of Erin*. T.674 on microfilm. (BBC) See F98.

Essay

E131 GIRLHOOD n.d.
Tccms on two grades of paper. On the first page in pencil: 'For: *The Leader*'. Slight pencil revisions. 8 pages. (Texas)

E132   THE IDEA OF A HOME n.d.

Tccms with blue ink revisions. The note at the end indicates the final pages are missing. Originally this was given as an address at Barnard College. 17 pages. (Texas)

E133   IRELAND n.d.

Signed typescript with heavy revisions on yellow second sheets which are matted on larger paper. In a case entitled 'Ireland (A Study)'. 18 pages. (Texas)

E134   ALFRED KNOPF n.d.

Typescript with few blue ink emendations. 8 pages. (Texas)

E135   *WAS* IT AN ART? n.d.

Typescript on white paper. Holograph note on page 4: 'Begin', underlined twice in red ink. From internal discussion, typewriter, and paper this appears to be one of Bowen's later articles. 9 pages. (Texas)

E136   REJECTED PAGES FROM THE EUDORA WELTY ARTICLE n.d.

Title for this group of pages is pencilled in holograph on cover sheet. Often Bowen saves rejected sheets. Holograph emendations in blue ink. Some cut pages. One group of three pages numbered in hand at the top right hand corner. Two pages are clipped together and the title 'Eudora Welty' is placed at the top of the page. A few holograph emendations. 17 sheets. (Texas)

E137   PAUL MORAND n.d. [1932]

Unsigned holograph on 8 x 10″ faintly-lined onionskin paper. This character sketch was enclosed in letter to Ottoline Morrell dated 1 Dec. 1932. 3 pages. (Texas)

E138   THE IDEA OF FRANCE 23 Nov. 1944

Tccms with black ink manuscript revisions. Essay about Bowen's personal views of France. 6 pages. (Texas)

E139   TOYS 7 Dec. 1944

Typescript and a few black ink revisions. 7 sheets. (Texas)

E140   PARIS PEACE CONFERENCE: 1946 | AN IMPRESSION. BY ELIZABETH BOWEN

Typescript with few black ink revisions; the content repeats some of the ideas in the three accompanying essays entitled 'Some Impressions'. 7 sheets.

    a.) *'Some Impressions. By Elizabeth Bowen* | I.'
Tccms with black ink emendations, 4 sheets.

    b.) *'Some Impressions. By Elizabeth Bowen.* | 2.'
Tccms with black ink emendations, 4 pages.

    c.) *'Some Impressions. By Elizabeth Bowen.* | 3.'
Tccms with black ink revisions, 4 pages. (Texas)

E141   HUNGARY 29 Oct. 1948
Two Tccms copies marked in ink and pencil on the top page of one copy: (Duplicate) *File Copy.* Few emendations. 10 pages. (Texas)

E142   WOMAN'S PLACE IN THE AFFAIRS OF MAN n.d. [1961]
Typescript, with manuscript emendations. Included with the typescript is ALS to Mrs. Morris. 4 pages. (Texas)

E143   BLANCHE KNOPF 1965
Typescript, with manuscript emendations. Photocopy. Date is written and underlined in blue ink at top of first page. This is a character sketch of Mrs. Knopf, and a brief account of the importance she played in the Borzoi story. Written the year of the Knopf House Fiftieth Birthday. 6 pages. (Texas)

Notebooks

E144   NOTES FOR LECTURES AT VASSAR 9 Feb. 1960
Signed manuscript in two spiral notebooks; with blue and red ink drawings and doodles on some pages. The earliest date of the first notebook, containing 70 pages, is 9 Feb. 1960; the last date in the second notebook, containing 14 pages, is 24 May 1960. (Texas)

E145   MISCELLANEOUS n.d. [1962]
Spiral notebook, 8 x 10″ sidebound from the University of Wisconsin. See A27, A29. (Texas) Contains in this order:

    a.) Early manuscript version, heavily deleted, of *The Little Girls,* with letters to 'Sheikie' signed 'Dicey from Applegate'. Some letters deleted and rewritten. Other scenes begun. These letters begin on p. 209 of the printed version. 5 pages.

b.) Notes from the *Junior Encyclopedia,* written on both sides of the paper, on Jacob and Wilhelm Grimm (1785–1863 and 1786–1859). 4 pages.

c.) Original efforts at the opening of *The Good Tiger.* Four efforts at the first sentence open the pages of this section of the notebook. 3 sheets.

d.) Opening the notebook from the back and upside down, one finds notes on *The Little Girls* for a class assignment. 5 sheets.

Novel

E146   ANNA n.d.

Unsigned manuscript with revisions on 8 x 10″ lined onionskin. Four chapters of unfinished work included in this holding: little or no internal evidence to indicate time of writing, but notes from bookseller indicate ca. 1932. The last chapter is about the relationship between St. Quentin and Anna. The subject matter focuses on the problems of writing, and on the difference between art and life. Chapter one contains 17 sheets, some cut; chapter two contains 13 sheets, some cut; chapter three contains 12 sheets and chapter four 16 sheets. (Texas)

Short Story

E147   THE BAZAAR. n.d.

Holograph in black ink on 7 x 10″ lined sheets, slightly corrected. 20 pages. (Texas)

E148   BEGINNING OF THIS DAY. n.d.

Typescript of story fragment with pencil emendations. 4 sheets. (Texas)

E149   CHRISTMAS GAMES. n.d.

Heavily revised typescript; 18 sheets, some cut. (Texas)

E150   FAIRIES AT THE CHRISTENING. n.d.

Tccms on two weights of paper with blue ink emendations. 21 sheets, some cut. (Texas)

E151   FLOWERS WILL DO. n.d.

Lightly corrected typescript with some internal changes indicating possibly two drafts compiled. The first pages of the story are a later draft. 23 sheets, only a few of which are numbered in pencil. (Texas)

E152   GHOST STORY? n.d.
Typescript of story fragment lightly emended in pencil with 11 sheets, some cut. (Texas)

E153   HOME FOR CHRISTMAS. n.d.
Typescript with pencil emendations. Title in pencil at top of first page. 12 sheets. (Texas)

E154   MISS JOLLEY HAS NO PLANS FOR THE FUTURE. n.d.
Slightly corrected holograph in black ink on 8 x 10" lined onionskin paper. 7 sheets. (Texas)

E155   THE MAN AND THE BOY. n.d.
Incomplete manuscript in black ink and heavily revised on 8 x 10" lined onionskin paper. 10 sheets, some cut. (Texas)

E156   NOW THE DAY IS OVER. n.d.
Incomplete typescript with holograph revisions in blue ink. 5 sheets. (Texas)

E157   ONLY YOUNG ONCE. n.d.
Lightly revised holograph in black ink on 8 x 10" ruled onionskin paper. From the handwriting it appears to be an early story. 10 sheets. (Texas)

E158   STILL THE MOON. n.d.
Typescript of story fragment with slight blue ink emendations. 5 sheets. (Texas)

E159   WOMEN IN LOVE. n.d.
Typescript with holograph emendations in blue ink. On the first sheet: 'T.V. ? By Elizabeth Bowen | *Women in Love*'. 26 pages, some cut. Tccms missing pp. 4, 7, 9, 11, 13, and 21. Two versions of p. 25. (Texas)

E160   STORY FRAGMENT. n.d.
Typescript with holograph revisions, and Bowen's signature. Unidentified story fragment. One page, numbered 14. (Texas)

E161 STORY FRAGMENT. n.d.
Typescript with pencil emendations. Beginning of story or character sketch of Amy Ticer. 4 pages, one of which is a duplicate with holograph revisions. (Texas)

E162 STORY FRAGMENT. n.d.
Typescript with a few pencil emendations. The beginning of a story or sketch of Ellen Nevin, whose mother is to be remarried. 2 pages. (Texas)

E163 STORY FRAGMENT. n.d.
Holograph with emendations in black ink, on 8 x 10" lined onionskin paper. Same handwriting as in E154, E155, and E157. Character sketch of a man. Break in story line. 4 pages. (Texas)

E164 STORY FRAGMENT. n.d.
Typescript with pencil emendations. Some cut sheets. In pencil at top, 'Strong Scene'. 9 sheets. Earlier typescript of same story fragment with pencil emendations. Also some cut sheets. 7 sheets. Two versions of story of Len Osten, his wife Rene, his cousin Flora, and his best friend Alec. (Texas)

E165 A THING OF THE PAST. n.d. [1944]
Typescript on pink paper. On the cover sheet in holograph: 'Beginning of a | short story | "A Thing of the Past" '. A few pencil emendations. An earlier version of E166. Story clipped together with 'The Last Bus', 4 sheets. (Texas) See E166.

E166 THE LAST BUS. 29 Nov. 1944
Typescript with ink emendations date typed on last page. 8 pages. (Texas)

Translations

E167 INDEX. n.d.
Holograph list in alphabetical order with volume, pages, etc. on the right-hand margin following each item. Alphabet ranges from A to U on lined onionskin paper. 17 sheets. (Texas)

E168 FLAUBERT, *Letters*. Vol. II n.d.
Clean typescript on partially and randomly numbered onionskin paper. 27 sheets. (Texas)

E169   FLAUBERT. n.d.
(Texas)
a.) Typescript and Tccms with holograph corrections of unidentified portions—numerous duplicate copies with one copy moderately emended in black ink. 49 sheets, beige paper.
b.) Tccms, 8 x 10" paper lightly emended in black ink. 3 sheets.
c.) Typescript on 8 x 10" paper lightly emended in black ink. 4 sheets.

E170   PROUST, *Le Temps Retrouvé*. n.d.
(Texas)
a.) Holograph translation on light brown, blue, and white paper with a note to typist. 43 sheets.
b.) Vol. I, page 7, holograph translation on lined onionskin paper in black ink. 7 sheets.
c.) Vol. 1, page 7, typescript lightly emended in pencil. 5 sheets.
d.) Vol. II, holograph and typescript, clean onionskin paper. 6 sheets.
e.) Vol II, follows E171d typescript with holograph emendation in first part only, on 8 x 10" paper. 25 sheets.

E171   JACQUES DE LACRATELLE, *Colère*; *suivi d'un Journal de Colère*. 1926
The holograph script is hurried and becomes less legible toward the end. Twenty-seven 8 x 10" lightly lined onionskin sheets; fourteen sheets in black ink and thirteen sheets in pencil. (Texas)

E172 UNSPECIFIED.
Holograph in black ink and pencil. 8 x 10" lined onionskin paper. 17 sheets. (Texas)

Miscellaneous Items about Elizabeth Bowen

E173   Peter Quennell 1926 [1935]
Untitled holograph essay on Elizabeth Bowen and in particular on *The House in Paris,* in Quennell's 'Trans-Siberian Notebook'. 6 sheets. (Texas)

E174   David Daiches [1938]
Critical commentary on Elizabeth Bowen. Signed holograph, 8½ x 10" paper. 2 pages. Housed in case with the incomplete holograph drafts and incomplete typescript of *The Death of the Heart.* (NYPL–B)

E175   John Lehmann [1945]
'British Reading—November'. Tccms, initialed review of *The Demon Lover*. 4 pages. (Texas)

E176   L. A. G. Strong 26 Oct. 1946
'Living Writers Series'. A talk on Elizabeth Bowen. T.522 on microfilm. (BBC) See F11.

E177   John Lehmann 31 May 1947
'Signposts in English Literature'. TccmsS slightly emended and dated May 1947 of BBC broadcast on Elizabeth Bowen. 3 pages. (Texas) See F14.

E178   John Lehmann 21 Oct. 1947
'Studies in English Letters'. Signed typescript of radio script for BBC on Elizabeth Bowen, dated 4 Sept. 1947. 6 pages. (Texas) T.280 on microfilm. (BBC) See F14.

E179   Ray Sands [26 July 1948]
'The Last September'. Book review sent from the South African Broadcasting Corporation, and broadcast from Durban and Pieternarilybury, 6 Sept. 1948. 3 pages. (Texas)

E180   L. P. Hartley 16 Nov. 1948
'Elizabeth Bowen: An Appreciation'. A talk broadcast on radio. T.200 on microfilm. (BBC) See F22.

E181   Pyke Johnson [21 Feb. 1949]
'The Askance Lady'. A parody of *The Heat of the Day*. Typescript dedicated to the Literary Guild and, respectfully, to Elizabeth Bowen. (Johnson) See E394.

E182   [Unsigned] Radio typescript on *The House in Paris* 21 May 1950
Written for NBC theater. 2 pages. Enclosed in envelope addressed to Mrs. Pyke Johnson, c/o Alfred A. Knopf, 501 Madison Avenue, New York. (Johnson)

E183   L. A. G. Strong 20 June 1950
'The Contemporary English Novel: The Work of Elizabeth Bowen'. Radio typescript. T.522 on microfilm. (BBC) See F11.

E184   Naomi Lewis 20 Nov. 1951

'The Other Side of the Door'. A radio talk on Elizabeth Bowen. W.H.21 on microfilm. (BBC) See F26.

E185   Joselyn Brooke n.d. [1952]
'Elizabeth Bowen'. Typescript with manuscript revisions, $8\frac{1}{2}$ x 11". Includes 'A Select Bibliography'. 39 pages. Typescript on Jocelyn Brooke and Bowen by the editor. 1 page. Galley proofs of monograph. 13 sheets. (Texas) See H15.

E186   L. P. Hartley 26 Mar. 1957
'London Calling Asia: English Writing'. Radio talk on Elizabeth Bowen. T.130 on microfilm. (BBC) See F22.

E187   William Plomer 8 Dec. 1963
'The Little Girls'. Photocopy of holograph biographical blurb for dust jacket of Jonathan Cape edition. 3 pages. Photocopy. 1 page. (Texas) See E111.

Letters from Elizabeth Bowen

The names of recipients are listed at the beginning of each entry, followed by a partial indication of content or subject matter. Letters are so treated individually, with one important exception: substantive material from letters written by Bowen's secretary to another assistant or to Bowen herself has been incorporated into descriptions of earlier Bowen letters, to avoid independent listings. This section is arranged alphabetically by recipient.

E188   Joe [Joseph] Randolph Ackerley. Promotional comment for his book *My Dog Tulip*, to be sent to American publisher. ALS Carbery, Church Hill. Hythe, Kent. 19 May 1965. 2 pages. (Texas)

E189   Audrey Anderson. Regarding script of *Impressions of Czechoslovakia* for broadcast. TLS 2 Clarence Terrace, Regent's Park N.W.1 3 Mar. 1948. 1 page. (BBC)

E190   Audrey Anderson. Accompanies script of broadcast, which is not housed with letter. TLS 2 Clarence Terrace, Regent's Park N.W.1 15 Mar. 1948. 1 page. (BBC)

E191   Helen Arbuthnot. Personal. Regarding broadcast of 'The Traitors' program. TLS Bowen's Court, Kildorrery, Co. Cork. 16 June 1952. 1 page. (BBC)

E192   Helen Arbuthnot. Personal. Confirming meeting time to prepare broadcast. TLS Bowen's Court, Kildorrery, Co. Cork. 24 July 1952. 1 page. (BBC)

E193 , [Terence Ian Fytton Armstrong] editor, *Literary Digest*. Regarding broadcast of 'The Power in the Cave'. TLS 2 Clarence Terrace, Regent's Park, N.W.1 6 June 1947. 1 page (Texas) See 'She', A25.

E194   Archibald Batty. Regarding BBC broadcast. TccL 23 July 1947. 1 page. (Texas)

E195   Miss P. Bentley-Goddard. Accepts Oxford University Press's plan to give Trollope pamphlet as its Christmas present to its friends. TccL 24 June 1946. 1 page. (Texas) See A16b.

E196   Ronald Boswell. Regarding Book Talk broadcast. TLS 2 Clarence Terrace, Regent's Park N.W.1 14 May 1945. 1 page. (BBC)

E197   Ronald Boswell. Regarding contract for Book Talk broadcast. TLS 2 Clarence Terrace, Regent's Park N.W.1 31 May 1945. 1 page. (BBC)

E198   Ronald Boswell. Regarding 'Sanditon' Competition. TLS 2 Clarence Terrace, Regent's Park N.W.1 9 July 1948. 1 page. (BBC) See F21.

E199   Barbara Bray. Regarding request to write for Third Programme. TLS Bowen's Court. Kildorrery, Co. Cork. 10 May 1954. 1 page. (BBC) Tccms on back of Bray's original letter. (Texas)

E200   Jocelyn Brooke. Thanking him for American edition of *The Scapegoat*. ALS 2 Clarence Terrace, Regent's Park N.W.1 4 Jan. 1949. 2 pages. (Texas)

E201   Jocelyn Brooke. Regretting that she will be unable to do the Anne Brontë broadcast. TLS 2 Clarence Terrace, Regent's Park N.W.1 28 Feb. 1949. 1 page. (Texas)

E202   Jocelyn Brooke. Personal. Refers to his *Images of a Drawn*

Sword. ALS 2 Clarence Terrace, Regent's Park N.W.1 12 May 1950. 4 pages. (Texas)

E203   Jocelyn Brooke. Invites Brooke to speak at the Summer School at Folkestone, of which she is Principal for the third time. TLS 2 Clarence Terrace, Regent's Park N.W.1 15 May 1950. 2 pages. (Texas)

E204   Jocelyn Brooke. Personal. Compliments him on *The Goose Cathedral.* ALS Bowen's Court, Kildorrery, Co. Cork. 30 Aug. [1950]. 2 pages. (Texas)

E205   Jocelyn Brooke. Thanking him for book. TLS 2 Clarence Terrace, Regent's Park, N.W.1 1 Jan. 1951. 1 page. (Texas)

E206   Jocelyn Brooke. Personal ALS Bowen's Court, Kildorrery, Co. Cork. 8 Sept. 1952. 4 pages. (Texas)

E207   Spencer Curtis Brown. Regarding the Anthony Trollope broadcast and possible publication by Oxford University Press. TccL 29 June 1945. 2 pages. (Texas)

E208   Spencer Curtis Brown. Regarding Trollope script and 'The Cat Jumps' broadcast in Spanish. TccL 12 July 1945. 1 page. (Texas)

E209   Spencer Curtis Brown. Returns signed contract with Oxford University Press. TccL 30 July 1945. 1 page. (Texas) See A16.

E210   Spencer Curtis Brown. Regarding publication of *The House in Paris* in German. TccL 9 Aug. 1945. 1 page. (Texas)

E211   Spencer Curtis Brown. Regarding publication of *The Demon Lover* in America. TccL 13 Aug. 1945. 2 pages. (Texas)

E212   Spencer Curtis Brown. Returns signed contract for American edition. TccL 3 May 1946. 1 page. (Texas) See A16b.

E213   Spencer Curtis Brown. Regarding copies of *Ivy Gripped the Steps.* TccL 10 May 1946. 1 page. (Texas) See A15b.

E214   Spencer Curtis Brown. Response to his letter of 9 Oct. TccL 15 Oct. 1946. 1 page. (Texas)

E215   Spencer Curtis Brown. Regarding three of his letters and contract for Flaubert introduction. TccL 31 Oct. 1946. 2 pages. (Texas)

E216   Spencer Curtis Brown. Regarding Uniform Edition contracts for *Ann Lee's* and *Encounters*. TLS 5 Nov. 1946. 1 page. (Texas)

E217   Spencer Curtis Brown. Regarding signed redrafted contract with Knopf. TccL 11 Nov. 1946. 1 page. (Texas)

E218   Spencer Curtis Brown. Approves publication of 'Notes on Writing a Novel' in condensed form in *Mademoiselle*, but asks if Vanguard Press may publish it in anthology prior to its appearance in *Collected Impressions*. TccL 13 Jan. 1947. 2 pages. (Texas)

E219   Spencer Curtis Brown. Regarding future essays: prefaces for Flaubert novels, and the John Irwin 'Kaleidoscope' series. TccL 28 Jan. 1947. 1 page. (Texas) See B20.

E220   Spencer Curtis Brown. Regarding a possible lecture series in the United States and returning the signed Cape Collected Edition contract. TccL 31 Jan. 1947. 1 page. (Texas)

E221   Spencer Curtis Brown. Regarding article for *NYTimes*. TccL 2 Apr. 1947. 1 page. (Texas)

E222   Spencer Curtis Brown. Returning signed contracts, and regarding payment for a *Vogue* article. TccL 22 May 1947. 2 pages. (Texas)

E223   Spencer Curtis Brown. Regarding two Flaubert prefaces. TccL 4 July 1947. 1 page. (Texas)

E224   Spencer Curtis Brown. Regarding *Shelbourne* contract. TccL 11 Aug. 1947. 1 page. (Texas) See A21.

E225   Spencer Curtis Brown. Personal. TccL 21 Aug. 1947. 1 page. (Texas)

E226   Spencer Curtis Brown. Regarding Albert Marre's request to obtain dramatic rights to *The Heat of the Day* for the New York City Drama Company. TccL 16 Apr. 1953. 1 page. (Texas)

E227   Mrs. Spencer Curtis [Jean] Brown. Regarding short story collection. TccL 5 July 1944. 1 page. (Texas)

E228   Mrs. Spencer Curtis [Jean] Brown. Apologizes for delay in sending stories to Cape. TccL 24 July 1944. 1 page. (Texas)

E229   Mrs. Spencer Curtis [Jean] Brown. Regarding collection of short stories. TccL 29 Aug. 1944. 1 page. (Texas)

E230   Mrs. Spencer Curtis [Jean] Brown. Regarding contract. TccL 18 Oct. 1944. 1 page. (Texas)

E231   Mrs. Spencer Curtis [Jean] Brown. Regarding forthcoming short stories. TccL 6 Nov. 1944. 1 page. (Texas)

E232   Mrs. Spencer Curtis [Jean] Brown. Regarding the last two stories for *The Demon Lover*. TccL 16 Jan. 1945. 1 page. (Texas)

E233   Mrs. Spencer Curtis [Jean] Brown. Regarding the publication of some of her books by Penguin. TccL 14 Mar. 1945. 1 page. (Texas)

E234   Rose Bruford. Regarding lecture. TccL 26 May 1954. 1 page. (Texas)

E235   Miss J. Burt. Regarding lecture at seminar. TccL 10 May 1954. 1 page. (Texas)

E236   Rufus Buxton. Regarding BBC broadcast. TccL 19 May 1947. 1 page. (Texas)

E237   Anne Caulder. Regarding 'Pink May' for BBC broadcast. TccL 6 May 1952. 1 page. (Texas)

E238   Sonia K. Chapter. Regarding Spanish edition of *The Death of the Heart*. TccL 24 Apr. 1944. 1 page. (Texas)

E239   Sonia K. Chapter. Regarding contract with Luis F. de Caralt. TccL 8 May 1944. 1 page. (Texas) See A10.

E240   Sonia K. Chapter. Regarding the possibility of expanding the market for Bowen's translations into South America. TccL 12 June 1944. 2 pages. (Texas)

E241   Sonia K. Chapter. Regarding Woodrow Wyatt's inclusion of her story 'The Shoes'. TccL 15 June 1944. 1 page. (Texas)

E242   Sonia K. Chapter. Regarding translation agreements with Portuguese firms. TccL 27 June 1944. 1 page. (Texas)

E243   Sonia K. Chapter. Regarding agreement with Luis de Caralt for a Spanish edition of *The Death of the Heart*. TccL 25 July 1944. 1 page. (Texas) See A10.

E244   Sonia K. Chapter. Regarding Spanish contract. TccL 22 Sept. 1944. 1 page. (Texas) See A10.

E245   Sonia K. Chapter. Regarding French translation of *To the North*. TccL 16 Jan. 1945. 2 pages. (Texas)

E246   Sonia K. Chapter. Regarding contracts with Penguin for *To the North* and *The House in Paris*. TccL 23 May 1945. 1 page. (Texas)

E247   Sonia K. Chapter. Regarding Bonnier contract for *To the North*. TccL 25 May 1945. 1 page. (Texas)

E248   Sonia K. Chapter. Regarding Fontaine contract, and requesting 'A Love Story' for the Maurice Fridberg collection. TccL 31 May 1945. 1 page. (Texas) See A17.

E249   Sonia K. Chapter. Regarding Bonnier contract. TccL 25 June 1945. 1 page. (Texas)

E250   Sonia K. Chapter. Regarding the Greek rights for 'Pink May'. ALS | cc AN 26 Nov. 1945. 2 pages. (Texas)

E251   Sonia K. Chapter. Regarding foreign translations and contracts. TccL 18 Jan. 1946. 2 pages. (Texas)

E252   Sonia K. Chapter. Regarding copies of *To the North*. TccL 11 Mar. 1946. 2 pages. (Texas)

E253   Sonia K. Chapter. Enclosing signed contracts. TccL 22 Mar. 1946. 1 page. (Texas)

E254   Sonia K. Chapter. Regarding Italian contract. TccL 28 Mar. 1946. 1 page. (Texas)

E255   Sonia K. Chapter. Regarding Dutch ministry's interest in *Bowen's Court*. TccL AN 18 Apr. 1946. 2 pages. (Texas)

E256 Sonia K. Chapter. Regarding copies of books for foreign publishers. TccL 17 June 1946. 2 pages. (Texas)

E257 Sonia K. Chapter. Accepts a Danish publishing firm's offer to print 'The Cat Jumps' in a collection of Irish short stories. TccL 24 June 1946. 1 page. (Texas) See D60.

E258 Sonia K. Chapter. Regarding one-page biography housed with letter. Two copies of letter. TccL 5 July 1946. 1 page. (Texas)

E259 Sonia K. Chapter. Regarding signed contracts with Swedish and Czech firms. TccL. 18 July 1946. 1 page. (Texas)

E260 Sonia K. Chapter. Regarding publication of 'In the Square' as a Christmas greeting in Denmark. TccL 30 Sept. 1946. 1 page. (Texas) See A15.

E261 Sonia K. Chapter. Contracts with Germany and Austria for *A House in Paris*. TccL 25 Oct. 1946. 1 page. (Texas) See A9.

E262 Sonia K. Chapter. Regarding contractual agreement. TccL 4 Nov. 1946. 1 page. (Texas)

E263 Sonia K. Chapter. Regarding stories that may appear in France. TccL 10 Feb. 1947. 1 page. (Texas)

E264 Sonia K. Chapter. Regarding German publication of *To the North*. TccL 19 May 1947. 1 page. (Texas)

E265 Sonia K. Chapter. Regarding article written originally for *Fontaine*. TccL 3 June 1947. 1 page. (Texas)

E266 Sonia K. Chapter. Regarding German publication of *The Demon Lover*. TccL 11 Aug. 1947. 1 page. (Texas) See A15.

E267 Sonia K. Chapter. Regarding French contract. TccL 29 Sept. 1947. 1 page. (Texas)

E268 Sonia K. Chapter. Regarding foreign rights in Germany. TccL 8 Oct. 1947. 1 page. (Texas)

E269 Sonia K. Chapter. Regarding anthology permissions. TccL 27 Apr. 1953. 1 page. (Texas)

E270   R. A. Chaput de Saintonge. Regarding trip to Germany. TccL 12 May 1953. 1 page. (Texas)

E271   Alan Collins. Regarding 'Careless Talk'. TccL 25 July 1944. 1 page. (Texas)

E272   Alan Collins. A thank you note. TccL 2 Oct. 1944. 1 page. (Texas)

E273   Alan Collins. Regarding publication in America of short story collection. TccL 21 Dec. 1944. 1 page. (Texas)

E274   Alan Collins. Enclosed subscription to Author's League of America. TccL 17 Jan. 1945. 1 page. (Texas)

E275   P. A. W. Collins. Refuses speaking engagement. TccL 26 May 1954. 1 page. (Texas)

E276   P. A. W. Collins. Declines speaking engagement. TccL 3 June 1954. 1 page. (Texas)

E277   A. E. Coppard. Accepts invitation to play 'A Game of Consequences'. ALS Waldencote Old Headington, Oxford 2 Nov. [1931]. 1 page. (Texas) See B6.

E278   A. E. Coppard. Regarding the writing of 'A Game of Consequences'. ALS Waldencote Old Headington, Oxford 28 July [1932]. 10 pages. (Texas) See B6.

E279   A. E. Coppard. Regarding 'A Game of Consequences.' ALS Bowen's Court, Kildorrery, Co. Cork [Summer 1932]. 2 pages. (Texas) See B6.

E280   A. E. Coppard. Accepts manuscript. [postmark: Corcorcaige 17 Aug. 1932] APC Bowen's Court, Kildorrery, Co. Cork. (Texas) See B6.

E281   A. E. Coppard. Personal note. [postmark: Ireland 5 Oct. 1932] APC Bowen's Court, Kildorrery, Co. Cork. (Texas)

E282   A. E. Coppard. [postmark: Oxford 9 Oct. 1932] Personal note. APC Bowen's Court, Kildorrery, Co. Cork. (Texas)

E283   A. E. Coppard. Regarding *To the North*. ALS Waldencote Old Headington, Oxford 15 Oct. [1932]. 4 pages. (Texas)

E284   A. E. Coppard. Personal note. ALS Waldencote Old Headington, Oxford 24 Oct. [1932]. 1 page. (Texas)

E285   A. E. Coppard. ALS Waldencote Old Headington, Oxford Monday 5th [8 Dec. 1932]. 6 pages. (Texas)

E286   A. E. Coppard. Accompanies stories written during the previous few years. The manuscripts of the stories are not housed with the letter. ALS Waldencote Old Headington, Oxford 5 July 1934. (Texas) See A8.

E287   A. E. Coppard. Regarding *The House in Paris*. ALS Bowen's Court, Kildorrery, Co. Cork. 31 Aug. [1935]. 6 pages. (Texas)

E288   A. E. Coppard. Regarding editorial work Elizabeth Bowen did for Faber and Faber. TLS 2 Clarence Terrace, Regent's Park, N.W.1 22 Mar. 1937. 1 page. (Texas) See B10.

E289   Sheila Crawley. Regarding signed contract for Uniform Edition. TccL 6 Mar. 1947. 1 page. (Texas)

E290   Sheila Crawley. Regarding Uniform Edition. TccL 18 Mar. 1947. 1 page. (Texas)

E291   Sheila Crawley. Acknowledging receipt of Cape contracts. TccL 16 July 1947. 1 page. (Texas)

E292   Sheila Crawley. Approves *Evening Standard's* second serial rights for 'The Demon Lover'. TccN n.d. 1 page. Tccms 28 Oct. 1947. 1 page. (Texas)

E293   Sheila Crawley. Approves *Evening Standard's* adaptation of 'The Demon Lover'. TccL 8 Nov. 1947. 1 page. (Texas)

E294   Patrick Crosbie. Regarding possibility of another book review by Bowen. TccL 9 Feb. 1954. 1 page. (Texas)

E295   Curtis Brown Ltd. Giving authority to sign on her behalf regarding appearances on radio or TV. TLS 22 Feb. 1957. 1 page. (BBC)

E296   Dorothy Daly. Regarding short stories. TccL 3 May 1945. 1 page. (Texas)

E297   Dorothy Daly. Regarding meeting with publisher for story contract. TccL 28 May 1945. 1 page. (Texas)

E298   Dorothy Daly. Regarding an article and a story. TccL 25 June 1945. 1 page. (Texas)

E299   Dorothy Daly. Regarding first and second serial rights for short stories. ALS | cc AN 26 Nov. 1945. 8 pages. (Texas)

E300   Dorothy Daly. Regarding anthology rights. TccL 18 Jan. 1946. 1 page. (Texas)

E301   Dorothy Daly. Authorization for Curtis Brown office in New York to sign on her behalf. ALS n.d. 2 pages. TccL 21 Jan. 1946. 1 page. (Texas)

E302   Dorothy Daly. Personal. TccL 28 Mar. 1946. 1 page. (Texas)

E303   Dorothy Daly. Regarding articles. TccL 26 July 1946. 1 page. (Texas)

E304   Dorothy Daly. Unable to write article for teenage anthology. TccL 30 Sept. 1946. 1 page. (Texas)

E305   Dorothy Daly. Regarding 'The Dolt's Tale'. TccL 4 Oct. 1946. 1 page. (Texas)

E306   Dorothy Daly. Suggests *NY* will not renew contract. *Sunday Times* is printing 'Sunday Afternoon', which she wrote at the request of Leonard Russell. TccL AN 15 Oct. 1946. 2 pages. (Texas) See A15.

E307   Dorothy Daly. Regarding anthology permission. TccL 18 Oct. 1946. 1 page. (Texas)

E308   Dorothy Daly. Regarding anthology permission. TccL 25 Oct. 1946. 1 page. (Texas)

E309   Dorothy Daly. Personal. TccL 20 Nov. 1946. 1 page. (Texas)

E310   Dorothy Daly. Personal. TccL 22 Nov. 1946. 1 page. (Texas)

E311 Dorothy Daly. Regarding *Reader's Digest* program. TccL 23 Dec. 1946. 1 page. (Texas)

E312 Dorothy Daly. Regarding reprinting her story 'I Died for [sic] Love'. TccL 3 Feb. 1947. 1 page. (Texas) See B17.

E313 Dorthy Daly. Regarding articles for *Vogue*. TccL 26 June 1947. 1 page. (Texas)

E314 Dorothy Daly. Regarding article for *Good Housekeeping*. TccL 17 July 1947. 1 page. (Texas)

E315 Dorothy Daly. Regarding *Vogue* article. TccL 19 Aug. 1947. 1 page. (Texas)

E316 Dorothy Daly. Regarding article. TccL 22 Aug. 1947. 1 page. (Texas)

E317 Dorothy Daly. Regarding publishing of Greene, Pritchett, and Bowen letters. TccL 21 Oct. 1947. 1 page. (Texas) See B21.

E318 Dorothy Daly. Regarding book review. TccL 15 Dec. 1947. 1 page. (Texas)

E319 Dorothy Daly. Regarding a story. TccL 9 June 1952. 1 page. (Texas)

E320 Tania Long Daniell. Rejects offer to write an article. TccL 2 Apr. 1947. 1 page. (Texas)

E321 G. M. Day. Regarding broadcast of *Castle Anna* in South Africa. TccL 12 May 1952. 1 page. (Texas).

E322 William Empson. Regarding Chinese broadcast. TLS 2 Clarence Terrace, Regent's Park, N.W.1 5 Aug. 1943. 1 page. (BBC)

E323 Betty Fergusson. Regarding contract with German Control Commission for *To the North*. TccL 30 May 1947. 1 page. (Texas)

E324 Betty Fergusson. Regarding Spanish contract for *The Hotel*. TccL 16 July 1947. 1 page. (Texas)

E325 Betty Fergusson. Personal. TccL 7 Oct. 1947. 1 page. (Texas)

E326   Betty Fergusson. Personal. TccL 8 Nov. 1947. 1 page. (Texas)

E327   Betty Fergusson. Acknowledges receipt of Norwegian translations. TccL 24 Nov. 1947. 1 page. (Texas)

E328   Betty Fergusson. Regarding photograph. TccL 15 Dec. 1947. 1 page. (Texas)

E329   Sean Fielding. Regarding short story 'Emergency in the Gothic Wing', for *Tatler*. TccL 14 Apr. 1954. 1 page. (Texas) See C458.

E330   Sean Fielding. Regarding same story. TccL 18 May 1954. 1 page. (Texas)

E331   Sheila Freeman. Regarding BBC broadcast of 'The Cat Jumps' in Spanish. TccL 23 Apr. 1945. 1 page. (Texas)

E332   Sheila Freeman. Regarding BBC broadcast. TccL 14 May 1945. 1 page. (Texas)

E333   Sheila Freeman. An instruction from Bowen to her secretary to 'Ask Miss F to note my address now Bowen's Court.' At the foot of a TLS from Freeman dated 21 Aug. 1945 which discusses BBC contract for an adaptation of 'Reduced', then called 'Henrietta Post', for William Plomer broadcast. AN [Aug. 1945] 1 page. (Texas) See F8.

E334   Sheila Freeman. Regarding broadcast of 'New Judgement: Anthony Trollope' for BBC. TccL 1 Feb. 1946. 1 page. (Texas) See F7.

E335   Sheila Freeman. Regarding BBC. TccL 11 Mar. 1946. 1 page. (Texas)

E336   Sheila Freeman. Regarding Bloomsbury feature for the BBC. TccL 24 June 1946. 1 page. (Texas)

E337   Sheila Freeman. Regarding BBC recording of 'New Judgement on Anthony Trollope'. TccL 15 Oct. 1946. 1 page. (Texas)

E338   Sheila Freeman. Regarding broadcast of 'The Tommy Crans'. TccL 31 Oct. 1946. 1 page. (Texas)

E339   Sheila Freeman. Regarding broadcast. TccL 1 Apr. 1947. 1 page. (Texas)

E340 Sheila Freeman. Regarding broadcast. TccL 19 May 1947. 1 page. (Texas)

E341 Sheila Freeman. Regarding BBC. TccL 22 May 1947. 1 page. (Texas)

E342 Sheila Freeman. Regarding TV broadcasts. TccL 29 May 1947. 1 page. (Texas)

E343 Sheila Freeman. Regarding BBC adaptation of stories. TccL 10 June 1947. 1 page. (Texas)

E344 Sheila Freeman. Regarding BBC. TccL 4 July 1947. 1 page. (Texas)

E345 Sheila Freeman. Regarding BBC broadcast of 'Tears, Idle Tears'. TccL 21 Aug. 1947. 1 page. (Texas)

E346 Kay Fuller. Regarding BBC Talk Series. ALS Bowen's Court, Kildorrery, Co. Cork. 27 Apr. 1949. 1 page. (BBC)

E347 Kay Fuller. Regarding broadcast 'In My Library'. ALS Bowen's Court, Kildorrery, Co. Cork. 13 July 1949. 3 pages. (BBC)

E348 Kay Fuller. Regarding broadcast 'In My Library'. TLS 2 Clarence Terrace, Regent's Park, N.W.1 5 Sept 1949. 1 page. (BBC)

E349 Kay Fuller. Regarding broadcast with Walter Allen. ALS Albergo d'Inghelterra, via Bocca di Leone 14 Rome. 8 Mar. 1955. 2 pages. (BBC)

E350 E. G. Gauner. Regarding 'Tipperary Woman'. TccL 16 Jan. 1945. 1 page. (Texas)

E351 E. G. Gauner. Regarding Contact Publications. TccL 29 June 1945. 1 page. (Texas)

E352 E. G. Gauner. Regarding *Vogue* article. TccL 14 July 1945. 2 pages. (Texas)

E353 Laurence Gilliam. Regarding broadcast 'Cinque Ports.' TLS 2 Clarence Terrace, Regent's Park, N.W.1 26 July 1946. 1 page. (BBC)

E354   Laurence Gilliam. Regarding interest in 'Cinque Ports' broadcast. TLS 2 Clarence Terrace, Regent's Park, N.W.1 23 Dec. 1946. 1 page. (BBC)

E355   Laurence Gilliam. Interest in 'Cinque Ports' broadcast. TLS 2 Clarence Terrace, Regent's Park, N.W.1 14 Mar. 1947. 1 page. (BBC)

E356   Sidney Gordon. Regarding Jane Austen article. TccL 10 May 1954. 1 page. (Texas)

E357   John Stuart Groves. Personal. APC 2 Clarence Terrace, Regent's Park, N.W.1 [postmark: 9 Apr. 1936]. (Texas)

E358   Mrs. Sewell Haggard. Regarding publication of short stories in America. TccLS 19 Feb. 1945. 1 page. (Texas)

E359   Mrs. Sewell Haggard. Regarding articles for American periodicals. TccL 25 Apr. 1953. 1 page. (Texas)

E360   Lionel Hale. Regarding adaptation of 'The Needle-case' to dramatic form. TccL 6 May 1952. 1 page. (Texas)

E361   Lionel Hale. Regarding same story. TccL 24 July 1952. 2 pages. (Texas)

E362   Lionel Hale. Regarding adaptation of story. TccL 1 Aug. 1952. 1 page. (Texas)

E363   Rayner Heppenstall. Personal. ALS Bowen's Court, Kildorrery, Co. Cork. 2 Oct. 1943. 2 pages. (Texas)

E364   Rayner Heppenstall. Personal invitation. ALS 2 Clarence Terrace, Regent's Park N.W.1 14 May 1945. 2 pages. (Texas)

E365   Rayner Heppenstall. Regarding radio version of short story 'Songs My Father Sang Me'. TLS 2 Clarence Terrace, Regent's Park N.W.1 3 May 1946. 1 page. (BBC)

E366   Rayner Heppenstall. Regarding script for 'Imaginary Conversations' broadcast. TLS 2 Clarence Terrace, Regent's Park N.W.1 11 Jan. 1948. 1 page. (BBC)

E367   Rayner Heppenstall. Regarding 'Imaginary Conversations' broadcast. TLS 2 Clarence Terrace, Regent's Park N.W.1 17 Mar. 1948. 1 page. (BBC)

E368   Rayner Heppenstall. Regarding 'Imaginary Conversations' broadcast. TLS 2 Clarence Terrace, Regent's Park N.W.1 9 July 1948. 1 page. (BBC)

E369   Rayner Heppenstall. Regarding 'The Inward Eye' series. TLS 2 Clarence Terrace, Regent's Park N.W.1 10 July 1950. 1 page. (BBC)

E370   Rayner Heppenstall. Regarding 'Imaginary Conversations' broadcast. ALS Bowen's Court, Kildorrery Co. Cork. 4 Sept. 1950. 2 pages. (BBC)

E371   Claire M. Higgins. Regarding permissions. TccL 20 Apr. 1954. 1 page. (Texas)

E372   Hettie Hilton. Regarding short story 'Oh Madam'. TccL 25 Apr. 1944. 1 page. (Texas)

E373   Hettie Hilton. Regarding 'The Most Unforgettable Character I Have Met'. TccL 8 May 1944. 1 page. (Texas)

E374   Hettie Hilton. Regarding 'Comfort and Joy'. TccL 16 May 1944. 1 page. (Texas)

E375   Hettie Hilton. Regarding short stories. TccL 2 June 1944. 1 page. (Texas)

E376   Hettie Hilton. Regarding 'Tipperary Woman'. TccL 22 Sept. 1944. 1 page. (Texas)

E377   Hettie Hilton. Regarding broadcast for BBC. TccL 7 July 1952. 1 page. (Texas)

E378   Hettie Hilton. Regarding stories broadcast in Boston. TccL 1 Aug. 1952. 1 page. (Texas)

E379   Gerard Hopkins. Enclosing her new book, which includes 'The Disinherited'. ALS Waldencote Old Headington, Oxford 5 July [n.y.]. 3 pages. (NYPL–B) See A8.

E380   Gerard Hopkins. Thanking him for criticism. ALS Bowen's Court Kildorrery, Co. Cork. 9 Aug. [1935]. 5 pages. (NYPL–B)

E381   Gerard Hopkins. Thanking him for criticism. ALS Bowen's Court Kildorrery, Co. Cork. 28 Aug. [n.y]. 6 pages. (NYPL–B) See A9.

E382   Mrs. B. C. Horton. Regarding BBC 'The Horrors of Childhood' series. ALS Bowen's Court, Kildorrery, Co. Cork. 29 May 1956. 1 page. (BBC)

E383   Mrs. B. C. Horton. Regarding 'Truth and Fiction' broadcasts. ALS Bowen's Court, Kildorrery, Co. Cork. 2 July 1956. 4 pages. (BBC) See A25.

E384   Mrs. B. C. Horton. Regarding 'Truth and Fiction' broadcasts. TLS Bowen's Court, Kildorrery, Co. Cork. 28 Aug. 1956. 2 sheets. (BBC)

E385   Mrs. B. C. Horton. Regarding 'Truth and Fiction' series. ALS Bowen's Court, Kildorrery, Co. Cork. 30 Aug. 1956. 2 pages. (BBC)

E386   L. T. Horton. Bowen agrees to speak to group in England. Western Union cablegram from Hopewell, New Jersey. 21 July 1959. (BBC)

E387   Godfrey James. Regarding broadcast 'Book Talks'. TLS 2 Clarence Terrace, Regent's Park, N.W.1 12 Apr. 1945. 1 page. (BBC)

E388   Godfrey James. Regarding script for 'Book Talks' broadcast. TLS Bowen's Court, Kildorrery, Co. Cork. 16 June 1945. 2 pages. (BBC)

E389   Godfrey James. Regarding 'Fiction Talk' script. ALS 2 Clarence Terrace, Regent's Park, N.W.1 12 July 1945. 1 page. (BBC)

E390   Margaret Storm Jameson. Regarding membership in P.E.N. TLS 2 Clarence Terrace, Regent's Park N.W.1 16 Jan. 1939. 1 page. (Texas)

E391   Peter Janson-Smith. Regarding German publication of her novels. TccL 24 June 1952. 1 page. (Texas)

E392   Pyke Johnson, Jr. Agreeing to read galley proofs of a novel by Elizabeth Sewell. ALS College Hill, Clinton, New York. Monday 6 Nov. 1950. 1 page. (Johnson)

E393 Pyke Johnson, Jr. Regarding meeting with Nelson Algren. ALS Hotel Florence, Missoula, Montana. 19 Nov. 1951. 2 pages. (Johnson)

E394 Pyke Johnson, Jr. Signed commentary and brief personal note by Elizabeth Bowen on the title page of typescript 'The Askance Lady' by Pyke Johnson, Jr., a parody of *The Heat of the Day* dedicated to the Literary Guild and, respectfully, to Elizabeth Bowen. Enclosed in Alfred A. Knopf airmail envelope and addressed to Mrs. Pyke Johnson n.d. (Johnson) See E181.

E395 Judith B. Jones. Information on bibliography in *A Time in Rome*. ALS The American Academy Via Angelo Masina 5 Rome 26 Oct. 1959. 3 pages. (Texas)

E396 [Anna Kallin] 'Niouta'. Telegram confirming program with Graham Greene and V. S. Pritchett. 28 Apr. 1948. (BBC) See B21.

E397 [Anna Kallin] 'Niouta'. Regarding 'Artist in Society' broadcast. TLS 2 Clarence Terrace, Regent's Park N.W.1 9 June 1948. 1 page. (BBC)

E398 [Anna Kallin] 'Niouta'. Regarding future program for the Coronation of Elizabeth II. TLS Bowen's Court, Kildorrery, Co. Cork. 17 Oct. 1952. 1 page. (BBC)

E399 R. E. Keen. Regarding possible broadcast. ALS Bowen's Court, Kildorrery, Co. Cork. 10 Apr. 1956. 2 pages. (BBC)

E400 Alfred A. Knopf. Personal. ALS 23 Nov. 1965. 2 pages. (Texas)

E401 Alfred A. Knopf. Personal and *Eva Trout*. ALS 22 Feb. 1968. 2 pages. (Texas)

E402 Alfred A. Knopf. Personal. ALS 20 Mar. 1968. 2 pages. (Texas)

E403 Alfred A. Knopf. Personal. ALS 2 May 1968. 2 pages. (Texas)

E404 Alfred A. Knopf. Regarding trip to New York and beauty of advance copy of *Eva Trout*. ALS 17 Sept. 1968. 3 pages. (Texas)

E405 William Koshland. Regarding corrections to be placed in Knopf edition of *A Time in Rome*. ALS c/o Curtis Brown Ltd 13 King Street

Covent Garden London W.C. 2 1 Oct. 1959. 5 pages. (Texas) See A24.

E406 William Koshland. Regarding corrected proofs of *A Time in Rome*. TLS The American Academy Via Angelo Masina 5 Rome 26 Oct. 1959. 2 pages. (Texas) See A24.

E407 William Koshland. Regarding copies of *A Time in Rome* ALS American Academy in Rome Via Angelo Masina 5 Rome 22 Dec. 1959. 3 pages. (Texas) See A24.

E408 Arthur Langford. Regarding possible translation and adaptation of 'Truth and Fiction' script for broadcasting in France. TLS White Lodge, Old Headington, Oxford 5 Dec. 1961. 2 pages. (BBC)

E409 John Lehmann. Regarding 'I Hear You Say So'. TLS 2 Clarence Terrace, Regent's Park N.W.1 29 June 1945. 1 page. (Texas)

E410 John Lehmann. Regarding corrected proofs of 'I Hear You Say So'. ALS 2 Clarence Terrace, Regent's Park N.W.1 6 July 1945. 1 page. (Texas)

E411 John Lehmann. Regarding reprinting of 'I Hear You Say So'. ALS Bowen's Court, Kildorrery Co. Cork. 6 Dec. 1945. 3 pages. (Texas)

E412 John Lehmann. Regarding second serial rights for story. TLS 2 Clarence Terrace, Regent's Park N.W.1 7 Feb. 1946. 1 page. (Texas)

E413 John Lehmann. Regarding story in *Wartime Stories from New Writing*, a German anthology. TL, signed for Bowen in another hand. 2 Clarence Terrace, Regent's Park N.W.1 13 March 1947. 1 page. (Texas)

E414 John Lehmann. Regarding the reprinting of story in German anthology. TLS 2 Clarence Terrace, Regent's Park N.W.1 22 May 1947. 1 page. (Texas)

E415 John Lehmann. Regarding story reprint. TL, signed for Bowen by her assistant Cooke. 2 Clarence Terrace, Regent's Park N.W.1 6 Aug. 1949. 1 page. (Texas)

E416 John Lehmann. Regarding an unknown writer's story that might be submitted to Lehmann. ALS Bowen's Court, Kildorrery, Co. Cork.

10 Oct. 1953. 2 pages. (Texas)

E417   Edward Howard Marsh. Regarding Peter Quennell's poems. ALS
32 Queen Anne's Gate, Westminster. 4 June [1923?]. (NYPL–B)

E418   Eileen Molnay. Regrets not being able to do broadcast. TLS
2 Clarence Terrace, Regent's Park N.W.1 26 Jan. 1950. 1 page. (BBC)

E419   Alison Kingsmill Moore. Regrets not being able to participate
in women's society of Dublin University. TccL 9 Feb. 1954. 1 page.
(Texas) See E609.

E420   Ottoline Morrell [Violet Anne Cavendish-Bentinck]. Personal.
ALS 'Waldencote Old Headington, Oxford' crossed from letterhead and
'6 Glebe Place S.W.3' added in holograph. n.d. 1 page. (Texas)

E421   Ottoline Morrell. Personal. Mentions *Friends and Relations*.
ALS Waldencote Old Headington, Oxford Sunday [1931]. 2 pages.
(Texas)

E422   Ottoline Morrell. Personal. ALS 'Waldencote Old Headington,
Oxford' crossed from letterhead and '6 Glebe Place S.W.3' added in
holograph. 18 Nov. [n.y.]. 1 page. (Texas)

E423   Ottoline Morrell. Personal. ALS 6 Glebe Place, Chelsea S.W.3
25 Nov. [1931]. 1 page. (Texas)

E424   Ottoline Morrell. Personal. ALS Bowen's Court, Kildorrery, Co.
Cork. 31 Mar. [n.y.]. 2 pages. (Texas)

E425   Ottoline Morrell. Personal. ALS Bowen's Court, Kildorrery, Co.
Cork. 6 Apr. [n.y.]. 1 page. (Texas)

E426   Ottoline Morrell. Personal. ALS Waldencote Old Headington,
Oxford. 26 Apr. [n.y.]. 2 pages. (Texas)

E427   Ottoline Morrell. Personal. ALS Waldencote Old Headington,
Oxford. 10 July [n.y.]. 4 pages. (Texas)

E428   Ottoline Morrell. Personal. ALS Bowen's Court, Kildorrery, Co.
Cork. 15 Aug. [1932]. 6 pages. (Texas)

E429   Ottoline Morrell. Personal. ALS Bowen's Court, Kildorrery,
Co. Cork. 7 Oct. [1932]. 4 pages. (Texas)

E430   Ottoline Morrell. Personal. ALS Waldencote Old Headington, Oxford. 14 Oct. [1932]. 2 pages. (Texas)

E431   Ottoline Morrell. Personal. Mentions review of *To the North*. ALS Waldencote Old Headington, Oxford. 24 Oct. [1932]. 2 pages, plus enclosed clipping. (Texas)

E432   Ottoline Morrell. Regarding literary portrait of Paul Morand. ALS Waldencote Old Headington, Oxford. [1 Dec. 1932]. 2 pages, plus enclosure. (Texas) See E137.

E433   Ottoline Morrell. Personal. ALS Waldencote Old Headington, Oxford. 15 Mar. [1933]. 4 pages. (Texas)

E434   Ottoline Morrell. Personal. ALS Bowen's Court, Kildorrery, Co. Cork. 2 Jan. [1934]. 2 pages. (Texas)

E435   Ottoline Morrell. Personal. Mentions *The House in Paris*. ALS Bowen's Court, Kildorrery, Co. Cork. 30 Sept. 1935. 3 pages. (Texas)

E436   Mrs. Morris. Regarding the essay 'Woman's Place in the Affairs of Man'. ALS Hampton House 28 East 70th St., New York, N.Y. 21 Oct. 1961. (Texas)

E437   P. H. Newby. Regarding request to do another program. ALS Bowen's Court, Kildorrery, Co. Cork. 27 Oct. 1941. 2 pages. (BBC)

E438   P. H. Newby. Regarding conversational program for BBC. TL, signed for Elizabeth Bowen by I. M. Cooke. 2 Clarence Terrace, Regent's Park N.W.1 10 July 1950. 2 pages. (BBC)

E439   D. E. Noël-Paton. Would like to do the tour for the British Council. TccL 18 May 1954. 1 page. (Texas)

E440   D. E. Noël-Paton. Regrets unable to do tour for British Council. TccL 1 June 1954. 1 page. (Texas)

E441   Stephen Potter. Regarding draft of 'New Judgement: Anthony Trollope' script for BBC program. TLS 2 Clarence Terrace, Regent's Park N.W.1 23 Mar. 1945. 1 page. (BBC) See A16.

E442   John Boynton Priestly. Regarding radio broadcast 'She'. ALS

2 Clarence Terrace, Regent's Park N.W.1 31 Oct. 1948. 4 pages. (Texas) See A25.

E443 Phoebe Prince. Regarding publishing 'The Demon Lover' in anthology. TccL 28 Jan. 1947. 1 page. (Texas) See G26.

E444 Phoebe Prince. Regarding permission for anthology. TccL 31 Jan. 1947. 1 page. (Texas) See G22.

E445 Phoebe Prince. Regarding contract for reprint of 'The Demon Lover' in Switzerland. TccL 19 May 1947. 1 page. (Texas)

E446 Phoebe Prince. Regarding reprint of 'Unwelcome Idea'. TccL 11 Aug. 1947. 1 page. (Texas)

E447 Phoebe Prince. Regarding reprint of excerpt from *Friends and Relations*. TccL 24 Nov. 1947. 1 page. (Texas)

E448 Phoebe Prince. Regarding reprint of 'Her Table Spread' in Sean O'Faoláin's book published by Collins. TccL 15 Dec. 1947. 1 page. (Texas) See C13.

E449 Alan Pryce-Jones. Personal. TccL 3 June 1954. 1 page. (Texas)

E450 William Rothenstein. Regarding *The Death of the Heart*. ALS 2 Clarence Terrace, Regent's Park N.W.1 [27 June 1959]. 2 pages. (Houghton Library) See A10.

E451 Jean [Rountree]. Regarding 'Truth and Fiction' series. ALS Bowen's Court, Kildorrery, Co. Cork. 9 July 1956. 2 pages. (BBC)

E452 Jean [Rountree]. Regarding 'Truth and Fiction' broadcasts. TLS Bowen's Court, Kildorrery, Co. Cork. 14 July 1956. 3 pages. (BBC)

E453 Christopher V. Salmon. Personal. ALS 2 Clarence Terrace, Regent's Park N.W.1 5 Sept. [1941]. 1 page. (BBC)

E454 Christopher V. Salmon. Accompanies story which is not kept with the letter. ALS 2 Clarence Terrace, Regent's Park N.W.1 3 Oct. 1941. 2 pages. (BBC)

E455 Eileen Sam. Regarding an enclosed broadcast. ALS 2 Clarence Terrace, Regent's Park N.W.1 10 Sept. 1942. 1 page. (BBC)

E456   William Sansom. Regarding permission to reprint story 'I Died for [sic] Love' in *Choice*. TccL 3 Feb. 1947. 1 page. (Texas) See B17.

E457   Det Schønbergske Förlag. Regarding reprinting 'Notes on the Novel' for Christmas gift. TccL 11 Aug. 1947. 1 page. (Texas) See A19.

E458   R. A. Scott-James. Regarding story 'A Walk in the Woods'. ALS 2 Clarence Terrace, Regent's Park N.W.1 17 Jan. 1938. 1 page. (Texas) See A11.

E459   R. A. Scott-James. Regarding future short story. TLS 2 Clarence Terrace, Regent's Park N.W.1 4 Oct. 1938. 1 page. (Texas)

E460   R. A. Scott-James. Personal. ALS 2 Clarence Terrace, Regent's Park N.W.1 29 Oct. 1938. 1 page. (Texas)

E461   R. A. Scott-James. Personal. ALS 2 Clarence Terrace, Regent's Park N.W.1 3 Apr. 1939. 2 pages. (Texas)

E462   J'nan Sellery. Regarding manuscripts and publication of correspondence. ALS Carbery, Church Hill, Hythe, Kent. 26 June 1967. 2 pages. (Sellery)

E463   William Shand. Thanking him for accompanying book. TccL Bowen's Court, Kildorrery, Co. Cork. 14 Apr. 1954. 1 page. (Texas)

E464   F. Sidgwick. Important letter regarding publication of her first novel. TccL 19 Nov. 1926. 4 pages. (Texas)

E465   L. Sieveking. Regarding radio adaptation of some stories from *The Demon Lover*. TL, signed by an assistant. 2 Clarence Terrace, Regent's Park N.W.1 8 Apr. 1946. 1 page. (BBC)

E466   L. M. Stapley. Regarding a possible radio broadcast. TccL 26 May 1954. 1 page. (Texas)

E467   W. F. Stirling. Regarding book review broadcasts for BBC. TLS 2 Clarence Terrace, Regent's Park N.W.1 25 June 1945. 1 page. (BBC)

E468   Leslie Stokes. Regarding broadcast of 'The Tommy Crans'. TLS 2 Clarence Terrace, Regent's Park N.W.1 8 Nov. 1946. 1 page. (BBC)

E469 Beryl M. Symons. Regarding request for Swiss reprint rights for 'Mysterious Kôr' by Atlantis Verlag. TLS 11 Aug. 1947. 1 page. (Texas) See D70.

E470 Major Thompson. Regarding return to London and the meeting of the Book Committee. TccL 4 Oct. 1946. 1 page. (Texas)

E471 Hilda Tweedy. Agrees to write article. TccL 19 Nov. 1952. 1 page. (Texas)

E472 Josephine Waldron. Accepts terms of Danish serial rights for 'The Evil That Men Do'. TccL 28 Oct. 1947. 1 page. (Texas) See A1.

E473 Josephine Waldron. Regarding Czech contract for *The House in Paris*. Tccms 24 Nov. 1947. 1 page. (Texas) See A9.

E474 Mollie Waters. Regarding the Japanese publication of *Why Do I Write*? TccL 29 Nov. 1961. 1 page (Texas) See B21.

E475 Graham Watson. Regarding possible book reviews. TccL 30 Apr. 1953. 1 page. (Texas)

E476 D. J. Wendon. Would be glad to speak on 'The Writer and the Novel'. TccL 3 Dec. 1953. 1 page. (Texas)

E477 D. J. Wendon. Pleased to speak at International Graduates Summer School at Oxford. TccL 1 June 1954. 1 page. (Texas)

E478 Ray B. West, Jr. Regarding invitation to America. TccL Bowen's Court, Kildorrery, Co. Cork. 20 Apr. 1954. 1 page. (Texas)

E479 Virginia Woolf. Regarding some of Elizabeth Bowen's travels. ALS Bowen's Court, Kildorrery, Co. Cork. 26 Aug. [n.y.]. 14 pages. (NYPL–B)

E480 Virginia Woolf. Personal. Mentions *The House in Paris*. ALS Waldencote Old Headington, Oxford. 31 July [1935?]. 6 pages. Leonard Woolf has pencilled '1937 or 8'. (NYPL–B)

E481 Virginia Woolf. Personal. ALS 2 Clarence Terrace, Regent's Park N.W.1 7 June [1936?]. 3 pages. Leonard Woolf has pencilled '1937 or 1938'. (NYPL–B)

E482   Virginia Woolf. Regarding an essay of Virginia Woolf's. ALS 2 Clarence Terrace, Regent's Park N.W.1 1 July 1940. 7 pages. (NYPL–B)

E483   Colin Young. Regarding an article. TccL 24 May 1952. 1 page. (Texas)

E484   Colin Young. Includes ts for *News Chronicle* article, but that is not housed with letter. TccL 4 June 1952. 1 page. (Texas)

E485   Colin Young. Regarding essay for *NYTimes*. TccL 19 June 1952. 1 page. (Texas)

E486   Colin Young. To assistant M. A. Crawford regarding essays for *NYTimes* and *News Chronicle*. TccL 23 June 1952. 1 page. (Texas)

E487   Colin Young. Regarding *NYTimes* article. TccL 30 June 1952. 1 page. (Texas)

E488   Colin Young. To assistant M. A. Crawford regarding titles of possible articles: 'The Roving Eye', 'Likeable Persons', 'Rediscovery'. TccL 29 July 1952. 1 page. (Texas)

E489   Colin Young. Regarding the article *Harper's* would like her to write about America. TccL 9 Mar. 1953. 1 page. (Texas)

E490   Colin Young. Regarding 'teen-age' article for *The American Weekly* enclosed. TccL 15 Apr. 1953. 1 page. (Texas)

E491   Colin Young. Regarding timing of article for the Coronation. TccL 16 Apr. 1953. 1 page. (Texas)

E492   Colin Young. Regarding articles and personal. TccL 10 June 1953. 1 page. (Texas)

Letters to Elizabeth Bowen

This list comprises only letters read by the compilers and does not pretend to be complete. This section is arranged alphabetically by sender, and multiple letters from a single correspondent are treated under a single entry number.

E493   Joe [Joseph Randolph] Ackerley. 8 Apr. 1936—3 Oct. 1938. (3 letters) Regarding three stories, including a Christmas story for *The Listener*. (Texas)

E494   Audrey G. Anderson. 26 Jan. 1948. Regarding lecture tour to Czechoslovakia. (Texas)

E495   Helen Arbuthnot. 13 June 1952—18 July 1952. (4 letters) Regarding 'Conversations on Traitors', BBC program. (Texas)

E496   Cynthia Asquith. 13 May 1934. Personal. (Texas)

E497   Edith Barnes. Sept. and Oct. 1952. (2 letters) Regarding anthology rights. (Texas)

E498   James Barrie. 22 Mar. 1956. Regarding Danish translation of the *Third Ghost Book*. (Texas)

E499   Archibald Batty. 21 July 1947—16 Sept. 1947. (3 letters) Regarding broadcasts of Bowen's stories. (Texas)

E500   John Bayley. n.d. Compliments *Eva Trout*. (Texas)

E501   Stella Benson. 1 Apr. [n.y.] Regarding a meeting. (Texas)

E502   H. N. Bentinck. 2 June 1948—2 Nov. 1951. (4 letters) Regarding BBC broadcasts. (BBC)

E503   Phyllida Bentley-Goddard. 28 Nov. 1945—Aug. 1946. (4 letters) Regarding 'Love Story', *Anthony Trollope*, and the Penguin edition of *The House in Paris*. (Texas)

E504   Anthony Berry. 28 May 1954. Requests Bowen's participation in panel choosing 'Novel of the Month'. (Texas)

E505   John Betjeman. 29 Oct. 1938—24 Feb. 1964. (2 letters) Regarding *The Death of the Heart* and Anglo-Irish novelist Norah Hoult. (Texas)

E506   Kitty Black. 11 Aug. 1955. Regarding dramatization of *The House in Paris*. (Texas)

E507   Ronald Boswell. 14 May 1945—8 July 1948. (5 letters) Regarding BBC broadcasts. (BBC)

E508   Lilian Bowes-Lyon. 3 Aug. 1938. Regarding meeting. (Texas)

E509   Maurice Bowra. 7 Sept. [n.y.]—25 Jan. 1969. (6 letters) Regarding *The House in Paris, A World of Love,* and *Eva Trout.* (Texas)

E510   Heather Bradley. 10 Nov. 1952. Regarding article for *NYTimes.* (Texas)

E511   Barbara Bray. 3 May 1954. Requests Bowen to write original radio play for Third Programme. (BBC)

E512   Eleanor Brockett. 19 Nov. 1952—13 Jan. 1953. (2 letters) Regarding transcription of *The Heat of the Day* into Braille, and anthology rights for two extracts from novels. (Texas)

E513   Leah Bronzite. 25 Aug. 1953—6 July 1954. (2 letters) Regarding broadcasts. (Texas)

E514   Jocelyn Brooke. 24 Feb. 1949—13 May 1950. (3 letters) Regarding broadcasts and his book *The Scapegoat.* (BBC) and (Texas)

E515   Francis Brown. 20 May 1953. Regarding an article in *NYTBR.* (Texas)

E516   Jean [Mrs. Spencer Curtis] Brown. 16 June 1944—6 June 1945 (4 letters) Regarding publication of short stories and the next novel. (Texas)

E517   Spencer Curtis Brown. 15 May 1924—10 Sept. 1964. (72 letters) Regarding publication contracts, broadcasts, finances, appearances, and articles. Concern most books from *Encounters* to *The Little Girls.* (Texas)

E518   Rose E. Bruford. 18 May 1954. Regarding lecture. (Texas)

E519   Jane Burt. n.d. [May 1954] Regarding a seminar on the short story. (Texas)

E520   Rufus Buxton. 14 May 1947—20 May 1947. (2 letters) Regarding Canadian radio broadcasts. (Texas)

E521   Arthur Calder-Marshall. n.d. Regarding stories that Bowen will edit. (Texas)

E522   Anne Caulder. 8 May 1952—25 Aug. 1952. (2 letters) Regarding adaptation of stories for BBC broadcasts. (Texas)

E523   Sonia K. Chapter. 11 Apr. 1944—11 June 1956. (65 letters) Regarding all foreign translation rights and contracts. (Texas)

E524   R. A. Chaput de Saintonge. 6 May 1953. Requests Bowen to make a trip to Germany for the Foreign Office. (Texas)

E525   Agatha Mallowan [Christie]. 2 Mar. [n.y.] Personal. (Texas)

E526   Alan C. Collins. 16 Aug. 1944—13 Dec. 1945. (3 letters) Regarding her next novel, a story for *NY,* and motion picture consideration of *To the North.* (Texas)

E527   Norman Collins. 1 Nov. 1938. Regarding *The Death of the Heart.* (Texas)

E528   P. A. W. Collins. 17 May 1954—Jan. 1955. (2 letters) Regarding lecture at Vaughan College, Leicester. (Texas)

E529   Ivy Compton-Burnett. 6 Oct. 1938—9 Feb. 1969. (5 letters) Regarding Bowen's novels. (Texas)

E530   B. Connell. 20 May 1952. Regarding an article for *New Chronicle.* (Texas)

E531   Cyril Connolly. 'Thurs' [n.d.] Personal. (Texas)

E532   K. Cooper. 13 July 1945. Regarding Anthony Trollope broadcast. (Texas)

E533   A. E. Coppard n.d. [Apr. 1926]—5 Sept. 1935. (11 letters) Regarding short stories and three novels. (Texas)

E534   Edward Crankshaw. 27 Apr. 1936. Regarding her review of his book in the *Spectator.* (Texas)

E535   M. A. Crawford. 5 June 1952—21 Oct. 1954. (9 letters) Regarding articles for periodicals. (Texas)

E536   Sheila Crawley. 4 Mar. 1946—5 Nov. 1947. (7 letters) Regarding contracts and serial rights. (Texas)

E537   Patrick Crosbie. 4 Jan. 1954. Regarding reviews for the *Cork Examiner*. (Texas)

E538   Clifford Curzon. 30 Oct. 1938. Praises *The Death of the Heart*. (Texas)

E539   Dorothy Daly. 2 May 1945—10 Dec. 1963. (57 letters) Regarding all aspects of short story publication. (Texas)

E540   Tania Long Daniell. 31 Mar. 1947. Regarding article. (Texas)

E541   Gladys M. Day. 9 May 1952. Regarding *Castle Anna*. (Texas)

E542   A. L. Distom. 16 Aug. 1946. Requesting article for *Daily Graphic* and *Daily Sketch*. (Texas)

E543   Osamu Doi. 29 May 1952. Regarding translation into Japanese of seven stories. (Texas)

E544   Anne Duffin. 30 Aug. 1962—19 Aug. 1964. (4 letters) Regarding foreign translation rights of Bowen's novels. (Texas)

E545   T. S. Eliot. 27 Feb. 1934—30 Apr. 1943. (12 letters) Regarding friendship and publications. (Texas)

E546   William Empson. 3 May 1943—28 June 1943. (2 letters) Regarding BBC broadcasts to China. (BBC)

E547   Betty Fergusson. 9 Apr. 1947—9 Dec. 1947. (7 letters) Regarding serial rights for foreign publication of short stories. (Texas)

E548   Sean Fielding. 1 Apr. 1954—20 May 1954. (3 letters) Regarding a story for *Tatler* Christmas number. (Texas)

E549   I. Harvey Flack, M.D. n.d. [Jan. 1954] Regarding 'Disappointment'. (Texas)

E550   Sheila Freeman. 19 Apr. 1945—20 Aug. 1947. (18 letters) Regarding broadcasts for BBC. (Texas)

E551   M. Frost. 2 Apr. 1954. Regarding invitation to participate in Iowa Writers' Workshop. (Texas)

E552   Kay Fuller. 19 Apr. 1949—18 Apr. 1955. (7 letters) Regarding talk broadcasts for England and the Commonwealth. (BBC)

E553   E. G. Gauner. 15 Jan. 1945—19 July 1945. (6 letters) Regarding articles for *Synopsis* and *Vogue.* (Texas)

E554   Robert Gibbings. 26 Jan. 1933. Regarding publication of article. (Texas)

E555   Laurence Gilliam. 22 July 1946—13 Mar. 1947. (3 letters) Regarding 'Cinque Ports' program for BBC. (BBC)

E556   Sidney Gordon. 5 May 1954. Regarding Jane Austen article. (Texas)

E557   Graham Greene. 13 Apr. [n.y.]—17 Jan. 1946. (2 letters) Regarding friendship and *The Hotel.* (Texas)

E558   David Gunston. 26 Mar. 1953. Regarding anthology of short stories. (Texas)

E559   Edith Haggard. 17 Jan. 1945. Regarding publication of short stories in America. (Texas)

E560   Lionel Hale. 1 May 1952—29 July 1952. (3 letters) Regarding adaptation of 'The Needlecase' to dramatic form. (Texas)

E561   Lawrence Hammond. 1 June 1956—13 Aug. 1956. (8 letters) Regarding broadcasting, television, and articles. (Texas)

E562   Stuart Hampshire. n.d. (3 letters) Regarding travels, WW II, and publications. (Texas)

E563   L. P. Hartley. 12 Apr. 1929—3 Apr. 1955. (11 letters) Regarding friendship, reviews, and literature. (Texas)

E564   John Hayward. 28 July 1935—21 Feb. 1955. (5 letters) Regarding friends and *The Cat Jumps, To the North,* and *A World of Love.* (Texas)

E565   Rayner Heppenstall. 16 Apr. 1946—12 Dec. 1957. (16 letters) Regarding broadcasts for radio and television. (BBC)

E566   Hettie Hilton. 8 Dec. 1942—6 July 1955. (27 letters) Regarding articles, motion picture contracts, television and radio broadcast contracts. (Texas)

E567   Gerard Hopkins. n.d. (6 letters) Regarding literary criticism, and praising *To the North, The House in Paris,* and *A World of Love.* (Texas)

E568   B. C. Horton. 26 Sept. 1949—1 Sept. 1959. (23 letters) Regarding broadcasts for BBC. (BBC)

E569   Violet Hunt Hueffer. n.d. Highly complimentary of *To The North.* (Texas)

E570   Julian Huxley. 2 Nov. 1938. Praises *The Death of the Heart.* (Texas)

E571   Godfrey James. 10 Apr. 1945—20 June 1945. (2 letters) Regarding 'Book Talk' broadcast. (BBC)

E572   Norah C. James. 25 Sept. 1944—17 Jan. 1945. (2 letters) Regarding publishing contract for short stories. (Texas)

E573   Margaret Storm Jameson. 18 Jan. 1939. Regarding membership in the P.E.N. (Texas)

E574   Peter Janson-Smith. 2 Jan. 1952—29 Sept. 1955. (15 letters) Regarding translations of her work. (Texas)

E575   Elizabeth Jenkins. 26 Feb. 1955—17 Feb. 1964. (2 letters) Praises *A World of Love* and *The Little Girls.*

E576   Judith B. Jones. 26 Oct. 1959. Regarding bibliography for *A Time in Rome.* (Texas)

E577   Anna Kallin. 14 Oct. 1952—4 Mar. 1953. (3 letters) Regarding program on radio for the Coronation. (BBC)

E578   William R. Kane. 23 June 1924. Regarding a letter to the editor. (Texas)

E579   R. E. Keen. 6 Apr. 1956. Regarding Third Programme broadcast. (BBC)

E580   William Sergeant Kendall. 27 Mar. 1924. Regarding 'Making Arrangements'. (Texas)

E581   Margaret Kennedy. 29 June 1931—7 Oct. 1938. (6 letters) Regarding literary friendships and praising Bowen's novels. (Texas)

E582   Alfred A. Knopf. Sept. 1935—14 Nov. 1968. (2 letters) Regarding publishing. (Texas)

E583   Blanche Knopf. 17 Nov. 1937. Regarding contract. (Texas)

E584   William Koshland. 26 Oct. 1959—29 Dec. 1959. (4 letters) Regarding publication of *A Time in Rome*. (Texas)

E585   Arthur Langford. 4 Dec. 1961—7 Aug. 1962. (3 letters) Regarding foreign broadcasts. (BBC)

E586   James Langham. 18 June 1947—4 July 1947. (2 letters) Regarding broadcast. (BBC)

E587   Birgit Laskowsky. 30 May 1954. Requests assistance for appraisal of her work on Elizabeth Bowen for Ph.D. in German. (Texas)

E588   Owen Leeming. 14 Aug. 1962. Regarding broadcast of 'The Apple Tree'. (BBC)

E589   John Lehmann. 24 Mar. 1941—1 Jan. 1954. (8 letters) Requests short story for publication, and editorial participation in *London Magazine*. (Texas)

E590   Rosamond Lehmann. 12 Oct. 1935—1 Jan. 1969. (17 letters) Regarding friendship, Bowen's novels and short stories, and reviewers' opinions. (Texas)

E591   Richard Lewin. 17 Oct. 1947. Request for broadcast script. (BBC)

E592   Cecil Day Lewis. n.d. (11 letters) Regarding friends and publications. (Texas)

E593   Jill Balcon Day Lewis. 20 Mar. 1955. Highly praises *A World of Love*. (Texas)

E594   P. J. Lewis. 5 May 1954. Regarding 'What Jane Austen Means to Me'. (Texas)

E595   Joan Ling. 10 July 1942—6 Nov. 1943. (2 letters) Regarding the dramatization of *The House in Paris*. (Texas)

E596   Mark Longman. 9 Feb. 1955. Regarding one of Bowen's future books. (Texas)

E597   Ian F. H. Low. 11 Feb. 1954. Regarding Bowen's possible participation in a column for *News Chronicle*. (Texas)

E598   E. V. Lucas. 1 Mar. 1936—22 Mar. 1936. (3 letters) Regarding *The House in Paris*. (Texas)

E599   Rose Macaulay. 10 Nov. 1926—22 Feb. 1949. (11 letters) Regarding friendship, praise of novels, criticism, and radio broadcasts. (Texas)

E600   Desmond MacCarthy. n.d. Regarding invitation to friend. (Texas)

E601   Margaret McLaren. 27 Jan. 1959—10 Sept. 1964. (6 letters) Regarding broadcasts using excerpts from novels, the adaptation of short stories, and international translations. (Texas)

E602   Bertha MacLennan. 7 Oct. 1959—12 Oct. 1959. (2 letters) Regarding translation of *The House in Paris*. (Texas)

E603   David Marcus. 1 Mar. 1954. Requests article for *Irish Writing*. (Texas)

E604   Edward Marsh. 29 May [n.y.]. Regarding poetry. (Texas)

E605   Ethel Colburn Mayne. 15 Dec. 1938. Regarding article in *Observer*. (Texas)

E606   James Meagher. 2 Mar. 1954. Regarding historical references centering on *Bowen's Court*. (Texas)

E607   William A. Menzies. 29 Nov. 1960—27 Apr. 1962. (3 letters) Regarding finances. (Texas)

E608 Eileen Molnay. 24 Jan. 1950. Regarding Home Service broadcast, 'The English Novel'. (BBC)

E609 Alison Kingsmill Moore. 16 Jan. 1954. Requests Bowen's appearance at the Elizabethan Society, which is the women's society of the University of Dublin. In 1948 Bowen had received an honorary Doctorate of Litt. from Trinity College, Dublin. (Texas) See E419.

E610 Ottoline Morrell. n.d. (8 letters) Personal, and laudatory of her writing. (Texas)

E611 John Morris. 14 Mar. 1956. Regarding publication of an article in anthology. (Texas)

E612 Raymond Mortimer. 25 Oct. 1935—14 Feb. 1955. (5 letters) Regarding reviews, travel, and laudatory of *A World of Love*. (Texas)

E613 Eleanor Motherwell. 19 Mar. 1954. Requests article for the *Irish Housewife*. (Texas)

E614 Iris Murdoch. n.d. Praises *Eva Trout*. (Texas)

E615 John Murray. 28 Sept. 1956. Thanks her for *Cornhill* article. (Texas)

E616 J. Middleton Murry. 15 Sept. 1923. Regarding a story she submitted to *Adelphi*. (Texas)

E617 Elizabeth Myers. 15 Mar. 1939—28 Apr. 1939. (2 letters) Regarding *The Death of the Heart* and a review by Bowen. (Texas)

E618 P. H. Newby. 4 Oct. 1949—18 Sept. 1950. (7 letters) Regarding radio broadcasts. (BBC)

E619 D. E. Noël-Paton. 12 May 1954—2 June 1954. (3 letters) Regarding a tour for the British Council of South America. (Texas)

E620 Sean O'Faoláin. n.d. 22 Apr. 1937. (3 letters) Regarding *Friends and Relations, Ann Lee's,* their friendship, and the need for Irish writers to write about Ireland. (Texas)

E621 Iris Origo. 10 Mar. 1960. Regarding errata in *A Time in Rome*. (Texas)

E622   P.E.N. 9 Jan. 1939—27 Jan. 1939. (2 letters) Regarding membership. (Texas)

E623   Logan Pearsall-Smith. 11 Dec. 1932. Regarding invitation. (Texas)

E624   B. F. Pejovio. 27 Jan. 1953. Regarding Serbo-Croatian translation of *The Death of the Heart*. (Texas)

E625   David Piper. n.d. Requests attendance at press reception. (Texas)

E626   William Plomer. 22 Jan. 1935—9 May 1963. (36 letters) Important correspondence on friendships, literature, writing, reviewing, etc. (Texas)

E627   Stephen Potter. 19 Mar. 1945. Regarding Anthony Trollope broadcast. (Texas)

E628   Phoebe Prince. 24 May 1946—12 Nov. 1947. (6 letters) Regarding second serial rights for publication. (Texas)

E629   V. S. Pritchett. 8 July 1947—25 Oct. 1951. (4 letters) Regarding their correspondence and literary ventures. (Texas)

E630   Alan Pryce-Jones. 27 May 1954. Requests Bowen to write an article for *TLS*. (Texas)

E631   Noreen Purdon. 21 Sept. 1949—24 Oct. 1949. (2 letters) Regarding radio broadcast in Australia, 'Famous Women'. (BBC)

E632   Ninette Quinn. 7 June 1962. Regarding anthology rights. (Texas)

E633   Joseph Reilly. 4 Feb. 1954. Requests permission to publish 'Tears, Idle Tears' in *Blarney Magazine* and requests another article after her American lecture tour in April. (Texas)

E634   Lennox Robinson. n.d.—6 June 1938. (4 letters) Regarding her work, election to the Irish Academy of Letters, and friendship. (Texas)

E635   W. Robinson. 19 June 1952. Regarding Cape Uniform Edition. (Texas)

E636   W. R. Rodgers. 12 Nov. 1947. Regarding feature article Bowen agreed to write for BBC. (Texas)

E637   William Rothenstein. 11 Jan. 1939. Praises *The House in Paris* and *The Death of the Heart*. (Texas)

E638   Jean Rountree. 29 Mar. 1956—9 July 1956. (3 letters) Regarding broadcasts. (BBC)

E639   Naomi Royde-Smith. 10 Mar. 1929—1 Feb. 1934. (3 letters) Regarding friendship and literature. (Texas)

E640   Peter S. 1 July 1955. Regarding *The Shelbourne*. (Texas)

E641   Edward Sackville-West. 9 Sept. 1943—6 Mar. 1955. (7 letters) Regarding friendships, literature, and praising her books. (Texas)

E642   Vita Sackville-West. 26 Oct. 1938. Praises *The Death of the Heart*. (Texas)

E643   Marquess of Salisbury. 10 Mar. [n.y.]. (2 letters) Personal, and laudatory of one of Bowen's novels. (Texas)

E644   Christopher V. Salmon. 27 May 1941—4 Mar. 1942. (9 letters) Requests stories for broadcasting. (BBC)

E645   Eileen Sam. 1 Sept. 1943. Regarding a script for broadcast. (BBC)

E646   William Sansom. n.d. [postmark 5 Feb. 1947]. Regarding second serial rights for 'I Died of Love'. (Texas)

E647   May Sarton. 25 July 1936—11 Dec. 1938. (8 letters) Regarding their friends, literature, and Bowen's works. (Texas)

E648   Det Schønbergske Förlag. 5 Aug. 1947. Requests permission to publish 'Notes on the Novel' as Christmas present from the publishers. (Texas)

E649   Ethel Sidgwick. 29 Jan. 1933—19 Dec. 1936. (3 letters) Requests story for *Home and Country*. (Texas)

E650   Frank Sidgwick. 12 Jan. 1923—26 Nov. 1926. (8 letters) Regarding publication of her writing and reviews. (Texas)

E651   Lance Sieveking. 24 Jan. 1946—15 Apr. 1946. (3 letters) Desires to adapt stories for broadcasts. (BBC)

E652   Stephen Spender. n.d. [1935—1955?]. (12 letters) Important correspondence on Bowen's writing, comparing her to Virginia Woolf. (Texas)

E653   L. M. Stapley. 17 May 1954. Regarding BBC broadcast for Far Eastern Service. (Texas)

E654   W. F. Stirling. 7 June 1945—6 July 1945. (2 letters) Request to write three book reviews for the Latin American Service of the BBC. (BBC)

E655   Leslie Stokes. 7 Nov. 1946. Regarding broadcast of short story on Third Programme. (BBC)

E656   Evelyn John Strachey. 17 June 1924—3 July 1924. (2 letters) Regarding a story for *Spectator*. (Texas)

E657   Beryl M. Symons. 10 June 1947—25 Aug. 1947. (3 letters) Regarding foreign reprint rights for essays. (Texas)

E658   Donald F. Taylor. 21 Dec. 1942. Regarding Norwegian film. (Texas)

E659   Elizabeth Taylor. n.d. [1945—1965?]. (12 letters) Refers to the problems of the woman writer and to the current books each writes. (Texas)

E660   N. G. Thompson. 13 Sept. 1946. Regarding committee meeting. (Texas)

E661   J. Patricia Thurgood. 24 Sept. 1959—19 Feb. 1960. (3 letters) Regarding 'A Day in the Dark'. (Texas)

E662   Hilda Tweedy. 24 Oct. 1952—27 Dec. 1952. (2 letters) Regarding article for the *Irish Housewife*. (Texas)

E663   Philip Unwin. 1 Dec. 1947. Requests book review. (Texas)

E664 Josephine Waldron. 23 Oct. 1947—11 Nov. 1947. (2 letters) Regarding second serial rights in translation. (Texas)

E665 H. J. Walker. 20 Jan. 1954. Regarding lecture on Jane Austen in German. (Texas)

E666 Hugh Walpole. 26 Nov. 1938. Regarding misquotation. (Texas)

E667 Mollie Waters. 15 Mar. 1960—31 Jan. 1964. (7 letters) Regarding second serial rights for translations. (Texas)

E668 Graham Watson. 20 Mar. 1953—28 Apr. 1953. (2 letters) Regarding book reviews. (Texas)

E669 Evelyn Waugh. n.d.—22 Feb. 1964. (5 letters) Covers material from *Friends and Relations* and *The Last September* to *The Little Girls*. (Texas)

E670 Veronica Wedgwood. 29 Aug. [n.y.]—29 Mar. 1955. (2 letters) Regarding Bowen's writings and hers, and their personal and literary friendships. (Texas)

E671 H. G. Wells. 18 Nov. 1932—25 Mar. 1945. (8 letters) Compliments and finds fault with Bowen's work. (Texas)

E672 Peggy Wells. 7 July 1947—18 Mar. 1948. (2 letters) Regarding adaptation of 'Look At All Those Roses' for broadcast. (BBC)

E673 Eudora Welty. n.d. (17 letters) Important personal letters. (Texas)

E674 D. J. Wenden. 21 Jan. 1954. Establishes date for lecture. (Texas)

E675 Ray B. West Jr. 21 Mar. 1954. Requests Bowen's participation in Writers' Workshop in Iowa City. (Texas)

E676 Virginia Woolf. 22 July [1932]—[Mar. 1939]. (38 letters) Regarding their roles as women writers and as friends. (Texas)

E677 Phoebe Y. 24 Mar. 1955—2 Aug. 1955. (3 letters) Regarding articles for periodicals. (Texas)

E678 Colin Young. 26 May 1952—11 Jan. 1954. (16 letters) Regarding publication of articles. (Texas)

This section lists only a portion of the many known broadcasts. Due to World War II and the concomitant loss of records, details of many broadcasts are not available; moreover, the specifics of a number of foreign broadcasts are not available. For instance, numerous short stories were read on the air in translation in Austria, China, Denmark, France, Germany, Sweden, and Switzerland. In 1943 Bowen wrote a Weekly Book Review for broadcast on the BBC Overseas Chinese Service. Details for only three remain. Through correspondence it is known that her works were broadcast on CBS and NBC radio and television, but details of these broadcasts are not available to the compilers.

The first part of this section lists Bowen's works as adapted for radio or television. Unless stipulated, all productions were adapted by Bowen. When adaptations were made by others, they were always approved by Bowen before production. Commentaries about Bowen or reviews of her work are included in this first part of the section. The second part lists Bowen's appearances on radio or television and is known to be incomplete. Under both Productions and Appearances items are listed chronologically.

Productions

F1 'New Judgement: Elizabeth Bowen on Jane Austen' (play) BBC Home Service, 8 March 1942. The part of Jane Austen was played by Fay Compton. Revised for new production by Stephen Potter. BBC Third Programme, 16 Aug. 1948. Recording repeated: BBC Third Programme, 22 Aug. 1948. See E115.

F2 'London Revisited: As Seen by Fanny Burney' No. 1 (play) BBC Home Service, 14 Nov. 1942. See E116.

F3 'Book Talk' (book review) BBC Overseas Chinese Service, 17 May 1943. A weekly literary review written by Bowen and read by Mrs. Su.

F4 'Book Talk' (book review) BBC Overseas Chinese Service 16 Aug. 1943. A weekly literary review written by Bowen and read by Mrs. Su.

F5 'Book Talk' (book review) BBC Overseas Chinese Service 13

Sept. 1943. A weekly literary review written by Bowen and read by Mrs Su.

F6 'The Cat Jumps' (dramatization and adaptation of short story) BBC Latin American Service, ca. Apr. 1945. Fifteen-minute dramatization in Spanish. BBC Overseas Service, France, 29 Sept. 1947. Same dramatization in French. BBC Home Service, 27 Dec. 1956. Read by Olive Gregg and possibly slightly abridged. See A8.

F7 'New Judgement: Anthony Trollope' (play) BBC Home Service. 4 May 1945. Recording repeated: BBC Home Service, 6 Sept. 1945; BBC Third Programme, 10 Feb. 1948; BBC Home Service, 26 Feb. 1950. Also transcribed for other services and broadcast for overseas distribution. See A16.

F8 'Henrietta Post' (dramatization of short story, 'Reduced') Adaptation by James Langham. BBC Home Service, 14 Sept. 1945. See A11a.

F9 'This is London: "Bloomsbury"' No. 12 (essay) BBC Overseas African Service, 1 July 1946. Research by Rufus Buxton.

F10 'Modern Short Stories: "The Demon Lover"' (short story) BBC Home Service, Midland Region, 27 Aug. 1946. Adapted for radio. Read by Evelyn Russell. 'Woman's Hour: "The Demon Lover"' BBC Light Programme, 6 Apr. 1951. Produced by Paul Stephenson. Read by Catherine Salkeld. BBC Home Service, 17 Dec. 1956. Read by Catherine Salkeld. 'Morning Story: "The Demon Lover"' BBC Radio 4, 10 Jan. 1974. Recorded from West Region. Adapted and read by Cecile Chevreau. See A15.

F11 'Living Writers—4 Elizabeth Bowen' (essay) By L. A. G. Strong. BBC Third Programme, 26 Oct. 1946. Recording repeated: BBC Home Service 3 Nov. 1946. Extracts from *The Last September*, 'Ann Lee's', and *The Death of the Heart* read by Strong. See E176. 'Contemporary English Writers—Elizabeth Bowen' BBC Overseas Latin American Service, 24 and 25 Apr. 1947. Read by Valdes. 'The Contemporary English Novel No. 3—Elizabeth Bowen' BBC Home Service, 20 June 1950. See E183.

F12 'The Tommy Crans' (short story) BBC Third Programme, 6 Nov. 1946. Recording repeated: BBC Home Service, 19 Nov. 1946. Read by Beatrice Curtis Brown. 'Morning Story: "The Tommy Crans"' BBC Radio 4, 22 Nov. 1973. Recorded from Northern Ireland and read by

Pitt Wilkinson. Shortened by a few seconds to accommodate time slot. See A8.

F13 'Ireland Today' (commentaries) CBS television, 22 May and 6 June 1947. Two-part program for which Bowen wrote the essays.

F14 'Book Review—Signposts in English Literature, No. 14 on Elizabeth Bowen' (book review) By John Lehmann. BBC European Service, Germany, 31 May 1947. 'Studies in English Letters on Elizabeth Bowen' By John Lehmann. BBC Overseas Far Eastern Service, 21 Oct. 1947. Revised version of German Service script, 31 May 1947. See E177, E178.

F15 'Love' (short story) BBC Overseas Service, France, 21 July 1947. See A11.

F16 'Tears, Idle Tears' (short story) BBC Home Service, 15 Sept. 1947. Read by Susan Richards. 'The Storyteller—"Tears Idle Tears" ' BBC Home Service, 15 Sept. 1964. Read by Mary Wimbush. See A11.

F17 'Cultural Magazine: Impressions of Czechoslovakia' (essay) BBC European Service, Czechoslovakia, 16 Mar. 1948. Read by Mrs. Krywultova. See E66.

F18 'Wednesday Matinee: "Look At All Those Roses" ' (adaptation of short story) Adapted by Peggy Wells. BBC Home Service, 5 May 1948. 'The Storyteller—"Look At All Those Roses" ' BBC Home Service, 25 May and 26 May 1964. Read by Nicolette Bernard. BBC Overseas Service, Sept. 1964. Transcribed in Italian. Shortened version. Overseas World Service, 14 Dec. and 15 Dec. 1966. 'Story Tellers: 5 "Look At All Those Roses" ' BBC Radio 4, 10 Aug. 1970. Series in which short stories (sometimes abridged) are read by artists. Jill Balcon reads Bowen's story. See A11.

F19 'Telling' (short story) BBC Third Programme, 5 June 1948. Recording repeated: 17 July 1948. Read by Alan Blair. See A5

F20 'Songs My Father Sang Me' (short story) BBC Third Programme, 8 Aug. 1948. Read by Arthur Calder Marshall. See A15.

F21 'Sanditon' (competition) BBC Third Programme, 21 Oct. 1948. Report on winning entry in competition to outline best ending for Jane Austen's unfinished story. Bowen was one of three judges. The

other two were Elizabeth Jenkins and Dr. R. W. Chapman. The winning
entry was read by Leslie Stokes. See E120.

F22   'An Appreciation of Elizabeth Bowen' (essay) By L. P. Hartley.
BBC Third Programme, 16 Nov. 1948. See E180. 'English Writing:
Talk on Elizabeth Bowen and Her Work' BBC Overseas Service, Lon-
don Calling Asia, 26 Mar. 1957. Quotations read by Jill Balcon and
John Scott. See E186. 'Life and Letters: The Work of Elizabeth
Bowen' BBC General Overseas Service, 9 Feb. 1964.

F23   'A Year I Remember—1918' (play) BBC Third Programme, 10
Mar. 1949. Produced by R. D. Smith with a cast of thirteen. Recording
repeated: 11 Mar. 1949. See E121.

F24   'New Books and Old' (book review) By Eric Gillett. BBC Light
Programme, 2 Apr. 1949. Review of *The Heat of the Day*.

F25   'The House in Paris' (novel) NBC ca. 21 May 1950. There is no
information regarding the adaptation. See A9.

F26   'The Other Side of the Door' (talk) By Naomi Lewis. BBC Light
Programme, 20 Nov. 1951. A talk on Elizabeth Bowen. See E184.

F27   'Woman's Hour: "The House in Paris" ' (abridgement of novel)
Adapted by Brenda Markham. BBC Light Programme, 20 Nov. to 10
Dec. 1951 weekly. Read by Patience Collier. See A9.

F28   'Pink May' (adaptation of short story). Adapted by Mary
Jones. BBC Overseas Service. Transcribed in Italian, July 1953. 'To-
night's Short Story: "Pink May" ' BBC Home Service Midland Region,
North Region, Northern Ireland, West Region, Wales, 21 Nov. 1960.
Read by Mary Wimbush. 'Morning Story: "Pink May" ' Adapted by
Cecile Chevreau. BBC Radio 4, 8 Nov. 1973. Recorded from West
Region. Read by Cecile Chevreau. See A15.

F29   'Death of the Heart' (extracts from novel) BBC Overseas European Service, 23 Mar. and 30 Mar., 6 Apr. and 13 Apr. 1954. Extracts
printed in European Programme Bulletin. BBC London Calling Asia.
Sent to Singapore on 18 June and 25 June and 2 July and 9 July 1954.
Also sent to Turkey. BBC Overseas European Service, France, 24 Feb.
and 2 Mar. and 9 Mar. and 16 Mar. 1966. Extracts printed in 'Ici
Londres'. See A10.

F30 'Talking of Books' (book review) By Arthur Calder Marshall. BBC Home Service, 6 Mar. 1955. Review of *A World of Love*.

F31 'Book in the Shade: "A World of Love" ' (dramatization of novel) Dramatization and presentation by Arthur Marshall. BBC Light Programme, 7 Aug. 1955. See A22.

F32 'Chapter One of "The House in Paris" ' (novel) BBC Home Service, 18 Sept. 1955. Read by Mary Wimbush. Third in the Sunday Morning Series of six readings from the opening chapters of distinguished novels. See A9, E11.

F33 'Between Two Worlds, Saturday Night Theatre: "The Heat of the Day" ' (adaptation of novel) Adapted by Mary Hope Allen. BBC Home Service, 29 Oct. 1955. 'The Monday Play: "The Heat of the Day" ' Dramatized by Mary Hope Allen. BBC Radio 4, 14 Feb. 1972. See A18.

F34 'The Critics' (book review) Unsigned. BBC Home Service. 26 Dec. 1955. Review of *A World of Love*.

F35 'The Death of the Heart' (dramatization of novel). Dramatized by Anne Allan and Julian Amyes. BBC television, 5 July 1956. See A10.

F36 'Friends and Relations' (serialization of novel) Prepared for serialization by Mary Hope Allen. BBC Home Service, 15 Apr. to 2 July 1957 weekly. Serialized into twelve installments. The last installment condenses two parts into one.

F37 'The Death of the Heart' (adaptation of novel) Adapted by Anne Allan and Julian Amyes. BBC Home Service, 9 Sept. 1957. See A10.

F38 'The House in Paris' (dramatization of novel) Dramatized by Anne Allan and Julian Amyes. BBC television, 1 Sept. 1959. See A9.

F39 'Something to Read' (discussion) BBC television, 7 Mar. 1960. Review and discussion of *The House in Paris*.

F40 'The World of Books' (book review) By Peter Duval Smith. BBC Home Service, 9 July 1960. Review of *A Time in Rome*.

F41 'Wilfred Pickles Tells a Story: "The Demon Lover" ' (short story) BBC television, 13 Sept. 1960. See A15.

F42 'The Inherited Clock' (dramatization of short story) Adapted by Mrs. Anthony Kearkey. BBC television, fall 1960. Cast: Crutchley as Clara, Mary Merrall as Aunt Addie, Fabia Drake as Rosanna, Paul Eddinton as Paul, Ronald Leigh Hunt as Henry Harley. BBC telerecording of Ilona Terence's adaptation was sent to Australia and New Zealand in 1964. See A15.

F43 'Reduced' (short story) BBC Home Service, 8 May 1962. Recorded from *Selected Short Stories* and read by Mary Wimbush. 'Morning Story: "Reduced"' Adapted and read by Cecil Chevreau. BBC Radio 4, 4 April 1974. Recorded from West Region. See A11.

F44 'Talk of Books' (book review) By Isabel Quigley. BBC General Overseas Service, 4 June 1962. Review of *The Death of the Heart*.

F45 'The Apple Tree' (short story) BBC Home Service, 14 Aug. 1962. Read by Olive Kirby. 'Story Time Tales of the Supernatural: "The Apple Tree"' BBC Radio 4, 21 Apr. 1970. Read by Patience Collier. See A8.

F46 'Women and Words' (discussion) Mary McCarthy talks with Peter Duval Smith. BBC television, 8 Jan. 1963. Recorded extract of conversation by Elizabeth Bowen in Jocelyn Brooke program. See F79.

F47 'Attractive Modern Homes' (short story) BBC Home Service, recorded 12 Dec. 1963 for future broadcast. Produced by Michael Bukht. 'The Storyteller: "Attractive Modern Homes"' BBC Home Service, 4 May 1964. Read by Cecile Chevreau. See A11.

F48 'The Critics' (book review) By Alan Brien. BBC Home Service Midland Region, North Region, Northern Ireland, West Region, Wales, 16 Feb. 1964. Review of *The Little Girls*.

F49 'The Storyteller: "The Easter Egg Party"' (short story) BBC Home Service, 29 June 1964. Read by Hilda Schroder. See A11.

F50 'The World of Books' (book review) By Brian Glanville. BBC Home Service Scotland, Midland Region, North Region, Northern Ireland, Wales, 7 Aug. 1965. Review of *A Day in the Dark*.

F51 'Holiday Books: *The Death of the Heart*' (book review) by C. V. Wedgwood. BBC Home Service, 4 Aug. 1965.

F52 'The Thirties in Britain—The Novel' (essay) By Walter Allen. BBC Third Programme, 30 Nov. 1965. Allen considers the characteristic writing of the decade in terms of the novels of Evelyn Waugh, Graham Greene, Lewis Grassic Gibbon, Wyndham Lewis, Christopher Isherwood, Henry Green, and Elizabeth Bowen. 'The Novel in the Thirties. A Reconsideration' Recording repeated: Third Programme, 24 May 1966.

F53 'Woman's Hour: Books and Writers' (book review) By Elizabeth Berridge. BBC Light Programme, 10 Mar. 1966. Review of *The Demon Lover*.

F54 'The Critics' (book review) Unsigned. BBC Radio 4, 26 Jan. 1969. Review of *Eva Trout*.

F55 'The Little Girls' (dramatization of novel) Dramatized and adapted by Norman Painting. Produced by Anthony Cornish. BBC Radio 3, 25 Apr. 1969. Recorded in Birmingham and repeated 27 May 1969. See A27.

F56 'The World of Books' (book review) By Eric Rhode. BBC Radio 4, 1 Jan. 1970. Review of *Eva Trout*.

F57 'Maria' (adaptation of short story) Adaptation and translation by Yves Leclerc. BBC European Service, France, 2 Jan. 1970. See A8.

F58 'Now Read On' (book review) By Lorna Pegram. BBC Radio 4, 20 Oct. 1970. Review of *The Good Tiger*.

F58.1 'Morning Story: "Firelight in the Flat"' (short story) BBC Radio 2, 24 Mar. 1971. Series of short stories read on radio. Recorded from Northern Ireland and read by Rosalind Shanks. See A8.

F58.2 'Tribute to Elizabeth Bowen' BBC Radio 4, 28 Feb. 1973. Ronald Harwood presents tribute. Excerpts from Elizabeth Bowen's work.

Appearances

F59 'Strength of Mind—Do Women Think Like Men?' (discussion) BBC Home Service, 17 Oct. 1941. One of a series of broadcasts between different people discussing the nature and authority of thought and what can be expected from thinking. This program, No. 3, was between Elizabeth Bowen, Phyllis Vallance, G. M. Young, and John Mabbott. See C121, E48.

F60 'The Living Image' (discussion) BBC Home Service, 4 Dec. 1941. Discussions on the relation between life and art. This program on books, No. 3, featured Hugh Sykes-Davis, Elizabeth Bowen, V. S. Pritchett, and H. L. Beales. See E113.

F61 'Strength of Mind—Convention and Value' (discussion) BBC Home Service, 5 Dec. 1941. A discussion between Lt. Crd. J. E. M. Noad, Elizabeth Bowen, RNVR Capt. Allan Pryce-Jones, and John Mabbott. See C123.

F62 'The Living Image' (discussion) BBC Home Service, 23 Jan. 1942. This program, No. 4, focused on a discussion of the relation between life and art through books, and featured Hugh Sykes-Davis, Elizabeth Bowen, V. S. Pritchett, and H. L. Beales. See E114.

F63 'Book Talk—New and Recent Fiction' (book review) BBC Home Service, 25 June 1945. See E118.

F64 'Book Talk—New and Recent Fiction' (book review) BBC Home Service, 16 July 1945. See E119.

F65 'Return Journey 2 "Hythe and Romney Marshes" ' (essay) BBC Home Service, 6 Jan. 1946. Script also by Elizabeth Bowen.

F66 'Quiz Team—9 Residents vs Authors' (quiz) BBC Light Programme, 8 Feb. 1946. Residents: Christopher Stone, Margaret Stewart, Daniel George, Anora Winn. Authors: John Dickson-Carr, Elizabeth Bowen, Capt. A. E. Dingle ('Sinbad'), and Pamela Frankau.

F67 'The Crisis (4)' (talk) BBC Third Programme, 23 Feb. 1947.

F68 'The Crisis (3)' (talk) BBC Third Programme, 28 Feb., 2 Mar. 1947. See E64.

F69 'Contemporary Thinkers' (talk) BBC radio, 5–6 Mar. 1947.

F70 'Kaleidoscope: "Meet Your Favorite Authors", No. 6' (interview) BBC television, 6 June 1947. Interview with Elizabeth Bowen. See B20.

F71 'The Reader Takes Over' (interview) Recorded by BBC for Canadian Broadcast Corporation, 6 June 1947. Bowen discusses one of her books with Henry Reed.

F72 'Books and Authors—"The Next Book" ' (interview) BBC Light Programme, 13 July 1947. Bowen talks with editor about 'the next book'. Recording repeated: 'Famous Writers II' BBC Overseas Service, Pacific Service, 14 Sept. 1950. An excerpt from a discussion on Books and Authors. Recording repeated: 'My Next Book' BBC Third Programme, 15 Jan. 1964. See C307.

F73 'The Reader Takes Over' (discussion) BBC North American Service and Transcription Service, 13 Aug. 1947 and 14 Aug. 1947. Discussion with Mr. Henry Reed, Mrs. E. Sturch, Mr. Robert Locke, and Elizabeth Bowen.

F74 'The Artist and Society' (discussion) BBC Third Programme, 10 July 1948. Scripted discussion with Graham Greene, Elizabeth Bowen, and V. S. Pritchett. See B21.

F75 'In My Library' (talk) BBC General Overseas Service, 2 Nov. 1949. Talk by Elizabeth Bowen. See E122.

F76 'ABC Women's Programme No. 7 "The Mechanics of Writing" ' (talk) BBC Overseas Service Pacific, 14 Nov. 1949. Talk by Elizabeth Bowen. See C375, E73.1.

F77 'Town Forum from Banbury' (interview) BBC Midland Region, 16 Dec. 1949. An audience puts spontaneous questions to Elizabeth Bowen, John Moore, The Radio Doctor (Dr. Gill), and Eric Gillett. Chairman: Bernard Storey. Recording repeated: 19 Dec. 1949.

F78 'Arts Magazine: "How I Write" ' (interview) BBC Wales, 10 May 1950. Interview with Glyn Jones. See E68.

F79 'A Conversation between Elizabeth Bowen and Jocelyn Brooke' (discussion) BBC Third Programme, 15 Dec. 1950. Recording repeated: 20 Dec. 1950. About her novels and the beliefs that lie behind them. See E123.

F80 'The Cult of Nostalgia' (essay) BBC Third Programme, 4 Aug. 1951. Recording repeated: 8 Aug. 1951. Bowen examines the tendency in modern English writing to turn back to childhood and the remembrance of things past. Recording repeated: BBC Overseas Service, Japan, 1951 and 1952. See C389.

F81 'Conversation on Traitors' (discussion) BBC Home Service, 21 Aug. 1952. Unscripted discussion on the nature of betrayal and the qualities that make a man a potential traitor. Speakers Nigel Balchin, Noel Annan, Alan Moorehead and Elizabeth Bowen. See E124.

F82 'For a Sovereign Lady—Some Thoughts on the Coronation' (discussion) BBC Third Programme, 31 May 1953. Recording repeated: 4 June 1953. Discussion between C. V. Wedgwood and Elizabeth Bowen. See E125.

F83 'English Writing' (talk) BBC Overseas Service, London Calling Asia, 1 Mar. 1955. Talk on her own writings including reading of an extract from *The Death of the Heart*. Read by Jill Balcon.

F84 'Contemporary British Novelists—We Write Novels' (discussion) BBC General Overseas Service, Transcription Service, 2 June 1955. Unscripted discussion with Walter Allen. Bowen discusses her approach to the novel. See E126.

F85 'Some Horrors of Childhood: 2 Not Rising to the Occasion' (talk) BBC Home Service, 19 July 1956. See C548.

F86 'Truth and Fiction: Story, Theme, and Situation' (talk) BBC Home Service, 26 Sept. 1956. The first of three talks on the novelist's craft. Repeat: 'The Single Vision: Story, Theme and Situation' BBC Home Service Midland Region, Northern Ireland, Scotland, West Region, Wales, 24 Mar. 1963. Recording repeated to Home Service, Midland Region, North Region, Northern Ireland, West Region, Wales, 20 Aug. 1963. See A25.

F87 'Truth and Fiction: People: the Creation of Character' (talk) BBC Home Service, 3 Oct. 1956. The second of three talks. See A25.

F88 'Truth and Fiction: Time, Period and Reality' (talk) BBC Home Service, 10 Oct. 1956. The third of three talks. See A25 and F100.

F89 'Desert Island Discs' (discussion) BBC Home Service, 11 Mar. 1957. Discussion with Ray Plomley to decide which eight records Bowen would choose to have with her if she were sent away on a desert island.

F90 'Writing About Rome' (talk) BBC Home Service, 14. Oct. 1959. Bowen describes how a visit to Rome with the intention of writing a book on an already familiar city clarified her vision of it. See E127.

F91 'Frankly Speaking' (interview) BBC Home Service, 16 Mar. 1960. Interview by John Bowen, N. Ewer, H. A. L. Craig. Recording repeated: 'A World of Sound from the BBC Archives: "A Sort of Agony (No. 5)—Secure against Death" ' BBC Home Service, 29 Mar. 1963. Recording repeated: 'The Writer's Craft No. 1' BBC Third Programme, compiled from Sound Archives, 10 Jan. 1964. See E128.

F92 'Bookstand' (discussion) BBC television, 7 Feb. 1962. Discussion between V. S. Naipaul and Bowen on *The Death of the Heart*.

F93 'Life and Letters: The Stories of Katherine Mansfield' (talk) BBC General Overseas Service, 7 Apr. 1963. Series recorded talk.

F94 'Before Publication—Introduced by Elizabeth Bowen' (novel) BBC Third Programme, 16 Feb. 1964. Excerpts from *The Little Girls* read by Bowen. See A27a.

F95 'Tonight' (interview) BBC television, 18 Feb. 1964. Derek Hart interviews Bowen about *The Little Girls*.

F96 'The World of Books' (review/interview) BBC Home Service, 14 Mar. 1964. Review of *The Little Girls*. Includes a recorded interview of Bowen by Robert Waller. Recording repeated: 'The Lively Arts No. 79' on North American Service. See E129.

F97 'This Time of Day' (interview) BBC Home Service North Region, Northern Ireland, West Region, Wales, 25 June 1965. Interview by Wendy Jones about *A Day in the Dark*.

F98 'The World of Books' (review) BBC Home Service North Region, Scotland, West Region, Wales, 26 June 1965. Bowen reviews *Daughters of Erin* by Elizabeth Coxhead. See E130.

F99 'Today: Companions of Literature' (interview) BBC Home Service North Region, Northern Ireland, Midland Region, Scotland, 7 July 1965. Interview between C. Day Lewis, Dan Zerdin, and Elizabeth Bowen.

F100 'Literary Friendships' (talk) BBC Home Service, 29 Aug. 1966.

Richard Church used edited extracts from 'Truth and Fiction: Time, Period and Reality'. See F88.

F101 'Take It or Leave It' BBC television, 17 Aug. 1968. Literary Panel Game. Chairman: Alan Brien. Reader: John Moffatt. Panelists: Elizabeth Bowen, Claire Tomalin, Cyril Connolly, and V. S. Naipaul.

F102 'Release' (interview) BBC television, 7 Jan. 1969. Interview by James Mossman about *Eva Trout*.

F103 'A Portrait of Virginia Woolf' (essay) BBC television, 18 Jan. 1970. Repeated 8 Aug. 1973. Contributions by Elizabeth Bowen, Lord David Cecil, Duncan Grant, Raymond Mortimer, George Rylands, and Quentin Bell.

F104 'Take It or Leave It' BBC television, 9 Oct. 1970. Literary Panel Game, broadcast from Manchester. Chairman: Alan Brien. Reader: Peter Eyre. Panelists: Elizabeth Bowen, A. S. Byatt, Cyril Connolly, and Peter Porter.

F105 'Take It or Leave It' BBC television, 20 Nov. 1970. Literary Panel Game, broadcast from Manchester. Chairman; Alan Brien. Reader: Peter Eyre. Panelists: Elizabeth Bowen, A. S. Byatt, Cyril Connolly, and Peter Porter.

F106 'Summer Review: An Imaginary Friend' (literary portrait) BBC television, 13 Aug. 1971. A literary portrait of John Woodby with contributions from Irene Handl, Elizabeth Bowen, V. S. Naipaul, John Betjeman, and Peter Cook.

Items are listed chronologically according to date of first publication.

G1 'All Saints' [1 May 1923]
Achievements in Fiction: A College Anthology, ed. Burton L. Cooper
and Lila K. Chalpin (Boston: Allyn and Bacon, 1971), pp. 224–28.
First printed in A1 (q.v.).

G1.1 'Coming Home' [1 May 1923]

Insights: A Selection of Creative Literature about Childhood, ed. The
Child Study Association of America, with introd. and commentary by
Anna W. M. Wolf (New York: Jason Aronson, Inc., 1973), pp. 408–
13. First printed in A1 (q.v.).

G2 'The Shadowy Third' [1 May 1923]
Achievements in Fiction: A College Anthology, ed. Burton L. Cooper
and Lila K. Chalpin (Boston: Allyn and Bacon, 1971), pp. 238–46.
First printed in A1 (q.v.).

G3 'Just Imagine' [Dec. 1926]
Best British Short Stories, ed. Edward J. O'Brien (London: Jonathan
Cape, 1927), pp. 82–93; (New York: Dodd Mead and Co., 1927), pp.
72–84; *Stories of To-Day and Yesterday,* ed. Frederick H. Law (New
York: Century Book Co., 1930), pp. 24–37. First printed in *Eve* (C8).

G4 'Telling' [Oct. 1927]
A Century of Creepy Stories, comp. Cynthia Asquith (London: Hutch-
inson & Co., 1934), pp. 193–200; *And Darkness Falls,* ed. Boris Karloff
(Cleveland and New York: World Publishing Co., 1946), pp. 421–27.
See A5a.

G5 'Maria' [28 Sept. 1928]
Introduction to Modern English and American Literature, ed. William
Somerset Maugham (New York: New Home Library, 1943), pp. 77–
86; *Modern English Short Stories, Second Series,* comp. Derek Hudson
(London: Oxford University Press, 1956), pp. 304–19. See A8.

G6 'An Evening in Anglo-Ireland'   [31 Jan. 1929]
1000 Years of Irish Prose, ed. Vivian Mercier and David H. Greene
(New York: The Devin-Adair Co., 1952), pp. 294–310. An excerpt
from *The Last September* (A4).

G7 'Joining Charles'   [11 July 1929]
Modern English Short Stories, First Series, comp. Phyllis M. Jones
(London: Oxford University Press, 1939), pp. 374–89 [re-issued in 1973
as *English Short Stories, 1888–1937*]; *Treasury of Short Stories*, comp.
Bernardine Kielty (New York: Simon and Schuster, 1947), pp. 483–92;
Reading Modern Short Stories, ed. Jarvis A. Thurston (Chicago: Scott,
Foresman & Co., 1955), pp. 155–65. See A5.

G8 'Foothold'   [11 July 1929]
By and About Women: An Anthology of Short Fiction, ed. Beth Kline
Schneiderman (New York: Harcourt Brace, Jovanovich, Inc., 1973),
pp. 139–57. First printed in A5.

G9 'The Cat Jumps'   [2 Sept. 1929]
A Century of Creepy Stories, ed. Cynthia Asquith (London: Hutchinson & Co., 1934), pp. 201–10; *Stories, British and American*, ed. J. B.
Ludwig and W. R. Poirier (Boston: Houghton Mifflin Co., 1953), pp.
132–41; *Types of Literature*, ed. Francis Connolly (New York: Harcourt Brace and Co., 1955), pp. 112–16. See A8.

G10 'The Tommy Crans'   [Feb. 1930]
The Best British Short Stories of 1933, ed. Edward J. O'Brien and John
Cournos (London: Jonathan Cape, Ltd., 1933), pp. 103–11, (Boston:
Houghton Mifflin Co., 1933), pp. 69–75; *Achievements in Fiction: A
College Anthology*, ed. Burton L. Cooper and Lila K. Chalpin (Bos-
ton: Allyn and Bacon, 1971), pp. 116–21. See A8.

G11 'Her Table Spread'   [May 1930]
The Short Story, comp. Seán O'Faoláin (London: William Collins,
1948), pp. 305–13; *Anchor Book of Stories*, selected with an introd. by
Randall Jarrell (New York: Doubleday & Co., 1958), pp. 75–83; *Short
Stories: A Study in Pleasure*, ed. Seán O'Faoláin (Boston: Little, Brown
& Co., 1961), pp. 333–41; *The Realm of Fiction: 65 Short Stories*, ed.
James B. Hall (New York: McGraw-Hill, Inc., 1965), pp. 285–92; *Fic-
tion 100: An Anthology of Short Stories* (New York: Macmillan, Inc.,
1974), pp. 88–92. See A8.

G12 'The Apple Tree'   [May 1930]
A Century of Creepy Stories, comp. Cynthia Asquith (London: Hutch-
inson & Co., 1934), pp. 181–92; *The Best Ghost Stories,* comp. Anne B.
Ridler (London: Faber and Faber, Ltd., 1948), pp. 340–53. See A8.

G13 'Reduced'   [12 June 1935]
The Best British Short Stories of 1936, ed. Edward J. O'Brien and John
Cournos (London: Jonathan Cape, Ltd., 1936), pp. 73–85, (Boston:
Houghton Mifflin and Co., 1936), pp. 49–59; *Tellers of Tales: One
Hundred Short Stories from the United States, England, France, Russia
and Germany,* ed. W. Somerset Maugham (New York: Doubleday and
Co., 1939), pp. 1381–89. See A11.

G14 'Elizabeth Bowen on Jane Austen'   [30 Apr. 1936]
Novelists on Novelists, ed. Louis Kronenberger (New York: Doubleday and Co., 1962), pp. 9–18. First printed as "Jane Austen" in B9
(q.v.).

G15 'Tears, Idle Tears'   [2 Sept. 1936]
The Best British Short Short Stories of 1937, ed. Edward J. O'Brien and
John Cournos (London: Jonathan Cape, Ltd., 1937), pp. 43–52, (Bos-
ton: Houghton Mifflin & Co., 1937), pp. 29–36; *Literature: Structure,
Sound and Sense,* ed. Laurence Perrine (New York: Harcourt, Brace
and World, Inc., 1970), pp. 93–99 [also published separately in *Story
and Structure,* 3rd. ed., with the same pagination]; *Women & Men To-
gether: An Anthology of Short Fiction,* ed. Dawson Gaillard and John
Mosier (Boston: Houghton Mifflin Company, [1978]), pp. 254–60. See
A11.

G15.1 'The Faber Book of Modern Short Stories'   [Oct. 1937]
Short Story Theories, ed. Charles E. May (Athens, Ohio: Ohio Uni-
versity Press, [1976]), pp 152–58. First printed as 'The Short Story'.
See A19.

G16 'Look at All Those Roses'   [10 and 17 Nov. 1937]
Short Story: A Thematic Anthology, ed. Dorothy Parker and Frederick
B. Shroyer (New York: Charles Scribner's Sons, 1965), pp. 97–104.
See A11.

G17 'The Easter Egg Party'   [Apr. 1938]
The Best British Short Stories of 1939, ed. Edward J. O'Brien and
John Cournos (London: Jonathan Cape, Ltd., 1938), pp. 66–78, (Bos-

ton: Houghton Mifflin & Co., 1938), pp. 42–52; *World's Best Stories, Humor, Drama, Biography, History, Essays, Poetry,* ed. Whit Burnett (New York: The Dial Press, 1950), pp. 623–33. See A11.

G17.1 'Innocence' [3 Oct. 1938]
The New Treasure Chest: An Anthology of Reflective Prose, ed. J. Donald Adams (New York: E. P. Dutton & Co., Inc., 1953), p. 369. An excerpt from *The Death of the Heart* (A10).

G18 'Number 16' [19 Jan. 1939]
The Best British Short Stories of 1939, ed. Edward J. O'Brien (London: Jonathan Cape, Ltd., 1939), pp. 55–65, (Boston: Houghton Mifflin & Co., 1939), pp. 59–67. See A11.

G19 'A Queer Heart' [Feb. 1939]
Reading Modern Short Stories, ed. Jarvis A. Thurston (Chicago: Scott, Foresman & Co., 1955), pp. 147–55; *Masters and Masterpieces of the Short Story,* ed. Joshua McClennen (New York: Henry Holt & Co., 1957), pp. 1–4; *Selected Modern Short Stories,* ed. Walter Gilomen (Bern, Switzerland: Francke Verlag, 1957), pp. 31–44; *Fifty Modern Stories,* ed. Thomas H. M. Blair (New York: Harper & Row, 1960), pp. 571–78; *British Short Stories: Classics and Criticism,* ed. Leonard R. N. Ashley and Stuart L. Astor (Englewood Cliffs, N. J.: Prentice-Hall, 1968), pp. 311–19; *Points of Departure: A Collection of Short Fiction,* ed. Herbert Goldstone, *et al.* (Englewood Cliffs, N. J.: Prentice-Hall, [1971]), pp. 40–49. See A11.

G20 'Bowen on Gorki' [5 Aug. 1939]
Storytellers and Their Art: An Anthology, ed. Georgianna Sampson Trask and Charles Burkhart (New York: Doubleday & Co., 1963), pp. 339–42. See 'Gorki Stories' in A19.

G21 'A Love Story' [July 1940]
Irish Harvest: An Anthology of Prose and Poetry, ed. Robert Greacen (Dublin: New Frontiers Press, 1946), pp. 82–98. See A11.

G22 'Unwelcome Idea' [10 Aug. 1940]
Turnstile One: A Literary Miscellany from 'The New Statesman and Nation', ed. V. S. Pritchett (London: Turnstile Press, 1948), pp. 90–95. See A11.

G23 'Summer Night' [20 Jan. 1941]
Stories of the Forties, ed. Reginald Moore and Woodrow Wyatt (London: Nicholson and Watson, 1945), pp. 98–126; *Modern Irish Short Stories,* selected with an intro. by Frank O'Connor (London: Oxford University Press, 1957), pp. 297–335. First printed in A11 (q.v.).

G24 'Sunday Afternoon' [July 1941]
A World of Great Stories, ed. H. Haydon and John Cournos (New York: Crown Publishers, 1947), pp. 206–12; *Women and Fiction 2: Short Stories by and about Women,* ed. Susan Cahill (New York: New American Library, 1978), pp. 137–44. See A15.

G25 'In the Square' [Sept. 1941]
Horizon Stories, ed. Cyril Connolly (London: Faber and Faber Ltd., 1943), pp. 112–21 (New York: Vanguard Press, 1946), pp. 23–34. See A15.

G26 'The Demon Lover' [6 Nov. 1941]
House of Fiction, ed. Caroline Gordon and Allen Tate, 2nd ed. (New York: Charles Scribner's Sons, 1950), pp. 483–88; *Reading Modern Fiction,* ed. Winifred Lynskey (New York: Charles Scribner's Sons, 1952), pp. 28–32; *England in Literature,* ed. Robert C. Pooley (Chicago: Scott, Foresman & Co., 1953), pp. 95–105; *Stories for the Dead of Night,* ed. Don Congdon (New York: Dell Publishing Co., 1957), pp. 116–23; *Love and Marriage: Twenty-Two Stories,* ed. Margaret Cousins (Garden City, N. J.: Doubleday and Co., 1961), pp. 223–32; *Fifty Years, A Retrospective . . .,* ed. Clifton Fadiman (New York: Alfred A. Knopf, 1965), pp. 521–26; *Romance, Modes of Literature Series,* ed. Ashley Brown and John L. Kimmey (Columbus, Ohio: Charles E. Merrill Co., 1969), pp. 214–19; *Mandala: Literature for Critical Analysis,* ed. Wilfred L. Guerin *et al.* (New York: Harper and Row, 1970), pp. 183–88; *Achievements in Fiction: A College Anthology,* ed. Burton L. Cooper and Lila K. Chalpin (Boston: Allyn and Bacon, 1971), pp. 8–13; *Studies in Short Fiction,* ed. Douglas A. Hughes (New York: Holt, Rinehart and Winston, Inc., 1971), pp. 430–35; *Three Stances of Modern Fiction: A Critical Anthology of the Short Story,* ed. Stephen Minot and Robley Wilson, Jr. (Cambridge, Mass.: Winthrop Publishers, Inc. 1972), pp. 175–81; *By Women: An Anthology of Literature,* ed. Marcia McClintock Folsom and Linda Heinlein Kirschner (Boston: Houghton Mifflin, 1976), pp. 20–25; *The Shape of Fiction,* 2nd ed., ed. Leo Hamalian and Frederick R. Karl (New York: McGraw Hill Co.,

1978), pp. 280–86. *Elements of Literature: Essay, Fiction, Poetry, Drama, Film,* ed. Robert Scholes, Carl H. Klaus, Michael Silverman (New York: Oxford University Press, 1978), pp. 194–99. See A15.

G27 'English Novelists' [Apr.-May 1942]
Impressions of English Literature, ed. W. J. Turner (London: William Collins, 1944), pp. 227–70 [the American issue by Hastings House is entitled *Romance of English Literature*]. First printed as A12.

G28 'The Cheery Soul' [24 Dec. 1942]
The Best from Fantasy and Science Fiction, ed. Anthony Boucher and J. Francis McComas, 2nd series (Boston: Little, Brown and Co., 1953), pp. 108–22. See A15.

G29 'Panorama du Roman' [1944]
Aspects de la Littérature Anglaise 1918–1945, présentés par Kathleen Raine et Max-pol Fouchet (Paris: Fontaine, 1944), pp. 30–39. First printed in *Fontaine* (C133).

G30 'Mysterious Kôr' [Jan. 1944]
English Stories from New Writing, Ljus English Library, #48, ed. John Lehmann (Stockholm: Ljus, 1946), pp. 12–31, (London: Purnell & Sons, 1951), pp. 234–48 [the American issue by Harcourt Brace is entitled *Best Stories from New Writing*]; *Synthesis: Response to Literature,* ed. Charles Sanders, *et al.* (New York: Alfred A. Knopf, [1971]), pp. 164–72. See A15.

G31 'The Happy Autumn Fields' [Nov. 1944]
Reading Modern Fiction, ed. Winifred Lynskey, rev. ed. (New York: Charles Scribner's Sons, 1957), pp. 28–41. See A15.

G32 'Songs My Father Sang Me' [27 Nov. 1944]
Modern Short Stories: The Fiction of Experience, ed. M. X. Lesser and John N. Morris (New York: McGraw-Hill Book Co., Inc., 1962), pp. 45–57. See A15.

G33 'Notes on Writing a Novel' [Autumn 1945]
Little Reviews Anthology, ed. Denys Val Baker (London: Eyre and Spottiswoode, 1946), pp. 111–23; *Modern Literary Criticism: An Anthology,* ed. with an intro. by Irving Howe (New York: Grove Press, 1958), pp. 50–64; *Myth and Method: Modern Theories of Fiction,* ed. with an intro. by James Edwin Miller (Lincoln: University of Nebraska

Press, 1960), pp. 33–50; *Aspects of Fiction,* ed. Howard E. Hugo (Boston: Little, Brown & Co., 1962), pp. 176–89; *Perspectives in Fiction,* ed. J. L. Calderwood and H. E. Tolliver (New York and London: Oxford University Press, 1968), pp. 217–31. See A19.

G34 'Ivy Gripped the Steps'   [Sept. 1945]
English Short Stories of Today, ed. Dan Davin, 2nd series (London: Oxford University Press, 1958), pp. 1–33; *English Short Stories in My Time,* comp. David Cecil (London: Oxford University Press, 1970), pp. 89–120; *Modern British Short Novels,* ed. Robert M. Davis (Glenview, Ill.: Scott, Foresman & Co., 1972), pp. 238–64. See A15.

G35 'The Cost of Letters'   [Aug. 1946]
Ideas and Places, by Cyril Connolly (London: Wiedenfeld and Nicolson, 1953), pp. 82–83 [also published in an American issue by Harper and Brothers]. First printed in *Horizon* (C189).

G36 'Out of a Book'   [Autumn 1946]
British and American Essays, 1905–1956, comp. Carl L. Anderson and George W. Williams (New York: Henry Holt & Co., 1959), pp. 78–84. See A19.

G37 'The Artist in Society—An Exchange of Views: [1947]
        Graham Greene, Elizabeth Bowen, V. S. Pritchett'
From the Third Programme: A Ten Years' Anthology, ed. John Morris (London: Nonesuch Press, 1956), pp. 97–112 [reprinted by Kennikat Press, under its own imprint, in 1970]. See B21.

G37.1 'Music of the Familiar'   [21 Feb. 1949]
The New Treasure Chest: An Anthology of Reflective Prose, ed. J. Donald Adams (New York: E. P. Dutton & Co., Inc., 1953), p. 370. An excerpt from *The Heat of the Day* (A18).

G38 'The Achievement of Virginia Woolf'   [26 June 1949]
Highlights of Modern Literature: A Permanent Collection of Memorable Essays from the New York Times Book Review, ed. Francis Brown (New York: New American Library, 1954), pp. 109–13. See A19.

G39 'The Writer's Peculiar World'   [24 Sept. 1950]
Highlights of Modern Literature: A Permanent Collection of Memorable Essays from the New York Times Book Review, ed. Francis Brown (New York: New American Library, 1954), pp. 32–34. See 'Disloyalties' in A25.

G40 'The Light in the Dark' [Dec. 1950]
The World in Vogue, ed. Bryan Holme *et al.* (New York: The Viking Press, 1963), pp. 291–92. First printed in *Vogue* (C384).

G41 'The Art of Respecting Boundaries' [1 Apr. 1952]
Arts of Living, ed. Ernest Dimnet *et al.* (New York: Simon & Schuster, 1954), pp. 140–47. First printed in *Vogue* (C393).

G42 'Hand in Glove' [27 Oct. 1952]
The House of the Nightmare, and Other Eerie Tales, ed. Kathleen Lines (London: Bodley Head, [1967]), pp. 50–61, (New York: Farrar, Straus and Giroux, Inc., [1968]), pp. 47–60; *Ladies of Horror: Two Centuries of Supernatural Stories by the Gentle Sex,* ed. Seon Manley and Gogo Lewis (New York: Lothrop, Lee & Shepard Co., 1971), pp. 160–72. See A28.

G43 'The Search for a Story to Tell' [14 Dec. 1952]
Highlights of Modern Literature: A Permanent Collection of Memorable Essays from the New York Times Book Review, ed. Francis Brown (New York: New American Library, 1954), pp. 30–32. See 'The Roving Eye' in A25.

G44 'English Fiction at Mid-Century' [21 Sept. 1953]
Arts at Mid-Century, ed. R. Richman (New York: Horizon Press, 1954), pp. 209–13. First printed in *New Republic* (C406).

G45 'A Day in the Dark' [Autumn 1955]
40 Best Stories from Mademoiselle 1935–1960, ed. Cyrilly Abels and Margarita G. Smith (New York: Harper's, 1960), pp. 192–200. *Botteghe Oscure Reader,* ed. George Garrett (Middletown, Conn.: Wesleyan University Press, 1974), 182–91. See A28.

G46 'The Claimant' [15 Nov. 1955]
The Third Ghost Book, ed. Cynthia Asquith (London: James Barrie, 1955), pp. 9–17. First printed in *Vogue* (C513).

G47 'Home for Christmas' [Dec. 1955]
Family Christmas Book, ed. Dorothy Wilson (New York: Prentice-Hall, Inc., 1957), pp. 2–3. First printed in *Mademoiselle* (C517).

G48 'Coming to London' [Mar. 1956]
Coming to London, ed. John Lehmann (London: Phoenix House, Ltd., 1957), pp. 74–81. First printed in *London Magazine* (C529).

G49   'Introduction'   [10 Sept. 1956]
[to *Stories by Katherine Mansfield* (B29)]
Discussions of the Short Story, ed. with an intro. by Hollis Spurgeon
Summers (New York: D. C. Heath & Co., 1963), pp. 89–93. See A25.

G50   'Rx for a Story Worth the Telling'   [31 Aug. 1958]
Opinions and Perspectives from the New York Times Book Review, ed.
with an intro. by Ernest Francis Brown (New York: Houghton Mifflin, 1964), pp. 230–34. First printed in *NYTBR* (C642).

G51   'The Teakettle'   [Jan. 1963]
*These Simple Things: Some Appreciations of the Small Joys in Daily
Life*, ed. by the editors of *House and Garden* (New York: Simon and
Schuster, 1965), pp. 11–18. First printed in *House and Garden* (C658).

| H | | BOOKS, DISSERTATIONS, THESES ABOUT (OR PARTIALLY ABOUT) ELIZABETH BOWEN |

H1   Adelman, Irving and Rita Dworkin, comp. *The Contemporary Novel: A Checklist of Critical Literature on the British and American Novel since 1945*. Metuchen, N. J.: The Scarecrow Press, Inc., 1972, pp. 60–64.

H2   Allen, Walter Ernest. *The English Novel*. New York: E. P. Dutton, 1954, pp. 100, 285, 413.

H3   Allen, Walter Ernest. *The Modern Novel in Britain and the United States*. New York: E. P. Dutton, 1964, pp. 188, 191–95, 262, 283. [Published in England as *Tradition and Dream: A Critical Survey of British and American Fiction from the 1920's to the Present Day*. London: Phoenix House, 1964.]

H4   Astaldi, Maria Luisa. 'Una Scrittrice: Elizabeth Bowen', *Nuove letture inglesi*. Florence: Sansoni, [1959], pp. 376–91.

H5   Atkins, John. 'Elizabeth Bowen: Connoisseur of the Individual', *Six Novelists Look at Society: An Inquiry into the Social Views of Elizabeth Bowen, L. P. Hartley, Rosamund Lehmann, Christopher Isherwood, Nancy Mitford, C. P. Snow*. London: John Calder, 1977, pp. 48–76.

H6   Austin, Allan E. *Elizabeth Bowen*. New York: Twayne Publishers, Inc., 1971.

H6.1   Baron, Wendy. *Miss Ethel Sands and Her Circle*. London: Peter Owen, 1977, pp. 225, 229–30, 264, 273–74.

H7   Bates, Herbert Ernest. *The Modern Short Story: A Critical Survey*. London: Thomas Nelson & Sons, 1941, *passim*.

H8   Beachcroft, T. O. *The English Short Story*. Rev. ed. London: Longmans, Green, & Co., 1967, II, 22–23.

H9   Beachcroft T. O. *The Modest Art: A Survey of the Short Story in English*. London: Oxford University Press, 1968, pp. 1, 88, 153, 177, 182–85, 190, 192, 221, 234.

H9.1   Berger, Josephine M. 'Elizabeth Bowen's Concept of the Short

Story: The Androgenous Mind in Literature'. Unpublished doctoral dissertation, St. John's University, 1977.

H10   Bergonzi, Bernard. *The Twentieth Century*, vol. 7 of *History of Literature in the English Language*. London: Barrie & Jenkins, 1970, pp. 254–58.

H11   Blodgett, Harriet Horowitz. 'Circles of Reality: A Reading of the Novels of Elizabeth Bowen'. Unpublished doctoral dissertation, University of California at Davis, 1968.

H12   Blodgett, Harriet Horowitz. *Patterns of Reality: Elizabeth Bowen's Novels*. The Hague: Mouton, 1975.

H13   Booth, Wayne C. *The Rhetoric of Fiction*. Chicago: University of Chicago Press, 1961, pp. 113, 172.

H14   Bowra, C. M. *Memories 1898–1939*. London: Weidenfeld and Nicolson, 1966, pp. 190–91.

H15   Brooke, Jocelyn. *Elizabeth Bowen*. London and New York: Longmans, Green, 1952. MS, E185.

H16   Brown, Spencer Curtis. 'Foreword', *Pictures and Conversations* by Elizabeth Bowen. New York: Alfred A. Knopf, 1975; London: Allen Lane, 1975, pp. vii–xlii.

H17   Burgess, Anthony. *The Novel Now: A Student's Guide to Contemporary Fiction*. London: Faber and Faber, 1967, pp. 119–21. [Published in the United States as *The Novel Now: A Guide to Contemporary Fiction* (New York: W. W. Norton & Company, 1967), pp. 119–21.]

H17.1 Byatt, A. S. 'Introduction', *The House of Paris*, by Elizabeth Bowen. Penguin Modern Classics. Harmondsworth: Penguin Books, 1976, pp. 7–16.

H17.2 Chessman, Harriet Scott. 'Talk and Silence in the Novels of Virginia Woolf, Elizabeth Bowen, and Ivy Compton-Burnett'. Unpublished doctoral dissertation, Yale University, 1979.

H18   Coles, Robert. 'Youth: Elizabeth Bowen's *The Death of the Heart*', *Irony in the Mind's Life: Essays on Novels by James Agee, Elizabeth Bowen, and George Eliot*. Charlottesville: University of Virginia Press, 1974, pp. 107–53.

H19 Collins, Arthur Simons. *English Literature of the Twentieth Century*. London: University Tutorial Press, 1951, pp. 257–61.

H20 Daiches, David. *The Present Age: After 1920*. London: The Cresset Press, 1958, pp. 115–16, 302–3, 305, 315.

H21 Davenport, Gary T. 'Four Irish Writers in Time of Civil War: Liam O'Flaherty, Frank O'Connor, Seán O'Faoláin, and Elizabeth Bowen'. Unpublished doctoral dissertation, University of South Carolina, 1972.

H22 Dostal, Sister Rose Margaret, O.S.U. 'Innocence and Knowledge in the Novels of Elizabeth Bowen'. Unpublished doctoral dissertation, University of Notre Dame, 1964.

H23 Foster, Jeannette H. *Sex Variant Women in Literature: A Historical and Quantitative Survey*. London: Frederick Muller, Ltd., 1958, pp. 279, 282–83, 287, 351, 363.

H24 Fraser, G. S. *The Modern Writer and His World*. London: Derek Verschoyle, 1953, pp. 121, 124, 126; New York: Frederick A. Praeger, 1965, pp. 149–51, 193, 394.

H25 Frierson, William C. *The English Novel in Transition: 1885–1940*. Norman: University of Oklahoma Press, 1942, pp. 283–89, 314–21.

H26 Gill, Richard. *Happy Rural Seat: The English Country House and the Literary Imagination*. New Haven and London: Yale University Press, 1972, pp. 178–93 *et passim*.

H27 Gindin, James. 'Ethical Structures in John Galsworthy, Elizabeth Bowen, and Iris Murdoch', *Forms of Modern British Fiction*. Ed. Alan Warren Friedman. Austin: University of Texas Press, 1975, pp. 15–41.

H28 Glendinning, Victoria. *Elizabeth Bowen: Portrait of a Writer*. London: Weidenfeld and Nicolson, 1977; New York: Alfred A. Knopf, 1978 [reprinted in paperback—New York: Avon Books, 1979].

H28.1 Glendinning, Victoria. 'Introduction', *Elizabeth Bowen's Irish Stories*. Dublin: Poolbeg Press, 1978, pp. 5–8.

H29 Hall, James W. *The Lunatic Giant in the Drawing Room*. Bloomington: Indiana University Press, 1968, pp. 17–55.

H30 Hanna, John Greist. 'Elizabeth Bowen and the Art of Fiction: A Study of Her Theory and Practice'. Unpublished doctoral dissertation, Boston University, 1961.

H31 Heath, William Webster. 'Elizabeth Bowen and the Tradition of the Novel'. Unpublished doctoral dissertation, University of Wisconsin, 1956.

H32 Heath, William Webster. *Elizabeth Bowen: An Introduction to Her Novels*. Madison: University of Wisconsin Press, 1961.

H33 Howard, Michael S. *Jonathan Cape, Publisher: Herbert Jonathan Cape, G. Wren Howard*. London: Jonathan Cape, Ltd., 1971, pp. 181–83.

H34 Karl, Frederick R. *A Reader's Guide to the Contemporary English Novel*. Rev. ed. New York: Farrar, Straus, and Giroux, 1972, pp. 107–30. [The first edition was entitled *The Contemporary English Novel* in the American issues (New York: Farrar, Straus, and Cudahy, 1962; New York: Noonday Press, 1962) and *A Reader's Guide to the Contemporary English Novel* in the English issue (London: Thames & Hudson, 1963).]

H35 Kendris, Thomas. 'The Novels of Elizabeth Bowen'. Unpublished doctoral dissertation, Columbia University, 1964.

H36 Kenney, Edwin J. *Elizabeth Bowen*. Irish Writers Series. Lewisburg, Pennsylvania: Bucknell University Press, 1974.

H37 Kiely, Benedict. *Modern Irish Fiction, A Critique*. Dublin: Golden Eagle Books, Ltd., 1950, pp. 152–58.

H38 Kirkpatrick, Larry. 'Elizabeth Bowen and Company: A Comparative Essay in Literary Judgment'. Unpublished doctoral dissertation, Duke University, 1965.

H38.1 Lawson, Judith Anne. 'Professionalized Susceptibilities: Imagination in the Early Novels of Elizabeth Bowen'. Unpublished doctoral dissertation, University of Iowa, 1979.

H39 Lehmann, John, ed. *The Craft of Letters in England*. London: The Cresset Press, 1956, pp. 46–51, 55–56, 62.

H40 Lehmann, John. *I Am My Brother*. London: Longmans, Green, 1960; New York: Reynal, 1960, pp. 148, 172, 188, 247.

H41 Lehmann, John. *In My Own Time: Memoirs of a Literary Life*. Boston & Toronto: Little, Brown & Co., 1969, *passim*.

H42 Lynskey, Winifred, ed. *Reading Modern Fiction*. New York: Charles Scribner's Sons, 1957, pp. 41–42.

H43 McCormick, John. *Catastrophe and Imagination*. London: Longmans, Green & Co., 1957, pp. 92, 93, 97, 159, 165, 177, 229, 292.

H44 McDowell, Alfred B. 'Identity and the Past: Major Themes in the Fiction of Elizabeth Bowen'. Unpublished doctoral dissertation, Bowling Green State University, Ohio, 1972.

H45 McGowan, Martha Jean. 'Lyric Design in the Novels of Elizabeth Bowen'. Unpublished doctoral dissertation, Boston University, 1971.

H46 Markovic, Vida E. 'Elizabet Bouin', *Engleski Roman XX Veka*. Belgrad: Nancna Rnjiga, 1965, pp. 2, 96–108, 243–45.

H47 Markovic, Vida E. 'Stella Rodney', *The Changing Face: Disintegration of Personality in the Twentieth-Century British Novel, 1900–1950*. Carbondale: Southern Illinois University Press, 1970; London and Amsterdam: Feffer and Simons, Inc., 1970, pp. 112–22.

H48 Miller, Donald William. 'Scene and Image in Three Novels by Elizabeth Bowen'. Unpublished doctoral dissertation, Columbia University, 1967.

H49 Miller, James E., Jr., ed. *Myth and Method: Modern Theories of Fiction*. Lincoln: University of Nebraska Press, 1960, pp. 33–50.

H49.1 Moon, Heath. 'Henry James and the English Cult of Nostalgia: The Past Recaptured in the Fiction and Autobiography of Elizabeth Bowen, Sir Osbert Sitwell, and L. P. Hartley'. Unpublished doctoral dissertation, University of California, Santa Barbara, 1979.

H50 Moser, Margarete. 'Elizabeth Bowen. Ihre Romane und Kurzgeschichten'. Unpublished doctoral dissertation, University of Vienna, 1955.

H51 Mullen, Thomas P. 'Progress Toward Disaster: A Study of the Novels of Elizabeth Bowen'. Unpublished bachelor's honors thesis, Amherst College, 1950.

H52 Nardella, Anna Gayle Ryan. 'Feminism, Art, and Aesthetics: A Study of Elizabeth Bowen'. Unpublished doctoral dissertation, SUNY—Stony Brook, 1975.

H53 Neuner, Hannelore. 'Studien zur Erzähltechnik der Romane Elizabeth Bowen'. Unpublished doctoral dissertation, University of Graz, Austria, 1953.

H54 Newby, P. H. *The Novel, 1945–1950*. London: Longmans, Green, 1951, pp. 19–20.

H55 Nicholson, Norman. *Man and Literature*. London: S.C.M. Press, 1943, pp. 160–61.

H56 Noble, Linda Rae Willis. 'A Critical Study of Elizabeth Bowen's Novels'. Unpublished doctoral dissertation, University of Oregon, 1975.

H57 O'Faoláin, Seán. *The Short Story*. New York: Devin-Adair, 1951, pp. 165–66, 202–4, 206–10, 229–31.

H58 O'Faoláin, Seán. *Short Stories: A Study in Pleasure*. Boston: Little, Brown, 1961, pp. 165–66, 341–45.

H59 O'Faoláin, Seán. *The Vanishing Hero: Studies in the Novelists of the Twenties*. London: Eyre and Spottiswoode, 1956, pp. 167–90; Boston: Little, Brown & Co., [1957], pp. 146–69 [reprinted in paperback as *The Vanishing Hero: Studies of the Hero in the Modern Novel*. New York: Grosset and Dunlap, 1958].

H60 Pendry, E. D. *The New Feminism of English Fiction: A Study in Contemporary Women Novelists*. Tokyo: Kenyusha Ltd., 1956, pp. 120–52.

H61 Perry, John O. 'Elizabeth Bowen' and 'The Cat Jumps', *Insight II: Analyses of British Literature*, ed. John V. Hagopian and Martin Dolch. Frankfurt: Hirschgraben, 1965, pp. 20–28.

H62 Prescott, Orville. *In My Opinion: An Inquiry into the Contemporary Novel*. New York and Indianapolis: Bobbs-Merrill, 1952, pp. 101–5.

H63 Rabinovitz, Rubin. *The Reaction Against Experiment in the English Novel, 1950–1960*. New York and London: Columbia University Press, 1967, pp. 39, 78.

H64 Reed, Henry. *The Novel Since 1939*. London: Longmans, Green & Co., 1946, pp. 20–21.

H65 Rempel, Mary-Lyle. 'The Theme of Isolation in the Novels of Elizabeth Bowen'. Unpublished master's thesis, Stanford University, 1963.

H66   Ritchie, Charles. *The Siren Years: Undiplomatic Diaries, 1937–1945.* London: Macmillan, 1975, pp. 115–79 *passim* [paperback edition entitled *The Siren Years: A Canadian Diplomat Abroad, 1937–1945.* Toronto: Macmillan of Canada, 1977].

H67   Roddy, Sonora Hudson. 'Point of View: The Snopes Trilogy. Development of Ambiguity in *The House in Paris*'. Unpublished master's thesis, University of Texas, Austin, 1971, pp. 28–43.

H68   Rowse, A. L. *The English Spirit: Essays in History and Literature.* New York and London: Macmillan & Co., 1946, pp. 256–59.

H69   Rule, Jane. 'Elizabeth Bowen', *Lesbian Images.* Garden City, N.Y.: Doubleday and Co., Inc., 1975, pp. 115–25.

H70   Rupp, Richard Henry. 'The Achievement of Elizabeth Bowen: A Study of Her Fiction and Criticism'. Unpublished doctoral dissertation, Indiana University, 1963.

H71   Sackville-West, Edward. 'Ladies whose bright pens. . .', *Inclinations.* London: Secker and Warburg, 1949; New York: Charles Scribner's Sons, 1949, pp. 78–103.

H72   Sarton, May. *I Knew a Phoenix.* New York: Rinehart, 1959, pp. 215–18.

H73   Sarton, May. 'Elizabeth Bowen', *A World of Light: Portraits and Celebrations.* New York: W. W. Norton & Company, Inc., 1976, pp. 191–213.

H74   Schaeffer, Alice Ann. 'A Study of Literary Method in the Novels of Elizabeth Bowen'. Unpublished master's thesis, Stanford University, 1963.

H75   Schirmer, Walter F. *Geschichte der englischen und amerikanischen Literatur: Von den Anfängen bis zur Gegenwart.* Tübingen: Max Niemeyer Verlag, 1967, pp. 281–82.

H76   Schneider, Dorothy Leona. 'The Novels of Elizabeth Bowen'. Unpublished master's thesis, Washington University, 1952.

H77   Scott-James, R. A. *Fifty Years of English Literature, 1900–1950.* London: Longmans, Green & Co., 1951, pp. 182–85.

H78   Soldani, Sister Louise N., S.S.A. 'To Live How One Can: A

Thematic Study of Elizabeth Bowen's Short Fiction'. Unpublished doctoral dissertation, University of Notre Dame, 1967.

H79   Spiel, Hilde. 'Der Blick nach Innen' [Towards the inner light], *Der Park und die Wildnis: Zur Situation der neueren englischen Literatur*. Munich: C. H. Beck'sche, 1953, pp. 100–104.

H80   Sprigge, Elizabeth. *The Life of Ivy Compton-Burnett*. New York: George Braziller, 1973, *passim*.

H81   Stanton, Robert J. *A Bibliography of Modern British Novelists*. Troy, New York: The Whitson Publishing Company, Inc., 1978, pp. 135–79.

H82   Stern, Joan Oberwager. 'A Study of Problems of Values and the Means by Which They Are Presented in the Novels of Elizabeth Bowen'. Unpublished doctoral dissertation, New York University, 1974.

H83   Stevenson, Lionel. *The History of the English Novel*. New York: Barnes and Noble, Inc., 1967, XI, 288–96.

H84   Strong, L. A. G. 'Elizabeth Bowen', *Living Writers: Being Critical Studies Broadcast in the B.B.C. Third Programme,* ed. Gilbert Phelps. London: Sylvan Press, [1947], pp. 58–69. [Revised and reprinted in *Personal Remarks*. London: P. Nevill, 1953; New York: Liveright Publishing Corp., 1953, pp. 140–45.]

H85   Temple, Ruth Z. and Martin Tucker. *A Library of Literary Criticism: Modern British Literature*. New York: Frederick Ungar Publishing Co., [1966], I, 108–16.

H86   Tindall, William Y. *Forces in Modern British Literature: 1885–1946*. New York: Alfred A. Knopf, 1947, pp. 207–9.

H87   Vinson, James, ed. *Contemporary Novelists*. New York: St. Martin's Press, 1972, pp. 132–36.

H88   Wall, Stephen. 'Aspects of the Novel 1930–1960', *The Twentieth Century: The Sphere History of Literature in the English Language,* ed. Bernard Bergonzi. London: The Cresset Press, 1970, VII, 254–58.

H89   Walsh, William. *The Use of Imagination: Educational Thought and the Literary Mind*. London: Chatto and Windus, 1959, pp. 148–63.

H90   Wild, Rebecca Smith. 'Studies in the Shorter Fiction of Elizabeth Bowen and Eudora Welty'. Unpublished doctoral dissertation, University of Michigan, 1965.

H91   Zeraffa, Michel. *Personne et Personnage*. Paris: Éditions Klincksieck, 1969, pp. 341–42, 359–61.

I   PERIODICAL ARTICLES ABOUT
(OR PARTIALLY ABOUT)
ELIZABETH BOWEN

I1   Adams, J. Donald. 'Speaking of Books', *NYTBR* (2 Dec., 9 Dec. 1956) : 2, 2.

I2   Unsigned, 'The Climate of Treason', *TLS* 2457 (5 Mar. 1949):152.

I3   Antonini, Giacomo. 'I poemi in prosa de Elizabeth Bowen', *La Fiera Letteraria* 10 #14 (3 Apr. 1955):1–2.

I4   Atkins, John. 'Dreams of Nowhere', *Books and Bookmen* 14 #8 (May 1969):8–10.

I5   Beck, Martha A. 'Vassar Student Talks about Elizabeth Bowen', *Mademoiselle* 51 (July 1960):6, 88.

I6   The Bellman (pseud.). 'Meet Elizabeth Bowen', *The Bell*, ed. Seán O'Faoláin 4 (Sept. 1942):420–26.

I7   Bentley, Phyllis. 'Is the British Novel Dead?' *SatRev* 19 (28 Jan. 1939):3–4.

I7.1   Bertolotti, Sonia. 'Studi su Elizabeth Bowen', *Cultura* 15 (1977): 120–31.

I8   Brandes, Lawrence. 'Aspects of E. M. Forster', *Literary Half-Yearly* (Dept. of Post-Graduate Studies in English, University of Mysore, India) 10 (July 1969):95–104.

I9   Breit, Harvey. 'Talk with Miss Bowen', *NYTBR* 55 (26 Mar. 1950):27 [reprinted in *The Writer Observed*. Cleveland: World Publishing Co., 1956; London: Alvin Redman, Ltd., 1956, pp. 107–10].

I10   Brierre, Anne. 'Littérature anglo-irlandaise', *La Revue des Deux Mondes* 140 (1 Jan. 1968):84–91.

I11   Brooke-Rose, Christine. 'Lady Precious Stream', *London Magazine* 4 (May 1964):83–86.

I11.1   Brothers, Barbara. "Pattern and Void: Bowen's Irish Landscapes and *The Heat of the Day*", *Mosaic* 12 #3 (Spring 1979):129–138.

I12 Cecil, David. 'Chronicler of the Heart: The British Writer, Elizabeth Bowen', *Vogue* (American edition) 122 (1 Nov. 1953):118–19.

I13 Coles, William. 'The Pattern of Responsibility in the Novels of Elizabeth Bowen', *Harvard Advocate*, 137 (Dec. 1952):20–22, 37–40.

I14 Colum, Mary M. 'Do We Learn from History?' *SatRev* 25 (5 Sept. 1942):3–4.

I14.1 Corn, Alfred. 'An Anglo-Irish Novelist', *YR* 67 (1977–78): 615–22.

I15 Crichton-Gordon, Mollie. 'Elizabeth Bowen, A Great Woman Novelist', *World Review* (Sept. 1946):44–45.

I16 Daiches, David. 'The Novels of Elizabeth Bowen', *EJ* 38 (June 1949):305–13.

I17 Davenport, Gary T. 'Elizabeth Bowen and the Big House', *Southern Humanities Review* 8 (Winter 1974):27–34.

I18 Davis, Robert M. 'Contributions to *Night and Day* by Elizabeth Bowen, Graham Greene, and Anthony Powell', *Studies in the Novel* 3 (1971):401–4.

I19 Deitch, J. 'Miss Bowen Scans a Turbulent Scene', *ChScMM* (6 Jan. 1951):13.

I20 Dorenkamp, Angela G. ' "Fall or Leap": Bowen's *The Heat of the Day*', *Critique: Studies in Modern Fiction* 10 #3 (1968):13–21.

I21 Fadiman, Clifton. 'The Decline of Attention', *SatRev* 32 (6 Aug. 1949):20–24.

I22 Fremantle, Anne. 'Thirty Years A-Growing', *Commonweal* 53 (23 Mar. 1951):593–94.

I23 Gordan, John D. 'New in the Berg Collection: 1959–1961', *Bulletin of the New York Public Library* 68 (Feb. 1964):81–82.

I24 Greene, George. 'Elizabeth Bowen: Imagination as Therapy', *Perspective* 14 (Spring 1965):42–52.

I25 Greene, Graham. 'The Dark Backward: A Footnote', *London Mercury* 32 (1935):562–65 [reprinted in *Collected Essays*. London: The Bodley Head, 1969, pp. 69–74].

I26 Hardwick, Elizabeth. 'Elizabeth Bowen's Fiction', *Partisan Review* 16 (Nov. 1949):1114–21.

I27 Harkness, Bruce. 'The Fiction of Elizabeth Bowen', *EJ* 44 (Dec. 1955):499–506.

I28 Hawkins, Desmond. 'Fiction Chronicle', *Criterion* 18 (1938):82–92.

I29 Heinemann, Alison. 'The Indoor Landscape in Bowen's *The Death of the Heart*', *Critique: Studies in Modern Fiction* 10 #3 (1968): 5–12.

I30 Hopkins, Gerard. 'Elizabeth Bowen', *Landmark* 16 (August 1934): 409–12.

I31 Hughes, Douglas A. 'Cracks in the Psyche: Elizabeth Bowen's "The Demon Lover" ', *Studies in Short Fiction* 10 (1973):411–13.

I32 Hutchens, John K. 'Elizabeth Bowen', *NYHTB* 26 (26 Mar. 1950):3.

I33 Kiely, Benedict. 'Elizabeth Bowen', *Irish Monthly* 78 (1950): 175–81.

I34 Langley, Lois. 'Bowen in the Looking-Glass', *Guardian* (24 June 1970):8.

I34.1 Lee, Hermione. 'The Placing of Loss: Elizabeth Bowen's *To the North*', *Essays in Criticism* 28 (1978):129–42.

I34.2 McDowell, Alfred. '*The Death of the Heart* and the Human Dilemma', *Modern Language Studies* 8 #2 (1978):5–16.

I35 MacLaren-Ross, J. 'A World of Women', *Punch* 228 (23 Mar. 1955):366–67.

I36 Marković, Vida E. 'Elizabet Bouin', *Savremenick* (Belgrade) 9 (1956):244–60.

I37   Melchiori, Georgio. 'Elizabeth Bowen', *Le spettatore italiano* 8 (May 1955):186–92.

I38   Mitchell, Edward. 'Themes in Elizabeth Bowen's Short Stories', *Critique: Studies in Modern Fiction* 8 #3 (Spring-Summer 1966):41–54.

I39   Monaghan, Charles. 'Elizabeth Bowen on What She Reads', *Book World* 2 (10 Nov. 1968):6.

I39.1   Moss, Howard. 'Interior Children', *NY* (5 Feb. 1979):121–22, 125–28.

I40   O'Faoláin, Seán. 'Elizabeth Bowen', *Britain Today* 3 (Mar. 1948): 16–19.

I41   Parrish, Paul A. 'The Loss of Eden: Four Novels of Elizabeth Bowen', *Critique: Studies in Modern Fiction* 15 #1 (1973):86–100.

I42   Pritchett, V. S. 'The Future of English Fiction', *Partisan Review* 15 (1948):1063–70.

I43   Pritchett, V. S. 'Prospects for the English Novel', *NYTBR* 54 (17 Apr. 1949):1, 21–22.

I44   Rubens, Robert. 'Elizabeth Bowen', *P.E.N. Broadsheet* 2 (Summer 1976):7–8.

I45   Rupp, Richard H. 'The Post-War Fiction of Elizabeth Bowen', *Xavier University Studies* 4 (1965):55–67.

I46   Sackville-West, Edward. 'An Appraisal: Ivy Compton-Burnett and Elizabeth Bowen', *Horizon* 13 (June 1946):367–85.

I47   Saul, George Brandon. 'The Short Stories of Elizabeth Bowen', *ArQ* 21 (Spring 1965):53–59.

I48   Sellery, J'nan. 'Elizabeth Bowen: A Check List', *Bulletin of the New York Public Library* 74 (Apr. 1970):219–74.

I49   Seward, Barbara. 'Elizabeth Bowen's World of Impoverished Love', *College English* 18 (Oct. 1956):30–37.

I50   Sharp, Sister M. Corona. 'The House as Setting and Symbol in

Three Novels by Elizabeth Bowen', *Xavier University Studies* 2 (1963): 93–103.

I51 Snow, Lotus. 'The Uncertain "I": A Study of Elizabeth Bowen's Fiction', *Western Humanities Review* 4 (Autumn 1950):299–310.

I52 Spender, Stephen. 'Books and the War—IV: The Short Story To-Day', *Penguin New Writing* 5 (Apr. 1941):140–42.

I53 Stokes, Edward. 'Elizabeth Bowen—Pre-Assumption or Moral Angle?' *Journal of the Australasian University Language and Literature Association* 11 (Sept. 1959):35–47.

I54 Strachey, John. 'The Golden Age of English Detection', *SatRev* 19 (7 Jan. 1939):12.

I55 Strickhausen, H. 'Elizabeth Bowen and Reality', *SR* 73 (Winter 1965):158–65.

I56 Sullivan, Walter. 'A Sense of Place: Elizabeth Bowen and the Landscape of the Heart', *SR* 84 (1976):142–149.

I57 Toki, Tomoko. 'Elizabeth Bowen no Shosetsu: Sono Kaigeteki Shuho ni tsuite' [A novel by Elizabeth Bowen: that method regarding pictorial description] *Oberon* 16 #1 (1975):111–32.

I58 Vallette, J. 'Elizabeth Bowen', *Mercure de France,* 307 (Sept. 1949):166–69.

I59 Van Duyn, Mona. 'Pattern and Pilgrimage: A Reading of *The Death of the Heart',* *Critique: Studies in Modern Fiction* 4 #2 (Spring-Summer 1961):52–66.

I60 Wagner, Geoffrey. 'Elizabeth Bowen and the Artificial Novel', *Essays in Criticism* 13 (Apr. 1963):155–63.

I61 Williams, Raymond. 'Realism and the Contemporary Novel', *Partisan Review* 26 (Spring 1959):200–13.

I62 Yoneda, Kazuhiko. 'Elizabeth Bowen's *Eva Trout*', *Eigo Seinen* [The Rising Generation] 119 (1973):202–3.

From among many other, more perfunctory obituaries, the following
have been selected and arranged in chronological order.

J1   Holloway, David. 'Elizabeth Bowen', *Daily Telegraph*, 23 Feb. and
24 Feb. 1973.

J2   Unsigned. 'Elizabeth Bowen, Novelist, Dead', *NYTimes*, 23 Feb.
1973, p. 39.

J3   Unsigned. 'Elizabeth Bowen: Writer of Subtlety and Distinction',
Times (London), 23 Feb. 1973, p. 19. Dame Veronica Wedgwood wrote
a supplementary letter, published in the *Times*, 27 Feb. 1973, p. 16.

J4   Weil, Martin. 'Elizabeth Bowen, 73; Wrote on British Middle Class',
Washington Post 24 Feb. 1973, p. B6.

J5   Connolly, Cyril. 'Elizabeth Bowen: A Poet Working in Prose', *Sunday Times* (London), 25 Feb. 1973, p. 12.

J6   King, Francis. 'Novelist Without Pretence', *Sunday Telegraph*, 25
Feb. 1973.

J7   Toynbee, Philip. 'Elizabeth Bowen', *Observer*, 25 Feb. 1973, p. 23.

J8   Pritchett, V. S. 'Elizabeth Bowen', *New Statesman*, 9 Mar. 1973,
p. 350.

J9   Moss, Howard. 'Elizabeth Bowen, 1899–1973', *NYTBR*, 8 Apr.
1973, pp. 2–3.

APPENDIX: CONTRACTS

With minor exceptions, the following list describes the contracts which are to be found among Elizabeth Bowen's papers at the Humanities Research Center at The University of Texas at Austin. (An asterisk indicates a contract which appears on a list of contracts in Bowen's hand; this list is at Texas, while the contracts themselves do not reside there.) In some cases, there are contracts with publishers for which a book, to date, has not be located. In most cases of contracts without books, it has been discovered that the contract was cancelled. Where an existing contract elucidates an unusual publishing history of a book, a note has been made under the entry for that book in Section A. The dates are those noted on the signed contract. Anthology or broadcast contracts are not listed.

A1	ENCOUNTERS	
	*Sidgwick and Jackson	July 1924
A3	THE HOTEL	
	Constable and Co., Ltd.	1 Apr. 1927
	Dial Press	1927
	Luis de Caralt, Barcelona	9 June 1944
	(in Spanish)	
A4	THE LAST SEPTEMBER	
	Dial Press	16 Oct. 1928
	Fontaine, Paris	28 May 1945
	(in French)	
	Arnoldo Mondadori, Milan	16 Oct. 1945
	(in Italian)	
A5	JOINING CHARLES AND OTHER STORIES	
	*Constable and Co., Ltd.	31 Jan. 1929
	*Simon and Schuster	14 Apr. 1947
A6	FRIENDS AND RELATIONS	
	Dial Press	21 Mar. 1931
	Victor Gollancz	24 Apr. 1931
A7	TO THE NORTH	
	Alfred A. Knopf	8 Nov. 1932
	Albert Bonnier, Stockholm	19 Apr. 1945

(English Continental Series)
Penguin Books, Ltd.   1 May 1945
Fontaine, Paris   28 May 1945
(in French)
Secy. of State for Foreign Affairs in England   22 May 1947
(in German)

A8   THE CAT JUMPS

Victor Gollancz   15 June 1934

A9   THE HOUSE IN PARIS

Victor Gollancz   25 July 1935
Albatross Verlag, Paris   5 Oct. 1935
(in English)
Librairie Gallimard, Paris   21 July 1939
(in French)
Penguin Books, Ltd.   1 May 1945
Luis de Caralt, Barcelona   7 Jan. 1946
(in Spanish)
Det Schønbergske Förlag, Copenhagen   15 Jan. 1946
(in Danish)
Arnoldo Mondadori, Milan   16 Oct. 1945
(in Italian)
Control Office for Germany and Austria   n.d.
(in German)

A10   THE DEATH OF THE HEART

Victor Gollancz   4 Oct. 1938
Albatross Verlag on behalf of Bernard Tauchnitz 20 Oct. 1938
(in English)
Librairie Plon, Paris   22 Nov. 1938
(in French)
Luis de Caralt, Barcelona   27 Apr. 1944
(in Spanish)
Det Schønbergske Förlag, Copenhagen   22 Feb. 1946
(in Danish)
Arnoldo Mondadori, Milan   25 Mar. 1946
(in Italian)
Sfinx Premystova, Prague   10 July 1946
(in Czech)

A11   LOOK AT ALL THOSE ROSES

| Victor Gollancz | 30 Dec. 1938 |
| Alfred A. Knopf | 11 Feb. 1941 |

A13 BOWEN'S COURT
    Alfred A. Knopf   12 Oct. 1937
    Longmans, Green & Co.   17 May 1939

A14 SEVEN WINTERS
    Longmans, Green & Co.   1943

A15 THE DEMON LOVER AND OTHER SHORT STORIES
    Jonathan Cape   6 Oct. 1944
    *Fontaine, Paris   28 May 1945
    (in French) Volume of short stories
    including more than English edition.
    Éditions de Jeune Parque, Paris   31 Jan. 1946
    (in French)
    Ernest G. Mortensens Forlag, Oslo   24 May 1946
    (in Norwegian)
    Albert Bonnier, Ltd., Stockholm
    (in Swedish)
    Secy. of State for Foreign Affairs in England   n.d.
    (in German)

A16 ANTHONY TROLLOPE
    Humphrey Milford, Publisher to the University   18 July 1945
      of Oxford
    Oxford University Press, New York   30 Apr. 1946

A17 SELECTED STORIES
    Maurice Fridberg, Hour-Glass Library   13 Mar. 1946

A18 THE HEAT OF THE DAY
    Jonathan Cape, Ltd.   26 Mar. 1940

A? VOLUME OF SHORT STORIES AT PRESENT UNTITLED
    Jonathan Cape, Ltd.   5 Feb. 1947

SELECTIVE INDEX

References are to item numbers in the bibliography. The first listing of a work as it appears in the bibliography becomes the main entry for that work, with subsequent entries cross-referenced to the main entry. Throughout the Index, titles of works by Bowen appear in capital letters. Entries for prefaces and introductions written by Bowen appear in capital letters under the titles of the works for which they were written. The titles of books reviewed by Bowen, of critical studies concerning Bowen, and of periodicals carrying reviews of Bowen's work are not indexed. Sections B and F are indexed selectively. The abbreviation "app." directs readers to entries in the Appendix.

E115, E122, E356, E556, E665, F21.
See also 'JANE AUSTEN', 'NEW
JUDGEMENT: ELIZABETH
BOWEN ON JANE AUSTEN',
'PERSUASION', 'SANDITON',
'WHAT JANE AUSTEN MEANS
TO ME'.
Austin, Allan E., H6
Authors' League of America, E274
'AUTOBIOGRAPHICAL NOTE',
E108
'AUTOBIOGRAPHICAL NOTE FOR
EVERYWOMAN', E109
'AUTOBIOGRAPHY', A25, A26,
C387
'AUTOBIOGRAPHY AS AN ART',
C387. *See also* 'AUTOBIO-
GRAPHY'.
Avaery, Ira, C537
Avon Books, A3b, A6b, A7b, A9b,
A10b, A18a, A22a, A27a, A30a
Ayrton, Michael, C272

B.B.C. *See* British Broadcasting
Corporation.
B. T. Batsford Ltd. (publisher), B27
'BACK DRAWING-ROOM, THE',
A2, A20, E2
'BADGE OF COURAGE, THE', C414
Bagg, D. B., A24a
Bain, A. W. & Co. *See* A. W. Bain &
Co. (publisher).
Baines, Frank, C638
Baker, Carlos, A22a
Baker, Denys Val, G33
Baker, Roger, A30b
Balchin, Nigel, C152, C248, C300,
C352, C463, C504, F81
Balcon, Jill. *See* Lewis, Jill Balcon
[Mrs. Cecil] Day.
Baldridge, Letitia, C624
Baldwin, James, C425
Baldwin, Monica, C605
Balzac, Honoré de, C177
Bamford, Francis, C191
Bancroft, T. O., C289
Bard, Mary, C362
Bardin, J. F., C276, C320
Baring, Maurice, E61

Barnard College, E132
Barnes, Edith, E497
Barnhof, Karl, C639
Baro, Gene, A24a, A25, A27a
'BARON THE UNFORGETTABLE',
C588
Baron, Wendy, H6.1
'BARRIE', A19, C109
Barrie and Rockliff (publishers),
B12a
Barrie, James, E498
Barry, Iris, A6b, A18a
Barry, Sarah, E52
Barsley, Michael, C178
Barton, Betsey, C342
Barton, Derek, C468, C580
Batchelor, Denzil, C303
Bates, H. E., C99, C186, C328, C453,
C540, C592, C620, H7
Batey, Charles, B30
Batty, Archibald, E194, E499
Bawden, Nina, C497, C502, C549,
C625
Bax, Clifford, C168, C196, C370
Bayer-Protich, Lubitsa, D16
Bayley, John, A18b, E500
Bayley, Viola, C480
Baylis, Ebenezer and Son, Ltd. *See*
Ebenezer Baylis and Son, Ltd.
'BAZAAR, THE', E147
Beachcroft, T. O., C198, C304,
H8, H9
Beales, H. L., F60, F62
Beardsley, Aubrey, C315
Beaton, Cecil, C172, C188
Beaty, David, C544
'BEAU IDEAL OF ESSAYISTS,
THE', C440
Beauclerk, Helen, C18
'BEAUTY OF BEING YOUR AGE,
THE', C655, E101
Beauvoir, Simone de, C304
Beck, Martha A., I5
Beck, Warren, C148
Becker, Marianne, C476
Bedoyere, Michael de la, C630
Beerbohm, Max, C200, C627
'Before Publication—Introduced by
Elizabeth Bowen', F94

317

'BLINDFOLD KING, THE', C471
Bliss, Trudy, C258
Bloch, Bertram, C555
Blodgett, Harriet Horowitz, H11, H12
Blond, Anthony. *See* Anthony Blond (publisher).
Bloom, Ursula, C616
Bloomfield, Anthony, C483
Bloomfield, Paul, A18b
Blunden, Edmund, C175
Blunt, Wilfrid, C614
Bogan, Louise, A10b, A11b, A13b
Boisier, Cecilia, D17
Bolton, Guy, C434
Bone, Stephen, C199
Boni and Liveright (publisher), A1b, A2b
Bonnier, Albert. *See* Albert Bonnier (publisher).
Bonsey, Lionel, C182
Boochever, Florence, A19b
'Book at Bedtime, A: "THE CAT JUMPS" ', E29. *See also* 'CAT JUMPS, THE'.
'Book in the Shade: *A WORLD OF LOVE*', F31. *See also* WORLD OF LOVE, A.
Book of Modern Ghosts, A, B28b. *See also, Second Ghost Book, The.*
Book-of-the-Month Club, A3b, A9b
'Book Review—Signposts in English Literature, No. 14 on Elizabeth Bowen', F14. *See also* 'Signposts in English Literature'.
Book Society, The, A10a, A18b, A22b
'BOOK TALK', E387, E388, E571, F3, F4, F5
'BOOK TALK—NEW AND RECENT FICTION', E118, E119, E386, E387, E388, F63, F64
Booker Award, A30b
Bookman, C365
'Books and Authors: "THE NEXT BOOK" ', E65, F72. *See also* 'NEXT BOOK, THE'.
Books for Libraries, Inc. (publisher), A2b, B34b
'BOOKS IN GENERAL', C392

Books of Today, C380
'BOOKS THAT GROW UP WITH ONE, THE', C377, E72
Bookseller, The, A3a, A7a, A21b
'Bookstand', F92
Booth, Wayne C., H13
Boothby, Robert, C269
Borden, Mary, C560
Boros, Eva C542, C569.1
Bosco, Henri, C226
Boston, Lucy M., C451
Boswell, Ronald, E196, E197, E198, E507
Botkin, B. A. C192
Botteghe Oscure, C506
Botteghe Oscure Reader, G45
Bottome, Phyllis, C184, C563
Boucher, Anthony, G28
Boulle, Pierre, C559
'BOUQUET', C76. *See also* 'DUBLIN III'.
Bowen, Henry Charles Cole, A13a
Bowen, John, C551, C634, E128, F91
'BOWEN ON GORKI', G20. *See also* 'GORKI STORIES'.
BOWEN'S COURT, A13, E13, E15, E255, E606
'BOWEN'S COURT', C644
Bowes-Lyon, Lilian, E508
Bowra, C. M., C314, H14
Bowra, Maurice, E509
'BOY WHO STOPPED BUMP IN NIGHT', C422
Boyd, Donald, C167
Boyd, Martin, C485
Boyle, Kay, A13b
Boynton, H. W., A2b
Bradbury, Malcolm, B37
Bradbury, Ray, C552
Bradenham, Hugh, A15a
Bradley, Heather, E510
Brady, Charles A., A22a
Braine, John, C588
Brand, Christianna, C273, C338, C502
Brande, Dorothea, A6b, A7b
Brandel, Marc, C297
Brandes, Lawrence, I8

Coles, William, I13
Colette, C629
Collected Essays, I21
COLLECTED IMPRESSIONS,
A19, E76, E218
Collier, Patience, F27, F45
Collier Publishing Company, A29a
Collier, Richard, C239, C292, C635
Collingwood, R. G., B5b
Collins, Sons and Co., Ltd., William.
See William Collins, Sons and Co.,
Ltd. (publisher).
Collins, Alan, E271–74, E526
Collins, Arthur Simons, H19
Collins, Catherine Pomeroy, A22
Collins, Norman, B20, C161, C317,
E527
Collins, P. A. W., E275, E276, D528
Collins, Wilkie, C266
Collis, John Stuart, C477
Collis, Maurice, C466
Colonial Press, Inc., The (printer),
A23
Colquhoun, Ithell, C499
Colum, Mary M., A10b, A13b,
I14
Columbia Broadcasting System, F13
'COME TO IRELAND', E87
'COMEBACK OF GOLDILOCKS
ET AL', C656
'COMFORT AND JOY', C145, E374
'COMING HOME', A1, A20, A23,
G1.1
Coming to London, G48
'COMING TO LONDON . . . VI',
C529, G48
'COMMONSENSE ON BURNS', C467
Compton, Fay, F1
Compton-Burnett, Ivy, C112, C138,
C226, C329, C350, C472, C608,
E98b, E529. *See also* 'IVY
COMPTON BURNETT I' and 'IVY
COMPTON-BURNETT II'.
'CONFESSIONS', C366
'CONFIDANTE, THE' (play), E117
'CONFIDANTE, THE' (short story),
A1, A20
Congdon, Don, G26

Connell, B., E530
Conner, Reardon, C51
Connolly, Cyril, A3a, C165, C236,
C402, E61, E531, F101, F104,
F105, G25, G35, J5
Connolly, Francis, G9
'CONQUEROR OF THE INFIDELS',
C498
'CONQUERORS IN THE HARDEST
BATTLE', C571
'CONRAD', A19, C26
Constantine of Bavaria, Prince, C462
Conroy, Jack, A15b, A18a
Consequences, B6, E33, E277, E278,
E279, E280
Constable & Co., Ltd. (publisher),
A3a, A4a, A5a, A6a, app.
Constable, Ltd., T. and A. (printer),
A2
Constant, Benjamin, C330
Contact, C160, C213, C268, C316,
E351
'CONTEMPORARY', C126
'CONTEMPORARY BRITISH
NOVELISTS', E126
'Contemporary British Novelists—
We Write Novels', F84. *See also*
'CONTEMPORARY BRITISH
NOVELISTS'.
'Contemporary English Novel, The,
No. 3—Elizabeth Bowen', F11
'Contemporary English Novel, The:
The Work of Elizabeth Bowen', E183
'Contemporary English Writers—
Elizabeth Bowen', F11
'Contemporary Thinkers', F69
'CONTESSINA, THE', A2, A20, C5
Continental Book Company
(publisher), A7a
'Conversation between Elizabeth
Bowen and Jocelyn Brooke, A',
F79. *See also* E123.
'Conversation on Traitors', E124, E192,
E193, E495, F81
'CONVERSATION PICTURE, A',
A8, C13, E31. *See also* 'HER
TABLE SPREAD'.
'CONVERSATION PIECE, A', C13.

Gamlin, Lionel, C212
Gardiner, H. C., A27a
Gardner, Arthur, C255
Gardner, Erle Stanley, C152
Garnett, David, B37, C519
Garrett, George, G45
Garve, Andrew, C444, C536
Gascoyne, David, E61
Gaskell, Elizabeth Cleghorn, B26, E81, E122
Gaskell, Jane, C609
Gauner, E. G., E350–52, E553
Gaury, Gerald de, C498
Gehman, Richard, C516
'GENIUS OF THE DEEP SOUTH', C452
Gentlemen's Quarterly, C646.1
Geoffrey Bles Ltd. (publisher), B35
Geoffrey Cumberlege (publisher), A16a
George C. Harrap & Co. (publisher), A21b
George, Daniel, C260, C338, C443, F66
Georges-Michel, Michel, C585
Gernsheim, Helmut, C245
Gersov, Anja Samooja, D49
'GHOST STORY?', E152
Gibbings, Robert, E554
Gibbon, Lewis Grassic, F52
Gibbon, Monk, C294
Gibbons, Stella, C215, C561
Gibson, Tony, C573
Gibson, Wilfrid, A10a
Gibson, William, C450
'GIFT FOR THE GAFFE', C666
'GIFT THAT SPEAKS, THE', C518
Gilbert, Anthony, C325
Gilbert, Edwin, C341
Gilbert, Michael, C603
Gilbert, Stuart, C176, C187
Giles, G. C. T., C176
Gilkes, A. N., C604
Gill, Brendan, A18a, C590
Gill, Maire, A14a
Gill, Richard, H26
Gillespie, Jane, C426
Gillespie, Susan, C222
Gillett, Eric, C207, F24, F77

Gilliam, Laurence, E353–55, E555
Gillon, Diana, C477
Gillon, Meir, C477
Gilomen, Walter, G19
Gindin, James, H27
'GIRL WITH THE STOOP, THE', A11, C82
'GIRLHOOD', E131
'GIRLS, THE', A19, C93
Glamour Magazine, C650
Glanville, Brian, F50
Glasgow, R. C. Robertson, C298
Glemser, Bernard, C232
Glendinning, Victoria, A33, H28, H28.1
'GLIMPSE OF THE PIT, A', C373
Globa, George, D6, D37
'GLORIOUS UNREGIMENTED WOMEN, THE', C456
G. P. Putnam's Sons (publisher), B5.1
Gyldendal Norsk (publisher), D46
Glyn, Anthony, C584
Godden, Jon, C258
Godden, Rumer, C197, C302, C588, E118
'GODDESS OF SUMMER, A', C478
Gogol, Nikolai, C277, C348
Gold, Herbert, A22a
'GOLDEN APPLES, THE', A25, A26, C380
Golden Cockerel Press, The, B6a
Golding, Louis, B20
Goldring, Douglas, C282
Goldsmith, Anthony, C116
Goldstone, Herbert, G19
Gollancz, Victor. *See* Victor Gollancz (publisher).
'GONE AWAY', A28, C162
Gooch, C. P., C480, C561
'GOOD EARL, THE', B16, E62
'GOOD GIRL, THE', A8, C14, D59
Good Housekeeping, E314
Good Living, C316
GOOD TIGER, THE, A29, E25, E145c, F58
Goolden, Barbara, C20, C430
Gordan, John D., I23
Gordimer, Nadine, C546
Gordon, Alexie, C258
Gordon, Caroline, G26

Gordon, Sidney, E356, E556
Gorell, Ronald, G. B., C324
Gorer, Geoffrey, C496
Gorham, Maurice, C370
Gorki, Maxim, C91, C309
'GORKI STORIES', A19, C91, G20
Gorman, Herbert, A13b, C106
Gould, Gerald, A2a, A3a, A5a, B5b
'GRACE', A19, C79
'GRAF SPEE'S JACKAL, THE', C502
Graham, Gladys, A2b, A5b
Graham, Winston, C549
Grainham, Sarah, C547
Grant, Ambrose, C219
Grant, Douglas, A22a
Grant, Duncan, F103
Grau, Shirley Ann, A27a
Greacen, Robert, G21
Greame, Paulette Lloyd, C630
Greave, Peter, C491
'GREAT KHAN, THE', C451
Green, F. L., C196
Green, G. F., C273
Green, Henry, C208, C318, F52
'GREEN HOLLY', A15a, C141
Greene, David H., G6
Greene, George, I24
Greene, Graham, A10a, B7, B21, C97,
    C245, C268, C288, C312, C473,
    C521, C626, E61, E69, E98a, E317,
    E396, E557, F52, F74, G37, I25
Greene, Hugh, C626
Greenslet, Ferris, C254
Greenwood Press, Inc., A3b
Gregg, Olive, E29, F6
Grevtorex, Clifford, C289
Grey, Jean, C534
Grierson, Edward, C541, C481
Griggs, G. P., C159
Grimault, Berthe, C589
Grimm, Jacob and Wilhelm,
    C659, E145b
Groves, John Stuart, E357
Grubb, Davis, C431
Guerin, Wilfred L., G26
Guest, John, C349
'GUIDE TO THE FUTURE, FOR
    THOSE SETTING OUT', C573
Gulbranssen, Trygve, C22

Gunston, David, E558
Gunther, John, C355
'GUSTO', C85
Guzzardi, Walter, A30a
Gwynn, Stephen, C76
Gwynne-Jones, Alan, C244

H. Wolff (printer), A9b, A10b,
    A11b, A15b
Haddon Craftsmen, Inc. (printer),
    A4c, A13c, A27a
Hadfield, Charles, C169
Hagan, William, A24a
Haggard, Edith (Mrs. Sewell), E101,
    E104, E358, E359, E559
Hale, Lionel, E360–62, E560
Hale, Nancy, A27a
Halio, Jay L., A27a, A30a
Hall, Cyril, C247
Hall, F. G., C360
Hall, J. C., C514
Hall, James B., G11
Hall, James W., H29
Hall, William Glenvil, C350
Hamilton, Alex, A28
Hamilton, Bruce, C188
Hamilton, Elizabeth, C443
Hamilton, Mrs. Robert, A5a
'HAMILTON ROWAN', A19, C132
Hamish Hamilton (publisher), B35.1
Hammersley, Violet, C525
Hammond, Lawrence, E561
Hampshire, Stuart, E562
'HAND IN GLOVE', A28, A33, B28,
    D72, E88, G42
Handl, Irene, F106
Hanley, Gerald, C591
Hanley, James, C84, C97
Hanna, John Greist, H30
Hansen, Aase, D41, D46
'HAPPINESS', C647
'HAPPY AUTUMN FIELDS, THE',
    A15a, A23, A28, A33, C139,
    D72, G31
'HAPPY FOUR LOST LADIES,
    THE', C449
Harben, Philip, C167, C223
Harcourt, Brace and Co., B9b, B37b

337

Lytton, Earl of, C305
Mabbott, John, F59, F61
Macallister, Hamilton, C595
Macaulay, Rose, C74, C203, C344,
C411, C555, E599
McBean, Angus, A4c, A18a, A22a,
A24b, A26, A27a, A30
McBrien, W. A., A27
MacCarthy, Desmond, C104, E600
McCarthy, Mary, C323, C335, F46
McClelland & Stewart Ltd., A4c, A22a
McClennen, Joshua, G19
McClintock, David, C532
McClintock, Mary Howard, C300
McCloy, Helen, C436, C459, C532,
C594
McClure, Jane, C496
McComas, J. Francis, G28
McCormick, John, H43
McCulloch, Derek, C317
McCullough, Donald, C364
Macdonald, Isobel, C346
MacDonald, Philip, C313
McDowell, Alfred B., H44, I34.2
McDowell, Frederich P. W., A27a,
A30a
McFadyean, Barbara, C297
McGerr, Pat, C490
MacGillivray, Arthur, A25
McGivering, Helen, A22b
McGowan, Martha Jean, H45
McGrady, H. H., A29a
McGrewy, Thomas, C56
McGuinness, Norah, A21b
McHugh, Vincent, A11b
MacInness, Colin, C612
Mackail, O. M. Denis, C109
Mackay, Mercedes, C421
Mackay, W. & J., Co. *See* W. & J.
Mackay & Co. (printer).
Mackenzie, Compton, C354, C429,
C446, C454, C546, C611
MacKenzie, Faith Compton, C416
McLaren, Margaret, E601
McLaren, Moray, C362
MacLaren-Ross, J., I35
McLaughlin, Richard, A22a, A25
MacManus, Francis, C385.1, E77
MacManus, M. J., C88

MacLean, Alistair, C511
MacLennan, Bertha, E602
Mac Liammóir, Michael, C448
MacLysaght, Edward, C88
Macmillan Co., B33
McNeill, Janet, C634
Macpherson, Donald, C20
Mac Veagh, Lincoln. *See* Lincoln Mac
Veagh (publisher).
Macy, John, A3b
Madame Solario, C569
Maddoch, Melvin, A27a
Mademoiselle, C385, C408, C469,
C506, C517, C651, E110, E218
Magalaner, Marvin, A21a
*Magazine of Fantasy and Science
Fiction*, C130
'MAGIC IN THE MIDDLE
DISTANCE', C634
Magnus, Peter, D34
Magny, Claude-Edmonde, D37
Mailer, Norman, C345
'MAINIE JELLETT', C140, E57
Mainwaring, Marion, C439
'MAKING ARRANGEMENTS', A2,
A20, C3, E2, E580
Malet, Oriel, C181, C314, C505,
C607
Mallet-Joris, Françoise, C631
Malling, Liv, D12
Mallowan, Agatha [Christie]. *See*
Christie, Agatha.
Malraux, Andre, C21
'MAN AND HIS LEGEND, A',
C398, E90
'MAN AND THE BOY, THE', E155
'MAN OF THE FAMILY, THE',
A8
'MAN WHO HAD EVERYTHING,
THE', C504
'MANCHESTER', A19, C38
Manchester, P. W., C356
*Mandala: Literature for Critical
Analysis*, G26
Manesse (publisher), D71
'MANKOWITZ RINGS THE BELL',
C540
Mankowitz, Wolf, C515, C540, C603
Manley, Seon, G42

345

346